ISSUES IN ACCOUNTING POLICY

A READER

ISSUES IN ACCOUNTING POLICY

A READER

Robert Bloom, Ph.D.
John Carroll University

Pieter T. Elgers, D.B.A., C.P.A.
University of Massachusetts

The Dryden Press
Harcourt Brace College Publishers

Fort Worth Philadelphia San Diego New York Orlando Austin San Antonio
Toronto Montreal London Sydney Tokyo

Acquisitions Editors	Elizabeth Storey, Bill Teague
Developmental Editor	Craig Avery
Project Editors	Emily Thompson, Matt Ball
Art Directors	Beverly Baker, Linda Miller
Production Manager	Ann Coburn
Photo & Permissions Editor	Elizabeth Banks
Product Manager	Annie Todd
Marketing Coordinator	Sam Stubblefield
Copy Editor	Katherine M. Morse
Composition	Thompson Type
Text Type	10/12 Bembo

Address for orders:
The Dryden Press
6277 Sea Harbor Drive
Orlando, FL 32887-6777
1-800-782-4479 or 1-800-433-0001 (in Florida)

Address for editorial correspondence:
The Dryden Press
301 Commerce Street, Suite 3700
Fort Worth, TX 76102

ISBN: 0-03-097924-2

Library of Congress Catalog Card Number: 94-72112

Printed in the United States of America

4 5 6 7 8 9 0 1 2 3 039 9 8 7 6 5 4 3 2 1

The Dryden Press
Harcourt Brace College Publishers

The Dryden Press Series in Accounting

Introductory

Bischoff
Introduction to College Accounting
Third Edition

Principles

Hanson, Hamre, and Walgenbach
Principles of Accounting
Sixth Edition

Computerized

Bischoff and Wanlass
The Computer Connection: General Ledger and Practice Sets to accompany Introductory Accounting
Second Edition

Wanlass
Computer Resource Guide: Principles of Accounting
Fourth Edition

Financial

Porter and Norton
Financial Accounting: The Impact on Decision Makers

Stickney and Weil
Financial Accounting: An Introduction to Concepts, Methods, and Uses
Seventh Edition

Beirne and Dauderis
Financial Accounting: An Introducion to Decision Making

Backer, Elgers, and Asebrook
Financial Accounting: Concepts and Practices

Managerial

Maher, Stickney, and Weil
Managerial Accounting: An Introduction to Concepts, Methods, and Uses
Fifth Edition

Ketz, Campbell, and Baxendale
Management Accounting

Intermediate

Williams, Stanga, and Holder
Intermediate Accounting
Fifth Edition

Advanced

Pahler and Mori
Advanced Accounting
Fifth Edition

Huefner and Largay
Advanced Financial Accounting
Third Edition

Financial Statement Analysis

Stickney
Financial Statement Analysis: A Strategic Perspective
Second Edition

Auditing

Rittenberg and Schwieger
Auditing: Concepts for a Changing Environment

Guy, Alderman, and Winters
Auditing
Third Edition

Theory

Bloom and Elgers
Foundations of Accounting Theory and Policy: A Reader

Bloom and Elgers
Issues in Accounting Theory and Policy: A Reader

Belkaoui
Accounting Theory
Third Edition

Taxation

Everett, Raabe, and Fortin
1995 Income Tax Fundamentals

Duncan
Essentials of U.S. Taxation
Second Edition

Reference

Miller and Bailey
Miller Comprehensive GAAS Guide
College Edition

Williams and Miller
Miller Comprehensive GAAP Guide
College Edition

Governmental and Not-for-Profit

Douglas
Governmental and Nonprofit Accounting: Theory and Practice
Second Edition

Ziebell and DeCoster
Management Control Systems in Nonprofit Organizations

The Harcourt Brace College Outline Series

Campbell, Grierson, and Taylor
Principles of Accounting I
Revised Edition

Emery
Principles of Accounting II

Emery
Intermediate Accounting I
Second Edition

Emery
Intermediate Accounting II

Frigo
Cost Accounting

Poteau
Advanced Accounting

PREFACE

Issues in Accounting Policy: A Reader is essentially a new book. Its predecessor, *Accounting Theory and Policy: A Reader* (both the first and second editions), has evolved into two new books, each with a different emphasis. The *Issues* volume focuses on the institutional framework for setting accounting standards in the United States and addresses a variety of current controversies in financial reporting. It is directed toward students at 150-hour schools as well as those in M.B.A. and M.S. programs. By contrast, the other volume, *Foundations of Accounting Theory and Policy: A Reader,* emphasizes theory rather than issues and is designed to appeal to students of accounting theory, whether in the United States or abroad. Although both books draw on articles from the academic and professional literature, *Issues* relies more heavily on the professional literature than does *Foundations.*

Both *Foundations* and *Issues* contain approximately thirty articles and may be used on a stand-alone basis as primary or supplementary materials in courses dealing with accounting theory and financial reporting issues, respectively. On the other hand, because no article appears in both volumes, they may be used together in a single course that addresses both theory and issues.

The articles selected for this book emphasize the nature of the standard-setting process in the United States. They address topics in the definition and measurement of the elements of business financial statements and examine selected financial reporting controversies from the current agendas of the Financial Accounting Standards Board (FASB) and the Securities and Exchange Commission (SEC). In addition, several papers consider accounting for multinational operations and international variations in accounting standards.

This book consists of two parts. Part I addresses the framework for the setting of accounting standards in the United States, including the following five sections: (A) historical perspectives on accounting and financial reporting, (B) events and value theories of accounting measurement, (C) positive accounting theory, (D) the conceptual framework, and (E) market efficiency and economic consequences. Part II, which examines issues in accounting measurement and disclosure, consists of seven sections: (A) measurement of income, (B) measurement of assets and liabilities, (C) measurement of shareholder equity and earnings per share, (D) reporting of pensions and other post-employment retirement benefits, (E) reporting for business combinations and consolidations, (F) international issues in financial reporting, and (G) expansion in the contents of financial reports.

We have selected articles primarily on the basis of how provocative and stimulating they are, not for their compatibility with our own views. Our intent is to provide a catalyst for discussion rather than to present, or lead the reader to, particular conclusions. For the same reason, our interstitial comments on individual articles are descriptive rather than evaluative.

The editors most gratefully acknowledge the invaluable suggestions and comments of the following professors on the original outlines for both *Foundations* and *Issues:*

Jeffrey Cohen, Boston College (United States)

Haim Falk, McMaster University (Canada)

Jayne Fuglister, Cleveland State University (United States)

Michael J. R. Gaffikin, University of Wollongong (Australia)

Eugene Imhoff, University of Michigan (United States)
Ross G. Jennings, University of Texas at Austin (United States)
Mayh Lo, Western New England College (United States)
K. V. Peasnell, University of Lancaster (United Kingdom)
Etzmun S. Rozen, Cleveland State University (United States)
Daniel B. Thornton, University of Calgary (Canada)

CONTENTS

CONTENTS

ISSUES IN ACCOUNTING POLICY

A READER

PART I

FRAMEWORK FOR SETTING ACCOUNTING STANDARDS

The papers included in Part I of this reader provide a frame of reference for understanding U.S. accounting standards that are used in evaluating specific financial reporting issues. Accounting standards typically are not the product of deductive reasoning based upon generally accepted theories of accounting. Rather, accounting standards are largely the result of a political process involving a variety of groups whose economic interests are potentially affected by financial reports. These groups include business managers, investors, auditors of financial reports, governmental regulatory agencies, and others. Accounting standard setting entails a balancing of the often competing economic interests of these sundry groups.

Part I consists of five lettered sections. In Section A, "Historical Perspectives in Accounting and Financial Reporting," there are two papers. The initial paper by Brief (1975) offers an historical perspective on current accounting controversies and suggests that perennial accounting disputes are rooted in uncertainty about the future. Brief argues that providing direct forecasts of cash flows and other future-oriented information in financial reports might cause the concept of profit to become obsolete as a measure of past performance or as a predictor of future performance. If the concept of profit becomes obsolete, the theoretical debates concerning accounting measurements of income and value also lose importance.

The second paper by Zeff (1984) reviews the circumstances leading to five major turning points in the process by which accounting principles have been established in the United States and attempts to identify the reasons for the new approaches to reforms. The review covers a period of more than five decades (1917–1972). Although many factors were influential in affecting the accounting standard-setting process, Zeff observes that a motivating force for each reform seems to have been the accounting profession's fear of government involvement.

Section B contains the only two articles in this volume that deal directly with theories of accounting. These papers are included because both the events and value approaches to accounting theory that these papers examine are represented in current accounting policy deliberations. Sorter (1969) argues that the myriad uses of accounting data as well as the array of decision models available make it impossible to produce income and asset measurements that are optimal for a wide range of users. As an alternative, Sorter proposes an "events" theory under which accountants would provide "information about relevant economic events that allows users to generate their own input values for their own decision models." The conventional accounting emphasis on income and valuations as well as aggregations generated by the accountant may be less useful than disaggregated data. Chasteen's (1984) paper, by contrast, rests on the presumption that accountants will continue to provide measurements of income and value. The paper describes and classifies in an algebraic framework models that deal with price changes: historical cost, current cost, and current exit value—with and without constant dollar adjustments—providing an introduction to these models for comparative analysis.

In Section C, two articles deal with positive accounting theory. Revsine (1991) observes that financial reporting rules are often arbitrary, complicated, and misleading. He suggests that this problem may be attributed to flexible reporting rules promulgated by standard setters who have been "captured" by reporting firms. Firms may desire such rules because the resulting latitude allows them flexibility in depicting their performance. Revsine identifies incentives that encourage managers, shareholders, auditors, and standard setters to prefer "loose" rather than "tight" reporting standards. He recommends reducing the resources devoted to developing additional standards, suggesting instead that existing standards could effectively be "frozen" and used as the basis for all future contracting and reporting.

Zimmerman (1980) discusses the rationale for positive research in accounting with a view to the development of a theory to explain, for example, why managers adopt one particular accounting method rather than another. Such a theory would provide a foundation for the measurement of the benefits and costs of alternative accounting methods. Zimmerman recognizes several pitfalls in the formulation of a positive theory, including the lack of a theory of the political process and an incomplete knowledge of auditors' incentives. Nonetheless, the author expects significant findings to emerge from research on this subject in the near future.

Section D evaluates the purpose and limitations of the FASB's Conceptual Framework project. Miller (1990) examines seven major events in the Conceptual Framework project in chronological order, beginning with the design of the project to derive an authoritative set of deductive concepts and ending with the production of the sixth and last concepts statement. Miller rejects the idea that the Conceptual Framework is primarily an integrated accounting theory, viewing it instead as a set of political declarations. Daley and Tranter (1990) consider the argument that, because the Conceptual Framework project has been completed, previously issued FASB standards may need to be reevaluated and made to conform with the ideas set forth in the Concepts Statements. The authors believe that the reason particular standards do not conform to the tenets of the Conceptual Framework is that the project unrealistically ignored the significant role of economic and political pressures in the development of accounting standards. The paper analyzes several controversial standards (including those dealing with pension plans, investment tax credits, and troubled debt restructurings) in order to question the applicability of the concept of neutrality defined in Concepts Statement No. 2. The authors argue that in the current setting in which accounting standards are designed, it is impossible for accounting standards to be "neutral."

Section E develops the implications for accounting policy of modern portfolio theory, security market information efficiency, and the potential economic and political consequences of accounting standards. Dietrick and Harrison (1984) define the capital asset pricing model and market efficiency and attempt to correct various misconceptions that have appeared in the business press. The authors emphasize that the beliefs and actions of individual managers, bankers, and investor analysts are irrelevant to the truth (or falsity) of the hypothesis of market efficiency. Brown (1990) notes widespread agreement among standard setters, managers, auditors, and users of financial reports that changes in accounting standards often have economic consequences. For this reason, cost/benefit considerations should affect accounting standards: changes should be made only when expected benefits exceed anticipated costs. Brown provides a useful catalog of costs and benefits that are likely to be associated with changes in accounting standards. He observes that the FASB gives paramount consideration to conceptual consistency, neutrality, and objectivity when formulating accounting standards, except in the presence of compelling evidence about potential unacceptable economic consequences.

With this framework in place, the reader will be better equipped to evaluate specific accounting issues covered in Part II.

I-A

HISTORICAL PERSPECTIVE ON ACCOUNTING AND FINANCIAL REPORTING

I-A1

THE ACCOUNTANT'S RESPONSIBILITY IN HISTORICAL PERSPECTIVE

Richard P. Brief

Several years ago it was reported (*The New York Times,* January 4, 1972) that many accountants, "like victims of an earthquake or the fist of Joe Frazier, . . . wander dazedly asking what happened; where did the force come from; why wasn't it foreseen; how could it have been avoided . . . ?" The article elaborated on the current state of the profession, indicating that "now, from within the profession itself, revolt is brewing. . . . And for more than 100,000 accountants themselves, the preservation of their professional credibility could not have higher significance. This credibility is under attack in the Congress, in the courts and within the profession itself." This revolt is not new. It has been brewing for nearly 100 years.

One way to gain insight into the vexing and unsettled questions connected with the responsibility of accountants is to approach the subject from an historical perspective. In the pages that follow we examine nineteenth and early twentieth century thought on various topics

---

The original version of this paper was written while the author was a Visiting Professor of Finance, Dartmouth College. It was presented at the annual meeting of the American Accounting Association in August, 1974, during a session sponsored by the Academy of Accounting Historians. Comments and suggestions by the discussants, Professor David Green, Jr. and Mr. Leonard Spacek, and by Mr. Walter Oliphant, Professor Louis Goldberg, and the reviewers of *The Accounting Review* changed the manuscript in important ways. Their help is appreciated. In addition, some of the ideas expressed in this paper are a joint product of several years of discussion with my colleague, Professor Joel Owen. Research support was provided by the Tuck Associates Program, Dartmouth College, and it is gratefully acknowledged. Naturally, the author is solely responsible for this paper.

Richard P. Brief, "The Accountant's Responsibility in Historical Perspective," *The Accounting Review,* April 1975, pp. 285–297. Reprinted by permission of the American Accounting Association.

which have been, and continue to be, of concern to accountants. It will become evident that "history repeats itself" and that most of the basic problems considered by accountants now are also those which have perplexed the profession for nearly a century. Thus despite all the changes in the business environment, controversy within the accounting profession today has remarkable similarities to the discussion taking place decades ago. Why do certain accounting problems appear to be perennial and why has regulation and legislation apparently not solved many of the fundamental disputes in accounting?

The thesis of this study is that accounting controversy persists because profit calculations involve "uncertainty about the future." Legislation and regulation cannot reduce this controversy because they cannot eliminate the element of uncertainty from the problem of profit determination. Consequently, until the subject of uncertainty is given a central position in accounting theory, the problems recognized in earlier times will continue to be deferred to later generations for resolution.

The paper is divided into three sections. The first surveys accounting thought on the subjects of disclosure and alternative techniques and questions concerning the scope of audit and audit certificate. Although there has been an enormous amount of legislation and regulation in these areas, many of today's problems are no different from those which preoccupied the profession during the last century. In the second section, the attitude toward the accountant's responsibility for forecasts and estimates is examined. Historically, an effort was made to minimize uncertainty-related problems by arguing that the accountant's main responsibility was for "prosaic facts" and "dry realities." The third section concludes that this emphasis on the past rather than the future conflicts with the idea of profit as a return for risk bearing. However, the modern corporate concept of profit is a product of lawyers, not of accountants, and legislation governing the payment of dividends has had a significant impact on the development of accounting.

Legislation and Problems of the Accountant's Responsibility

This section considers two broad topics relating to the accountant's responsibility: full disclosure and alternative techniques and the scope of the audit and audit certificate. Nineteenth century accountants were concerned with the improvement of practice in these areas and many of them, like their twentieth century counterparts, advocated more effective regulation to reduce the degrees of freedom in accounting behavior. The profession was almost unanimous in its belief that accountants should take the lead in promulgating reform. However, there was a diversity of opinion on the specific changes in practice that were needed and some cautioned that certain kinds of regulation would have undesirable consequences.

Full Disclosure and Alternative Techniques

In the last quarter of the nineteenth century debate over the interpretation of the legal requirement that "dividends must not be paid out of capital" and the determination of "profits available for dividends" were inextricably connected to the depreciation problem and other familiar subjects (Brief, 1970). During this period accountants attempted for the first time to formulate theory, to codify methodology, and to clarify their responsibility. The development of accounting was marked by angry argument, caustic rhetoric, and more important, a very sophisticated and penetrating dialogue on a wide range of subjects.

Underlying much of the debate was the belief that reported profits had an effect on investor behavior. The nature of this relationship was boldly and sarcastically described in 1837 (*Railway Magazine,* p. 2): "Let it only be seen by six months working of that line [Grand Junction] that a profit will accrue to proprietors of 8 or 10 percent per annum and there is little hazard in predicting that other lines of great intercourse will be amply supported." Thus, when a railroad charged £14,625 to capital and paid a dividend by arguing that "the efficiency and the value of the engines have been materially increased" after the severe winter of 1838, the sufficiency of disclosure and capitalization policy were criticized by the *Railway Magazine,* which stated: "a more puny and meagre document we have never witnessed" (1838, p. 189). The subject of accounting error, its economic effect, and the accountant's responsibility for this error were a source of continuing argument throughout the period (Brief, 1965).

Many accountants advocated that the profession should take the lead in writing new legislation to improve business practices. One writer put it this way (*The Accountant,* December 12, 1885):

> Is there a single word in the whole of the Acts restraining the payment of dividends out of capital? There is not; what is said seems to amount to this, that the payment of dividends out of capital can be made. . . . What are accountants doing towards drawing up formal suggestions on this and other equally important points on which the Companies Acts are notoriously at fault? Not going to sleep, let us hope.

In addition, a very competitive attitude towards others, notably lawyers, also is observed in the profession's formative years. This attitude is illustrated by the common complaint that "Existing law is deplorably defective, and . . . the Chartered Accountants acting through their Institute should be the first to move in the matter, and not allow the work to be done, and the honour to be appropriated by other and less capable hands" (*The Accountant,* December 19, 1885).

At an early date *The Accountant* (April 30, 1881) stated that "If a balance sheet be correct although condensed he [the auditor] is bound to sign it" because the auditor should not publicly disagree with management. But *The Accountant* also advocated full disclosure of the amounts charged to depreciation, the method of valuation, etc.:

> A shareholder is entitled to know, not what is the true value of his shares, for that in most instances is a matter of opinion, but *how* the value of fixed assets has been estimated—whether at cost, at a valuation . . . , or otherwise, and what sums have been placed in reserve or written off for depreciation, running out of leases or other decreases in value . . .

However, although the editor argues that "Much of the information . . . might be given if the legislature made its publication compulsory upon all," he also believed that "it is difficult to enforce full information without committing an act of injustice towards companies, as opposed to private concerns, which need never print any balance-sheets" (June 4, 1881).

Although many accountants, in the nineteenth century as in the twentieth, argued that legislation which increases the amount of disclosure in financial statements and reduces the number of alternative methods is a desirable goal, others, like the editor of *The Accountant,* also considered some of the undesirable by-products of achieving these objectives. The extreme position was that "as I don't approve of too much grandmotherly legislation in a free country where a people should learn from their own experience how to take care of themselves, I don't approve of the State preventing undertakings being floated with an inducement of this sort" [returning interest on capital during construction] (*The Accountant,* December 4, 1886). In the same vein, when the editor of *The Accountant* discussed (October 8, 1881) the balance sheet of John Crossley and Son, Limited, which was criticized on the basis of inadequate disclosure by the *Citizen* newspaper, he reasoned, in effect, that inadequate disclosure would increase a firm's cost of capital:

> Here, indeed, the entire assets are lumped together in one line, and we infer that no outsider is expected to take shares; in fact, none but a semi-private concern would issue such a balance sheet. Any ordinary company would assuredly separate its freehold and plant, its stock-in-trade, its book-debts, and its cash, though it might include "minerals" perhaps with freeholds. The *et cetera* at the end of the liabilities means the reserves, no doubt, against discounts, bad debts and any other drawbacks. But the true answer of the public to such a balance sheet, however respectably audited, is to respectfully let the company's shares alone. *We therefore, consider that the "dissatisfied shareholder" must be deemed a goose.* (italics added)

Dicksee, doubtless the most influential nineteenth century accountant, also questioned the effect of legislating accounting practices (*The Accountant,* March 1, 1902):

> even with regard to such important questions as the value of assets, provision for depreciation, the assessments of profits earned, and the distribution of unrealised profits, the Courts have shown a marvelous disinclination [to provide] principles for the safe guidance of the auditor. . . . No doubt it has acted wisely in adopting this course, however, because any attempt to state explicitly what the duties of auditors are in all cases would afford the best possible excuse in such cases for the insufficiency of the audit that has been performed.

And seventeen years earlier Matheson, responding to a criticism of failing to specify exact methods in his book on depreciation, had the same apprehensive attitude about fixed rules (*The Accountant,* January 3, 1885):

> [regarding] the absence from my book of exact rates of depreciation for different classes of plant, I am more on my ground, and I venture to assert that any positive statements of rates would be more likely to mislead than inform . . . fixed rules are impossible, and examples, if offered for imitation, dangerous.

More recently, a strikingly similar view was expressed by the Chief Accountant of the Securities Exchange Commission, John C. Burton: "He was not happy with the old 18-man, part-time board. 'By writing precise rules,' he asserted, 'the board made it possible for people to observe the letter and avoid the spirit with the blessing—and often the assistance—of their auditors' " (*The New York Times,* June 25, 1972).

There were other arguments against regulation and they concerned the depreciation problem. For example, one writer said that legal requirements to charge depreciation before declaring dividends would be "injurious to companies and the public. . . . It would stop all enterprise because it would be absolutely impossible for companies to pay dividends in the early years of their existence" (*The Accountant,* December 14, 1889). Similarly, Lord Justice Lindley, in the landmark 1889 decision in *Lee v. Neuchatel* (41 LR Ch. 1, 19) went so far as to argue that the legal requirement to charge depreciation regularly and periodically would "paralyze the trade of the country."

Still another argument against legally requiring depreciation, which the business historian might usefully consider, was made by "an eminent accountant in the north of England." He argued (*The Accountant,* November 29, 1884) that the provision for depreciation ("money retained out of profits"):

> enables managers and directors to undertake continual new work without consulting their shareholders. It is only another way of providing fresh capital or avoiding a call, which might be resisted by those interested if it came in that form; and further in cases where you have several classes of shares upon which the capital is not equally paid up, or where you have debenture holders as well as ordinary shareholders, the rights of the respective parties are prejudicially affected by what can only be styled the misappropriation of funds intended for a specific object.

There were differences of opinion among accountants over basic questions and they were vigorously debated. However, judicial and statutory authority did not play a significant role in resolving these differences (Brief, 1966). Rather, the profession attempted to establish the limits of its own responsibility and the aims were, according to Dicksee (1915, p. xiv), somewhat Utopian:[1]

> If it should be thought that the standard I have throughout advocated is somewhat Utopian in character, and unattainable in practice, I can only reply that I maintain that, to me, an incomplete investigation seems worse than useless, and I am convinced that it is only by voluntarily accepting, and even increasing the responsibilities of our position that we can hope to maintain and to increase the large measure of public confidence we at present enjoy.

Throughout the period, accountants fought to establish the profession as a permanent institution, but the battle still rages to determine whether "the honour [will be] appropriated by other and less capable hands."

> It is now likely that unless accountants and their corporate clients take the initiative in reducing the number of acceptable accounting practices, financial disclosure will become much more a matter of law. There seems to be increasing pressure to limit the diversity of accounting methods by establishing an arbitrary set of rules. . . . If the accounting profession does not do so, "its position of eminence may be lost to those who seize the larger opportunity"[2] (Chatfield, 1974, p. 280).

---

[1]The quote is taken from the preface to the first edition (1892) which was reprinted in subsequent editions.

[2]Chatfield is quoting from Mautz and Sharaf (1961, p. 200). Similar comments can be found elsewhere. For example, Hawkins (1963, p. 168) commented, "Once more, the possibility of further government intervention in industrial reporting matters is imminent, principally because of the accounting profession's inability to narrow the areas of difference in accounting principles and management's resistance to its critics' demands for improved corporate disclosure." The same idea is echoed by *Business Week* (April 22, 1972). "Before such sweeping moves are widely demanded, the Wheat proposals give the accounting profession another chance to demonstrate that workable accounting and auditing procedures can be set in the private sector, with the broad-based cooperation of accountants, financial executives, security analysts, and educators."

Although the business setting has changed, nineteenth century debate on disclosure and alternative methods has a modern tone and many of the issues before the profession in the present day are those which concerned its original members. How can disclosure be improved? How much disclosure is desirable? How can the range of accounting alternatives be reduced? What are the effects of regulation? Then, as now, accountants were searching for satisfactory answers to these questions. Nineteenth century debate on the audit certificate is also relevant to today's problems.

SCOPE OF AUDIT AND AUDIT CERTIFICATE

The pure laissez-faire attitude in the last century towards the scope of the audit was illustrated in the early legal case of *Turquand* v. *Marshall* which was decided in 1869 (20 LT 766):

> As to the publication of false balance sheets and including in them debts which were hopelessly bad, it was difficult to say where a debt was hopeless; and besides, if any shareholders were deceived into buying shares he might have his separate remedy, but each would have a different case, and the whole body could not sue.

The debtor in this case was the Confederacy! However, although the courts generally did not interfere in business affairs, accountants and other groups were more active in their advocacy of reform, and the audit and related problems quickly became a major issue which was actively discussed.

As early as 1883 there was an interesting controversy on the audit, sparked by a series of articles in a magazine called *Vanity Fair.* Significantly, *The Accountant* reprinted them in entirety, even though the comments were harshly critical of accounting practice.

Apparently, *Vanity Fair* thought that "auditors' certificates might be longer and better" and "legislation is needed" to achieve this objective. However, the editor of *The Accountant* argued that "In a simple matter such as an auditor's certificate we fail to see why any legal interference is called for. What the public and shareholders want is a readable assurance from the accountants, stating in plain English what they really have done" (October 27, 1883). With great sarcasm, the editor elaborated on this point (November 3, 1883):

> We would suggest that in future the auditors' certificates should, in accordance with the defense now made for them, run thus:—We having been allowed to audit not from month to month, but only once a year; having had too little time to make an exhaustive report, because the documents are required for the printer; knowing that shareholders are generally impatient to get through the business; being paid a fee out of all proportion to the work required to be done; and being aware that the voting power is in the absolute control of the Board—certify that, so far as we, under these disabilities, can ascertain and dare disclose the facts, it is all right. This would at any rate let shareholders know from the certificate, as we know from the general chorus of certifiers, what the true meaning and value of the certificate really amounts to. Our complaint was and is that at present they do not know this, but that they are led and are meant to imagine that bladders are lanterns and auditors' certificates proofs of all excellences and complete solvency and security.
>
> We are not to be drawn off the scent by any invitation to discuss the powers of auditors or the technicalities of auditing. That is not the question. The question is—What is worth, and what, therefore, the use of an auditorial certificate

> in its various forms as it is now commonly given? We say it is worth next to nothing. Our critics say, not that it is worth much, but that it is very hard to make it worth anything. Very well. Then we and our critics are agreed. The certificate *is* worth next to nothing, and this being so, it is a delusion and a snare.

Then, in response to a letter, the editor of *The Accountant* argued that to remedy the audit's deficiencies, a direct approach was called for: "Cease making those damnable faces which are called Auditors' Certificates." Rather than paraphrase, these remarks are quoted in entirety in order to give the flavor of the lively debate which took place during the profession's first decade of development:

> There is however one correspondent of *The Accountant* who signs himself "Anti-Twaddle," and who deserves special remark. He is very rude, but not more rude than illogical and ungrammatical. He too sets forth the difficulties of the poor auditor, and so feelingly that he has evidently suffered from them. The auditor gets no power, no time, and no money to talk of; he is not responsible except for the verification of figures put before him; he is the slave of the directors, who do not like to look at the worst side of affairs, and he has to satisfy also the shareholders, for we believe that if they have sometimes a strong objection to knowing the truth, they have at least as often as strong an objection to having lies told to them. And it is quite clear that, if this venerable Aunty were herself set to audit accounts and to frame thereon an auditorial certificate, she would unhesitatingly avoid any difference of opinion with directors, would carefully abstain from looking at the worst side of affairs, would very generously indulge the shareholders' strong objection to knowing the truth, and would, in spite of the insufficient time, power, and money, frame and publish a certificate that would make everything pleasant for everybody, and above all for Aunty. This is exactly what we complain of.
>
> And yet, in spite of this injurious disclosure of the way in which certificates are moulded from the dirty mud of facts by the Sculptor-Director, and invested with artistic merit by the Ghost-Auditor, Aunty wants to have herself fastened on all concerns by an Act of Parliament which shall supersede directors and everybody else, and make Aunty a first charge on the concern, just as though she were an official liquidator or trustee. And she proposes that *we* should get her Act passed for her! No; we cannot do this. On the contrary, we say—Amend your certificates and not your Statutes; tell the truth if you know it, and shame the Director. If you don't know and can't find out—why say that; but in any case, cease making those merely damnable faces which are now called Auditors' Certificates. (November 3, 1883)

Some leading accountants took a constructive view of this criticism. Thomas Welton, President of the Institute of Chartered Accountants in England and Wales in 1891–2, believed that *The Accountant's* remarks on the auditors' certificate "would do great good even if they did no more than induce shareholders to more closely scan the wording of these documents . . ." (October 27, 1883). But the basic complaint was that accountants lacked authority to impose exacting standards. For example, the problem of requiring firms to charge "adequate" depreciation was of great concern in those days and Pixley (1887, p. 127) complained that "It is in the earlier years of a company's existence the auditor has the greatest difficulty in inducing Directors to charge an amount sufficient to provide for the past depreciation of the period." A similar comment appears in the preface to the second edition of the first book on depreciation (Matheson, 1910, p. ix–x): "Auditors, and especially those who have to deal with joint stock or other concerns, where the remuneration of the management is made wholly or partly dependent upon declared profits, know in what varied forms resistance to an adequate charge against profits for Depreciation is presented."

This conflict between the accountant and management, and its effect on the accountant's responsibility to shareholders, was recognized in the first years of the profession's existence, and questions relating to the auditor's independence were connected to the proxy system which permitted persons in fiduciary positions to vote on matters affecting their own interest. Once again, *The Accountant* (October 27, 1883) identified a critical problem:

> The audit of Public Companies' accounts was designed to control and check the action of directors in their administration of the affairs of Public Companies: and yet, as a rule, the auditors who are chosen for this purpose owe their employment to the very directors whom they are presumed so to control and check in the interests of the shareholders. This is one of the evils arising out of the proxy system, which I trust we may some day see abolished, as being utterly pernicious and vicious in root and branch. It should be laid down as an invariable rule that directors, trustees, or other persons in fiduciary positions should never be allowed the direct or indirect use of proxies in voting, or in fact to vote personally, on any subject affecting the performance of the duties imposed upon them by the trusts under which they act, or on the passing of the accounts as presented by them to their proprietary or *cestui que* trust.

This problem of the auditor's autonomy remains a topic of current interest, and recent suggestions for reform (Hawes, 1974) echo *The Accountant's* earlier argument:

> At a time when auditors are subject to a staggering number of lawsuits, intense pressures from managements to adopt accounting treatment that will put the best face on the financial statements and the difficult task of codifying accounting principles, legislation is needed to make stockholder approval of the appointment of auditors mandatory.
>
> Such legislation would underscore the fact that the auditor's client is the stockholders and thus would have an important therapeutic effect on the corporation.

This historical review of the audit certificate and scope of audit has demonstrated that many modern problems are not new. From the first, accountants recognized the limitations of the audit certificate and they raised questions concerning the auditor's independence. Many recommended more effective regulation but some took a more straightforward approach: "Amend your certificates and not your statutes." In summarizing this section, one conclusion is inescapable. After nearly a century of debate,

> there is still no comprehensive, integrated statement of concepts on which accountants and statement readers can agree and rely. There is still no consensus as to the exact meaning of the standard audit opinion that financial statements

present the results of operations "fairly" in accordance with generally accepted accounting principles. One result is that accounting methods have changed much more slowly than the accounting environment. And the profession has not solved its basic problems of disclosure, consistency and statement comparability (Chatfield, 1974, pp. 298–99).

The thesis of this paper is that accounting controversy persists because profit calculations involve "uncertainty about the future." The next section surveys the attitude toward the accountant's responsibility for estimates and forecasts.

ATTITUDE TOWARD ACCOUNTANT'S RESPONSIBILITY FOR ESTIMATES AND FORECASTS

In the discussion that follows it should be borne in mind that a formal framework for studying decision problems under uncertainty has become generally available only in the last decade or so. Therefore, nineteenth century accountants quite naturally made an effort to avoid uncertainty-related problems. Nevertheless, these early theorists did begin to discuss topics related to the subject, and their attitude towards them had a significant influence on the progress in accounting.

HISTORICAL ATTITUDE TOWARD UNCERTAINTY

One of the earliest references to the problem of uncertainty in accounting can be found in a series of articles on audits which appeared in several 1881 issues of *The Accountant*. Referring to balance sheet audits, the editor asserted (April 23, 1881) "that the real object to be aimed at is such a verification that will be practically sufficient." The auditor's task is then compared to a judge and jury who are often obliged to be content with "little more than a reasonable probability." Thus, at the end of a period "some matters outstanding . . . must be introduced by estimation . . . to make the apparent profit a real measure of what has been accomplished in the period under review." However, the auditor should not "indulge in forecasts or in expressions of feeling, but rather adhere as coldly and impassively as he can to facts—hard, dry realities."

This logical contradiction between the necessity to make estimates and the adherence to dry realities is not resolved, but the writer does suggest a "trend analysis" for specific problems like estimating "probable losses" such as "bad and doubtful debts." Since the facts "keep changing almost hourly," the auditor should study past trends and advocate reserves in good years to be used in years when losses exceed the average. However, when a loss is certain, "no rule can be laid down," but "broad principles" which "favour moderation in the distribution of dividends, and . . . ample reserves is [sic] desirable. Yet he should likewise remember the possibility of excess in the latter direction" which might induce shareholders "to part with their shares at an insufficient valuation."

The principle of conservatism and the auditor's responsibility for estimates is discussed again (June 4, 1881):

> Generally he [the shareholder] should be enabled to see in the balance sheet which of the assets are matters of opinion, and which are matters of fact. When

> this part of the subject is clear, little doubt can rest upon the estimate of profit or loss, which may be deemed correct or otherwise according to the spirit in which matters of opinion are apparently handled.
>
> Estimates are often proper things to make use of, where they relate to subsidiary matters, and enables the balance sheet to be speedily prepared, but all estimates should be slightly to the disadvantage of the company, rather than tending the other way.

In the first paper on the ethics of accountancy in 1888 (*The Accountant,* December 12, 1888), John Mather flatly opposed any idea of chance or uncertainty in accounting. However, once again, the views on this subject are not perfectly consistent:

> What is called the "glorious uncertainty of the Law"—illustrated not only in the varying interpretations of enactments, but often in the evidence of opposing experts in law suits—conveys an idea that rarely attaches to the figures, statements, or certificates of Chartered Accountants. And it is our hope and belief, that as we succeed in gradually raising the standard of the skill and the ethics of the profession, any such idea of chance or uncertainty will be still more foreign to its work in the future.

In other words, "There seems a general agreement that . . . the accountant may not prophecy 'unless he knows' . . . he must avoid the tempting region of fancy and stick to the prosaic facts." Stated differently, "in most cases an accountant is no better able than other people to forecast the business prospects of an undertaking which, however sound at the outset, may ultimately fail through mismanagement, change of fashion, invalidity of patents, or numberless unforeseen causes." Yet, according to Mather, the accountant, "in the opinion of many . . . is fully justified in dealing with those facts in their bearing upon the future. . . ." But how can the accountant do this if he must stick to the prosaic facts?

Further insight into the accountant's conflicting attitudes towards uncertainty is provided by Dickinson twenty-six years later. In concluding a discussion of the accountant's responsibility for earnings projections Dickinson (1914, pp. 226–27) said that:

> It should be clear, therefore, from the above considerations that any estimate of future earnings must necessarily depend upon so many contingencies that it would hardly seem desirable that it should be put forth without calling specific attention to the assumptions involved; and an estimate with such qualification attached would hardly be of much service to the promoter and would not be incorporated in the prospectus.

However,

> *In as much as the community is being educated to consider that statements emanating from a public accountant deal only with facts,* it may be said in conclusion that in such a case as that supposed, the accountant's duty should end with the submission on request of a carefully prepared estimate, accompanied by all necessary qualifications, without, however, any certificate there to. . . . (italics added)

Even though Dickinson rejects the inclusion of estimates in the prospectus, his proposal that all estimates should be accompanied by the assumptions on which they are based reflects modern thinking on the subject. Of greater significance, however, is his remark concerning the effort *to educate* the community that financial statements deal only with facts. It suggests that a conscious attempt was made by the profession to convince the public that the accountant is responsible only for "facts," and it also helps to explain why so many generations have come to regard accounting as an essentially historical discipline.

At the same time, accountants understood the tenuous nature of their argument. Even Dickinson (p. 236) recognized that "Every balance sheet is a matter of opinion." But he failed to make any explicit connection between the problems which require the accountant to exercise his "opinion" and the conditions which give rise to these problems—namely, uncertainty about the future.

These references to the uncertainty problem are generally in terms of estimating balances in asset and liability accounts at the end of each period. This perspective is consistent with a balance sheet approach to income determination. However, there were also discussions about another class of estimation and forecasting problems in accounting and they concerned the relationship between reported profits and future profits.

The first of these provides an amusing illustration of the "interim reporting problem." In 1883 The Hotels and City Properties Share Trust, Limited issued a four-month report and estimated the year's results by doubling the figures for the interim period. *The Accountant* (October 27, 1883) published a scathing criticism of this report:

> Mr. Daniels has furnished the public with the result of working the Royal during the best four months of the year. But are we to understand that he pledges his professional reputation that *any* appreciable profit can be made during the remaining eight months, when Southend is little better than a howling wilderness, and when a stray Londoner at the Royal is looked upon with as much curiosity as if he were a friendly Zulu? During those dark and dreary months is there not an entire absence of excursionists, and as a rule are not the only occupants and best customers of that spacious bar which the prospectus says is a great source of profit, the neglected piermaster and the boatman?

In another reference to this general subject, Montgomery (1909, p. 324) seems to argue that the purpose of reporting the results of operations in past periods is to predict profits of future periods:

> the certificate, therefore, should be a clear and unconditional certificate of accomplished facts, and not a mere estimate of possible—or even probable—future results, misnamed a "certificate." To the limited extent already mentioned it may be permissible, and even desirable, to modify the past results so that they may more usefully serve the purpose for which they are primarily intended—namely, provide a reliable index of future profits. But at the same time a certificate should relate not to the future, but to the past. . . .

Although Montgomery argues unequivocally that financial statements should reflect "accomplished facts," i.e., financial statements should be historical, he also points out that the primary purpose of reporting past results is to provide an index (estimate) of future profits. Clearly, the methods used to calculate past performance will influence this "index," but questions about this relationship were not raised.

EFFECT ON MODERN ACCOUNTING THOUGHT

The early ideas on uncertainty and its relevance to accounting have not changed very much in the twentieth century. There are few extended discussions of the subject in modern texts and theoretical treatises and most references to the uncertainty problem are vague and ambiguous.

For example, van Pelt (1972, pp. 13–4) defines profitability as the "excess of revenues . . . over *known* costs . . ." (italics added), but also states that "estimates . . . will be required for the purpose of allocating costs." The *APB Accounting Principles* (1973, 1, p. 15) states that "Accountants have considered themselves primarily historians, not prophets. . . . However, *even* present accounting practices require estimates of the future" (italics added). How are estimates used in allocating costs? Which accounting practices require estimates of the future? What quantities must be estimated? What assumptions are the estimates based on? What estimating procedures are used? Questions such as these, and there are many others, have rarely been asked.

This historical review of the accountant's attitude towards uncertainty shows that the profession has always recognized that many of the numbers in financial statements are based on estimates of uncertain future events. At the same time, it also indicates that many accountants repeatedly stated that the accounts should reflect "prosaic facts" and "dry realities." This attitude toward uncertainty dominated thought; accountants, as well as the public, have been educated to believe that financial statements are essentially historical.

In the final section this attitude towards uncertainty is at least partly explained by the legal origin of the modern corporate concept of profit.

UNCERTAINTY AND THE CORPORATE CONCEPT OF PROFIT

It is uncertainty about the future that makes profit a return for risk bearing (Edwards and Bell, 1961, p. 9). It is also uncertainty about the future that provides the *logical* motivation for calculating the "profit of a period," and the common procedure in accounting of assuming certainty about the future completely obscures the information content of period earnings reports (Brief and Owen, 1970, p. 167). Thus, by assuming that the future is known with certainty (or by deemphasizing and minimizing the importance of uncertainty), accountants have eliminated, or at least have obscured, that which they set out to measure.

However, as a practical matter, the origin of the modern corporate concept of profit is in dividend law, not accounting, and the purpose of this legislation was to protect the rights of creditors and different classes of shareholders. This legal origin of the profit concept had an important influence on accounting.

Kehl (1941, p. 14) indicates that "During the 1600's charters began including dividend regulations among their provisions. The most common limitation required that dividends be paid from profits. Such was the restriction used in 1620 in the charter of James I to the New River Company." And "By 1700, there had already been adopted in England two statutory standards, one or the other of which still controls dividend distributions under present day statutes in a great many American states" (Kehl, p. 4).

This legislation governing the payment of dividends produced the "capital impairment rule" and the "profits tests" which were the first statutory references to the modern corporate concept of profit. Dividends cannot be paid out of capital and/or dividends must be paid out of the *profit of a period.*

Historically, railroads, utilities, and other quasi-public enterprise used a cash receipts-less-disbursements method of calculating profit. This method implied that the value of assets was "permanent." And although it became evident that this assumption was not valid, the cameralistic origin of the method seems to have blocked accounting reform for this class of enterprise.

The profit calculations of other firms are more difficult to assess. At the beginning of the nineteenth century the "inventory method" was employed. This method was a balance sheet (direct valuation) approach to profit determination. Eventually, this method was replaced by the modern accounting concept of profit that assumes a going concern and computes profit by "matching" revenues and expenses. All of these approaches have been sanctioned by the courts at various times (Brief, 1966).

Leake (1912, p. 2) correctly observed that "when commerce was carried on by individuals, each on his own account, in a vast number of small undertakings, and there was no regular income tax, it was a matter of small moment . . . whether the surplus of receipts . . . was economic profits." On the other hand, the coming of modern corporation and the development of capital markets interacted with dividend law to make the concept of a year's profit one of the most important ideas in economics and, as May (1936, II, p. 307) put it, "the central question of modern accounting." Yet, Hatfield's comment (1927, p. 241) about the profit concept is as valid today as it was nearly fifty years ago:

> It is a peculiar fact that while all business is carried on for the purpose of securing profits, while the distribution of profits is continually the subject of controversy in the courts, while the ascertainment of profits enters largely into the discussion of every economist, the term is still vaguely and loosely used and without definition by either economist, man of affairs, jurist, or accountant.

Thus, whereas dividend law conditioned businessmen, investors, and creditors to think in terms of the concept of "profit of a period," traditional accounting models that attempt to explain operationally the meaning of this concept in the context of the modern firm have been unsatisfactory. And as long as the term, "profit," is vaguely and loosely used and without definition, all areas of accounting responsibility that touch on questions concerning profit calculations must be a continuing source of controversy and dispute. This controversy will not subside until accountants become willing to acknowledge that in theory it is uncertainty about the future, not dividend law, that gives rise to the problem of determining the profit of a period.

CONCLUSION

Accounting thought in the nineteenth century is especially relevant to contemporary issues because the laissez-faire business environment produced a free and uninhibited exchange of views. The courts at this time were reluctant to interfere in business affairs and, unless fraud were an issue, business practices were determined by businessmen. Similarly, the statutes did not lay down specific rules governing accounting practices, and quasi-judicial administrative bodies such as the Securities Exchange Commission did not yet exist.

The last two decades of the nineteenth century were a "golden age" in accounting and most of the major issues connected with the subject of the accountant's responsibility were brought out in the period. Questions concerning full disclosure, alternative techniques, scope of audit and the meaning of the audit certificate were widely discussed in the first few years after the profession was formally established.

However, nineteenth century accountants did not "solve" most of the problems which they debated. One explanation for the perennial nature of controversy is the accountant's early attitude toward uncertainty. During the last century, the profession began to emphasize the historical nature of accounting calculations even though many theorists recognized that forecasts and estimates were inherent in most problems.

Thus one explanation for the persistence of accounting controversy is the failure to recognize that profit calculations involve uncertainty about the future. But given the legal origin of the profit concept, it is not surprising to find that accountants became more concerned with statutory and judicial references to profit than with the more abstruse questions associated with an uncertain future. What implications can be drawn from this historical study of the accountant's responsibility?

First, many modern proposals for reform can be traced directly to the nineteenth century. Indeed, the basic perspective of the accountant's responsibility has not changed very much, and recent suggestions for improving practice often repeat earlier ideas. Thus even though the economic environment was very different 100 years ago, the basic problems in accounting today closely resemble those which confronted the profession in the last century. Therefore, regulation and legislation do not seem to have produced many of the improvements in practice which were expected.

Second, there is recent evidence that the accounting profession's attitude toward uncertainty may be changing. The report of the Study Group on the Objectives of Financial Statements (1973) gives explicit attention to the problem of forecasting future cash flows. And the Forecasting Task Force of the MAS Development and Liaison Subcommittee of the AICPA (1974) considered questions concerning past profit as an "index" of future profit. This work could produce a radical change in the concept of profit.

If direct forecasts of cash flows and other information about the future are given in financial reports, the modern corporate concept of profit might become obsolete as a measure of either past performance or as an index of future performance. In the last analysis, a firm's performance depends on its cash flows, and if information about cash flows were provided by accountants, what purpose would be served by reporting profit figures that are based on conventional methods in accounting? And what purpose would be served by forecasting future profits, if direct estimates of future cash flows already were available? Questions like these will inevitably arise when more attention is devoted to the subject of uncertainty.[3]

Third, if the traditional opposition to forecasting and estimation overrides the current effort being made in some quarters to integrate forecasting and estimation problems within the mainstream of accounting theory, then the lesson of history will not have been learned. For most debate in accounting inevitably must lead to a discussion of uncertainty about the future. This is the one area of thought which nineteenth century accountants were unable to deal with, and twentieth century accountants have not yet faced the problem squarely.

[3]See, e.g., Thomas (1974).

REFERENCES

American Institute of Certified Public Accountants, Study Group on the Objectives of Financial Statements, *Objectives of Financial Statements* (1973).

American Institute of Certified Public Accountants, Forecasting Task Force of the MAS Development and Liaison Subcommittee, March 28, 1974 Exposure Draft, *Standards for Systems for the Preparation of Financial Forecasts* (1974).

APB Accounting Principles, Current Text as of June 30, 1973 (Commerce Clearing House, 1973).

Brief, R. P., "Nineteenth Century Accounting Error," *Journal of Accounting Research* (Spring 1965), pp. 167–77.

———, "The Origin and Evolution of Nineteenth Century Asset Accounting," *Business History Review* (Spring 1966), pp. 1–23.

———, "Depreciation Theory in Historical Perspective," *The Accountant* (December 26, 1970), pp. 737–39.

——— and Owen, J., "The Estimation Problem in Financial Accounting," *Journal of Accounting Research* (Autumn 1970), pp. 167–78.

Chatfield, M., *A History of Accounting Thought* (Dryden Press, 1974).

Dickinson, A. L., *Accounting Practice and Procedure* (Ronald Press, 1914).

Dicksee, L. R., *Auditing,* 10th ed. (Gee & Co., 1915).

Edwards, E. O. and Bell, P. W., *The Theory and Measurement of Business Income* (University of California Press, 1965).

Hatfield, H. R., *Modern Accounting—Its Principles and Svme of Its Problems* (D. Appleton & Co., 1927).

Hawes, D. W., "Towards a More Muscular Audit," *New York Times,* April 14, 1974.

Hawkins, D. F., "The Development of Modern Financial Reporting Practices Among American Manufacturing Corporations," *Business History Review* (Autumn 1963), pp. 135–168.

Kehl, D., *Corporate Dividends—Legal and Accounting Problems Pertaining to Corporate Distributions* (Ronald Press, 1941).

Leake, P. D., *Depreciation and Wasting Assets* (Henry Good & Son, 1912).

Matheson, E., *Depreciation of Factories,* 4th ed. (E. & F. Spon, 1910).

Mautz, R. K. and Sharaf, H. A., *The Philosophy of Auditing,* American Accounting Association Monograph Number Six (American Accounting Association, 1961).

May, G. O., *Twenty-Five Years of Accounting Responsibility 1911–1936,* B. S. Hunt, ed. (American Institute Publishing Co., 1936).

Montgomery, R. H. ed., *Dicksee's Auditing,* 2nd ed. (New York, 1909).

Pixley, F. W., *Auditors: Their Duties and Responsibilities,* 4th ed. (Henry Good & Son, 1887).

Thomas, A. L., *The Allocation Problem: Part II,* Studies in Accounting Research #9 (American Accounting Association, 1974).

van Pelt III, J. V., "The Future of Accepted Accounting Principles," A Digest of the 1971–72 Gold Medal Award Winning Article, *Management Accounting* (August 1972), pp. 11–14.

I-A2

SOME JUNCTURES IN THE EVOLUTION OF THE PROCESS OF ESTABLISHING ACCOUNTING PRINCIPLES IN THE U.S.A.: 1917–1972

Stephen A. Zeff

Several junctures in the evolution of the process of establishing accounting principles in the United States may be discerned. It is my purpose in this paper to identify the factors that seem to have been influential in shaping these events. The several junctures may be enumerated as follows:

1. Vote of the membership of the American Institute of Accountants (AIA), in 1918, to reject the capitalization of interest cost.
2. Vote of the AIA membership, in 1934, to adopt six "rules or principles" of accounting.
3. Decision by the Institute's Council, in 1938–39, to reorganize the Committee on Accounting Procedure, create a research department, and authorize the Committee to issue a series of bulletins on accounting without reference to Council.

Editor's Note: This paper served as the basis for a plenary address given at the 1983 Annual Meeting of the American Accounting Association. It was subsequently submitted and reviewed for publication. Useful comments on an earlier draft were received from Richard Macve, Gary J. Previts, Andrew Barr, Paul Grady, and Reed K. Storey. The author is, of course, solely responsible for what remains.

Steven A. Zeff, "Some Junctures in the Evolution of the Process of Establishing Accounting Principles in the U.S.A.: 1917–1972," *The Accounting Review* (July 1984), pp. 447–468. Reprinted by permission of the American Accounting Association.

4. Decision by the Institute's Council, in 1959, to supplant the Committee on Accounting Procedure by an Accounting Principles Board, and also to replace the Institute's research department by an accounting research division.
5. Decision by the Institute's Council, in 1972, to adopt the recommendations of the Wheat Study, terminate the Accounting Principles Board and the accounting research division, and support the creation of a Financial Accounting Foundation, whose purpose would be to underwrite a Financial Accounting Standards Board.

A theme that runs through the discussion of these events is that the actions of the Institute were precipitated by criticism voiced from inside or outside the profession, or by efforts of academics to influence the course of accounting principles. Especially in the 1930's, and even in the 1950's and 1970's, the American Accounting Association played a role.

Since accounting principles—which affect the behavior of independent auditors and their clients—have been set in the private sector, it is not surprising that, at each juncture, the American Institute of Accountants has been seen to seek support from authoritative bodies. At different times, these agencies have been in the government (e.g., the Federal Trade Commission, Federal Reserve Board, and Securities and Exchange Commission) or in the private sector (e.g., the New York Stock Exchange). In this context, the American Accounting Association has not been a support agency, but the Association has nonetheless been viewed by the Institute with concern and respect. Through its own initiatives, the Association could dilute the force of Institute pronouncements as well as suggest weaknesses (especially of the conceptual kind) in the Institute's program for establishing accounting principles.

"INTEREST AS A COST" IN 1917–18

In the early part of the second decade of the century, a number of articles began to appear in accounting journals which advocated the capitalization of interest. The controversy was precipitated, according to Wells [1978, p. 130], by the publication Arthur Lowes Dickinson's "The Fallacy of Including Interest and Rent as Part of Manufacturing Cost" [1911]. Dickinson was senior partner in the American firm of Price, Waterhouse & Co.

The FASB's Discussion Memorandum on "Accounting for Interest Costs" traces the background of the "interest as a cost" controversy:

> Towards the end of the nineteenth century, the issue of accounting for interest arose as part of a larger concern with developing realistic product costs to serve as a basis for establishing selling prices and measuring manufacturing efficiency. The increasing complexity of business, the increasing reliance on machinery, and the consequent need to invest large amounts of capital for long periods of time greatly increased the amount of overhead. The inclusion of overhead in product cost therefore became a major accounting issue [FASB, 1977, para. 174].

Along with the accounting treatment of depreciation, the manner of accounting for interest was born of the Industrial Revolution. The FASB adds,

> By the turn of the century, the general practice was to include in product costs virtually all costs of any nature, including interest. By 1910, however, most writ-

> ers had concluded that manufacturing expenses should be distinguished from selling and administrative expenses, and that only manufacturing expenses should be included in product cost [FASB, 1977, para. 174].

Academics and practitioners were arrayed on both sides of the question of whether to include interest in production cost, and feelings were strong. Clark [1923, p. 255] was justified in observing that "The discussion of this question is a strange mixture of dogmatic assertion and arguments from expediency." The matter seemed to have been settled in 1917, when, acting at the request of the Federal Trade Commission (FTC), the newly formed American Institute of Accountants published a memorandum devoted mostly to auditing procedures, but which carried the following dictum regarding the composition of overhead cost:

> That no selling expenses, interest charges, or administrative expenses are included in the factory overhead cost ["Uniform Accounts," 1917, p. 276].

But opposition to the Institute's position persisted. At the Institute's annual meeting in September 1917, Clinton H. Scovell, one of the leaders of the opposition, objected to the Institute's memorandum, published five months earlier, on the ground that it was unfavorable to the inclusion of interest in overhead. J. Lee Nicholson, another leader of the opposition, succeeded in persuading the Institute President to appoint a special committee "to gather statistics and facts and opinions on the treatment of interest and to report at the next meeting" ["Proceedings . . . ," 1917, p. 71]. The words of one observer testified to the hostile climate in which the action was taken:

> A great many accountants felt that the appointment of such a committee was slaying the slain, but in order that both sides of the question should be heard the whole institute approved the passing of the resolution. For some years there has been a small but vociferous minority of the membership which has clung to the generally discarded idea that interest was properly an element of cost" [Richardson, 1918, p. 292].

At the Institute's next annual meeting, the committee's report was presented. Instead of fulfilling its charge to marshal "statistics and facts and opinions," the committee, in language hardly indicative of judicial balance, haughtily dismissed the arguments of the opposition, finding that "the inclusion in production cost of interest on investment is unsound in theory and wrong, not to say absurd, in practice" ["Report . . ." 1918, p. 112].

It was a time when the leaders of the Institute were sensitive to the uses to which commercial bankers might put financial statements,[1] and the proposal to include interest in the cost of production probably was seen by most auditors as being inimical to a conservative and objective valuation of assets.[2]

At the Institute's 1918 annual meeting, the defenders of doctrine were so supremely confident of the rightness of their position that they sought and obtained the Institute membership's

---

[1]Although the Institute's 1917 memorandum on balance-sheet audits had been solicited by the Federal Trade Commission, the document was published in the *Federal Reserve Bulletin* after having been approved by the Federal Reserve Board.

[2]Previts and Merino [1979, p. 184] view the dispute as a conflict between the entity and proprietary theories.

approval, not mere acceptance, of its report.[3] The following sentence, appearing in a footnote appended to the committee's report in the Institute's *1918 Year-Book,* clearly implies that Institute members were expected not to approve the inclusion of interest in production cost in financial statements:

> Adoption of the report [by the Institute membership] did not debar any [Institute] member from including interest in cost of production when compiling . . . internal statistics—provided always that such statistics must not be used to color financial statements ["Report . . . ," 1918, p. 112].

Why did the Institute's leaders act so categorically on the proper treatment of interest in the accounts? A likely reason was to establish credibility with the Federal Trade Commission and the Federal Reserve Board. Edward N. Hurley, FTC chairman, had become interested in promoting uniform accounting practices in certain industries, and he had horrified Institute leaders by suggesting that "consideration might be given to the possibility of developing a register of public accountants whose audit certificates would be acceptable to the Commission and the [Federal Reserve] Board" [Carey, 1969, p. 130]. For its part, the Federal Reserve Board was "keenly interested in the credit worthiness of organizations whose commercial paper was discounted by Federal Reserve banks. The Board, therefore, had an immediate and vital interest in the reliability of certified financial statements of such enterprises" [Carey, 1969, p. 132]. Evidently, the Institute sought to present a united front on the treatment of interest.

Scovell, Nicholson, and others of like mind on the interest question rightly concluded that the Institute hierarchy was unsympathetic to their cause (also see Carey [1969, p. 311]). In October 1919, they were among the leaders of the 37 men who met in Buffalo, New York to found the National Association of Cost Accountants, and in 1920 the new Association appointed a committee to study the question of including interest in production cost. At the Association's 1921 International Cost Conference, the committee's report was presented and the subject was discussed at length ["Interest as an Element of Cost," 1921]. No conclusion was reached, but at least a friendly forum for an exchange of views was provided.

While it is true, as Moonitz [1970] points out, that there were several concerted initiatives in the 1910's and early 1920's to influence accounting practice, the one involving the possible inclusion of interest in production cost is the best example from that period of an organized and persistent opposition to Institute doctrine. It was the first time that the membership of a national accounting body had taken a position on a matter of accounting principle. Had the Institute not then been under pressure from the FTC and Federal Reserve Board (FRB), it is very likely that no committee would have been formed by the Institute in 1917 to put an end to the controversy, and that no position would have been submitted to a vote of the Institute membership in 1918.

---

[3]In 1979, I brought the fact of the Institute membership's 1918 disapproval of interest capitalization to the attention of the Financial Accounting Standards Board, which was then considering a Statement on the subject. When Statement No. 34, "Capitalization of Interest Cost," was issued by the Board in October 1979, the following sentence was included in a footnote to paragraph 25:

> Although the [1918] vote of the Institute's membership is of historical interest, it has not been incorporated into the body of authoritative pronouncements currently in force.

So much for the weight accorded the Institute membership's approval of accounting principles!

AIA APPROVAL OF SIX "RULES OR PRINCIPLES"

The second juncture in the evolution of the process of establishing accounting principles covered the period 1926–34. William Z. Ripley, a Harvard economics professor, wrote an exposé of corporate financial reporting in the September 1926 issue of *The Atlantic Monthly.* Entitled "Stop, Look, Listen!", the article contained specific criticisms of reporting practices that Ripley regarded as deceptive. In the article, he referred to "enigmatic accounting" [p. 388] and directed much of his criticism to understated depreciation provisions and overstated asset valuations. His brief embraced both measurement and disclosure issues, including "the failure to disclose the method of the valuation [of assets], whether it be of property or of stock in trade" [p. 390]. Ripley concluded on an ominous note:

> Let the word go forth that the Federal Trade Commission is henceforward to address itself vigorously to the matter of adequate and intelligent corporate publicity . . . [p. 399].

Ripley's article made an immediate impact. George O. May, senior partner in Price, Waterhouse & Co., commented critically on Ripley's article in a letter to *The New York Times* [1926a] and reacted more fully to Ripley's indictment in an address given a month after Ripley's article appeared [1926b].[4] May described the source of his concern as follows:

> Unless some effective steps are taken to meet criticisms such as those voiced by Professor Ripley, the result will be some sort of bureaucratic control, and I am satisfied that through proper cooperation methods can be devised, without resort to government, which will be more effective and at the same time less burdensome and vexatious than control by a governmental body is likely to be [May, 1926c, p. 42].

Not only did May dislike the prospect of government intervention, his words were well calculated to goad the profession into taking some concerted action to raise the standards of professional performance. In his address at the Institute's annual meeting in 1926, May proposed that the Institute sponsor a cooperative effort involving the leading stock exchanges, investment bankers, and commercial bankers so that

> standards might be established for balance-sheets and income accounts which would be welcomed by many corporation executives and accountants who desire to be guided by the best practice, if they can be assured what that practice is [May, 1926b, p. 324].

The succeeding paragraphs in May's address make it clear that his recommended standards would deal more with disclosure than with measurement. May was an Englishman, and he had received his accounting training in Exeter. In Britain (prior to 1981), the succession of Companies Acts largely confined their provisions on accounting to matters of disclosure, leaving the questions of how to value assets and determine net income to companies and their auditors. In his 1926 address, May favored the disclosure of the methods used to value capital assets

---

[4]May's talk was given at the annual meeting of the American Institute of Accountants. Carey [1969, Chap. 10] and May [Grady, 1962, Chap. 6] have discussed the series of initiatives by May and the Institute resulting from Ripley's critical writings on accounting and financial reporting.

and of any "extraordinary or extraneous profit" included in the profits of the year [pp. 324–325]. Of paramount importance would be the disclosure of any methods used "other than those commonly accepted" [p. 325].

May's philosophy, as set forth in the famous letter dated September 22, 1932 from the Institute's Committee on Cooperation with Stock Exchanges to the Committee on Stock List of the New York Stock Exchange, was that

> [w]ithin quite wide limits, it is relatively unimportant to the investor what precise rules or conventions are adopted by a corporation in reporting its earnings if he knows what method is being followed and is assured that it is followed consistently from year to year [AIA, 1934, p. 9].

His committee proposed that corporations listed on the New York Stock Exchange (NYSE) formulate and approve a list of accounting methods used in the preparation of their financial statements; give assurances that the methods so adopted will be followed consistently from year to year, but that any material deviations should be disclosed; and furnish the list to the Exchange so that any stockholder might, upon payment of a fee, request a copy (1932 letter, in AIA [1934, p. 13]). In addition, May's committee recommended that the Exchange "make universal the acceptance by listed corporations of certain broad principles of accounting which have won fairly general acceptance, and within the limits of such broad principles to make no attempt to restrict the right of corporations to select detailed methods of accounting deemed by them to be best adapted to the requirements of their business"[5] (1932 letter, in AIA [1934, pp. 12–13]). May's "broad principles" encompassed the following:

1. Unrealized profit should not be credited to income, and expenses ordinarily chargeable against income should not be charged instead against unrealized profit.
2. Except for quasi-reorganizations, capital surplus (in today's jargon, additional paid-in capital) should not be charged with amounts that ordinarily would be charged to income.
3. "Earned surplus [today, retained earnings] of a subsidiary company created prior to acquisition does not form part of the consolidated earned surplus of the parent company and subsidiaries."
4. While "it is perhaps in some circumstances permissible" for treasury stock to be shown as an asset, the dividends declared on such stock may not be credited to the company's income.
5. "Notes or accounts receivable due from officers, employees, or affiliated companies must be shown separately and not included under a general heading such as Notes Receivable or Accounts Receivable"[6] (1932 letter, in AIA [1934, p. 14]).

[5]The committee used the terms "principles," "practices," and "conventions" interchangeably, and at the 1934 Institute annual meeting, where the members were asked for their approval, the term "rules or principles" was employed. In a later article, May made clear that his committee did not use "principles" to suggest "fundamental principles," as in deductive logic. Instead, he preferred the following definition: "A general law or rule adopted or professed as a guide to action; a settled ground or basis of conduct or practice" [May, 1937, p. 423]. In 1939, when the Institute's Committee on Accounting Procedure reaffirmed the earlier "rules or principles," they were described as "rules formerly adopted." (Also see Grady [1962, pp. 73–74].)

[6]When these five "broad principles" were submitted for membership vote at the 1934 Institute annual meeting, a sixth was added, dealing with what is known as "treasury stock subterfuge." It was also approved by the membership.

Although the Institute's membership voted approval in 1934 of the committee's proposed principles, the Exchange did no more than agree to the list. Moreover, the Exchange never did impose a requirement on listed companies to compile a list of their accounting methods to be placed on public record. Yet much of what May's committee sought to achieve in this regard was implemented by the Securities and Exchange Commission (SEC) when it mandated the disclosure of certain accounting methods in the registration statements of listed companies [Blough, 1967, p. 3]. A further step was taken in 1972, when the Accounting Principles Board issued Opinion No. 22, requiring companies to disclose a summary of their "significant accounting policies" as an integral part of their annual financial statements.

Although the correspondence contained in *Audits of Corporate Accounts* [AIA, 1934] led to a successful collaboration between the Institute and the New York Stock Exchange, May's very substantial effort to ward off the intervention of the federal government in the establishment of accounting principles failed. Ripley's writings had spurred May and the Institute on, but the forces unleashed by the Great Depression were irreversible.

AIA Decision to Empower the Committee on Accounting Procedure to Issue Pronouncements

Once the Securities and Exchange Commission came into existence in 1934, the leading edge of George O. May's effort to raise the standard of accounting practice seemed to lose its sharpness, as if the Institute leadership had been intimidated into silence by the new layer of federal bureaucracy and its broad statutory powers over accounting and auditing practice. At the same time, May was philosophically opposed to identifying "accepted principles of accounting" until an informed consensus was clearly discernible; this credo, coupled with his preference to allow corporations to adopt accounting methods that they believed to be "best adapted to the requirements of their business," did not portend an active, forceful program of raising the standard of accounting practice. May was not about to become the dictator of best practice.[7]

In 1933, May was named chairman of a new Institute committee, the Special Committee on Development of Accounting Principles, and in its first report, issued in October 1934, the committee bespoke a reluctance to forge ahead as confidently as had May's Special Committee on Cooperation with Stock Exchanges. A few excerpts from the committee's report exemplified the new mood:

> Since principles of accounting cannot be arrived at by pure reasoning, but must find their justification in practical wisdom, the committee believes that the Institute should proceed with caution in selecting from the methods more or less commonly employed those which should be accorded the standing of principles or accepted rules of accounting. . . . The committee believes that the policy of the Institute should be to act with care and deliberation, and to endeavor whenever possible to secure the concurrence of some body possessing high authority in the rules or principles which it lays down ["Report . . . ," AIA, 1935, p. 276].

This was the only report to emerge from the committee, and it was not reappointed in 1936, when its assignment was transferred to the new Committee on Accounting Procedure, of which May became chairman in 1937.

---

[7]For a discussion of May's philosophy, see Storey [1964, pp. 13–15] and May [1943].

Eric L. Kohler, editor of *The Accounting Review,* journal of the American Association of University Instructors in Accounting (AAUIA), who wrote several biting editorials during the 1930's, professed a profound disappointment with the 1934 report of the Special Committee on Development of Accounting Principles:

> Little apparently may be hoped from the Committee. . . . Its recommendations are surface considerations and give no indication of any sound approach to the more general problem for which a solution is now so urgently necessary. In fact, it in substance confesses that it does not propose to exert any originality except that which will be required to restrain, shall we say, a securities and exchange commission that may get out of hand [Kohler, 1934b, pp. 335–336].

To be sure, the Institute committee was restating May's view that the profession required an authoritative ally in order to develop principles, as had been done with the FTC, FRB, and NYSE. But in 1934, the committee did not seem disposed to take the lead. In his editorials, Kohler began to adopt a cynical view toward the leaders of the Institute (see Kohler [1934a]), and he characterized himself as being among "the accounting radicals who advocate that accountants should not only think for themselves but also formulate their own rules without reference to outside agencies" [Kohler, 1935, p. 372]. In December 1934, Kohler sternly criticized the Institute and issued a "call to arms" to his colleagues in the Association:

> For years [the Editor] has assailed the smugness of the profession and its inability to set standards for its own conduct and for the information of the public that relies upon its findings. . . . For years it has failed to see the problems before it: problems for the complexity of which it alone has been responsible. . . .
>
> To instructors of accounting, this condition of affairs should offer a challenge. Now, more than ever, the voice of enlightened opinion within the profession is needed. Shall we as accountants recognize that the responsibilities of the profession are large, particularly to third persons? Or shall we drift as we have done in the past, waiting, at first hopefully and now fearfully, for someone else to tell us what to do? Is it impossible for us to take any initial responsibility for defining our accountability to the business and financial world and to the investing public? [1934a].

It is hardly farfetched to believe that the Institute's apparent abdication as a leading force in the establishment of accounting principles was the principal catalyst for the reorganization of the AAUIA as the American Accounting Association in 1935–36. In the new Association's declaration of objectives, published early in 1936, its leaders rejected the view that "the only practicable means of improvement [in accounting practice] is the slow, evolutionary process involving persuasion and example through which the worst accounting practices may be gradually eliminated" [AAA, 1936, p. 2]. The new Association's program was defined as follows:

> Specifically, there should be a definitive, understandable explanation of what a set of accounting statements purports to signify. . . . Such a body of principles would furnish an essential basis of judgment in constructing and appraising financial statements. . . . The essential of such a statement is that it constitute an integrated conception of the function of accounting as a means of giving financial expression to business facts [pp. 2–3].

One of the four official purposes of the new Association was

> To develop accounting principles and standards, and to seek their endorsement or adoption by business enterprises, public and private accountants, and governmental bodies [Zeff, 1966, p. 40].

This was a new objective that did not appear in the Constitution of the AAUIA. Thus was the impetus for the series of AAA statements on accounting principles, the first of which appeared in 1936.

There is ample reason to believe that the Institute leadership was not comfortable with the bold initiatives of the reborn Association. SEC Commissioner George C. Mathews was invited to attend the first meeting of the Association's 1936 executive committee, at which the Commissioner "asserted the need for an authoritative literature for use by governmental agencies" [Zeff, 1966, p. 43]. In June 1936, the Association's executive committee issued "A Tentative Statement of Accounting Principles Affecting Corporate Reports" and awaited the profession's reaction. Although numerous academics gave speeches and wrote articles that were critical of one or more sections of the principles statement, official comment from the Institute was nil. The Institute was evidently not pleased that the upstart organization of teachers was attempting to establish accounting principles that might, in the end, affect the performance standards expected of practitioners [Zeff, 1966, pp. 45–46]. Carman G. Blough, the SEC Chief Accountant, in a talk at the inaugural annual meeting of the Association, praised the body's principles statement as "a real contribution to the accounting profession" [1937, p. 30]. When, in early 1938, the Institute published a monograph entitled *A Statement of Accounting Principles,* written by three well-known academics [Sanders, Hatfield and Moore, 1938], a number of members of the Association believed that the Institute was trying to counter the recent achievement of the Association. The monograph had been commissioned in early 1935 by the Haskins & Sells Foundation, and the research was apparently completed before the Institute offered to publish it [Zeff, 1966, p. 47].

Annoyance at the growing role of the Association in the principles sphere was but one factor in impelling the Institute to regain the lead as a principles setter in 1938. The major factor was growing pressure being exerted by the SEC. Again, the specter of governmental intervention spurred the Institute's leadership.

During 1937–38, leaders of the Institute discussed whether, and if so, how, the Institute might reassert its leadership in the establishment of accounting principles. The SEC had been urging the Institute to take a more active role in promoting uniformity in accounting practice, and in April 1938, in one of Carman Blough's final acts as Chief Accountant, the Commission issued Accounting Series Release No. 4 which challenged the profession to provide "substantial authoritative support" for accepted accounting practices (see Zeff [1972, pp. 134–139]).

George O. May, for his part, proposed that his Committee on Accounting Procedure, rather than awaiting questions that might be raised by others (including the SEC), should act on its own initiative to give advice on matters meriting the Committee's attention. Previts and Merino report that May petitioned the Institute's executive committee in September 1937 to expand the Committee's membership, establish a research capability, and authorize it to initiate discussion on any problem area [1979, pp. 260–261] (also see Horne [1941, p. 47]).

The Institute's leadership moved cautiously in taking up May's suggestion. There was a concern that the Institute would suffer embarrassment if it were seen to issue pronouncements that failed to win the support of other authorities, or even of its own membership. May himself recognized the possible vulnerability of an Institute committee working alone in such sensitive waters. In a letter dated June 1, 1938 to Institute Secretary John L. Carey, May wrote:

> I feel it would be very unfortunate to have opinions put forward by the Institute which would be in direct conflict with those expressed by either the Securities and Exchange Commission or the New York Stock Exchange, or by an official body of accounting teachers, though I am quite prepared to express and maintain such dissent if it seems really necessary.

Other Institute leaders were impatient for signs of some progress. For example, on May 25, 1938, Will-A. Clader, a member of Council and a former Institute vice-president, wrote, in a letter to Frederick B. Andrews, also a member of Council and a former Institute President:

> For some reason the Institute's powers that be appear to be fearful of giving official approval to accounting principles. . . . I am getting old fast and fear that I may not see the day when the profession will have arrived to the point when it will have the final word in the accounting treatment of financial transactions.

Clader was concerned that Institute committees, including the Committee on Accounting Procedure when commenting on technical questions, were required to state that their views were given for information only "and that care must be taken so that there is no indication that they received the approval of the Institute or its governing body." Some, such as Clader, had suggested that the Institute's executive committee might allow statements drafted by technical committees to be issued under its imprimatur, but that idea was dismissed by Clem W. Collins, Institute President, in a letter to Clader dated June 2, 1938:

> The views of the members of the Executive Committee on such a controversial subject, would have no binding effect upon the profession or the members of the Institute if they did not represent the consensus of opinion and the prevailing best practice of the practitioners. It is quite conceivable that the views of the men constituting the Executive Committee might not represent that preponderance of opinion and practice; therefore until the profession has been given an opportunity to discuss proposed principles and procedures and to freely express opinions in regard thereto, I do not feel that any official group in the Institute should attempt to lay down the law.

Finally, acting on a proposal put forth in July 1938 by Patrick W. R. Glover, a partner in the major firm of Barrow, Wade, Guthrie & Co. and a member of the Institute's executive committee, the Institute leadership agreed to take a decisive step [Zeff, 1972, p. 135]. Glover's proposal contained the major points advanced by May in his recommendation to the executive committee nine months earlier, and he added the proviso that the Committee should be authorized to issue bulletins without reference to the executive committee. In his Committee's report to Council in September 1938, May's proposal of September 1937 was reiterated. As approved by the Institute's Council, the plan provided for an enlargement of the Committee on Accounting Procedure from eight to 22 members, including the President as *ex officio* chairman, and authority to issue pronouncements in its own name. In 1939, also reflecting the proposals made by May and Glover, the Institute formed a research department to assist the

Committee on Accounting Procedure in studying alternative solutions to accounting problems. These actions underscored the position that the Institute could not risk forfeiting its leadership in the establishment of accounting principles, especially in view of the restiveness of the SEC.

The essence of the compromise was that all interested parties and organizations whose support for pronouncements was required would be represented on the Committee. Three academics were named to the enlarged Committee: A. C. Littleton, William A. Paton, and Roy B. Kester, all of whom had led the reorganization of the AAA in 1935–36. Littleton and Paton were the Association's codirectors of research in 1938. (In all subsequent years, academics were included on the membership of the Committee.) The New York Stock Exchange was covered by the fact that George O. May, whose firm served as accounting adviser to the Exchange, was selected as vice-chairman of the Committee. (In actual fact, May chaired the Committee's meetings and led its work.) Since Carman G. Blough had concluded his service as SEC Chief Accountant on May 31, 1938 and had joined Arthur Andersen & Co. as a manager, he was an obvious candidate for Committee membership, and, indeed, his name appeared on the inaugural roll.[8] William W. Werntz, Blough's successor as SEC Chief Accountant, was invited to attend an early meeting of the Committee. Finally, a member was taken from each of the major public accounting firms, so that the likelihood of an important firm's disavowing the Committee's recommendations might be minimized. Another reason, of course, was to tap the substantial expertise in the larger firms, those whose clients were subject to the SEC's jurisdiction. The Committee membership in 1938–39 read like a "Who's Who" of the best-known technical experts in the U.S. accounting profession:

Clem W. Collins (Institute President), Chairman, Collins, Peabody and Young (Denver)

George O. May, Vice-Chairman, Price, Waterhouse & Co. (New York)

Frederick B. Andrews, F. B. Andrews & Company (Chicago)

George D. Bailey, Ernst & Ernst (Detroit)

Carman G. Blough, Arthur Andersen & Co. (Chicago)

Samuel J. Broad, Peat, Marwick, Mitchell & Co. (New York)

Arthur H. Carter, Haskins & Sells (New York)

Charles B. Couchman, Barrow, Wade, Guthrie & Co. (New York)

A. S. Fedde, Fedde & Company (New York)

Henry B. Fernald, Loomis, Suffern & Fernald (New York)

Stanley G. H. Fitch, Patterson, Teele & Dennis (Boston)

Henry A. Horne, Webster, Horne & Blanchard (New York)

Frederick H. Hurdman, Hurdman and Cranstoun (New York)

Lincoln G. Kelly, Lincoln G. Kelly & Company (Salt Lake City)

Roy B. Kester, Columbia University

[8]A measure of the importance of having the immediate past SEC Chief Accountant on the Committee is the fact that Blough was only a manager at Arthur Andersen & Co. He is probably the only representative of an accounting firm to serve on a standard-setting body prior to becoming a partner.

Lewis Lilly, McLaren, Goode & Co. (San Francisco)

A. C. Littleton, University of Illinois

Warren W. Nissley, Arthur Young & Company (New York)

William A. Paton, University of Michigan

Charles F. Rittenhouse, Charles F. Rittenhouse & Company (Boston)

Walter A. Staub, Lybrand, Ross Bros. & Montgomery (New York)

Victor H. Stempf, Touche, Niven & Co. (New York)

Thus began the precedent of inviting one member to the Committee from each of the major national firms.[9] (This practice was continued with respect to the Big Eight firms on the Accounting Principles Board.) The Institute leadership was careful to provide representation on the Committee from both small and large firms, and from the Midwest, Rocky Mountains, and West Coast, as well as the East. Seven of the members were chairmen of other Institute committees. All angles were considered.

The Institute's first Director and Coordinator of Research was Thomas H. Sanders, an accounting professor at the Harvard Business School, who had served as a consultant to the SEC in 1934–35 and was the lead author of the Institute's 1938 publication, *A Statement of Accounting Principles.*

Hence, by 1939, the Institute's machinery was in place. Between 1934, when the Institute membership had approved the six "rules or principles," and 1938–39, when the Institute reconstituted its Committee on Accounting Procedure and launched a research department, it had largely abandoned its leadership role in the establishment of accounting principles. The aggressiveness of the American Accounting Association in filling this void had been influential in inducing the Institute to find a way to recapture its leadership position. But the major influence had to be seen as the SEC. Yet notwithstanding the almost pathological fear by accounting practitioners of governmental intervention in their affairs, the Institute did not seize the initiative, following the passage of the securities acts, to develop and publicize its views on accounting principles. Kohler was probably right in believing that the leaders of the practicing profession, especially May, were exceedingly reluctant to "force" a consensus on accounting principles when a diversity of views prevailed among leading practitioners and other authorities. Throughout its life, the Committee on Accounting Procedure labored under this philosophical conflict—i.e., whether an authoritative professional body might insist upon the acceptability of only one accounting method when several enjoyed the support of leading CPA's and large corporations. The issue was not faced squarely until 1964, when the Institute, following 18 months of intensive study and debate, resolved to endow Opinions of the Accounting Principles Board with greater authority in the forging of "generally accepted accounting principles" (see Carey [1970, Chap. 5]). A burden was imposed on auditors to justify material departures from principles accepted in APB Opinions, and the APB was charged to "move toward the reduction of alternative practices in accounting" [*Report of the Special Committee on Opinions of the Accounting Principles Board,* 1965, p. 7].

[9] With the merger of several firms in 1947 to form Touche, Niven, Bailey & Smart, and the merger in 1950 of Barrow, Wade, Guthrie & Co. into Peat, Marwick, Mitchell & Co., the eight largest firms came to be known as the Big Eight, a term whose popularity is traceable to Wise [1960].

AICPA DECISION TO SUPPLANT CAP WITH APB

Several factors seem to have driven the Institute's decision, made in 1959, to replace the Committee on Accounting Procedure (CAP) with the Accounting Principles Board (APB).

First: Certain accounting problems had become increasingly difficult to resolve and had been causing serious divisions within the Committee on Accounting Procedure.

In several problem areas, the number of dissents and qualified assents (which often were tantamount, in their substance, to dissents) seemed to threaten further progress, and not a few of the dissenters and qualified assenters were representatives of the largest public accounting firms. Prominent instances were as follows:

"Accounting for the Use of Special War Reserves," Accounting Research Bulletin (ARB) No. 26 (October 1946)—three dissents (Haskins & Sells, Price Waterhouse, and Arthur Young).

"Emergency Facilities," ARB No. 27 (November 1946)—six dissents (including Price Waterhouse, Arthur Young, Touche Niven, and Barrow, Wade & Guthrie) and a qualified assent.

"Income and Earned Surplus," ARB No. 32 (December 1947)—three dissents (including Alexander Grant) and a qualified assent.

Letter dated October 14, 1948 from the Committee on Accounting Procedure reaffirming its ARB No. 33, "Depreciation and High Costs"—four dissents (including the chairman who was from Peat Marwick).

"Presentation of Income and Earned Surplus," ARB No. 35 (October 1948)—two dissents (Haskins & Sells and Ernst & Ernst) and four qualified assents.

"Depreciation and High Costs," Chapter 9(A) of ARB No. 43 (June 1953)—six dissents (including Peat Marwick and Price Waterhouse).

"Unamortized Discount, Issue Cost, and Redemption Premium on Bonds Refunded," Chapter 15 of ARB No. 43 (June 1953)—one dissent and four qualified assents (Peat Marwick, Haskins & Sells, Touche Niven, and Price Waterhouse).

"Accounting for the Costs of Pension Plans," ARB No. 47 (September 1956)—six qualified assents (including Price Waterhouse, Ernst & Ernst, Haskins & Sells, and Lybrand, Ross Bros. & Montgomery).

"Declining-Balance Depreciation," ARB No. 44 (Revised) (July 1958)—five qualified assents (including Arthur Andersen, Ernst & Ernst, Price Waterhouse, and Haskins & Sells).

Not only did these disagreements betray a difference in philosophy over the role of the Committee in narrowing the range of acceptable methods, but they also revealed fundamental disagreements over the proper methods of asset valuation and income determination. The latter discord suggested the need for more basic inquiries into the premises underlying broad accounting principles.

On at least four occasions during the Committee's history—1939, 1940, 1949, and 1956—it was proposed that the Committee develop a framework of fundamental principles that might serve to unite its members on the particulars of specific pronouncements, but no progress was ever reported (see Zeff [1972, pp. 141–143]). In his proposal for a reinvigorated accounting principles program in 1957, Institute President Alvin R. Jennings singled out research, especially fundamental research, as requiring a significant investment of resources [Jennings, 1958, pp. 31–33]. From this suggestion was born the accounting research division (of which Maurice Moonitz was the first director) to succeed the Institute's research department, which had been serving numerous other committees as well as the Committee on Accounting Procedure.[10]

Among the accounting research division's initial projects were, of course, the studies on postulates and basic principles by Moonitz and Robert T. Sprouse (see Zeff [1982]). Yet, upon the completion of this research phase, in 1962, the APB peremptorily dismissed the two studies as "too radically different from present generally accepted accounting principles for acceptance at this time" [APB, 1962]. The only fundamental research that reached fruition during the tenure of the APB were Accounting Research Study No. 7. *Inventory of Generally Accepted Accounting Principles for Business Enterprises* [Grady, 1965] and APB Statement No. 4, "Basic Concepts and Accounting Principles Underlying Financial Statements of Business Enterprises" [APB, 1970]. Except for small portions of both studies (Chapters 2 and 9 in the former, and Chapter 4 in the latter), neither went beyond an exposition of accepted practice.

Second: Representations had been made by the Controllers Institute of America (later to become the Financial Executives Institute) that company managements had not been given sufficient opportunity to comment on proposed bulletins prior to their issuance. (See Zeff [1972, pp. 145–148 and 168].) Since 1938, all of the members of the Committee on Accounting Procedure had been either accounting practitioners or academics, and the view had come to the fore that controllers and perhaps other interested parties should be integrated into the process of establishing accounting principles. In fact, the immediate past president of the Controllers Institute, Dudley E. Browne, was appointed in 1957 to the Institute's Special Committee on Research Program (which was formed in 1957 to study the implications of Jennings' presidential speech), evidently to underscore the newly acknowledged importance of the company controller in such matters. (From its founding, the APB always had between one and three financial executives as members. The Comptroller General of the United States was one of its charter members, and in the Board's final three years, 1971–73, one of its members was a financial analyst. Furthermore, the APB's exposure process and manner of consultation with interested parties eventually became considerably more elaborate than had been that of the Committee on Accounting Procedure.)

Third: The view had been gaining credence that the efforts of the American Accounting Association in the area of accounting principles reflected a more progressive spirit than did those of the Committee on Accounting Procedure. The AAA's Supplementary Statement No. 2, "Price Level Changes and Financial Statements" [1951], and the 1957 Revision of the Association's series of principles statements, "Accounting and Reporting Standards for Corporate Financial Statements," kept alive the interest, furthered more by academics than by practitioners,

[10] Almost as soon as the Institute's research department was created in 1939, it was serving more than one demanding master. Although it had been established to assist the Committee on Accounting Procedure, by 1939–40 it was also conducting studies for the new Committee on Auditing Procedure. The number of Institute committees which it served continued to grow, and Carman G. Blough said that, in the 1950s, "As Director of Research, I complained because I had to spread my little staff of four CPA's over some 25 committees of the Institute, and we were not able to give enough time and attention to the Committee on Accounting Procedure" [Interview conducted by the author in January 1967]. Hence, the charge to the newly created accounting research division in 1959 was that its exclusive responsibility was to the Accounting Principles Board.

of general price-level accounting. The former had been cited by several members of the Committee on Accounting Procedure, when, in 1953–54, an effort was made to reverse the Committee's negative stand toward accounting recognition of changing prices (see AIA [1953, Chap. 9(A)]). (Later in the decade, the AAA studies by Jones [1955] and Mason [1956] attracted considerable interest among policy makers.) Also, in the debate over the "all-inclusive" vs. "current-operating-performance" conception of the income statement, the SEC made a point (at least as late as 1951) of citing the AAA's support of the former, which the SEC favored, while at the same time criticizing the Committee on Accounting Procedure's espousal of the latter (see Barr [1979, pp. 45, 49–51 and ftn. 3]; King [1948; 1951]; and SEC [1948, p. 112]).

Even George O. May, whose leadership of the Committee during its early years established the Committee's practice of addressing accounting principles on an issue-by-issue basis, conceded in 1958 that the AAA's approach might well be emulated by the Institute:

> The American Accounting Association from the time of its first pronouncement has sought to relate specific provisions to a broad concept. It would seem that the Institute must successfully undertake a similar task before it can claim with reason to be either the leading authority or one of the leading authorities upon the subject [Grady, 1962, p. 278].

The Association's series of principles statements, especially the eight supplementary statements issued on specific topics between 1950 and 1954, caused some to believe that the Institute's program could benefit from a firmer conceptual basis in its pronouncements, underscoring the need, mentioned above, for more fundamental research. It is noteworthy, therefore, that one of the individuals named to the Institute's Special Committee on Research Program in 1957 was R. K. Mautz, of the University of Illinois, who had been chairman of the AAA committee that had prepared the 1957 Revision of the Association's series of principles statements.

Fourth: The Institute's leaders were feeling the sting of Leonard Spacek's outspoken criticism of the profession's record in establishing accounting principles. In one speech, given in early 1957, he accused the Committee on Accounting Procedure of yielding to industry pressure on a proposed pronouncement. Institute Executive Director John L. Carey reported that "A wave of indignation greeted [Spacek's] speech" [1970, p. 77]. The Institute appointed a special committee to investigate Spacek's allegations, and it concluded that his assertions were unfounded [AIA, 1957]. In his presidential address the following October, in which he proposed a major research program to support the Institute's ongoing effort to establish accounting principles, Alvin R. Jennings went out of his way to defend the profession's record of independence [1958, p. 33]. Although Jennings did not identify the source of the challenge to the profession's independence, it can easily be inferred that he had Spacek in mind. Moreover, Spacek was among the ten individuals named by Jennings to the Special Committee on Research Program.

It is evident that Spacek's criticisms of the Institute's accounting principles program, as well as his proposal for an accounting court made in a widely reported speech in August 1957 [Spacek, 1958], were consequential in the Institute's high-level review in 1957–58 of its process of establishing accounting principles.

Fifth: The Committee on Accounting Procedure had crossed swords several times with the SEC's Chief Accountant, and the confrontations had evoked disquiet on both sides. The SEC was displeased with the Committee's preference for the "current-operating-performance" conception of the income statement, and several members of the Committee (as well as a number of widely known practitioners and academics—e.g., Grady, Spacek, and Paton) were upset at the SEC's unwillingness to allow the effects of changing prices to enter into the determination of companies' net incomes.[11] (This latter concern led some to believe that a vigorous attempt to lay a groundwork of fundamental accounting principles might be the only avenue to genuine progress.) Furthermore, the SEC had made it known that the Committee had not done enough to limit the alternatives available to management (see Storey [1964, pp. 48–51] and Zeff [1972, pp. 150–160]). The Institute was, as always, sensitive to the need to retain its credibility with the SEC. Among the individuals appointed to the Special Committee on Research Program were Andrew Barr, the SEC Chief Accountant,[12] and two of the three former SEC Chief Accountants, Carman G. Blough and William W. Werntz. Blough had been the Institute's respected Director of Research since 1944, and Werntz was the Chairman of the Committee on Accounting Procedure in 1957–59.

Other factors may have been at work, but I believe that the foregoing five factors were the most important. Some critics complained that a few of the larger accounting firms had begun to nominate less senior partners to the Committee on Accounting Procedure, and it was not unknown for members to call their home offices to ascertain the views of their more senior partners—who would not have heard the Committee's debate—prior to casting their vote. When the Institute's executive committee appointed the members of the inaugural Accounting Principles Board, it insisted that the accounting firms could be represented only by their firm-wide managing partners. Some firms balked at this restriction, but no exceptions were allowed (save for the chairman of the Board, Weldon Powell, who had also been chairman of the Special Committee on Research Program).

Criticism in the financial press was infrequent and thus seems to have been largely absent as a factor.

One can therefore say, after reviewing the factors enumerated and discussed above, that the Institute was reacting both to internal and external criticisms. In the main, it hoped that a much more heavily research-based approach to establishing accounting principles would facilitate a resolution of the growing number of seemingly intractable problems.

AICPA Decision to Appoint a Study on Establishment of Accounting Principles (The Wheat Study)

As has already been noted, the APB failed to fulfill its founders' hopes that fundamental research would reduce complex accounting problems to basic notions on which leading professionals could find agreement. Neither the Grady [1965] study nor the Board's Statement No. 4 [1970] was followed up by normative research that might have recommended a set of fundamental principles or accounting objectives. And except for its much more elaborate procedure for obtaining comments on its tentative positions (meetings with industry groups, symposia, public hearings, and a more extensive distribution of exposure drafts), the Board operated in a manner not greatly dissimilar from that of the Committee on Accounting Procedure.

[11] For the opinion of the then Chief Accountant of the SEC, see King [1952].

[12] It has been exceedingly rare for the SEC Chief Accountant to serve as a voting member on Institute policy committees. One supposes that the Commission regards such service, except in unusual circumstances, as having the potential to compromise, at least in appearance, the SEC's independence from those organizations that are subject to its regulation.

Yet notwithstanding its new procedures and the fortified research commitment by the Institute, the APB compiled a record of dissents and qualified assents on matters involving asset valuation and income determination which exceeded that of the Committee on Accounting Procedure. Of the 12 substantive, single-issue Opinions issued by the Board through 1970 (see Exhibit 1), major disagreements among the Board members occurred on nine (i.e., excluding Opinions 5, 7, and 8).[13] These nine Opinions contained 35 dissents and 27 qualified assents, including in the former figure 13 dissents by Big Eight firm partners and eight dissents by academics. Indeed, of the 21 votes cast by the academics in the nine Opinions, 12 were either dissents or qualified assents. Three of the nine Opinions (Nos. 2, 11, and 16) secured only the barest majority (i.e., two-thirds) required for passage. In Opinion No. 4, on the investment credit, the amount of space used to present the views of the five dissenters and eight qualified assenters well exceeded the space used to express the majority view.

The circumstances attending the approval of Opinions 16 and 17 appalled a number of APB members and close observers of the Board's operations (see Seligman [1982, pp. 416–430]). Pressure from both industry and government was especially intense and unrelenting, and, in one celebrated instance, a Board member astonished his colleagues by changing the vote he had cast at an earlier Board meeting at which a business combinations/goodwill Opinion was approved in principle by exactly a two-thirds majority. The previous meeting of the Board had been regarded as the climax of 18 difficult months of trying to fashion an Opinion that would secure at least a two-thirds majority, and it is not an exaggeration to say that the member's announcement of his change of mind provoked general consternation in the Board. In the end, the Board divided business combinations and goodwill into two Opinions, and the required majorities were somehow achieved.

Hard on the heels of the Institute's publication of Opinions 16 and 17 in August 1970, the senior partners of three Big Eight firms wrote letters to the Institute President, Marshall S. Armstrong, in which they strongly criticized the Board's performance. In a letter dated November 11, 1970, Ralph E. Kent, managing partner of Arthur Young & Company, wrote that "A number of developments over the past several months have raised some doubts in my mind as to whether the present APB organization is the most appropriate ongoing mechanism for the establishment of accounting principles." Harvey E. Kapnick, chairman of Arthur Andersen & Co., in a letter dated November 16, 1970, wrote that "The Accounting Principles Board, in our view, has not successfully carried out its mission nor does it currently give promise of doing so." And Robert M. Trueblood (who had long been critical of the Board), chairman of the policy group of Touche Ross & Co., in a letter dated November 17, 1970, wrote that "we are presently reconsidering our entire participation in the affairs of the Board."

In the face of this barrage of criticism, Armstrong called an extraordinary conference of 35 prominent CPA's from 21 major accounting firms to discuss what should be done. The meeting was held in January 1971. Out of this conference came the recommendation that two study groups be appointed—one on the process of establishing accounting principles and the other on the objectives of financial statements (which came to be known as the Wheat and

[13]In fact, three Board members—two academics and a partner in a Big Eight firm—were prepared to file qualified assents to Opinion No. 7 owing to their belief that the Opinion proposed a kind of accounting for lessors that was inconsistent with the accounting for lessees specified in Opinion No. 5. At the eleventh hour, they were persuaded to withdraw their qualification in exchange for the insertion of paragraph 18, in which the Board acknowledged a possible inconsistency and said it "will continue to give consideration to this question." Yet the Board never addressed the alleged inconsistency in its later pronouncements.

EXHIBIT 1

Dissents and Qualified Assents in the 12 Substantive Single-Issue Opinions of the Accounting Principles Board through 1970

	Total		Big Eight Firm Partners		Academics		
Opinion No. and Title	Dissents	Qualified Assents	Dissents	Qualified Assents	Dissents	Qualified Assents	No. of Academics on APB
1 New Depreciation Guidelines and Rules	0	5	0	3	0	1	3
2 Accounting for the "Investment Credit"	6	1	4	1	0	0	3
4 Accounting for the "Investment Credit"	5	8	1	6	2	1	3
5 Reporting of Leases in FinancialStatements of Lessee	1	2	1	0	0	1	3
7 Accounting for Leases in FinancialStatements of Lessors	0	0	0	0	0	0	3
8 Accounting for the Cost of Pension Plans	0	0	0	0	0	0	2
9 Reporting the Results of Operations	0	5	0	3	0	1	2
11 Accounting for Income Taxes	6	1	2	1	1	0	2
14 Accounting for Convertible Debt and Debt Issued with Stock Purchase Warrants	4	2	2	1	1	0	2
15 Earnings per Share	3	5	2	2	0	1	2
16 Business Combinations	6	0	1	0	2	0	2
17 Intangible Assets	5	0	1	0	2	0	2
Totals	36	29	14	17	8	5	29
Totals for all but Opinions 5, 7, and 8	35	27	13	17	8	4	21

Note: Opinion No. 3, "The Statement of Source and Application of Funds," has been omitted as it did not affect the basic financial statements. Opinions 6, 10, and 12 dealt with a variety of matters, and Opinion 13 made a portion of Opinion 9 applicable to commercial banks.

Trueblood Study Groups, respectively, after the names of their chairmen). In March 1972, the Wheat Study reported its unanimous recommendation that a Financial Accounting Standards Board, largely independent from the AICPA, be established [Study on Establishment of Accounting Principles, 1972], and within two months the Institute's Council adopted the Study's recommendations. The Accounting Principles Board was terminated on June 30, 1973.

In the Institute leadership's deliberations in late 1970 and early 1971, it was noted that the American Accounting Association had, in August 1970, appointed a Committee on Establishment of an Accounting Commission, whose purpose was "to study the feasibility and desirability of a commission to inquire into the formulation of accounting principles" [AAA,

1971, p. 609]. The Association committee had been in touch with officers of the Institute and former members of the APB, so its existence was well known to the Institute hierarchy. Indeed, the Institute leadership was plainly nettled at the Association for trespassing on its turf. Both the Kent and Trueblood letters to Armstrong referred to the Association's initiative, and the AAA committee was mentioned during the high-level conference chaired by Armstrong in January 1971. The AAA committee recommended the establishment of a commission of inquiry, and in February 1971 the AAA's executive committee unanimously approved its report. But the Institute asked the Association to defer taking any action until after the report of its Wheat Study was received, and the Association acceded to this request. No further action was ever taken on the report of the Association's committee, but in its very creation and operation the committee had an impact on the actions taken by the Institute. In terms of practical effect, David Solomons, who had chaired the Association's committee, was named to the Wheat Study, and he became the principal draftsman of the Study's report. George H. Sorter, a member of the Association's committee, was appointed as research director for the Trueblood Study, and the 1968–69 and 1970–71 Association Presidents, Sidney Davidson and James Don Edwards, were made members of the nine-man Trueblood Study Group.

The report of the Association's committee [AAA, 1971] and the letters from Kent, Kapnick, and Trueblood, as well as other inquiries (e.g., see *AICPA Study . . .* [1972]), pointed to a number of deficiencies in the operation of the Board. An alleged lack of independence (a question raised in relation to the Committee on Accounting Procedure in the 1950's), possibly opening practitioner members to pressure from their firms' clients, was an issue. Others contended that the Board, e.g., in Opinion No. 15 on earnings per share, was producing rule books rather than statements of principles (see Paton [1971, p. 42]). Another concern felt strongly by a number of critics was the Board's failure (following on the failure of the Committee on Accounting Procedure) to establish fundamental principles, or objectives, to guide its work on specific topics. The Board's Statement No. 4, issued in early 1970, contained a strong dissent by one Board member (a Big Eight firm partner), and its status as a Statement rather than as an Opinion (which had been the original plan) was criticized by Maurice Moonitz, who had been a Board member in 1963–66, when the project was launched [1971]. As a Statement, the pronouncement could be ignored by practitioners.

One reason, seldom mentioned, why the APB foundered in its early years was the unexpected decision of the Institute's executive committee, in 1959, to insist that the accounting firms could be represented on the Board only by their firm-wide managing partners. One surmises that the reason behind the executive committee's decision was that (as suggested above) some firms were seen as not taking the work of the Committee on Accounting Procedure seriously, by sending partners of lesser stature to represent them. But the executive committee's policy was misconceived. Several of the managing partners had little interest in or aptitude for "theoretical" debates. Being the highest authority in their respective firms, they were disposed to pronounce their views rather than engage in a give-and-take discussion. Often they were not prepared for Board meetings, owing to the press of work in their firms. With strong-willed managing partners on the Board, a spirit of compromise was difficult to achieve. Especially when it was time for the Board to consider the Moonitz and Sprouse studies on accounting postulates and principles, the elder statesmen from the Big Eight firms were hardly of a mind to reexamine accounting from the ground up. Owing in part to this constitution of the Board's membership, relatively little genuine progress was made until 1964, when the Institute's executive committee, evidently having concluded that its membership policy was not working, began to replace most of the managing partners with their firms' senior technical partners.

After reviewing the history of the Committee on Accounting Procedure and the APB, Moonitz has concluded that "The evidence is clear that a professional accounting body, acting by itself, is incapable of obtaining agreement on a set of accounting standards" [1974, p. 67], as allies are needed to offset the power of management. While some have believed that outside pressures, such as those coming from government or industry, led to the downfall of the APB (e.g., see Zeff [1978]), George R. Catlett, a Board member from 1965 to 1971, disagreed:

> The Board's demise stemmed directly from the confusion and controversy stirred by efforts to halt alleged abuses and regulate accounting by means of arbitrary and uncoordinated rules based on a chain of questionable compromises [1980].

Former APB members and close observers despaired of the "questionable compromises" that were required in order to obtain even fragile majorities in certain Opinions. This experience led some to recommend a Board of considerably smaller size.

To be sure, the APB had been held to a higher standard than the Committee on Accounting Procedure, as it was expected to deal in a definitive way—i.e., severely reduce or eliminate the range of accepted practices—in highly controversial areas, such as pensions, leases, price-level accounting, and income tax allocation. But because the APB *was* expected to make hard choices, outside pressures (exacerbated by constant media coverage) intensified. While the "questionable compromises" cited by Catlett served to debilitate the Board, it cannot be gainsaid that pressures from industry, the financial sector, and government played a significant role in the demise of the APB.

CONCLUSION

No common explanation may be found to describe the factors motivating the actions at all of the five junctures, especially as they cover a period of more than five decades. Perhaps the strongest force was the profession's fear of active involvement by government in the establishment of accounting principles. Criticism from within the Institute (in 1917, 1957 and 1970) also was a precipitating factor. Although Ripley's writings represented criticism from outside the profession, his call for government intervention endowed his words with special meaning for the Institute. The surge of the reborn American Accounting Association in 1936, coupled with Kohler's critical editorials, made a mark on Institute affairs in the 1930's, and the series of AAA principles statements, culminating in the 1957 Revision, together with the appointment in 1970 of the AAA's Committee on Establishment of an Accounting Commission, were contributing factors in later decades.

This is not to suggest that the Institute's leaders could be caricatured as reluctant plutocrats who could be moved only by fear of losing their control over events. Ripley's criticism gave George O. May the opportunity to fill a void in the Institute's leadership and launch a campaign to raise the standards of accounting and auditing practice. A call to ideals motivated the critics (e.g., Scovell, Kohler, Spacek and Trueblood) as it did those who engineered reforms (e.g., May, Glover and Powell). The tactics used by the several actors were different, but the cause was the same: to find a better way.

REFERENCES

Accounting Principles Board, "Statement by the Accounting Principles Board" (AICPA, 1962).

———, "Basic Concepts and Accounting Principles Underlying Financial Statements of Business Enterprises," *Statement No. 4* (AICPA, 1970).

AICPA Study on Establishment of Accounting Principles, Cases in Public Accounting Practice, Volume 11 (Arthur Andersen & Co., 1972).

American Accounting Association, "Statement of Objectives of the American Accounting Association," *The Accounting Review* (March 1936), pp. 1–4.

———, Committee on Concepts and Standards Underlying Corporate Financial Statements, "Price Level Changes and Financial Statements," *Supplementary Statement No. 2* (AAA, 1951).

———, Committee on Accounting Concepts and Standards, "Accounting and Reporting Standards for Corporate Financial Statements," *1957 Revision* (AAA, 1957).

———, Committee on Establishment of an Accounting Commission, "The Role of the American Accounting Association in the Development of Accounting Principles," *The Accounting Review* (July 1971), pp. 609–616.

American Institute of Accountants, *Audits of Corporate Accounts* (AIA, 1934).

———, Committee on Accounting Procedure, "Restatement and Revision of Accounting Research Bulletins," *Accounting Research Bulletin No. 43* (AIA, 1953).

———, Report of Special Committee Investigating Certain Phases of the Work of the Committee on Accounting Procedure and the Committee on Relations with the Interstate Commerce Commission (1957), reproduced in *A Search for Fairness in Financial Reporting to the Public, 1956–1969* (Arthur Andersen & Co., 1969), pp. 469–487.

Barr, Andrew, "Relations Between the Development of Accounting Principles and the Activities of the SEC," in William W. Cooper and Yuji Ijiri, Eds., *Eric Louis Kohler, Accounting's Man of Principles* (Reston Publishing Company, 1979), pp. 41–61.

Blough, Carman G., "The Need for Accounting Principles," *The Accounting Review* (March 1937), pp. 30–37.

——— "Development of Accounting Principles in the United States," in *Berkeley Symposium on the Foundations of Financial Accounting* (Schools of Business Administration, University of California, Berkeley, 1967), pp. 1–14.

Carey, John L., *The Rise of the Accounting Profession: From Technician to Professional, 1896–1936* (American Institute of Certified Public Accountants, 1969).

———. *The Rise of the Accounting Profession: To Responsibility and Authority, 1937–1969* (American Institute of Certified Public Accountants, 1970).

Catlett, George R., "Accounting: More Words, Less Reality," *The New York Times* (September 21, 1980).

Clark, J. Maurice, *Studies in the Economics of Overhead Costs* (The University of Chicago Press, 1923).

Dickinson, A. Lowes, "The Fallacy of Including Interest and Rent as Part of Manufacturing Cost," *The Journal of Accountancy* (December 1911), pp. 588–593.

Financial Accounting Standards Board (FASB), "Accounting for Interest Costs," Discussion Memorandum (FASB, 1977).

Grady, Paul (Editor), *Memoirs and Accounting Thought of George O. May* (The Ronald Press Company, 1962).

———, *Inventory of Generally Accepted Accounting Principles for Business Enterprises* (AICPA, 1965).

Horne, Henry A., "Accounting Procedure and Research," in *Experiences with Extensions of Auditing Procedure and Papers on Other Accounting Subjects,* Presented at the Fifty-third Annual Meeting of the American Institute of Accountants, 1940 (American Institute of Accountants, 1941), pp. 46–53.

"Interest as an Element of Cost," *Year Book 1921* (National Association of Cost Accountants, 1921), pp. 45–96.

Jennings, Alvin R., "Present-Day Challenges in Financial Reporting," *The Journal of Accountancy* (January 1958), pp. 28–34.

Jones, Ralph Coughenour, *Price Level Changes and Financial Statements, Case Studies of Four Companies* (American Accounting Association, 1955).

King, Earle C., "The Income Statement—Problem Child of Accountancy," *The New York Certified Public Accountant* (June 1948), pp. 413–418.

———, "What Are Accounting Principles?", *California Certified Public Accountant* (November 1951), pp. 12–27.

———, "Dissent," in Report of Study Group on Business Income, *Changing Concepts of Business Income* (The Macmillan Company, 1952), pp. 122–123.

Kohler, Eric L., "A Nervous Profession," *The Accounting Review* (December 1934a), p. 334.

———, "Standards Must Come," *The Accounting Review* (December 1934b), pp. 334–336.

———, "Standards: A Dialogue," *The Accounting Review* (December 1935), pp. 370–379.

Mason, Perry, *Price Level Changes and Financial Statements, Basic Concepts and Methods* (American Accounting Association, 1956).

May, George O., "Publicity of Accounts" (1926a), in Bishop Carleton Hunt, Ed., *George Oliver May: Twenty-five Years of Accounting Responsibility, 1911–1936* (American Institute Publishing Co., Inc., 1936), pp. 49–52.

———, "Corporate Publicity and the Auditor," *The Journal of Accountancy* (November 1926b), pp. 321–326.

———, "A Proper Courage in the Assumption of Responsibility by the Accountant" (1926c), in Bishop Carleton Hunt, Ed., *George Oliver May: Twenty-five Years of Accounting Responsibility, 1911–1936* (American Institute Publishing Co., Inc., 1936), pp. 40–48.

———, "Principles of Accounting," *The Journal of Accountancy* (December 1937), pp. 423–425.

———, *Financial Accounting, A Distillation of Experience* (Macmillan Co., 1943).

Moonitz, Maurice, "Three Contributions to the Development of Accounting Principles Prior to 1930," *Journal of Accounting Research* (Spring 1970), pp. 145–155.

———, "The Accounting Principles Board Revisited," *The New York Certified Public Accountant* (May 1971), pp. 341–345.

———, *Obtaining Agreement on Standards in the Accounting Profession,* Studies in Accounting Research No. 8 (American Accounting Association, 1974).

Paton, W. A., "Earmarks of a Profession—and the APB," *The Journal of Accountancy* (January 1971), pp. 37–45.

Previts, Gary John, and Barbara D. Merino, *A History of Accounting in America* (Ronald Press-Wiley, 1979).

"Proceedings of the Annual Meeting Held at the New Willard Hotel, Washington, D.C., September 18 and 19, 1917," *1917 Year-Book of the American Institute of Accountants* (AIA, 1917), pp. 67–72.

"Report of Special Committee on Interest in Relation to Cost," *1918 Year-Book of the American Institute of Accountants* (AIA, 1918), pp. 110–112.

"Report of the Special Committee on Development of Accounting Principles," *1934 Year-Book of the American Institute of Accountants* (AIA, 1935), pp. 276–279.

Report of the Special Committee on Opinions of the Accounting Principles Board, Presented to Council of the American Institute of Certified Public Accountants (AICPA, Spring 1965).

Richardson, A. P., "Standardization of Accounting Procedure," *The Journal of Accountancy* (October 1918), pp. 292–295.

Ripley, William Z., "Stop, Look, Listen!", *The Atlantic Monthly* (September 1926), pp. 380–399.

Sanders, Thomas Henry, Henry Rand Hatfield and Underhill Moore, *A Statement of Accounting Principles* (American Institute of Accountants, 1938).

Securities and Exchange Commission, *14th Annual Report* (Government Printing Office, 1948).

Seligman, Joel, *The Transformation of Wall Street: A History of the Securities and Exchange Commission and Modern Corporate Finance* (Houghton Mifflin Company, 1982).

Spacek, Leonard, "Professional Accountants and Their Public Responsibility" (1957), in *A Search for Fairness in Financial Reporting to the Public, 1956–1969* (Arthur Andersen & Co., 1969), pp. 17–38.

———, "The Need for an Accounting Court," *The Accounting Review* (July 1958), pp. 368–379.

Storey, Reed K., *The Search for Accounting Principles* (American Institute of Certified Public Accountants, 1964).

Study on Establishment of Accounting Principles, *Establishing Financial Accounting Standards* (American Institute of Certified Public Accountants, 1972).

"Uniform Accounts," *Federal Reserve Bulletin* (April 1, 1917), pp. 270–284.

Wells, M. C., *Accounting for Common Costs* (Center for International Education and Research in Accounting, University of Illinois, 1978).

Wise, T. A., "The Auditors Have Arrived," *Fortune,* Part I (November 1960), pp. 151–157, 186, 191–192, 196, 198; Part II (December 1960), pp. 144–148, 239–240, 242, 244.

Zeff, Stephen A., *The American Accounting Association—Its First Fifty Years* (American Accounting Association, 1966).

———, *Forging Accounting Principles in Five Countries: A History and an Analysis of Trends* (Stipes, 1972).

———, "The Rise of 'Economic Consequences,' " *Journal of Accountancy* (December 1978), pp. 56–63.

———, *The Accounting Postulates and Principles Controversy of the 1960s* (Garland, 1982).

Resource note: Quotations are taken from correspondence that has been photocopied from the files of the American Institute of Certified Public Accountants and other sources, and these are in the possession of the author.

I-B

EVENTS AND VALUE THEORIES

I-B1

AN "EVENTS" APPROACH TO BASIC ACCOUNTING THEORY

George H. Sorter

In 1966, after two years work, a committee of the American Accounting Association issued *A Statement of Basic Accounting Theory.*[1] Undoubtedly, the most startling recommendations were the sanctioning of current costs and the advocacy of two column (historical and current) reports. To this member of the committee, however, even more startling was that the near unanimous agreement on the recommendations was arrived at by following two very divergent paths originating from two very dissimilar basic concepts about accounting. This split is not confined to committee members but rather seems representative of a more widespread and pervasive difference in the world outside. The majority view of the committee and the predominant faction outside believes in what I here define as the "value" approach to accounting. The minority view, of which I am sometimes the only member, I describe as the "events" approach. This view although implied by some in the past[2] has never to my knowledge been explicitly stated but might have far-reaching implications. This paper seeks to describe and contrast the two schools, present arguments for and illustrate the consequences of an "events" approach to accounting theory; and examine the logic leading to the conclusions embodied in the *Statement of Basic Accounting Theory.* Hopefully, this will provide not only insights and help for the analysis and evaluation of the committee's monograph but perhaps also stimulate discussion and criticism of a new approach and suggest new avenues of research and experimentation to make accounting more responsive to present day conditions.

George H. Sorter, "An 'Events' Approach to Basic Accounting Theory," *The Accounting Review,* January 1969, pp. 12–19. Reprinted by permission of the American Accounting Association.

[1]American Accounting Association, *A Statement of Basic Accounting Theory,* A Report Prepared by the Committee on Basic Accounting Theory (American Accounting Association, 1966).

[2]This idea, like so many others had its origin primarily in the writings and thought of Professor William J. Vatter whom I hasten to absolve from any of its shortcomings.

TWO VIEWS—VALUE AND EVENTS

THE VALUE THEORY

The "Value" school within the committee, or as they would probably prefer to be termed the "User need" school, assumed that users' needs are known and sufficiently well specified so that accounting theory can deductively arrive at and produce optimal input values for used and useful decision models. Most of the value theorists visualize accounting's purpose as producing optimum income and capital value or values.[3] This leads to the popular sport of proper matching of costs and revenue. The assumption is that "proper matching" associates costs and revenue to produce the right income figure or figures—the figure or figures optimal for users' decision models.

Several criticisms may be leveled at this value approach.

1. There are many and varied uses of accounting data and it is therefore impossible to specify input values that are optimal for the wide range of possible uses.
2. For each specified use different users utilize a wide range of different decision models, that they have so far been unable to describe, define, or specify. Further, neither economists nor accountants have been able to advance the theoretically correct decision models.
3. The value theory is unnecessarily restrictive. Thus, events such as leases or commitments have, until recently, tended to be excluded from the accounting universe, partially at least, because they did not affect income or net asset values.

   The orientation of accounting toward producing income and asset values which are nothing but simple attempts to adjust for the lag between cash outflows and cash inflows has impeded the development of more sophisticated lag models made possible by more sophisticated techniques.
4. The value theory is not useful in explaining many current developments in accounting. Income theory, for instance, does not provide a basis for the current sub-aggregates that are utilized in the income statement such as sales, cost of sales, etc. It has also not been helpful in explaining the advocacy of the Fund Statement or in helping the conglomerate and a host of other current problems.

THE EVENTS THEORY

Proponents of the "Events" theory suggest that the purpose of accounting is to provide information about relevant economic events that might be useful in a variety of possible decision models. They see the function of accounting at one level removed in the decision-making process. Instead of producing input values for unknown and perhaps unknowable decision models directly, accounting provides information about relevant economic events that allows individual users to generate their own input values for their own individual decision models. In other words, given the state of the arts, less rather than more aggregation is appropriate and the user, rather than the accountant, must aggregate, and assign weights and values to the data

[3]Not all value theorists are income oriented. Chambers for example can be considered a "value" but certainly not an "income" theorist.

consistent with his forecasts and utility functions. "Events" proponents suggest that the loss of information generated by aggregation and valuation by the accountant is greater than the associated benefit. While they would agree that the accountants' suggested weights and values deserve to be communicated, they would insist that these weights be communicated in disaggregated form so that users always had the non-weighted raw data available as well.

This viewpoint seems particularly appropriate today when little is known about how accounting data is used but may even be preferred when more knowledge about decision models becomes available. It is possible to visualize reasonable decision models that are consistent with an "events" approach rather than a "value" approach. An investor, for instance, attempting to forecast the value of a firm at some future point may utilize two methods: (1) He may base his estimate of future values on the trend, size, and variability of current income or other aggregated values. (2) Alternatively, he may wish to use current accounting data to predict specific future events and then base his estimate of future values on these predicted events. In other words, he may wish to predict income or he may wish to predict sales, cost of sales, taxes, etc. The first model is more consistent with a value approach, the second with an events approach.

The criticism must be met that the "events" approach relies just as heavily upon knowledge of users' models as does the "value" approach. The argument goes as follows. Decisions as to what events are relevant (surely not all events can be recorded) must be made and can only be made with users' needs in mind. Thus, the users' needs must still be known. This is correct. But it seems clear that less need be known about decision models to decide whether or not an event might be relevant for a model than to have to decide how the data fits a specific decision model and what specific weights should be assigned.[4] In the lease example, under an "events" approach, it is only necessary to decide that information about leases, commitments or orders are relevant to a host of decision models for such information to be included in accounting reports. It is unnecessary to justify how, if at all, this information should be weighted in an income valuation model.

TO AGGREGATE OR NOT TO AGGREGATE

As has been indicated, the real difference between the two schools lies in what level of aggregation and valuation is appropriate in accounting reports and who is to be the aggregator and evaluator. The question as to who is to aggregate or value is not unique to accounting. As Ijiri points out ". . . any aggregation generally involves loss of information in that the resulting total 'value' may be composed of many—possibly infinitely many—different *components*."[5] It is interesting to note that in two widely different areas there have recently been thrusts toward presenting less aggregated data. In modern statistics it is no longer considered good form to merely report confidence intervals. Instead the plea is for full presentation of the underlying data or distributions.[6] Only the user can decide what is or is not significant, given his loss function. In weather forecasts, we are no longer told that it will or will not rain or snow. Instead

[4]". . . a goal which by itself may not be so capable of definition as to determine a single perfect solution may nevertheless be clear enough and important enough to rule out some solutions . . ." from: Guido Calabresi, "Fault, Accidents, and the Wonderful World of Blum and Kalven," *Yale Law Journal* (December 1965), p. 222.

[5]Yuji Ijiri. *The Foundations of Accounting Measurement* (Prentice-Hall, Inc., 1967), p. 120.

[6]See Howard Raiffa and Robert Schlaifer, *Applied Statistical Decision Theory* (Harvard University, Division of Research, Graduate School of Business, 1961), p. 68.

we are given probability estimates and must ourselves decide whether or not to carry umbrellas or to send out work crews. We are given the underlying raw data and must assign values consistent with our individual utility functions.

Accounting income has variously been thought of as a measure of how much can be spent and still be as well off as before, as a measure of managerial efficiency or as a basis for forecasting future values. But each of these depends on individual expectations, individual preference functions and individual decision models, not on some never clearly defined concept of "proper matching of costs and revenues." Unfortunately this attempt to match, the assigning of weights to generate values, the attempt to aggregate into an income figure, destroys potentially useful information about important underlying events and increases possible measurement errors and biases. Every item on an income statement is the result of at least two processes—the underlying event and the accountants' allocation of the event to a particular time period. This allocation has the purpose of matching in order to derive a "true" income figure or figures. Lifo and Fifo for example are used in an attempt to produce better income figures. Both, however, destroy information about the consumption event. If either Lifo and Fifo is used consumption of two identical units bought at different prices will necessarily be described differently. A user interested in comparing consumption activity for two periods is unable to distinguish between variations caused by the measurement process, be it Lifo or Fifo, and real differences in the consumption levels.

Deferred taxes attempts to secure proper matching of costs and revenues and thereby destroys information about current tax payments. Conventional absorption costing in an attempt to secure proper matching destroys information about production inputs and outputs since cost of goods sold and inventory become dependent on both the level of production and of sales.

The loss of information due to aggregation also holds for the balance sheet. Necessarily, every balance sheet account is an aggregation of two or more types of events (the events recorded on the debit and credit sides of the account). Very often the events so aggregated vary greatly in type, measureability and variability and therefore destroy much information about specific events. For instance, if current costs or values are used, acquisition and consumption activities as well as environmental changes are combined and the reconstructibility of each specific event is impaired. Acquisitions and amortizations or acquisitions and dispositions are events differing widely in possible measurement error. By combining them in asset and liability accounts information about each is destroyed.

As already indicated, income and capital valuations are attempts to deal with lags between cash outflows and cash inflows. These appear to be unnecessarily crude and primitive given current advances in methodology and measurement technique. The presentation of less aggregated data suggested by the "events" approach might stimulate investigation of more complicated but more useful lag and forecast models that could vary for different industries, firms, time periods, or individuals.

SOME CONSEQUENCES OF AN EVENTS APPROACH

This is not the proper medium in which to describe some possible long-range consequences of the "events" approach. In a subsequent manuscript, I intend to speculate on the type of accounting reports appropriate to this approach. Even under the existing accounting framework there are several implications of "events" theory which might help to explain this point of view.

THE BALANCE SHEET

It is currently the fashion to say that the balance sheet or position statement has lost most, if not all, of its significance. But not for event theorists. We view the balance sheet not as a value statement nor as a statement of financial position but rather as an indirect communication of all accounting events that have occurred since the inception of the accounting unit. This indirect communication is provided by summing the effect of all events on the names used in describing these events and then recording the subsequent balances. Inventory, thus, does not report either value or costs but rather describes the acquisition and consumption activities that have occurred. This view has several advantages. It does not purport to report something that is not achieved (i.e., value) and it does facilitate the understanding and analysis of what is described. If the inventory figure, for instance; is visualized as a representation of the inventory, under value theory the accountant must somehow rationalize the particular costs or value figure that he uses. If historical cost is used, the validity of a representation of inventory that ignores value inevitably crops us. If value is used the argument centers about the justification of this rather than some other value. It is certainly difficult to justify either historical costs or any one representation of value. This difficulty does not create so grave a problem for the "event" theorist. Suppose original cost is used. Under an events notion this means simply that acquisition and consumption events, but not environmental changes, are recorded. Original costs need not be justified. One may certainly deplore the absence of information about environmental events (i.e., value changes) but one accepts information about the events that are described (i.e., acquisition and consumption) and uses them in whatever fashion is appropriate.

An "events" approach to the balance sheet could lead to operational rules about balance sheet construction and presentation. The following represents a possible rule. *A balance sheet should be so constructed as to maximize the reconstructability of the events being aggregated.* Various users may thus generate information about particular events they are interested in. One purpose of the balance sheet is to facilitate the preparation of Funds Statements and like reports that provide information about important events.

THE INCOME STATEMENT

For value theorists the purpose of an income statement quite simply is to report income value or values. Under an "events" approach the purpose of the income statement is to provide direct communication concerning the operating events or activities of the firm. Accounting utilizes two forms of communication: an indirect or effect communication of all events (the Balance Sheet) and direct, specific or event communication of certain critical events (Income Statement, Cash Statement, Production Statement, Funds Statement, etc.). The concern of event theorists is not primarily with the final income figure but rather with describing critical operating activities of a firm. The preferred title would be "Statement of Operating Events." Events theory can suggest an operational rule for income statements. For instance, *each event should be described in a manner facilitating the forecasting of that same event in a future time period given exogenous changes.* The deferred tax question would then be resolved by investigating which quantification more reliably forecasts future tax payments. Both Lifo and Fifo would be rejected because they impede the ability to forecast acquisitions and consumptions of inventory in the future.

The "events" school can justify the present organization of the income statement which reports several sub-aggregates such as sales, cost of sales, etc., because these are considered critical operating events. Perhaps this is one instance when an events orientation has already affected the accounting structure.

THE FUNDS STATEMENT

Value theorists, rigidly faithful to their doctrine, have the most difficulty in justifying this statement. They state rather feebly that ". . . the basic purpose of the Funds Statement is to account for the change in working capital during the period covered by the statement."[7] Such a concept certainly underrates the utility of this statement and leads to trivial discussions as to the proper definition of working capital. The "events" school thinks of this statement as "A Statement of Financial and Investment Events." The Working Capital account merely represents a useful technique to organize the events and prepare the statement. The important consideration is whether a financing or investment event is relevant and should be reported, not whether working capital is affected by a given event. This again demonstrates the flexibility of an "events" approach. Different financing or investment events may or may not be relevant for specific firms or at specific times. The content of the Funds Statement thus need not remain invariate for all times or for all firms.

"A STATEMENT OF BASIC ACCOUNTING THEORY" AND THE EVENTS THEORY

Most of the recommendations contained in *A Statement of Basic Accounting Theory* flow more logically from an "events" rather than from a "value" orientation. Why are standards or guidelines necessary at all if a "value" approach is adopted? If users' needs are in fact well specified then accounting should provide the values that make the decision models operate optimally. The only relevant standard then would be the ability of the data to perform in the model. There would be no need for values to be verifiable or free from bias if they work well in a specified model. If, however, users' needs are not well specified suggesting an "events" approach, then it is necessary to employ standards that limit the range and define the description of relevant events.

The need for two-column reporting under a "value" approach is not clear. Presumably, the need arises because different columns are useful for different users; that is, historical cost data is useful for the stewardship function and current cost data for the investment function. This rather inadequate rationale has led to the assumption that the historical costs column was only advocated as a stop-gap measure until current value could sweep the day. This was not the intent of the committee.

Multi-column reporting seems eminently compatible with an "events" view of accounting. The two column reports advocated by *ASOBAT* is a step in that direction. As the monograph states, "The historical information reflects market transactions, the current cost information reflects market transactions plus 'unrealized' market influences, and the difference shows the effect of unrealized environmental influences."[8] Since the historical cost column in-

[7]Perry Mason, " 'Cash Flow' Analysis and the Funds Statement," *Accounting Research Study No. 2* (American Institute of Certified Public Accountants, 1961).

[8]American Accounting Association, *op. cit.,* p. 31.

cludes descriptions of events other than market transactions (i.e., depreciation, amortization, and other significant accruals) and because market transactions and environmental changes are not the only events that have relevance to the firm, the two columns advocated do not go far enough, but they represent a start.

Separate events should be reported in separate columns because (1) they vary in measurability, (2) they vary in controllability, and (3) they vary in importance from period to period. There is no question that market transactions and environmental changes, for instance, vary in measurability. Market transactions can be relatively satisfactorily described by single numbered quantifications (with relatively little measurement error). There is apt to be little variance around that single number. The same, however, cannot be said about environmental changes or forecasts where description by ranges or distributions could be more appropriate and where measurement errors could be material. As long as a single column is used there will be a tendency to continue to measure events by a single measurement process which is inappropriate for certain types of events and we shall continue to be faced with troubles in assessing measurement biases or errors.

These events also vary in controllability by the managers of a firm. Clearly, market transactions are more controllable than environmental changes but less controllable than conversions. If accounting reports are to be useful in evaluating management then a separation of events by controllability should help in fulfilling this objective.

Finally, the importance of the different classes of events may vary from period to period. An investor may predict a period of stability where certain environmental changes are expected to be minimal and in order to forecast adequately from accounting data he must then be able to separate the effect of environmental changes from market transactions. This he can do in multi-column reporting. As the importance of different types of events vary, users, according to their estimate of the future, can attach different weights to the different types of events.

At first blush, multi-column reporting seems a drastic departure from current practices—but is it really? Presently we use multi-row reporting. We break down the income statement into many sub-aggregates such as sales, cost of sales, S&A expenses, taxes, etc. We break down the balance sheet into many rows by classes of equities and assets. Very little research has been done as to what explains the current level of sub-aggregation and extreme proponents of the "value" school would have a hard time rationalizing the present format of the income statement. Presently the income statement is organized around a functional event structure, and the balance sheet around a functional effect structure. Multi-column reporting would add a "source of events" classification to both reports and instead of accounting reports consisting of a 7 by 1 matrix they would consist of a 7 by 5 matrix. This move from one matrix to another does not seem that revolutionary, and would be facilitated by an events approach.

CONCLUSION

Admittedly, the above represents only a rough and underdeveloped first approach toward a new orientation for accounting theory. Why, then, is it presented here and now? Only in the hope of encouraging the research activities suggested by this approach and also in the further hope that it might stimulate a reexamination of some essential if rarely expressed implicit tenets of present accounting thought. The areas of possible research opportunities indicated by an events approach are many. The following represent a few:

1. Test whether line by line predictions of events, i.e., the prediction of sales, cost of sales, etc., are more efficient in explaining the future value of a firm than the use of more aggregated figures such as income.
2. Investigate the present format of accounting reports to see how useful these formats could be, i.e., to what extent do the various subcategories of the income statement and balance sheet covary? To what extent do they provide additional information?
3. Attempt to develop more sophisticated models to explain the lag between cash outflows and cash inflows, i.e., utilizing fund statements, production statements, and others in an attempt to predict cash flows.
4. Investigate the information loss due to the aggregations presently used by accountants. How much information is lost by aggregating and combining events to produce one income figure or to produce the different balance sheet amounts? A subsequent extension of this would be an investigation of the information loss due to expressing all economic activities in dollar terms.
5. Construct useful accounting reports based on an events approach.

Ultimately this paper will find its justification if what is presented here as the conclusion will serve as an introduction to the research activities and the reexamination advocated.

I-B 2

A TAXONOMY OF PRICE CHANGE MODELS

Lanny Chasteen

Classification is an important element of any discipline. How theories relate to or compete with each other, how apparently competing theories contain common threads, and how some theories extend or build upon others contribute to a better understanding of that discipline.

The accounting literature is rich with models that deal with the effects of changing prices on a firm. The merits of the conventional historical cost model versus some form of current value have been debated. The effects of an unstable measuring unit for standards of comparison have been examined. More formal expositions have been couched in terms of a concept of capital maintenance for interpreting the nature of cash flows in income determination. The role of capital maintenance in long-run income determination and the roles of capital maintenance and asset valuation in periodic income determination have been examined [Shwayder, 1969; Gynther, 1970].

Dissatisfaction with a particular price change model which specifies either explicitly or implicitly (1) a valuation method (or a measured attribute) for assets and liabilities and (2) a capital maintenance concept has led to alternative models. In addition, variations or modifications have resulted when some aspect of a given theory appeared deficient. As a result, there exist many distinctly different price change models and variations thereof. Without proper classification these permutations make direct comparisons difficult.

This paper has a modest purpose: to classify the existing models so that analysis and comparison are more efficient. This taxonomy can be a useful instructional tool either by providing an overview prior to an in-depth study of the models or by providing closure after

Lanny Chasteen, "A Taxonomy of Price Change Models," *The Accounting Review,* July 1984, pp. 515–523. Reprinted by permission of the American Accounting Association.

the various models have been studied. An algebraic approach, similar to that taken by Chambers [1966, 1978], Barton [1975], and others, is used for exposition. (A numerical example appears in the Appendix.) Apart from a brief description of each model's rationale, no in-depth examination will be made. Adequate examination has appeared previously in the literature.

The first section of this paper gives the assumptions and price change data on which the models are based. The historical cost models, current cost models, and current exit value models are presented in the next three sections. A brief summary concludes the paper.

ASSUMPTIONS AND PRICE CHANGE DATA

1. A firm begins operations at a time $t = 0$ with monetary assets of M, nonmonetary assets acquired at a price of N, and monetary liabilities of L. Thus, at $t = 0$ the firm's financial position is given by $M + N = L + R$, where R equals equity and $R > 0$.
2. No transactions occur from $t = 0$ to $t = 1$.
3. During the time interval from $t = 0$ to $t = 1$, the following price changes occur:

	At $t = 0$	**At $t = 1$**
General price index	1	$1 + p$
Current cost of nonmonetary assets	N	$N(1 + s_1)$
Current exit value of nonmonetary assets	N	$N(1 + s_2)$

   where p = proportional change in the general level of prices (÷100), s_1 = proportional change in the asset's current cost (÷100), and s_2 = proportional change in the asset's current exit value (÷100).
4. For simplicity, assume that p, s_1, and $s_2 > 0$ and that p, s_1, and s_2 are not necessarily equal.

The various price change models can be classified in one of two ways:

1. The models may be grouped according to their capital maintenance (investment recovery) concept and the asset valuation methods may be varied. The three capital maintenance concepts which appear in the literature are the nominal dollar, constant dollar (general purchasing power), and physical capital concepts. The three asset valuation methods are historical cost, current cost, and current exit value.
2. The models may be grouped according to their asset valuation method and the capital maintenance concepts may be varied.

The first approach is appealing in that, for a given capital maintenance concept, all models which use that concept give identical amounts of long-run earnings. The second approach, however, is used in this paper because it appears to be a better method of presenting variations or modifications to a given model. The two terms which describe each model—an attribute to be measured (an asset valuation method) and a capital maintenance concept—will appear as follows:

Attribute Measured/Capital Maintenance Concept

HISTORICAL COST MODELS

HISTORICAL COST/NOMINAL DOLLARS (*HC/N$*)

The $t = 1$ financial position under the traditional *HC/N$* model is represented as follows:

$$(1) \qquad M + N = L + \underbrace{R}_{(t\,=\,1\text{ capital})}$$

The model is a conceptual description of GAAP. If the nonmonetary asset was inventory or an equity security investment, the asset might be reported at $N(1 + s_1)$ or $N(1 + s_2)$, if s_1 or s_2 were negative.

HISTORICAL COST/CONSTANT DOLLARS (*HC/C$*)

The traditional *HC/C$* model as developed by Sweeney [1936], *Accounting Research Study No. 6,* and APB *Statement No. 3* is as follows:

$$(2) \qquad M + N(1 + p) = L + \underbrace{R(1 + p)}_{(t\,=\,1\text{ capital})} - \underbrace{p(M - L)}_{(\text{income (loss)})}$$

This model also may be expressed in general purchasing power units other than $t = 1$ units. For example, SFAS *No. 33* permits average-for-the year dollars in the supplementary *HC/C$* disclosures. In terms of our one-period example, $t = 0$ dollars also could be used.

Two variations on this model are the Ijiri [1976] interpretation and the "one-line adjustment" approach. The Ijiri variation is:

$$(3) \qquad M + N(1 + p) = L + \underbrace{R(1 + p)}_{(t\,=\,1\text{ capital})} + \underbrace{Np - Rp}_{(\text{income (loss)})}$$

Ijiri offers a different interpretation from the traditional *HC/C$* model. He describes Np as a "price-level holding gain" and Rp as a "price-level capital charge."

The one-line adjustment model was proposed as early as the mid-1950s [Chambers, 1978] and has been supported by Grady [1975] and Price Waterhouse [Agrawal and Rosenzweig, 1982]. It may be represented as follows:

$$(4) \qquad M + N = L + \underbrace{R(1 + p)}_{(t\,=\,1\text{ capital})} - \underbrace{Rp}_{(\text{(loss)})}$$

This model may be interpreted as a surrogate for the traditional *HC/C$* model, and its primary rationale is based on simplicity.

All three of the above models incorporate a general purchasing power concept of capital maintenance and, therefore, report identical cumulative income over the life of a firm. The models in equations (2) and (3) also give identical periodic income amounts; thus they differ only in interpretation. The model in equation (4) in effect calculates a purchasing power loss from holding both net monetary assets *and* nonmonetary assets. By comparison, the traditional *HC/C$* model in equation (2) reduces this loss by the restatement of N to $N(1 + p)$ by assuming that the asset's specific price increase is at least equal to p.[1]

CURRENT COST MODELS

Three distinct current cost models appear in the literature: current cost/nominal dollars, current cost/constant dollars, and current cost/physical capital (productive capacity). Each of these current cost models adopts a different concept of capital maintenance, and, as discussed below, there are several additional variations for the physical capital model.

CURRENT COST/NOMINAL DOLLARS (*CC/N$*)

The *CC/N$* model is as follows:

$$M + N(1 + s_1) = L + \underbrace{R}_{(t\,=\,1\text{ capital})} + \underbrace{Ns_1}_{(\text{income})} \tag{5}$$

Two theories or hypotheses underlie this model. The first is the superiority of this model over the *HC/N$* model in evaluating firm management's operating activities and holding activities [Edwards and Bell, 1961]. Though not demonstrated with the present transactionless example, this model disaggregates a firm's replacement or current cost income into two elements: (1) current operating profit (revenues less the current costs of earning the revenues) and (2) holding gains (Ns_1).[2] This model also has been described as the "cost-savings hypothesis" model [Samuelson, 1980].

The second hypothesis is based on prediction [Revsine, 1973]. Under certain circumstances, current operating profit may be a good predictor of future operating profit and future dividend-paying ability. The holding gain component may provide signals about increased future cash flows.[3]

---

[1]To illustrate, *SFAS No. 33* does not permit the restatement of nonmonetary assets to exceed realizable value. Said another way, the restated amount cannot exceed the amount of accessible general purchasing power embodied in the asset.

[2]In the transactionless example assumed in this paper, current cost measurements are made in end-of-period current cost. The use of average current cost also has been proposed and thus may be considered as a variation in the subsequent discussion of current operating profit and recognized holding gains. Unrealized holding gains on assets held at a financial position date, however, are measured at end-of-period current cost under the average current cost variation.

[3]Although not germane to this paper, the issue of current cost of assets presently owned versus current cost of technologically superior assets has been addressed in the literature, and thus variations on these themes exist with respect to current cost valuation.

CURRENT COST/CONSTANT DOLLARS (*CC/C$*)

This model, which conceptually underlies the supplementary current cost disclosures required by *SFAS No. 33,* is as follows:

$$M + N(1 + s_1) = L + \underbrace{R(1 + p)}_{(t\,=\,1\text{ capital})} + \underbrace{N(s_1 - p) - p(M - L)}_{(\text{income (loss)})} \tag{6}$$

In (6), $N(s_1 - p)$ is the holding gain (specific price increase), net of inflation, and $p(M - L)$ is the purchasing power loss.[4] The *CC/C$* model attempts to overcome criticisms of the *HC/C$* model's treatment of nonmonetary assets by using specific input prices. Furthermore, the model considers the effects of general price level changes on a firm's monetary assets and liabilities. Thus, this model incorporates the same current cost information reported in the *CC/N$* model with two additions: a general purchasing power gain or loss on monetary items and holding gains "net of inflation."[5]

CURRENT COST/PHYSICAL CAPITAL (*CC/PC*)

The basic *CC/PC* model, sometimes referred to as a replacement value model, is as follows:

$$M + N(1 + s_1) = L + \underbrace{R + Ns_1}_{(t\,=\,1\text{ capital})} \tag{7}$$

The model's algebraic representation is similar to the above *CC/N$* model except that the holding gains are considered a capital maintenance adjustment instead of an element of income.

The *CC/PC* model interprets current operating profit arising from earnings activities as "distributable income"—the maximum amount that can be distributed as a dividend each period and allow the firm to replace its productive capacity. Because a firm which uses this model and which pays periodic dividends equal to periodic earnings still may not be able to replace the assets used in its earnings activities when current costs continually rise over time, the issue of "backlog depreciation" [FASB, 1976] may be considered as a variation within the context of this model.

May [1976] has extended the distributable income notion to situations where the income calculation also incorporates increased costs of resources which may never appear on a financial position statement. May defines "current period residual income" as (a) year-end net assets (adjusted for dividends paid and additional paid-in capital) at year-end replacement costs, minus (b) beginning-of-year net assets (as reported) *plus* adjustments equal to the *difference* between (i) year-end costs and (ii) beginning-of-year costs *of the maximum investment required* in each resource employed in the business to sustain current levels of operations indefinitely. Whereas current operating profit provides an estimate of long-run average periodic cash flows

[4]In *SFAS No. 33,* these two elements are disclosed but are not included in income from continuing operations.

[5]Although Edwards and Bell [1961] and Revsine [1973] assume, for the most part, a stable general price level, they acknowledge the need to consider general price level changes.

and maximum average *future* periodic dividends, in nominal dollars, current period residual income provides an estimate of the maximum *current period* dividend consistent with maintaining current capacity to generate net cash flows [May, 1976; AAA, 1977].

Other variations on the *CC/PC* model are an incorporation of purchasing power gains and losses on monetary items based on *specific* price changes [Gynther, 1966], "gearing adjustment," valuation of assets based on whether they are considered essential or nonessential to the continuing operations of a firm, and the "value to the business" or "deprival value" theory.

Specific purchasing power gains and losses on monetary items also can be incorporated in the following model:

$$M + N(1 + s_1) = L + \underbrace{R + Rs_1}_{(t\,=\,1\text{ capital})} - \underbrace{s_1(M - L)}_{(\text{income (loss)})} \tag{8}$$

Since a purchasing power gain or loss generally is calculated with reference to the assets that the firm normally purchases, s_1 is used in equation (8). Thus, the model in (8) considers the effect of specific price changes on both nonmonetary items and monetary items.

Proponents of the gearing adjustment maintain that current cost increases (holding gains) on operating assets represent income to equity holders to the extent that these assets are financed by long-term monetary liabilities. The gearing adjustment is calculated by allocating the holding gain (specific price increase) on nonmonetary assets between income and capital as follows:

$$\text{Income portion} = \left(\frac{L}{L + R}\right)Ns_1$$

$$\text{Capital maintenance portion} = \left(\frac{R}{L + R}\right)Ns_1$$

Thus, the income to be distributed allows the firm to maintain its present debt/equity ratio, given certain assumptions about additional financing.

The gearing adjustment causes difficulty in classification. Although the model is a variation on the current cost/physical capital theme, the gearing adjustment, in principle, results in a *mixed* concept of capital maintenance. That is, a portion of the holding gain is considered income (a nominal dollar concept of capital) and a portion is considered a capital adjustment (a physical capital concept).

SSAP No. 16 sets forth current cost disclosure requirements for certain U.K. companies and incorporates both a specific price change adjustment (see equation (8)), and the gearing adjustment. Assuming that M and N are operating assets and that L is long-term monetary debt, the current cost model under *SSAP No. 16* would be as follows[6]:

$$M + N(1 + s_1) = L + \underbrace{R + Ns_1\left(\frac{R}{L + R}\right) + Ms_1\left(\frac{R}{L + R}\right)}_{(t\,=\,1\text{ capital})} + \underbrace{Ns_1\left(\frac{L}{L + R}\right) - Ms_1\left(\frac{R}{L + R}\right)}_{(\text{income})} \tag{9}$$

[6]Technically, *SSAP No. 16* limits the portion of $Ns_1(L)/(L + R)$ to be included in income to the portion realized. This realized portion is reported as a reduction in current cost expenses.

Valuation of assets based on whether they are considered essential or nonessential to the continuing operations of a firm is another variation on the *CC/PC* model. Under this theory, essential assets are valued at current cost; holding gains on essential assets are considered capital maintenance adjustments. Assets not essential to continuing operations are valued at exit value [Australian Accounting Standards Committee, 1975]. This recommendation appears to be an extension of the use of several valuation bases, depending on the particular financial statement element involved [MacNeal, 1970; Backer, 1974].

Under the "value to the business" or "deprival value" theory, assets are valued at current cost unless replacement is not desirable, in which case they are valued at the higher of value in use (present value) or value in exchange (current exit value). Since replacement would not be desirable if current cost exceeded the higher of present value or current exit value, the valuation rule simplifies to the lower of current cost or realizable value. Although this theory usually is associated with the *CC/PC* model, presumably it also could apply to the *CC/N\$* and the *CC/C\$* models. For example, *SFAS No. 33* requires that recoverable value—present value or current exit value, as appropriate—be used to measure assets if recoverable value is less than current cost.

One final point should be made about the *CC/PC* model. This model appears to have more variations than any of the others. One reason for this, according to Chambers, is that because the concept of physical capacity is hard to quantify in financial terms, no firm meaning can be assigned to the maintenance of physical capacity [Chambers, 1978]. Consequently, perceived deficiencies or shortcomings in the *CC/PC* model have resulted in "patchwork."

CURRENT EXIT VALUE MODELS

The current exit value attribute may be combined with either a nominal dollar or a constant dollar concept of capital.

CURRENT EXIT VALUE/NOMINAL DOLLARS (*EV/N\$*)

The *EV/N\$* model is as follows:

$$M + N(1 + s_2) = L + \underbrace{R}_{(t\,=\,1\text{ capital})} + \underbrace{Ns_2}_{(\text{income})} \tag{10}$$

The holding gain (Ns_2) is similar to the holding gain under the *CC/N\$* model, except that it is based on exit prices instead of entry prices.

CURRENT EXIT VALUE/CONSTANT DOLLARS (*EV/C\$*)

This model has been proposed by Sterling [1970, 1975] and Chambers [1966, 1978]. The Sterling model is:

$$M + N(1 + s_2) = L + \underbrace{R(1 + p)}_{(t\,=\,1\text{ capital})} + \underbrace{N(s_2 - p) - p(M - L)}_{(\text{income})} \tag{11}$$

It is identical in formulation to the *CC/C$* model except that the nonmonetary assets are valued at exit prices instead of current cost.

The Chambers model is:

$$M + N(1 + s_2) = L + \underbrace{R(1 + p)}_{(t\,=\,1\text{ capital})} + \underbrace{Ns_2 - Rp}_{(\text{income})} \qquad (12)$$

Since $Ns_2 - Rp$ in (12) equals $N(s_2 - p) - p(M - L)$ in (11), Chambers and Sterling, while in basic agreement on the propriety of exit value, arrive at income by different means [Chambers, 1975]. Sterling's income number is comprised of a holding gain, net of inflation, plus a purchasing power gain or loss on monetary items. Chambers, on the other hand, prefers to call Ns_2 a "price variation adjustment" and Rp a "capital maintenance adjustment." Under Chambers' formulation, a purchasing power loss (Rp) is calculated on the firm's $t = 0$ net asset position.

SUMMARY

The algebraic approach in this paper has classified most of the price change models that have appeared in the accounting literature. The classification scheme presented here would appear to be useful for identifying common threads and distinct differences among price change models as well as for identifying modifications or extensions to a particular model.

APPENDIX

This Appendix presents a numerical example for each of the twelve model equations which appear in the body of this paper. Let

$$M = \$200 \qquad \frac{L}{L+R} = \frac{1}{3} \qquad s_1 = .24$$

$$N = \$1000 \qquad s_2 = .30$$

$$L = \$400 \qquad \frac{R}{L+R} = \frac{2}{3} \qquad C = \text{capital at } t = 1$$

$$R = \$800 \qquad p = .10 \qquad I = \text{income (loss)}$$

The beginning ($t = 0$) financial position statement is:

$$\underset{M}{\$200} + \underset{N}{\$1000} = \underset{L}{\$400} + \underset{R}{\$800}$$

Ending ($t = 1$) financial position statements for each price change model are:

(1) $\$200 + \$1000 = \$400 + \underset{C}{\$800}$

(2) $\$200 + \$1000(1.10) = \$400 + \$800(1.10) - .10(\$200 - \$400)$
$\$200 + \$1100 = \$400 + \underset{C}{\$880} + \underset{I}{\$20}$

$$\begin{aligned} (3)\quad \$200 + \$1000(1.10) &= \$400 + \$800(1.10) + \$1000(.10) - \$800(.10) \\ \$200 + \$1,100 &= \$400 + \$880 + \$20 \\ &\qquad\qquad C \qquad I \end{aligned}$$

$$\begin{aligned} (4)\quad \$200 + \$1000 &= \$400 + \$800(1.10) - \$800(.10) \\ \$200 + \$1000 &= \$400 + \$880 - \$80 \\ &\qquad\qquad C \qquad I \end{aligned}$$

$$\begin{aligned} (5)\quad \$200 + \$1000(1.24) &= \$400 + \$800 + \$1000(.24) \\ \$200 + \$1240 &= \$400 + \$800 + \$240 \\ &\qquad\qquad C \qquad I \end{aligned}$$

$$\begin{aligned} (6)\quad \$200 + \$1000(1.24) &= \$400 + \$800(1.10) + \$1000(.24 - .10) - .10(\$200 - \$400) \\ \$200 + \$1240 &= \$400 + \$880 + \underbrace{\$140 + \$20} \\ &\qquad\qquad C \qquad\qquad I \end{aligned}$$

$$\begin{aligned} (7)\quad \$200 + \$1000(1.24) &= \$400 + \$800 + \$1000(.24) \\ \$200 + \$1240 &= \$400 + \$1040 \\ &\qquad\qquad C \end{aligned}$$

$$\begin{aligned} (8)\quad \$200 + \$1000(1.24) &= \$400 + \$800 + \$800(.24) - .24(\$200 - \$400) \\ \$200 + \$1240 &= \$400 + \$992 + \$48 \\ &\qquad\qquad C \qquad I \end{aligned}$$

$$\begin{aligned} (9)\quad \$200 + \$1000(1.24) &= \$400 + \$800 + \tfrac{2}{3}(\$1000)(.24) + \tfrac{2}{3}(\$200)(.24) \\ &\quad + \tfrac{1}{3}(\$1000)(.24) - \tfrac{2}{3}(\$200)(.24) \\ \$200 + \$1240 &= \$400 + \$992 + \$48 \\ &\qquad\qquad C \qquad I \end{aligned}$$

$$\begin{aligned} (10)\quad \$200 + \$1000(1.30) &= \$400 + \$800 + \$1000(.30) \\ \$200 + \$1300 &= \$400 + \$800 + \$300 \\ &\qquad\qquad C \qquad I \end{aligned}$$

$$\begin{aligned} (11)\quad \$200 + \$1000(1.30) &= \$400 + \$800(1.10) + \$1000(.30 - .10) - .10(\$200 - \$400) \\ \$200 + \$1300 &= \$400 + \$880 + \$220 \\ &\qquad\qquad C \qquad I \end{aligned}$$

$$\begin{aligned} (12)\quad \$200 + \$1000(1.30) &= \$400 + \$800(1.10) + \$1000(.30) - \$800(.10) \\ \$200 + \$1300 &= \$400 + \$880 + \$220 \\ &\qquad\qquad C \qquad I \end{aligned}$$

REFERENCES

Agrawal, S. and K. Rosenzweig (1982), "One-line Adjustment Methods of Accounting for the Effects of Inflation," *Collected Abstracts of the AAA Annual Meeting* (AAA, 1982), p. 29.

Accounting Principles Board (1969), *Financial Statements Restated for General Price-Level Changes,* Statement No. 3 (AICPA, 1969).

Accounting Research Division (1963), *Accounting Research Study No. 6,* "Reporting the Financial Effects of Price-Level Changes" (AICPA, 1963).

American Accounting Association (1977), Subcommittee on the Conceptual Framework for Financial Accounting and Reporting, *Response to Discussion Memorandum, Parts II and III of the FASB* (AAA, 1977).

Australian Accounting Standards Committee (1975), "A Method of Current Value Accounting," Preliminary Exposure Draft (AASC, 1975).

Backer, M. (1974), "A Model for Current Value Reporting," *CPA Journal* (February 1974), pp. 27–33.

Barton, A. (1975), *An Analysis of Business Income Concepts,* ICRA Occasional Paper No. 7, International Centre for Research in Accounting (University of Lancaster, 1975).

Chambers, R. J. (1966), *Accounting, Evaluation and Economic Behavior* (Prentice-Hall, 1966).

——— (1975), "NOD, COG and PuPu: See How Inflation Teases," *Journal of Accountancy* (September 1975), pp. 56–62.

———(1978), "The Use and Misuse of a Notation: A History of an Idea," *Abacus* (December 1978), pp. 122–144.
Edwards, E. and P. Bell (1961), *The Theory and Measurement of Business Income* (University of California Press, 1961).
Financial Accounting Standards Board, (1976), *Conceptual Framework for Financial Accounting and Reporting: Elements of Financial Statements and Their Measurement,* FASB Discussion Memorandum (FASB, 1976).
———(1979), SFAS No. 33, *Financial Reporting and Changing Prices* (FASB, 1979).
Grady, P. (1975), "Purchasing Power Accounting," *Price Waterhouse Review* (1975), pp. 3–5.
Gynther, R. (1966), *Accounting for Price-Level Changes* (Pergamon Press, 1966).
———(1970), "Capital Maintenance, Price Changes, and Profit Determination," *The Accounting Review* (October 1970), pp. 712–730.
Ijiri, Y. (1976), "The Price-Level Restatement and Its Dual Interpretation," *The Accounting Review* (April 1976), pp. 227–243.
MacNeal, K. (1970), *Truth in Accounting* (Scholars Book Company, 1970).
May, R. G. (1976), "Some *A Priori* Properties of Conventional and Current-Cost Income Numbers Vis a Vis Security Analysis," Proceedings of the Second Annual *Duke University Accounting Symposium* (Duke University, 1976), pp. 92–114.
Peat, Marwick, Mitchell and Co. (1980), *Current Cost Accounting: A Guide to SSAP 16* (PMM & Co., 1980).
Revsine, L. (1973), *Replacement Cost Accounting* (Prentice-Hall, 1973).
Samuelson, R. A. (1980), "Should Replacement-Cost Changes Be Included in Income?" *The Accounting Review* (April 1980), pp. 254–268.
Schwayder, K. (1969), "The Capital Maintenance Rule and the Net Asset Valuation Rule," *The Accounting Review* (April 1969), pp. 304–316.
Sterling, R. R. (1970), *Theory of the Measurement of Enterprise Income* (University of Kansas, 1970).
———(1975), "Relevant Financial Reporting in an Age of Price Changes," *Journal of Accountancy* (February 1975), pp. 42–51.
Sweeney, H. (1936), *Stabilized Accounting* (Harper and Row, 1936).

I-C

POSITIVE ACCOUNTING THEORY

I-C1

THE SELECTIVE FINANCIAL MISREPRESENTATION HYPOTHESIS

Lawrence Revsine

Before the advent of modern technology and communication, decisionmaking was simpler in one critical respect—direct observation provided the basis for most judgments. For example, manufacturing efficiency was assessed by an owner who personally monitored the workforce; similarly, municipal decisions were made in town meetings by citizens who debated individually experienced events.

As business and society grew more complex, it became difficult to make financial decisions by directly observing the important variables. This complexity gave rise to financial reporting since "abstractions" (or surrogates) became necessary to summarize events and to provide information for more complex analyses. Although originally a *consequence* of societal complexity, the surrogates—by facilitating broader spans of control—eventually bred even more complexity. Today virtually all financial decisions in both the private and the public sector use accounting surrogates rather than directly observed events as the basis for action. Not surprisingly, managers, as well as public policy makers, gradually learned that while the events that affect performance often cannot be controlled, the way that people *perceive* these events can be controlled. Manipulating the surrogates provides decision-makers with a means for influencing peoples' perceptions of managerial performance.

The author gratefully acknowledges the helpful comments of James R. Boatsman, Ronald A. Dye, Dan Givoly, James J. Leisenring, Thomas Lys, Paul B. W. Miller, Arthur R. Wyatt and Stephen A. Zeff and financial support from the KPMG Peat Marwick Foundation. The viewpoints expressed in this paper are not necessarily those of the above named individuals and organization.

Lawrence Revsine, "The Selective Misrepresentation Hypothesis," Reprinted by permission of the American Accounting Association.

Financial reporting rules in both the private and public sector are often arbitrary, complicated, and misleading. Most critics view this situation as accidental, a result of bad judgments by standard setters and regulators. By contrast, this paper advances the hypothesis that the problem is not accidental, but instead results from contrived and flexible reporting rules promulgated by standard setters who have been "captured" by the intended regulatees and others involved in the financial reporting process.[1] Regulatees desire such rules because the resulting latitude allows them flexibility in depicting their performance.[2] Interestingly, other participants—shareholders, auditors, standard setters/public policy makers, and even academics—frequently derive simultaneous benefits from these misrepresentations. Thus, the often articulated financial reporting objective (FASB, 1980, para. 63)—correspondence between accounting numbers and the events those numbers purport to represent—is not always followed in practice. Instead, I argue that financial reporting is sometimes better characterized by the phrase *selective financial misrepresentation*. This selective financial misrepresentation hypothesis cuts across both public[3] and private sectors since participants in both sectors are motivated to support standards that selectively misrepresent economic reality when it suits their purpose.

I will illustrate the incentives that motivate various parties to misrepresent financial events. One must understand these incentives in order to appreciate the pitfalls that confront financial standards setters.

---

[1]For those unfamiliar with the term, regulatory "capture" describes a process where the ostensible purpose of regulation—protection of consumers—is eventually reversed and regulatees become the beneficiaries (Stigler, 1971). This happens largely because of personnel movement between the regulatory agency and the regulatees.
While it regrettably conjures a pejorative image, the phrase "regulatory capture" is not intended to impugn the integrity of standard setters. Instead, the point is that everyone is influenced by their background and becomes comfortable with familiar perspectives and experiences. This is inevitable and natural. Unfortunately, in the regulatory sphere, it is also antithetical to the intended purpose of regulation.

[2]Those who transact with managers understand that flexible financial reporting standards facilitate opportunistic behavior (see Jensen and Meckling, 1976). Contracts are presumably adjusted to reflect these anticipated costs. Since the cost of the anticipated opportunistic behavior is borne by the presumed perpetrators (in the form of lower salaries, etc.), there is an incentive on the part of managers and others to lower these "agency costs." Detailed reporting standards and audited statements can be viewed as mechanisms for reducing the costs by tying contract terms to the agreed-upon standards.
All parties to the transaction also understand that monitoring contracts is costly. Because of this, there is evidence that contracts are simply linked to GAAP and not adjusted for "artificial" effects like the impact of changed reporting rules (e.g., Simon 1983, Healy *et al.* 1987). If contracts are simply linked to GAAP, there is an immediate incentive on the part of potential perpetrators to favor reporting standards that facilitate opportunistic behavior. Thus, a preference for flexible reporting rules is plausible even where agency costs are totally borne by the prospective perpetrators.

[3]As used in this paper, "public sector financial reporting" extends beyond reporting by government agencies. It also includes accounting rules for enterprises whose performance can lead to direct economic losses for individuals who are neither owners nor direct transactors. Publicly regulated enterprises like S&Ls are a prime example. The distinguishing feature in such settings is that the market forces by which individuals can protect themselves from financial misrepresentations are limited. Specifically, an investor with superior analytic ability could have avoided S&L stocks (or sold them short) in response to the misleading regulatory accounting principles (or RAP accounting) statements. However, once the securities market as a whole impounds these effects, there is no convenient, efficient market mechanism for knowledgeable individuals to protect themselves from the social costs (e.g., higher taxes) occasioned by the S&L bailout. Thus, "public sector" refers to those areas in which market mechanisms are either partially or totally ineffective.

THE PROBLEM

Managers, shareholders, auditors and standard setters all derive benefits from selective financial misrepresentation. The motives for misrepresentation by each of these groups are presented in this section.

MANAGERS

Virtually all U.S. companies have management compensation plans tied to reported earnings numbers; consequently, managers have a natural incentive to increase reported profit since higher profit means higher compensation. However, external factors that are beyond managers' control sometimes drive real economic performance to levels too low for bonus attainment. But if flexible accounting rules are permitted, managers can shift income between years and thereby increase total bonus payouts. To facilitate these income shifts, managers prefer "loose" reporting standards over "tight" standards.[4]

Historical cost accounting for investments in marketable securities exemplifies a required "loose" financial reporting standard. To illustrate, under historical costing, real economic gains from investment activities do not appear in the financial statements when they occur. Instead, such gains are recognized only when managers choose to sell the securities, perhaps years after the gains initially arose. By adroitly timing sales of appreciated investments, managers can use the belatedly reported gains to offset current period operating shortfalls.

The LIFO inventory method also exemplifies potential "looseness" benefits. Although LIFO lowers earnings in periods of rising prices (relative to FIFO and average cost), the existence of LIFO "reserves" and other characteristics provides a reservoir for inter-period income shifts. That is, dipping into LIFO layers and carefully timing purchases at year-end provide opportunities for managers to achieve desired income targets.

Managers' preferences for "loose" financial reporting standards also arise for reasons other than bonuses. These include, for example, enhancing reported performance in an attempt to 1) impress shareholders and 2) protect their jobs by forestalling takeovers.

"Loose" reporting methods have been repeatedly criticized; however, the alternatives that are more closely related to economic reality (e.g., market-value accounting for marketable securities and inventories) have been consistently and overwhelmingly rejected by the financial community. The selective misrepresentation hypothesis helps us understand why these economically rational arguments are repeatedly rejected; specifically, various sectors of the financial community simply do not want reporting "improvements" since the changes reduce possibilities for opportunistic behavior. It is obviously politically unacceptable for them to say so; as a result, innovative smokescreens are used to defeat proposals for change. (A typical smokescreen is that market value numbers are either unauditable or too volatile, depending upon the context.) Standard setters frequently acquiesce to the smokescreens, perhaps because they have been "captured" by their constituency.

In summary, the selective misrepresentation hypothesis argues that managers prefer reporting methods that provide latitude in income determination (e.g., requiring choices among mutually acceptable alternatives) rather than methods that tightly specify statement numbers

[4]A loose standard is defined as one that provides managers with income timing latitude.

under given economic conditions. By providing managers with control over when they can report externally driven events, loose reporting standards can be used by managers to increase compensation, and to hide perquisite consumption, incompetence, or laziness. Whether these efforts are totally successful is unclear. It is reasonable to presume that those who negotiate managers' employment contracts anticipate such opportunistic behavior and reduce the compensation package accordingly.[5] Notice that the demand for "loose" standards is further increased insofar as managers bear some or all of the agency costs. Since they have already been "charged" for the anticipated opportunistic actions, they must now engage in them in order to achieve the benefits they "paid" for. Since loose standards facilitate opportunistic actions, the demand for such standards increases.

SHAREHOLDERS

One might initially presume that shareholders would object to reporting methods that allow managers to receive unwarranted rewards. However, the financial misrepresentation hypothesis suggests otherwise since shareholders often derive simultaneous benefits from these "loose" reporting methods. To illustrate, consider the following. Most earnings-based incentive plans have maxima and minima: for managers to receive a bonus, earnings must exceed some threshold level; but there are simultaneous upper limits on bonus payments. Given these incentive plan characteristics, it is often surmised that managers will try to smooth reported earnings in order to maximize their bonuses.[6] If they do so successfully, the *reported* earnings pattern would appear less volatile than the *real* earnings pattern. This appearance of lower volatility could, perhaps, lower the market's perception of default risk. The lower is the perceived default risk, the higher is firm value. As a consequence, shareholders would also benefit from managers' choices of "loose" accounting standards. Indeed, following the misrepresentation hypothesis, rather than objecting to such standards, shareholders might have a decided preference for them.

The flexibility afforded by "loose" reporting standards also provides opportunities to circumvent loan covenant and bond indenture restrictions. If covenants are successfully evaded, these activities would lower actual default risk and, again, convey positive benefits to shareholders. Recent theoretical papers (e.g., Dye, 1988) have used variations on this theme to explain why shareholders continue to allow managers to write employment and bonus contracts tied to "loose" numbers; while managers might utilize this "looseness" to enhance their remuneration, simultaneous benefits also accrue to shareholders.

AUDITORS

Following the selective misrepresentation hypothesis, auditors may likewise prefer reporting rules that sometimes distort economic reality. The explanation relates to auditors' obvious

[5]This perspective is consistent with the "agency theory" view of managerial behavior. See Jensen and Meckling (1976) and Watts and Zimmerman (1986).

[6]There is some research evidence that demonstrates income smoothing behavior by managers. Additionally, there are numerous well-publicized incidents where managers have been willing to misrepresent financial performance (via misdated invoices and manipulation of purchase and sales cut-offs) in order to achieve income smoothing objectives. Getschow (1979) describes such activities by managers at H. J. Heinz over the period 1972–1978; Guyon (1983) reports on similar smoothing activities at PepsiCo from 1978 through 1982; finally, Ingersoll (1984) discusses other types of manipulations at Datapoint Corp. during fiscal year 1981.

preferences for retaining clients: repeat audit engagements are especially profitable owing to the steepness of the learning curve. Thus, the hypothesis suggests that auditors' preferences for reporting methods will be influenced by the degree of client harmony elicited by various alternatives.

Depending upon the issue, these auditor preferences can take one of two forms. First, there will be instances where auditors will push for rigid standards that make no pretense of capturing economic circumstances. The immediate expensing of research and development expenditures (FASB, 1974) illustrates this avenue. This rigid approach reduces possibilities for frictions with clients where future outcomes are highly uncertain. When reporting procedures *require* immediate expensing, the threat of client loss arising from disputes is eliminated since all other auditors are compelled to apply the same standard.

Second, in instances where the reporting dilemma is driven more by theory debates rather than by uncertain future events, auditors will opt for reporting standards that simultaneously encompass *both* rigid computational metrics and flexibility. Historical cost accounting provides a perfect illustration of such a system. Readily auditable, "objective," past events measured using well-defined computational procedures (e.g., sum-of-years-digits depreciation) form the basis for historical cost statement numbers. Such numbers are defensible in court and, as such, would be preferred by auditors in the litigious climate they face (Arthur Andersen, 1984, p. 6). However, because of its simultaneous reliance on arbitrary allocations, historical cost accounting presents numerous alternatives for reporting similar phenomena. Full cost versus successful efforts accounting in the oil and gas industry provides one familiar example. Measurement and reporting latitude of this sort allows auditors flexibility and thereby facilitates more harmonious relations with clients.

Historical cost based inventory options like LIFO and FIFO also illustrate the simultaneous confluence of rigid computational metrics and flexibility. The alternative financial measures inherent to the initial LIFO/FIFO choice and the ability to periodically change methods, provide the negotiating room which enables auditors to placate clients and thereby avoid losing future billings.

The preceding analysis helps explain a curious anomaly. Sometimes auditors welcome certain inflexible methods (e.g., mandatory charge-offs of R&D expenditures) that don't necessarily capture economic circumstances. At other times, they reject methods that nicely capture the relevant economics, for instance, market value accounting for inventories and marketable securities. Why? The selective misrepresentation hypothesis suggests one explanation: client harmony. Sometimes harmony requires "slack" in the system as a desirable safety-valve, while under other circumstances rigidly specified rules provide a convenient shield for the auditor to hide behind.

STANDARD SETTERS

Even standard setters have sometimes revealed a preference for reporting methods that obscure reality. Following the selective misrepresentation hypothesis, the motive here is a combination of self-protection and altruism.

The issue of troubled loan restructuring provides an example. Statement Number 15 (FASB 1977) has been widely, repeatedly, and justifiably attacked for ignoring real economic losses in certain loan restructurings. However, many believe that this misrepresentation was purposeful. The issue arose after renegotiation of loan terms because of the New York City financial crisis in the mid 1970s. A candid recognition of the amount of genuine economic losses owing to the renegotiations would have eliminated much of the reported bank capital that must be maintained under regulatory guidelines. If the FASB had required realistic accounting rules for these restructurings, additional capital infusions might have been necessitated, lending limits exceeded, and potential use of Federal funds required to honor deposit insurance guarantees at failed banks.[7] The FASB's apparent agenda was to avoid precipitating a capital crisis for banks while simultaneously giving the appearance of having dealt with a highly visible problem. Notice that the general public is the ostensible beneficiary in this scenario since the avoidance of a bank capital crisis presumably made continued credit available to the economy. Indeed, the Office of the Comptroller of the Currency implicitly utilized the FASB (1977) model to achieve similar misrepresentation objectives in assessing adequacy of loan loss reserves for Third World debt (Comptroller's Handbook, 1990, Section 215.1). As before, the selective financial misrepresentation led to outcomes that, one surmises, were deemed by the standard setters to enhance aggregate social welfare.

While the troubled loan restructuring example illustrates financial misrepresentation actions precipitated by standard setters, a more familiar example of public policy manipulation using selective misrepresentation is provided by the savings and loan accounting rules. Regulatory accounting principles (RAP) are widely acknowledged to have been politically motivated mechanisms invented by regulators to misrepresent S&L financial performance and thereby delay the closing of insolvent associations (e.g., Berton, 1985). Keeping these insolvent S&Ls open avoided increasing the Federal budget deficits of the early 1980s. As the economic performance of S&Ls worsened, eventually even the notoriously lenient RAP rules could not disguise the unhealthy financial conditions confronting numerous thrifts. Consequently, additional misrepresentations were necessary. One example is provided by a 1984 stock dividend that was declared and paid to member associations by the Federal Home Loan Mortgage Corporation (Freddie Mac). The intent of the dividend, critics charge, was to bolster regulatory capital of the recipient S&Ls.[8] To achieve this end, the Federal Home Loan Bank Board and other interested parties lobbied the FASB to allow the stock dividend to be treated as income.

Not surprisingly, seven of the then Big Eight accounting firms also advised the Board to permit income treatment for the stock dividend (Berton, 1985); they argued that the stock dividend conveyed ownership rights that the thrifts did not previously have. Despite the conflict between income treatment and established accounting principles relating to stock dividends, the FASB (1985a) ultimately permitted the stock dividend to be included in income. This incident illustrates perhaps best of all the breadth of the benefits conveyed by accounting standards that permit selective misrepresentation. Here the beneficiaries included S&L managers (they kept their jobs), shareholders (the S&Ls stayed in business), auditors (they were able to placate their clients), standard setters (they thought they performed a social service), and public policy makers (they were able to avoid increasing the Federal deficit).

---

[7]In the 1970s, capital adequacy was not determined by strict formulae; instead a range of factors—some subjective like management quality—were used by regulators (see, for example, Crosse and Hempel, 1980, pp. 78–79).

[8]This objective was stated openly by the Federal Home Loan Bank Board, which initiated the transaction:

> Transferring the appreciated value of Freddie Mac in the form of a stock dividend to these institutions will allow them to recognize on their balance sheets a substantial portion of the value of the Corporation (U.S. League, 1984).

The undiscounted cost of the S&L industry collapse to be borne by taxpayers over the next forty years is currently estimated to be between $750 billion and one trillion dollars (Veribanc, 1991, p. 3). A considerable portion of the blame must be attributed to selective financial misrepresentations. Despite this, regulators and public policy makers continue to repeat the mistakes. Consider Federal Reserve Board Chairman Alan Greenspan's reaction to the SEC proposal that banks use current market value accounting for financial assets. In opposition, Greenspan raises the familiar argument that mark-to-market accounting injects volatility (Duke and Salwen, 1990). Of course, that is precisely the justification *for* the proposal. According to the SEC's chairman, "if you are in a volatile business, then your balance sheet and income statement should reflect that volatility" (Linden, 1990). Obviously, volatility in reported bank earnings and reported capital creates potential problems for the Federal Reserve Board; this apparently motivates the opposition since the Fed's latitude in responding to other economic conditions could be restricted by the mark-to-market volatility.

ACADEMICS

It has even been suggested (Watts and Zimmerman, 1979) that accounting theories and proposals for "improvements" in financial reporting advanced by the academic community are also sometimes motivated by a demand for selective misrepresentation. Succinctly, the argument is that the financial community understands that accounting rules can be used to effect wealth transfers. As events dictate, a demand for theories that facilitate such transfers emerges; in this view, academic (and other) accounting writers succumb to standard market forces and supply the demanded theories. Their remuneration is in the form of enhanced prestige and consulting fees.

To summarize, the selective misrepresentation hypothesis is dramatically inconsistent with the accounting profession's publicly articulated description of the financial reporting process. Because selective misrepresentation potentially leads to a resource allocation that is very different from the more traditional view implied by financial reporting standards, it is important to examine which view is more consistent with available evidence.

THE EVIDENCE

Obtaining evidence about embarrassing activities is difficult, especially when the subject is selective financial misrepresentation; after all, the perpetrators have professional reputations to uphold. Despite the obstacles, piecemeal evidence supporting the hypothesis has been accumulated. In addition, the behavior of participants in the financial reporting process allows observers to make inferences that are often very consistent with the misrepresentation hypothesis.

Before summarizing the evidence, it is important to understand that the primary purpose of financial reporting is to provide a basis for contracting and decision making. Therefore, the degree and frequency of misrepresentation must indeed be selective. Some reasonably close correspondence between economic events and accounting messages must predominate in order to instill confidence in affected parties. Without this correspondence, accounting numbers are unlikely to play any major role in contracting (Holmstrom, 1979). Stated somewhat differently, the fact that existing financial reporting rules predominantly reflect underlying economics is *not* inconsistent with selective misrepresentation. If the misrepresentations were pervasive, accounting would be discredited and the opportunity to use the numbers to effect wealth transfers would be limited.

Empirical evidence regarding selective misrepresentation must be inferred. One cannot easily discover the motives prompting advocacy of controversial, income increasing reporting methods for things like debt-for-debt swaps, debt-for-equity swaps, or defeasances. Empirical researchers are limited to studying the circumstances in which managers have utilized these (and other) devices and determining whether their adoption is consistent with the motivations for misrepresentation.

Research of this sort has been undertaken. Watts and Zimmerman (1978) and Deakin (1989) provide evidence consistent with the notion that managers lobby standard setting bodies to approve reporting methods that maximize managers' welfare. Similarly, Dhaliwal (1980) found that managers in highly leveraged firms lobbied against accounting standards that decreased reported income and (presumably increased risk of covenant violation). Further evidence suggests that once desired methods are permitted, managers adopt them in circumstances under which they derive benefits. For example, debt-for-equity swaps that increase earnings tend to occur during periods of low profitability (Hand, 1989) and are most likely "when the earnings shortfall is small and transitory" (Lys and Sivaramakrishnan, 1988); furthermore, these swaps are associated with increases in executive compensation (Defeo, Lambert and Larcker, 1989). Discretionary transactions frequently associated with income management were also found to increase compensation of bank executives (Clinch and Magliolo, 1991). A study of in-substance defeasances suggests that firms undertook these controversial transactions in order to smooth annual earnings or avoid bond covenant restrictions (Hand, Hughes and Sefcik, 1990). Johnson and Dhaliwal (1988) find that, in their sample, firms abandoning LIFO are characterized by low earnings performance and strained financial conditions. Healy (1985) found that when managers' bonuses are tied to profits, income-decreasing accruals tend to occur where upper and lower bonus constraints are binding; by contrast, income increasing accruals are concentrated in periods where these constraints are not binding. This behavior is consistent with bonus maximization across periods. Using a different methodology, McNichols and Wilson (1988) focused on income decreasing accruals. They found that, for their sample, income-decreasing accruals tend to occur when income is unusually high or low; these results are again consistent with multi-period bonus maximization. Similarly, DeAngelo (1988) found that incumbent managers engaged in a proxy fight use income-increasing accruals. She suggests that this behavior is motivated by self-protection. In a study that examines factors influencing the choice of RAP by S&L managers, Blacconiere *et al.* (1991) report results that are also consistent with managerial self-protection. Elliott and Shaw (1988) examined discretionary accounting write-offs and found that managerial behavior conforms to "big bath" bunching of expenses and losses. Givoly and Revsine (1991) found evidence that the timing of the adoption of new reporting principles is consistent with income smoothing and acceleration of "good" earnings news.

To summarize, research evidence is consistent with the notion that managers use latitude in existing financial reporting to benefit themselves. In several of these studies, this behavior simultaneously benefits shareholders. This reinforces the point that misrepresentation conveys potentially widespread benefits. Indeed, this characteristic of "shared benefits" may be crucial to the survival of selective misrepresentation.

Academic research on auditor's preferences for principles that facilitate selective misrepresentation is sparse. One exception is Puro (1984). She finds that auditors' FASB lobbying activity regarding standardization of accounting treatment (i.e., eliminating alternatives) is consistent with self-interest. Another example is provided by Hill and Ingram (1989, p. 678) who infer from their results that auditors' willingness to let their S&L clients adopt RAP rather than GAAP accounting was "influenced by their perceptions of [RAP's] key role in maintaining the continued existence of their S&L clients." Less rigorous scrutiny of auditors' behavior on other issues also provides evidence that is consistent with selective misrepresentation. Perhaps the clearest illustration is in the area of accounting for marketable securities. By definition, market prices exist for these assets; despite the existence of such non-arbitrary non-manipulatable measures, lower of cost or market is the accepted reporting method. In addressing this anomaly, Arthur Wyatt, a former member of the FASB, stated (Wyatt, 1989):

> One can question why so little progress has been made in this [marketable securities] accounting problem area. The answer certainly goes beyond a simple resistance to change. Preparers of financial statements, and many auditors, are adamantly opposed to any accounting practice that injects volatility into the measure of reported earnings. It might be more accurate to say that the opposition is to volatility in reported earnings over which the preparer has no control. My perception is that today there can be little optimism that any research, whether undertaken by academics or others, would persuade preparers and many practitioners to agree that marketable securities should be measured at market rather than at historical cost.

Wyatt thus contends that existing practice is dictated by a desire to minimize volatility in income determination. Favoring reporting methods that minimize volatility, of course, is simply another way of describing a preference for selective misrepresentation.[9]

Another example that has already been discussed simultaneously illustrates both auditors' and standard setters' occasional preferences for misrepresentation. The issue relates to the lobbying to obtain income treatment for the Federal Home Loan Mortgage Corporation preferred stock dividend. As noted previously, there are also other inexplicable, apparently politically motivated, pronouncements and regulatory rules of this sort.

IMPLICATIONS AND A PROPOSAL FOR CHANGE

In the private sector, accounting and financial reporting evolved as a consequence of increasingly complex industrial structures, sophisticated contracting, and diffused ownership. Similarly, in the public sector as laws and regulatory policies grew more and more intricate and significant, accounting gradually assumed greater importance as a means for assuring compliance.

Inevitably, decision-makers in both sectors learned that clever manipulation of the surrogates—financial accounting data—could be utilized to perpetrate wealth transfers or circumvent social controls. Because accounting cannot be perfect, and because it is too costly to monitor each event, transfers of this sort must be accepted as an unavoidable element of modern

[9] Another example of this desire to minimize volatility is illustrated by Statement Number 87 on pensions (FASB, 1985b). Numerous exceedingly complicated smoothing devices permeate this standard. Eliminating volatility is explicitly discussed in the Statement, e.g., paragraphs 173–190.

contracting.[10] In the private sector, market forces anticipate and ameliorate important aspects of the transfers through the pricing process. For example, managers' salaries are presumably adjusted downward to absorb the expected losses associated with perquisite consumption, bonus manipulation and other wealth transfers. Accordingly, some of the losses discussed in this paper are not always a "surprise" to those on the other side of the transaction.

The moderating effect of these offsetting market forces coupled with the existence of selective financial misrepresentation requires reconsideration of the benefits of standard setting in the private sector. Standard setting is costly.[11] The financial community has previously borne this cost willingly since accounting standards facilitate contracting. But given the growing use of selective financial misrepresentation and the increasingly successful efforts to add standards that allow misrepresentation, the resulting rules may, at best, merely facilitate wealth transfers and, at worse, lead to dead-weight social losses.

Since the costly reporting standards allow misrepresentation, logic suggests that we should consider reducing the resources devoted to developing these complicated standards. If the task is fruitless, and countervailing market forces exist in the private sector, why should society expend resources? Instead, existing standards could effectively be "frozen" and used as the basis for all future contracting and reporting. (Indeed, the FASB's new "super-majority" voting rule might have been conceived as a step in this direction.) The resources saved by down-scaling the often ineffective private standard setting process could be redeployed to bolster the standard setting process in the public sector. (Recollect from footnote 3 that the definition of "public sector" used in this paper includes private enterprises whose performance can lead to direct economic losses for individuals who are neither owners nor direct transactors. Examples include publicly regulated banks and S&Ls.) Developing financial reporting rules for this sector should be the FASB's prime responsibility.

This redeployment of FASB effort is justified since market discipline is muted in the public sector and perpetrators of financial misrepresentations confront fewer obstacles. Accordingly, standards serve a more critical role here as is evidenced by the fact that the S&L misrepresentations identified in this paper have been used to circumvent social contracts underlying deposit insurance. That is, in exchange for the deposit guarantee, thrifts were compelled to maintain a cushion of capital. The manipulation of the accounting rules used to measure this capital subverted the intent of the agreement and raised the social risk of the insurance to unintended levels. As the costs of these accounting misrepresentations escalate, it becomes evident that something must be done. Nations built upon the rule of law must do more than just provide safety and environmental protection for their citizens. Fiscal misdeeds must also be prevented.

But can public sector financial reporting standards be upgraded without repeating the selective misrepresentation mistakes from the private sector? Realistically, the answer is "not completely." However, clear improvements are possible. To accomplish this, the FASB (or whatever other group assumes the primary public sector standard setting role) must be insulated from

[10]Following Jensen and Meckling (1976), these are now widely referred to as "agency costs."

[11]Funding the operations of the SEC and the FASB is only a small part of the total cost of standard setting. In addition, there are the costs associated with individual comprehension of the new standards, formal training, implementation of the standard, and adaptive behavior (including opportunistic adaptive behavior) on the part of market participants and other affected parties.

regulatory capture. This requires a four-step process: 1) educating the public, 2) improving the process for selecting and monitoring standards setters, 3) establishing new funding arrangements, and 4) creating independence for the standard setters.

EDUCATING THE PUBLIC

The public must first understand the losses that financial misrepresentation causes. As one example, the role of selective misrepresentation in the Savings and Loan fiasco is unclear to many, even in retrospect.[12] Part of the blame rests with accounting educators since misrepresentation issues receive little attention in most university courses and few academics try to alert the public as abuses unfold. Once we do a better job of communicating the problem to our various constituencies, more sophisticated public policy control devices will be widely demanded.

Take the case of the Gramm-Rudman-Hollings budget deficit law. The clear intent here was ultimately to bring Federal *operating* deficits down. Yet the law is easily circumvented because of the naive accounting rules that it utilizes (Bowsher, 1990). Asset sales (Conrail, etc.) and commingling of disparate activities (e.g., Social Security surpluses) have been used as accounting devices to subvert its objective. When the general public understands the true extent of financial misrepresentation, more sophisticated and less manipulatable control devices will be perceived to be necessary and ultimately implemented. This is the first step.

IMPROVING SELECTION AND MONITORING

The phenomenon of regulatory capture compounds the problem of selective financial misrepresentation; accordingly, certain changes in the selection and monitoring of financial regulatory bodies are urgently needed. As an example of existing insensitivity to such concerns, a majority of the composition of the FASB is comprised of former regulatees, specifically, individuals from CPA firms and industry. The oversight board that reviews the activities of the FASB—the Financial Accounting Foundation—is comprised primarily of *current* regulatees, thereby exacerbating the problem (Miller and Redding, 1988).[13] A more notorious public regulatory example is the Federal Home Loan Bank Board, the originator of many of the RAP rules that precipitated the S&L debacle. As public understanding grows, so too will pressure to reform the regulatory appointment and oversight process. An effort to balance representation between those knowledgeable about financial issues and others possessing a broader perspective can lead to clear improvements.

ESTABLISHING NEW FUNDING ARRANGEMENTS

Since business organizations fund the FASB, it is not surprising that these regulatees expect to participate in oversight activities. But this intrusion worsens the selective misrepresentation problem. One solution is to continue the existing FASB funding arrangement but bar the

---

[12] A recent, supposedly exhaustive, review of the S&L crisis (Rosenbaum, 1990) failed even to mention manipulation of accounting regulatory rules as one of the culprits.

[13] A longstanding, prominent observer of the FASB recently wrote a blistering letter to the President of the Financial Accounting Foundation accusing the Foundation of damaging the standard-setting system (Miller, 1991).

funding organizations (and their members) from oversight activities. However, those who pay the bill usually expect accountability; therefore, if this approach were enforced, funding would inevitably cease.

Another approach is to have the relatively modest (under $20 million) annual FASB operating costs funded by user fees. For example, a small Federal tax on all security market transactions, private placements, loans and other financing contracts would easily fund standard-setting operations. Since the FASB's operating costs pale in comparison to the recent costs arising from public sector selective financial misrepresentation, once the social benefits of improved standards are understood, it should be relatively easy to alter the funding base.

(Of course, Federal funding raises the possibility of Congressional intrusion since, as stated above, those who pay the cost expect to influence the outcome. But Congressional intrusion already exists in the form of government hearings, SEC oversight of FASB activities, and similar pressures. Since the ultimate responsibility for formulating financial reporting rules already resides in the governmental sector, i.e., through the SEC,[14] Federal funding is unlikely to drastically alter the degree of Congressional intrusion.)

CREATING INDEPENDENCE

Above all else, those who set public sector financial standards must be insulated from the regulatees—that is, from ourselves and our elected representatives. After all, it was Congress that instigated the S&L RAP rules that kept insolvent associations open in the early 1980s and thereby deferred (and worsened) the problem. It was also Congress that acquiesced to putting more than half of the initial Resolution Trust financing "off-budget," thereby understanding the true deficit and circumventing the budget deficit law (Thomas, 1989).

Mechanisms for establishing the requisite independence for standard setters already exist in the public sector. Examples include life-tenure for Supreme Court justices and 14 year terms for Federal Reserve Board governors. By providing similar continuity for public sector financial standard setters, the public might be somewhat better protected from Congressional pressure for politically inspired financial misrepresentations. That is, long term job protection should insulate these individuals from pressures to initiate opportunistic standards advanced by interested parties. Making standards setters impervious to such pressures is an important element in reducing the incidence of selective financial misrepresentation.

---

[14]These powers are given to the SEC in Section 19(a) of the Securities Act of 1933 as Amended:

> the Commission shall have authority, for the purposes of this title, to prescribe the form or forms in which required information shall be set forth, the items or details to be shown in the balance sheet and earning statement, and the methods to be followed in the preparation of accounts, in the appraisal or valuation of assets and liabilities, in the determination of depreciation and depletion, in the differentiation of recurring and nonrecurring income, in the differentiation of investment and operating income, and in the preparation, where the Commission deems it necessary or desirable, of consolidated balance sheets or income accounts of any person directly or indirectly controlling or controlled by the issuer, or any person under direct or indirect common control with the issuer. The rules and regulations of the Commission shall be effective upon publication in the manner which the Commission shall prescribe.

CONCLUSION

Financial reporting standards should enhance economic efficiency, rather than aiding those who wish to gain at another's expense. But the repeated wealth transfers perpetrated using financial standards in the private sector call into question the justification for incurring these standard setting costs. Since market forces anticipate and ameliorate elements of the private sector wealth transfers, further refinement of existing reporting rules in that sector seems less urgent than a tightening of standards in the public sector.

In outlining the selective financial misrepresentation hypothesis, this paper advances the notion that society may have overinvested in standard setting activities in the private sector and underinvested in these activities in the public sector. One can hope that a better understanding of selective financial misrepresentation will motivate important reforms.

REFERENCES

Arthur Andersen & Co., *Objectives of Financial Statements for Business Enterprises,* 1984.

Berton, Lee, "Accounting at Thrifts Provokes Controversy as Gimmickry Mounts," *The Wall Street Journal,* March 21, 1985.

Blacconiere, Walter G., Robert M. Bowen, Stephen E. Sefcik, and Christopher H. Stinson, "Determinants of the Use of Regulatory Accounting Principles by Savings and Loans," *Journal of Accounting and Economics* (June, 1991), pp. 167–201.

Bowsher, Charles A., "Cooking the Books Is a Bad Recipe to Cool Deficit," *Journal of Accountancy* (February, 1990), pp. 23, 25.

Clinch, Greg, and Joseph Magliolo, "Executive Compensation Effects of Accounting-Oriented Discretionary Transactions in Commercial Banks," working paper, University of Pennsylvania (May 1991).

Comptroller's Handbook for National Bank Examiners, March 1990.

Crosse, Howard, and George H. Hempel, *Management Policies For Commercial Banks,* 3rd ed. (Englewood Cliffs, N.J., 1980).

Deakin, Edward B., "Rational Economic Behavior and Lobbying on Accounting Issues: Evidence from the Oil and Gas Industry," *The Accounting Review* (January, 1989), pp. 137–151.

DeAngelo, Linda E., "Managerial Compensation, Information Costs, and Corporate Governance: The Use of Accounting Performance Measures in Proxy Contests," *Journal of Accounting and Economics* (January, 1988), pp. 3–36.

Defeo, Victor, Richard Lambert, and David Larcker, "The Executive Compensation Effects of Equity-for-Debt Swaps," *The Accounting Review* (April, 1989), pp. 201–227.

Dhaliwal, Dan S., "The Effect of the Firm's Capital Structure on the Choice of Accounting Methods," *The Accounting Review* (January, 1980), pp. 78–84.

Duke, Paul Jr., and Kevin G. Salwen, "SEC Proposal Draws Criticism from Greenspan," *The Wall Street Journal,* November 8, 1990.

Dye, Ronald A., "Earnings Management in an Overlapping Generations Model," *Journal of Accounting Research* (Autumn, 1988), pp. 195–235.

Elliott, John, and Wayne Shaw, "Write-Offs as Accounting Procedures to Manage Perceptions," *Journal of Accounting Research,* Supplement, 1988, pp. 91–119.

Financial Accounting Standards Board, "Accounting for Research and Development Costs," *Statement of Financial Accounting Standards No. 2* (1974).

———, "Accounting by Debtors and Creditors for Troubled Debt Restructurings," *Statement of Financial Accounting Standards No. 15* (1977).

———, "Qualitative Characteristics of Accounting Information," *Statement of Financial Accounting Concepts No. 2* (1980).

———, Technical Bulletin No. 85-1, "Accounting for the Receipt of Federal Home Loan Mortgage Corporation Participating Preferred Stock" (March, 1985). (1985a)

———, "Employers' Accounting for Pensions," *Statement of Financial Accounting Standards No. 87* (1985). (1985b)

———, "Statement of Cash Flows," *Statement of Financial Accounting Standards No. 95* (1987).

Getschow, George, "Initial Study of Some Heinz Units Finds $5.5 Million in Profit-Juggling Practices," *The Wall Street Journal,* July 2, 1979.

Givoly, Dan, and Lawrence Revsine, "Managerial Opportunism and the Adoption Timing of New Accounting Principles," working paper, Northwestern University (May, 1991).

Guyon, Janet, "PepsiCo Chief Kendall Steps up Role at Firm before '86 Retirement," *The Wall Street Journal,* July 29, 1983.

Hand, John, "Did Firms Undertake Debt-Equity Swaps for an Accounting Paper Profit or True Financial Gain?", *The Accounting Review* (October, 1989), pp. 587–623.

———, Patricia J. Hughes, and Stephan E. Sefcik, "Insubstance Defeasances: Security Price Reactions and Motivations," *Journal of Accounting and Economics* (May 1990), pp. 47–89.

Healy, Paul, "The Impact of Bonus Schemes on the Selection of Accounting Principles," *Journal of Accounting and Economics* (April 1985), pp. 85–108.

———, Sok-Hyon Kang, and Krishna G. Palepu, "The Effect of Accounting Procedure Changes on CEO's Cash Salary and Bonus Compensation," *Journal of Accounting and Economics* (April 1987), pp. 7–34.

Hill, John W., and Robert W. Ingram, "Selection of GAAP or RAP in the Savings and Loan Industry," *The Accounting Review* (October, 1989), pp. 667–679.

Holmstrom, Bengt, "Moral Hazard and Observability," *The Bell Journal of Economics* (Spring, 1979), pp. 74–91.

Ingersoll, Bruce, "SEC Accuses Datapoint of Overstating Revenue and Net Income for Fiscal 1981," *The Wall Street Journal* (June 19, 1984).

Jensen, Michael, and William Meckling, "Theory of the Firm: Managerial Behavior, Agency Costs and Ownership Structure," *Journal of Financial Economics* (1976), pp. 306–60.

Johnson, W. Bruce, and Dan S. Dhaliwal, "LIFO Abandonment," *Journal of Accounting Research* (Autumn, 1988), pp. 236–272.

Linden, Dana Wechsler, "If Life Is Volatile, Account for It," *Forbes,* November 12, 1990, pp. 114–115.

Lys, Thomas, and Konduru Sivaramakrishnan, "Earnings Expectations and Capital Restructuring: The Case of Equity-for-Debt Swaps," *Journal of Accounting Research* (Autumn, 1988), pp. 273–299.

McNichols, Maureen and G. Peter Wilson, "Evidence of Earnings Management from the Provision for Bad Debts," *Journal of Accounting Research,* Supplement, 1988, pp. 1–31.

Miller, Paul B. W., and Rodney J. Redding, *The FASB: The People, the Process and the Politics,* 2nd ed. (Homewood, IL, 1988).

———, Letter to Shaun F. O'Malley, February 13, 1991.

Puro, Marsha, "Audit Firm Lobbying before the Financial Accounting Standards Board: An Empirical Study," *Journal of Accounting Research* (Autumn, 1984), pp. 624–646.

Rosenbaum, David E., "A Financial Disaster with Many Culprits," *The New York Times,* June 6, 1990.

Simon, Daniel T., "Compensation Effects and Accounting Changes: An Empirical Examination," (Unpublished Ph.D. dissertation, Northwestern University, 1983).

Stigler, George J., "The Theory of Economic Regulation," *Bell Journal of Economics and Management Science* (Spring 1971), pp. 3–21.

Thomas, Paulette, "Thrift Regulators Could Further Raise Bailout Debt apart from U.S. Budget," *The Wall Street Journal,* October 10, 1989.

U.S. Congress, "Securities Act of 1933 as Amended" [H. R. 5480] 73d Congress.

U.S. League of Savings Institutions, *Washington Notes* (Washington, D. C., December 7, 1984).

Veribanc, Inc., *Veribanc News Release* (Wakefield, Massachusetts, April 4, 1991).

Watts, Ross and Jerold Zimmerman, "Towards a Positive Theory of the Determination of Accounting Standards," *The Accounting Review* (January 1978), pp. 112–134.

———, "The Demand for and Supply of Accounting Theories: The Market for Excuses," *The Accounting Review* (April 1979), pp. 273–305.

———, *Positive Accounting Theory* (Englewood Cliffs, N.J., 1986).

Wyatt, Arthur, "Interface between Teaching/Research and Teaching/Practice," *Accounting Horizons* (March, 1989), pp. 125–128.

I-C2

POSITIVE RESEARCH IN ACCOUNTING

Jerold L. Zimmerman

The last fifteen years have witnessed an emerging interest in positive research in accounting. In the last five years the attention of some researchers has turned to developing a positive theory of the determination of accounting standards. That is a theory, that can explain managers' voluntary choice of accounting procedures and how the regulated standards have changed over time. If and when constructed, a positive theory of the determination of accounting standards will be able to *explain* the existing set of generally accepted accounting standards and *predict* how that set will be altered with changes in the underlying variables. Such a positive theory will allow us to explain and predict the actions of the various parties to the standard setting process, including the actions of managers, auditors, accounting policy makers, politicians and other regulators. The purpose of this paper is to discuss what positive research in accounting is and how it has evolved (section A), to present a capsule summary of the current research (section B), and to offer some predictions of what is likely to be learned from this inquiry (section C).

Research support was provided by the Center for Research in Government Policy and Business and the Managerial Economics Research Center, University of Rochester. Many of the thoughts and views expressed in this paper are the product of a prolonged and fruitful collaboration with Ross Watts. The comments of Phil Meyers, Subrata Sen, Jerold Warner and in particular Michael Jensen and Ross Watts are gratefully acknowledged.

Jerold L. Zimmerman, "Positive Research in Accounting," in *Perspectives in Research,* ed. R. Nair and T. H. Williams, University of Wisconsin, Madison, May 1980, pp. 107–128. Reprinted by permission of the University of Wisconsin-Madison.

A. Positive Research

Milton Friedman's monograph entitled, *Essays in Positive Economics* (1953), discusses in detail positive research in economics. A positive science[1] is described as "a body of systematized knowledge concerning *what is*" (J. M. Keynes, *The Scope and Method of Political Economy* cited by Friedman). That is, positive research seeks to develop a theory that can explain observed phenomena. A positive theory of the determination of accounting standards seeks to answer such questions as:

1. Why do some firms choose straight-line and others accelerated depreciation for financial reporting?
2. Why do some oil companies choose full-cost accounting and others successful-efforts accounting for exploration costs?
3. Why do public accountants support a quasi-private as opposed to a government-operated accounting standards board?
4. Why does the Securities and Exchange Commission (SEC) continue to subcontract (with veto power) to the accounting profession the overt policy-making role?

Answers to these questions, in terms of a set of empirically tested hypotheses, form a positive theory of accounting. Such a theory can address such questions as:

1. Is the Financial Accounting Standards Board (FASB) likely to alter generally accepted accounting standards for financial reporting if a 10–5–3 depreciation system is adopted for tax purposes?
2. Is the SEC's Reserve Recognition Accounting (RRA) proposal likely to be implemented?
3. Is the FASB likely to survive a major financial debacle involving financial reporting?

A positive theory is of the form, "If A then B," that is capable of being refuted. A positive theory of the manager's choice of depreciation accounting would be—"If bond covenants (written in terms of accounting numbers) become binding, then managers are more likely to switch from accelerated to straight-line depreciation for book purposes" (Holthausen, 1980). Notice that this statement can be refuted by the evidence. Furthermore, this theory, if not refuted, explains why managers switch depreciation methods.

The nature of positive research in accounting has changed over the last fifteen years. The best way to illustrate this change is to use three of the more widely cited empirical accounting papers:

1. Ball and Brown (1968), that examines the information content of annual earnings.
2. Ball and Watts (1972), that examines the time series properties of annual earnings.
3. Kaplan and Roll (1972), that tests the stock price reaction to accounting procedure changes [see also Ball (1972) and Sunder (1975)].

All of these classic papers do not address the question of why managers (or policy makers) choose the accounting standards that they do. All of them examine "what"-type questions.

---

[1] For a discussion of the difference between positive and normative research see Friedman (1953), Jensen (1976), and Zimmerman (1978).

What is the association between stock prices and earnings, stock prices and accounting changes, etc. Ball and Watts (1972) did not address the positive question of why earnings follow a random walk. Kaplan and Roll (1972) did not address the positive question of why managers change accounting procedures, although the Kaplan and Roll findings suggest that managers probably do not change accounting standards to "fool" the market.

Two other examples will serve to illustrate how positive research in accounting is changing. Dyckman and Smith (1979), Collins and Dent (1979) and Lev (1979) addressed the question of whether there was a security price reaction to the FASB's proposed elimination of full costing for oil and gas in 1977. Basically, these papers did not address the question of why some firms used full cost and others successful efforts. Collins and Dent and Lev found a stock price reaction which, in turn, led them to ask why it occurred.[2] Subsequent research by Collins, Rozeff and Dhaliwal (1981) is starting to probe the question of why, in an efficient capital market, oil and gas producers care about whether exploration costs are deferred or written off for financial accounting.

Another example concerns inflation accounting (ASR 190 and SFAS 33). The research findings to date have not found any evidence that replacement cost disclosures in 1977 contained information (see *Journal of Accounting and Economics,* 2:2). Primarily, these studies have not addressed the positive question of why the SEC and FASB adopted the form of inflation accounting that they did.

Both of these examples, oil and gas and inflation accounting, illustrate how positive research is evolving. The earlier empirical research on capital market efficiency and the time series behavior of earnings provides the basic foundation upon which the current positive propositions are being constructed. For example, the research on capital market efficiency has formed the basis for the current positive research in accounting by providing evidence on the ability of the capital markets to adjust for "cosmetic" changes in accounting procedures.

Another distinguishing feature between the earlier and later research is the nature of the questions addressed and the propositions tested. The earlier research usually did not seek to develop and test a model of an individual's choice of accounting standards (an exception is the income smoothing literature, discussed below). Often, the early studies sought to establish if an association did (or did not) exist between two variables and did not seek to explain why such an association did (or did not) exist. Often, straw men were tested. For example, Ball (1972) tested whether the "monopolistic hypothesis" (i.e., the market is misled by accounting changes) was consistent with the evidence.

The more recent research, on the other hand, seeks to develop models of accounting choice. Starting with the assumption of individual rationality (i.e., expected utility maximization), this research seeks to identify the relevant costs and benefits of alternative accounting procedures. For example, in addressing the question of why managers expend resources lobbying before standard setting boards on proposed accounting standards, Watts and I started with the assumption that managers, shareholders, and regulators/politicians are rational (see Watts and Zimmerman, 1978). We then tried to identify how accounting standards affect the firm's cashflows and hence shareholder wealth.[3]

---

[2]Dyckman and Smith (1979) did not find a statistically significant stock price reaction.

[3]Note that maximizing shareholders' expected wealth is not strictly equivalent to maximizing shareholders' expected utility.

The same approach was used in Zimmerman (1979). Given individual rationality, I sought to explain why cost allocations are such a pervasive phenomena in virtually all organizations. That is, how do cost allocations affect the firm's cashflows? What benefits are derived from allocating costs over direct costing for internal reporting purposes?

Besides assuming individual rationality, the recent research makes assumptions regarding the alternatives faced by the individual which includes assumptions about relative costs and benefits. For example, constructing a model of how compensation plans affect the manager's choice of depreciation methods requires the researcher to make assumptions regarding (1) the set of available depreciation models, (2) the bookkeeping costs of making the change, (3) the costs borne by the outside directors in monitoring manager's behavior, (4) the effects of alternative depreciation methods on the time series properties of reported earnings and management compensation payments, etc. The research then proceeds to derive testable implications, which if empirically supported, tell us something about the incentives of individuals and the costs and benefits of the alternatives.

Although the earlier empirical research in accounting (except the income smoothing literature) did not seek to develop and test models of an individual's choice of accounting standards, the current positive research draws heavily upon the earlier findings, in particular, the capital market studies. The next section illustrates how the early attempts to develop a positive theory of accounting choice were thwarted by making assumptions about capital market efficiency that were later refuted by positive research. In particular, some early attempts to develop a positive theory will be contrasted with current positive research efforts.

B. A Capsule Summary of the Recent Positive Research in Accounting[4]

1. Income Smoothing Hypothesis

The first serious attempt to construct a positive theory of the manager's choice of accounting procedures was undertaken by Gordon (1964), and Gordon, Horowitz, and Meyers (1966) at the University of Rochester. In my opinion, these papers were the first two papers in a line of inquiry that sought to develop a systematic explanation of the manager's choice of accounting procedures. For the first time, a model of managerial choice was formulated *and* subsequently tested.[5] But more important, these authors understood the role of data is constructing a positive theory and subjected their hypothesis to the rigors of empirical testing. Gordon's original work (1964) and the paper by Gordon, Horowitz and Meyers (1966) became the seminal papers on the income smoothing hypothesis.

Unfortunately, the income smoothing hypothesis was based on the faulty positive proposition (discovered by subsequent research) that capital markets are inefficient (Watts and Zimmerman, 1980c, chap. 5). In particular, Gordon (1964) assumed that a firm's stock price is a

[4]Due to space limitations, this section cannot be complete nor totally representative of the literature.

[5]On a historical note, Hepworth (1953) speculated that managers would smooth income for tax reasons and to placate shareholders. Hepworth did not propose smoothing as a general phenomena nor did he propose to test his ideas.

direct, mechanical function of the growth and variance of reported earnings. That is, the extreme form of the Gordon assumption would say that firms with identical future cashflow distributions would *not* have the same market values if they had different growth rates and/or variances of reported earnings. Accounting procedures can affect both of these parameters. Using two other assumptions: that managers maximize utility and their utility depends on the stock price, Gordon deduced that managers choose accounting procedures that maximize the growth but minimize the variance in reported earnings, thereby maximizing share price.

Numerous other researchers have attempted to extend and test the smoothing model but have met with mixed results (see Gonedes and Dopuch, 1974, pp. 109–110). Ex post, the major problem with building a positive theory on the Gordon assumptions has been that one of his key, underlying assumptions is inconsistent with the evidence.

2. Positive Theories of Managers' Choices of Accounting Procedures

Ross Watts and Michael Jensen in a 1973 working paper re-examined the positive question of why managers choose the accounting procedures that they do. But their work, unlike the smoothing literature, assumed that the stock price depends on the firm's future cashflows and not mechanically on reported earnings. Based on the then current research into the efficiency of capital markets, they assumed that the market would value two firms with identical future cashflow distributions identically, even though they used different accounting procedures. Hence, the search for a positive theory of accounting focused on how accounting procedures affect the firm's cashflows. Watts (1974) further elaborated the beginnings of such a theory. The ideas in Watts (1974) in conjunction with the insights provided in Jensen and Meckling (1976) on agency theory formed the foundation for the current positive research in accounting of which Watts (1977) and Watts and Zimmerman (1978) are representative.

The current state of the positive theory of the manager's choice of accounting procedures can be briefly summarized as:

1. The production process of the firm requires the combination of various factors of production which are usually owned by different parties (capital, labor, management, etc.). The self-interest of each of these parties gives rise to a set of agency problems and hence the view of the firm as "a nexus of contracts" which is the least cost solution to the agency problem (Jensen and Meckling 1976, and Fama 1980).
2. Accounting numbers are useful devices in some of the contracts that are written to reduce the agency costs of certain conflicts (Jensen and Meckling 1976; Watts 1977; Watts and Zimmerman 1978, 1979; and Smith and Warner 1979). In particular, accounting numbers are used in debt contracts (Leftwich 1980 and Holthausen 1980) management compensation contracts (Watts and Zimmerman 1978) and corporate by-laws (Watts and Zimmerman, 1979).
3. Besides being used in some of the private contracts among the factor input owners of the firm, accounting numbers are also used by government to regulate and tax the firm (Watts 1974, 1977; and Watts and Zimmerman 1978, 1979). Government regulation takes two forms. Direct regulation, usually of the rates charged by public utilities, is the more commonly thought of form. (See Jarrell (1979) for tests of how accounting numbers were initially used by the first state public utility

> commission). Besides direct regulation, individuals using the powers of the state can transfer wealth from the firm via affirmative action, OSHA, EPA, antitrust, price controls, etc. These latter activities impose what we call "political costs" on the firm which managers attempt to reduce via lobbying, public relations, and lower reported earnings. Accounting numbers are often used in these struggles to transfer corporate wealth (see Benston, 1980, for a more complete review of this literature).

Accounting numbers affect the firm's cashflows and hence stock prices by altering agency costs (which include bookkeeping costs), taxes, the effects of regulation, and political costs (e.g., antitrust, price controls, etc.). That is, changes in accounting procedures (e.g., switching from accelerated to straightline depreciation for financial accounting only) affect the firm's net cashflows beyond the bookkeeping costs of making the changes. In particular, the firm's net cashflows are affected if the accounting change alters the numbers in debt and management compensation contracts, the firm's revenues if it is a regulated utility, and the costs incurred by the firm from increased government investigative and regulatory activities if the change increases government scrutiny of the firm.

Since reported accounting numbers are used for different purposes simultaneously, it is unlikely that a single accounting procedure is optimum for all purposes. For example, higher reported profits relax prior constraints in lending agreements but at the same time draw the attention of regulators. Managers must then make trade-offs and compare the potential costs of additional regulation and bookkeeping against the benefits of less binding debt covenants.

The set of accounting procedures that result are those that maximize the value of the firm (Gordon 1964 and Watts 1974).[6] Also, the choice of the optimum set of accounting procedures is conceptually no different from the manager's choice of the optimum financing policy, production mix, advertising policy, etc.

The difficult aspect and the role played by positive research is to delineate and measure the costs and benefits of alternative accounting procedures. Yet, it is the knowledge of these costs and benefits and how they vary across the firms that makes a positive theory valuable. In essence, the manager chooses a portfolio of accounting procedures (e.g., straight-line depreciation, flow-through for the investment tax credit, LIFO, etc.) that, in his best judgment at the time, maximizes the manager's welfare. By observing the cross-sectional and time series variation in manager's choices of accounting procedures, inferences can be made regarding the relative costs and benefits of alternative procedures. Knowledge of these costs and benefits will allow us to construct a positive theory that not only explains the manager's current choice of accounting procedures, but can then be used to predict the manager's future accounting choices and reactions to proposed accounting standards. For example, a positive theory of accounting informs policy makers of the likely costs individuals will incur from the elimination of a currently accepted accounting procedure. A positive theory would also suggest to auditors and managers whether the firm is currently using the optimum set of accounting procedures.

[6]Some readers may question the conclusion that managers choose financial accounting procedures that maximize firm value. Yet, few would question the proposition that *tax* accounting procedures are chosen to minimize the net present value of the firm's tax liability and thereby maximize the value of the firm.

The beginnings of such a positive theory are starting to emerge. Besides the paper already cited, Hagerman and Zmijewski (1979) and Zmijewski and Hagerman (1980) derive and test a cross-sectional model of managers' choice of four accounting policies (depreciation, inventory, pension amortization and investment tax credit). Although they did not include the effects of accounting numbers on bond covenants as independent variables in their model, they still find proxies for political costs and the existence of management compensation plans to be statistically significant predictors of the manager's choice of accounting procedures.

Watts (1977) and Watts and Zimmerman (1980a) hypothesize that if accounting numbers are useful in reducing agency costs, then we should observe that the earliest firms (e.g., firms in the twelfth and thirteenth century) voluntarily provided financial numbers and provisions for auditing these numbers. Watts and Zimmerman (1980a) find evidence that the early English firms (the merchant guilds) voluntarily kept accounts that were routinely audited by the owners in the thirteenth century. Furthermore, the evidence in Watts and Zimmerman (1979) suggests that accounting procedures changed in response to major institutional changes (e.g., utility regulation, taxation, the securities acts).

Holthausen (1980) attempts to explain why firms would *voluntarily* switch back to straight-line depreciation for financial reporting purposes. He hypothesizes that bond indentures and management compensation plans are likely to be affected by the switchback and hence provide managers with the incentive to make this voluntary change. In particular, if the contraints in these contracts start to become binding, managers are likely to switch back. His empirical tests do not support these hypotheses.[7]

Leftwich (1980) develops the hypothesis that *mandatory* changes in accounting procedures affect the firm's lending agreements and hence the value of the firm. He tests this hypothesis using the Accounting Principles Board Opinion on Business Combinations and a sample of actively merging firms that would most likely be affected by this mandatory ruling. The tests are consistent with his hypothesis.

Collins, Rozeff and Dhaliwal (1981) use a multiple regression methodology similar to Leftwich's (1980) and Holthausen's (1980). Collins, Rozeff, and Dhaliwal are able to explain a statistically significant proportion of the cross-sectional variation in the abnormal returns of the full-cost oil producers around the release of the exposure draft to SFAS 19 that proposed the elimination of full costing. Their independent variables include information on debt and management compensation contracts as well as other firm-specific variables such as size, the effect of the proposed elimination of full costing on stockholder equity, etc.

These studies, taken as a whole, provide encouraging support for the development of a positive theory of the manager's choice of accounting procedures—a theory that ultimately will be able to explain the cross-sectional and time series variation in managers' choices of accounting procedures. Besides understanding how accounting numbers affect shareholder wealth, a positive theory should explain how accounting numbers affect auditors and regulators, the other major participants in the standard setting process. The next section briefly reviews some of the positive research analyzing the auditors' and regulators' incentives to participate in the standard setting process.

---

[7]Holthausen relies on stock price changes at the time of the switchback to test his hypotheses. If the magnitude of the wealth effects of the switchback are small or anticipated by the market prior to the change, then his tests are likely to be weak.

3. A Positive Theory of Accounting That Incorporates Auditors and Regulators

Turning first to positive research on auditing, Watts and Zimmerman (1980a) trace the historical development of auditing from the thirteenth century in England to the present day.[8] By using agency theory to examine the market forces that give rise to auditing, we are able to reject the null hypothesis that auditing arose because the government required audits. The evidence is consistent with the hypothesis that auditing arose to reduce the agency costs from the conflicts of interests among the parties to the firm. Furthermore, the evidence is consistent with the hypothesis that professional auditors, as opposed to part-time auditors, arose in part to solve the moral hazard problem (see Benston, 1975).

In another paper, Watts and Zimmerman (1980b), a model of auditors' lobbying behavior was developed and tested. In particular, the model suggests that accounting standards affect the auditor's wealth directly by altering the quantity of auditing mandated by the regulatory process and indirectly by altering the wealth of the auditor's clients. The wealth of the auditor's clients are affected (see subsection 2 above) by altering the accounting numbers used in the client's existing contracts, political costs, bookkeeping costs, etc. Given that the auditor maximizes his wealth, he has incentives to lobby for/against a proposed accounting standard. Tests of the model are consistent with its predictions.

Benston (1980) presents an analysis of the market for accounting and auditing services and summarizes the relevant literature. The primary purpose of his paper is to analyze the Congressional proposal to increase government regulation of auditing and accounting. While no hypotheses are derived or empirical tests conducted, the incentives of auditors, politicians, and regulators are discussed.

Benston also has written extensively on the incentives of government officials to regulate financial disclosure (Benston (1980) reviews much of this previous work; also see Benston, 1969, 1973, 1975 and 1976). His analysis and empirical tests primarily are directed at the public policy question of whether the benefits of the SEC exceed its costs. While Benston does not formulate or test hypotheses regarding why the regulators do what they do, important insights and inferences emerge from this work. For example, based on Benston's findings (along with the expanding research in the economics of regulation [Posner, 1974]) future positive research on the incentives of regulators to regulate accounting should *not* be based on the assumption that regulators are operating in the "public interest" (i.e., there is no evidence to support such an assumption).

Finally, DeAngelo (1979) develops and tests a model of the incentives of the auditor and his client. Based on her analysis, she is able to explain the form of the contract between the auditor and client. Preliminary tests appear consistent with her hypothesis.

In summary, there has been some positive research into the demand for auditor services and the incentives of auditors to participate in the process by which accounting standards are determined. However, our knowledge of these incentives is far less than the current state of knowledge of the manager's incentives. Part of the difference in our state of knowledge is likely due to the wealth of data on corporations (stock prices, COMPUSTAT, 10-Ks, etc.) and the corresponding lack of data on auditors.

---

[8]The books by Zeff (1972), Carey (1969, 1970) and Moonitz (1974) are among the most complete historical accounts of the U.S. standard setting process. They provide useful descriptive material on the actual behavior of auditors and regulators in the standard setting process.

If our understanding of auditors' incentives is miniscule, then our understanding of the policy makers' and regulators' incentives is virtually non-existent.[9] Part of the problem in developing testable implications regarding policy makers/regulators is that the economic theory of the political process is still in its embryonic stage. For example, economists are unable to explain why the SEC exists in the U.S. and not in the U.K., why farmers get farm subsidies while extractive industries get tax breaks (i.e., the form of the government subsidy), or why the airlines were "deregulated" when they were and not the railroads. Answers to the preceding questions require an economic theory of regulation, a theory that can explain existing institutions—why they exist and take the forms they do. The economic theory of the firm (e.g., Alchian and Demsetz 1972; Jensen and Meckling 1976; Fama 1980, etc.) is much further developed. Hence it can provide a better foundation for developing positive propositions regarding how accounting affects the manager's wealth than the economic theory of regulation can provide regarding how accounting affects the regulator's/politician's wealth.

C. The Future of Positive Research in Accounting

This brings me to the final topic. What progress towards developing a positive theory of accounting choice are we likely to achieve and what payoffs will this line of inquiry produce given this progress?

Projecting research progress over the next five to ten years is a precarious business. Progress will depend on the quantity and quality of research efforts devoted to this pursuit. I expect the quantity of research to expand. There are a growing number of high quality, empirically trained, accounting researchers tiring of conducting event studies of information content. Some of these individuals are starting to apply the event-study methodology to address policy questions. For example, Collins and Dent (1979), Dyckman and Smith (1979), and Lev (1979) examined SFAS 19. Gheyara and Boatsman (1980); Ro (1980); and Beaver, Christie, and Griffin (1980) examined ASR 190 replacement cost disclosures. Questions regarding why accounting procedures are chosen naturally arise out of such event studies. The following two questions arise from SFAS 19 and ASR 190: (1) why were the full cost firms affected by SFAS 19, and (2) given no evidence that investors used the replacement cost disclosures, why did the SEC mandate ASR 190? Such positive questions lead other researchers to attempt to answer them. For example, Collins, Rozeff, and Dhaliwal (1981) try to explain why the full cost firms were affected by SFAS 19.

Given the low-cost availability of "good" data (e.g., CRSP and COMPUSTAT) and a fairly robust technique (see Brown and Warner 1980; e.g., security price research), positive research in accounting will continue to address why various accounting procedures are chosen and accounting standards sanctioned.[10]

---

[9]See Watts (1977) and Zimmerman (1977) for a review of the "Crisis Hypothesis" of political actions. One of the earliest references to this crisis theory is in James Madison's Federalist Paper No. 47, 1788 (see Cooke 1961, pp. 333–4).

[10]For example, instead of examining the information content of management forecasts (Patel 1976; and Gonedes, Dopuch, and Penman 1976), some researchers will ask the question—why do some managers release forecasts while others do not?

The quality of future positive research also is likely to improve. Accounting researchers' econometric skills are generally quite good and getting better. In my opinion, the average quality of the empirical work in the leading accounting journals is not significantly below the average quality of the empirical work in the leading finance and economics journals.

Besides better econometric skills, accounting researchers' finance and economics training is improving. If the past is any guide to the future, then it will be out of economics and finance that future positive propositions in accounting are most likely to emerge. Thus, if an individual wants to conduct positive research in accounting, he should maintain a working knowledge of finance and microeconomics (primarily industrial organization, property rights, and managerial economics).

Based on the increasing quantity and quality of positive research in accounting, I expect the current research to continue to expand. Within the next five to ten years we should have a fairly detailed model of how accounting numbers affect the firm's cashflows. This will increase our understanding of why managers choose the accounting procedures that they do and why they lobby on proposed standards as they do.

Our understanding of how accounting standards affect auditor wealth will not be as well developed as our understanding of how accounting affects the manager's wealth, but will certainly be further along than it is now. We will have a better idea of why auditors tend to specialize by industry and why they provide the non-audit services (tax, management advisory services, etc.) that they do. That is, our understanding of the economics of the audit firm will be greater than it is today. However, due to the lack of data and small sample sizes, I do not expect that positive models of the auditor's lobbying behavior on accounting standards will ever achieve the predictive ability that positive models of managers' lobbying behavior will achieve.

Over the next five or ten years, a positive model incorporating politicians and policy makers is likely to emerge. But again, due to small sample sizes and the lack of a theory of the political process, the explanatory power of models of politicians' actions will not achieve the same predictive ability as models of managers' or even auditors' choice of accounting standards. For example, I do not expect to see a model that predicts why the SEC required replacement costs and not price level adjustments in the near future, or a model of why the SEC promulgated RRA and did not affirm SFAS No. 19. As previously discussed, answers to such questions require a theory of the political process and the answers to some very difficult theoretical questions.

Besides a lack of theory of the political process, there are other obstacles that retard the development of positive propositions in accounting. Three of the more difficult problems are outlined. First, a theory of finance is not as fully developed as one would like. If accounting numbers are used in contracts to control capital structure and dividend payments (see Smith and Warner 1979), questions of optimal capital structure and dividend policy have important implications for accounting. Hence progress in accounting will depend on progress in finance (and economics) and to some extent vice versa.

Second, most accounting standard changes and voluntary changes in accounting procedures by managers are likely not to be of sufficient magnitude to affect stock prices for most listed firms. This reduces the usefulness of the event study technique and requires the researcher to devise alternative test procedures.

Third, developing testable implications in accounting requires the researcher to make simplifying assumptions regarding (unobservable) *relative costs*. As discussed earlier, accounting numbers are used for multiple purposes, forcing managers to trade-off the costs and benefits of the different purposes. The accounting researcher, who cannot observe the costs and benefits but only the outcome of the manager's decision process, must make assumptions about the *relative costs* of the various purposes in order to derive testable implications. For example, in Watts and Zimmerman (1978), we had to make assumptions about the relative magnitudes of the costs price-level accounting would impose vis-a-vis management compensation plans, compared to the costs price-level accounting would impose vis-a-vis political costs. That is, would managers (whose earnings are lower under price-level accounting) favor the proposed standard because of the lower political costs or oppose the standard because of the adverse effect on compensation plans? We *assumed* the political cost effects would dominate for larger firms. This assumption was justified using a relative transactions cost argument. Without this assumption no predictions could be made regarding how managers would lobby on the price-level issue. It is important to recognize that assumptions regarding relative costs must be made to derive testable implications. At times these assumptions appear arbitrary and ex post. But if they yield testable implications that are consistent with the evidence in replications, then progress towards a positive theory of accounting is achieved and our understanding of the relative magnitudes of the costs and benefits enhanced.

Given the modest progress towards a positive theory of accounting that I expect, what payoffs are we likely to receive? There are basically three groups who might benefit from progress towards a positive accounting theory. First, students will be better equipped to deal with the problems they will face. For example, after teaching the flow-through and deferral methods of the investment tax credit, how do we inform our students as to the relative advantages of the two methods? Some instructors argue that the choice doesn't matter if you adopt an extreme form of the efficient markets hypothesis. Other instructors argue one method is better than the other because it is more conservative, or better matches revenues to expenses, etc. That is, they try to rationalize one method using some combination of the standard normative litany. A positive theory will allow us to explain how these two methods affect the firm's cashflows and hence how the manager should make the choice.

The second group that one would like to believe would benefit from a positive theory of accounting are policy makers. To the extent it allows policy makers to form better estimates of the costs (and benefits) firms incur due to the policy makers' actions, the policy makers could make more "informed" choices. However, until we have a better understanding (i.e., a positive theory) of how policy makers select the actions they do, it is difficult to speculate on what they would find useful.

The third beneficiary of a set of empirically tested positive propositions are economics and finance researchers. Finance researchers have found the explanation of firms' capital structures to be an elusive problem. The firm's accounting procedures and capital structure are both endogeneous decision variables and are likely to be interrelated if agency costs are an important determinant of both. To the extent that positive propositions of accounting choice are formulated and tested, they will have implications regarding the firm's capital structure and finance theory.

Positive propositions in accounting will also be of interest to economists. Agency theory, problems of moral hazard, and the theory of the decentralized firm—all managerial economics topics—are likely to be better understood to the extent that the manager's choice of accounting procedures can be explained. Any progress in explaining how the accounting policy makers behave will be of interest to economists working on a theory of regulation.

Numerous other examples can no doubt be constructed of how a positive accounting theory can contribute to answering more general economic questions.

To conclude, I am optimistic and excited about the future positive research possibilities in accounting. There is virtually an unlimited supply of interesting positive research questions that can be addressed with our existing methodology due to the rate at which the SEC and FASB continue to promulgate standards. Furthermore, this research is of interest not only to academics in accounting, finance, and economics but to our students and the accounting profession (even though the profession may find some of the results disturbing).

REFERENCES

Alchian, Armen and Harold Demsetz, 1972. Production, information costs, and economic organization. *American Economic Review* LXII: 777–795.

Ball, Ray, 1972. Changes in accounting techniques and stock prices. Empirical Research in Accounting: Selected Studies, 1972, Supplement to *Journal of Accounting Research* 10:1–37.

Ball, Ray and Phillip Brown, 1968. An empirical evaluation of accounting income numbers. *Journal of Accounting Research* 6:159–177.

Ball, Ray and Ross L. Watts, 1972. Some time series properties of accounting income. *Journal of Finance* XXVII:663–682.

Beaver, William H., Andrew A. Christie, and Paul A. Griffin, 1980. The information content of SEC accounting series release No. 190. *Journal of Accounting and Economics* 2:2.

Benston, George J., 1969. The effectiveness and effects of the SEC's accounting disclosure requirements. In *Economic Policy and the Regulation of Corporate Securities,* Henry Manne (ed.), Washington: American Enterprise Institute for Public Policy Research.

Benston, George J., 1973. Required disclosure and the stock markets: An evaluation of the securities and exchange act of 1934. *American Economic Review* LXIII (March): 132–155.

Benston, George J., 1975. Accountants' integrity and financial reporting. *Financial Executive* XLIII (August): 10–14.

Benston, George J., 1976. *Corporate Financial Disclosure in the U.K. and the U.S.A.* Saxon House/Lexington Books (D.C. Heath) and the Institute of Chartered Accountants in England and Wales (London).

Benston, George J., 1980. The market for public accounting services: Demand, supply & regulation. *Accounting Journal* 3: forthcoming.

Brown, Stephen J. and Jerold B. Warner, 1980. Measuring security price performances. *Journal of Financial Economics,* 8:3 (September): 205–258.

Carey, J. L., 1969. *The rise of the accounting profession, from technician to professional 1896–1936.* New York: American Institute of Certified Public Accountants.

Carey, J. L., 1970. *The rise of the accounting profession to responsibility and authority 1937–1969.* New York: American Institute of Certified Public Accountants.

Collins, Daniel W. and Warren T. Dent, 1979. The proposed elimination of full cost accounting in the extractive petroleum industry. *Journal of Accounting and Economics* 1 (March): 3–44.

Collins, Daniel W., Michael S. Rozeff, and Dan S. Dhaliwal, 1981. The economic determinants of market reaction to proposed mandatory accounting changes in the oil and gas industry: A cross-sectional analysis. *Journal of Accounting and Economics,* forthcoming.

Cooke, Jacob E., 1961. *The Federalist.* Middletown, CT: Wesleyan University Press.

DeAngelo, Linda, 1979. The market for audit services and the economic determinants of the auditor-client contractual form, unpublished working paper, University of Washington.

Dyckman, Thomas R. and Abbie J. Smith, 1979. Financial accounting and reporting by oil and gas producing companies: A study of information effects. *Journal of Accounting and Economics* 1 (March): 45–75.

Fama, Eugene F., 1980. Agency problems and the theory of the firm. *Journal of Political Economy* 88 (April): 288–307.

Friedman, Milton, 1953. *The methodology of positive economics, Essays in Positive Economics.* Chicago: University of Chicago Press.

Gheyara, Kelly and James Boatsman, 1980. Market reaction to 1976 replacement cost disclosures. *Journal of Accounting and Economics,* 2:2.

Gonedes, Nicholas and Nicholas Dopuch, 1974. Capital market equilibrium, information production, and selecting accounting techniques: Theoretical framework. Studies on Financial Objectives: 1974. *Journal of Accounting Research* Supplement: 48–129.

Gonedes, Nicholas, Nicholas Dopuch, and Stephen Penman, 1976. Disclosure rules, information production, and capital market equilibrium: The case of forecast disclosure rules. *Journal of Accounting Research* 14 (Spring): 89–137.

Gordon, Myron J., 1964. Postulates, principles and research in accounting. *Accounting Review* 39 (April): 251–263.

Gordon, Myron J., Bert N. Horowitz, and Phillip T. Meyers, 1966. Accounting measurements and normal growth of the firm. In *Research in Accounting Measurements,* Jaedicke, Ijiri and Nielsen (eds.), American Accounting Association, 221–231.

Hagerman, Robert L. and Mark E. Zmijewski, 1979. Some determinants of accounting policy choice. *Journal of Accounting and Economics* 1:141–162.

Hepworth, S. R., 1953. Smoothing periodic income. *Accounting Review* 28 (January): 32–39.

Holthausen, Robert W., 1980. Theory and evidence on the effect of bond covenants and management compensation contracts on the choice of accounting techniques: The case of the depreciation switch-back. Unpublished Ph.D. dissertation, University of Rochester.

Jarrell, Gregg A., 1979. Pro-producer regulation and accounting for assets: The case of electric utilities. *Journal of Accounting and Economics* 1:93–117.

Jensen, Michael C., 1976. Reflections on the state of accounting research and the regulation of accounting. Presented at the Stanford Lectures in Accounting, May 1976, Stanford University, Palo Alto, California.

Jensen, Michael C., and William H. Meckling, 1976. Theory of the firm: Managerial behavior, agency costs and ownership structure. *Journal of Financial Economics* 3:4 (October): 305–360.

Kaplan, Robert S. and Richard Roll, 1972. Investor evaluation of accounting information: Some empirical evidence. *Journal of Business* 45 (April): 225–257.

Leftwich Richard, 1980. Private determination of accounting methods in corporate bond indentures. Unpublished Ph.D. dissertation, University of Rochester.

Lev, Baruch, 1979. The impact of accounting regulation on the stock market: The case of oil and gas companies. *Accounting Review* 54 (July): 485–503.

Moonitz, Maurice, 1974. *Obtaining agreements on standards in the accounting profession.* SAR #8, Sarasota, FL: American Accounting Association.

Patell, James M., 1976. Corporate forecasts of earnings per share and stock price behavior: Empirical tests. *Journal of Accounting Research* 14 (Autumn): 246–276.

Posner, Richard A., 1974. Theories of economic regulation. *Bell Journal of Economics and Management Science* 5:2 (Autumn): 335–358.

Ro, Byung T., 1980. The adjustment of security returns to the disclosure of replacement cost information. *Journal of Accounting and Economics* 2:2.

Smith, Clifford and Jerold Warner, 1979. Financial contracting: An analysis of bond covenants. *Journal of Financial Economics* 7:117–162.

Sunder, Shyam, 1975. Stock price and risk related to accounting changes in inventory valuation. *Accounting Review* 50:305–315.

Watts, Ross L., 1974. Accounting objectives. Unpublished working paper No. 7408, University of Rochester.

Watts, Ross L., 1977. Corporate financial statements, a product of the market and political processes. *Australian Journal of Management* 2:53–75.

Watts, Ross L. and Michael C. Jensen, 1973. Outline of theory, policy and accounting. Unpublished manuscript, University of Rochester.

Watts, Ross L. and Jerold L. Zimmerman, 1978. Towards a positive theory of the determination of accounting standards. *Accounting Review* 53:112–134.

Watts, Ross L. and Jerold L. Zimmerman, 1979. The demand for and supply of accounting theories: The market for excuses. *Accounting Review* 54 (April): 273–305.

Watts, Ross L. and Jerold L. Zimmerman, 1980a. The markets for independence and independent auditors. Unpublished manuscript, University of Rochester.

Watts, Ross L. and Jerold L. Zimmerman, 1980b. Auditors and the determination of accounting standards. Unpublished working paper GPB 78–06, University of Rochester.

Watts, Ross L. and Jerold L. Zimmerman, 1980c. Notes on empirical research in accounting. Unpublished manuscript, University of Rochester.

Zeff, Stephen A., 1972. *Forging accounting principles in five countries.* Champaign, IL: Stipes Publishing Company.

Zimmerman, Jerold L., 1977. The municipal accounting maze: An analysis of political incentives. *Journal of Accounting Research* Supplement: 107–144.

Zimmerman, Jerold L., 1978. On the 'statement of accounting theory and theory acceptance.' Proceedings of the 1978 American Accounting Association Annual Meetings, Denver, Colorado.

Zimmerman, Jerold L., 1979. The costs and benefits of cost allocations. *Accounting Review* 54 (July): 504–521.

Zmijewski, Mark E. and Robert L. Hagerman, 1980. An income strategy approach to the positive theory of accounting standard setting/choice. Unpublished manuscript, State University of New York at Buffalo.

I-D

CONCEPTUAL FRAMEWORK

I-D1

THE CONCEPTUAL FRAMEWORK AS REFORMATION AND COUNTERREFORMATION

Paul B. W. Miller

Although a great deal has been published about the Conceptual Framework (CFW) project conducted by the Financial Accounting Standards Board (FASB), more remains to be said.[1] In contrast to those that consider the framework to be innocuous or weak, this paper's thesis is that it contains much that would lead to substantial reform in accounting practice. It also asserts that the first three concepts statements implied such radical changes that a counterreformation was created to turn FASB back onto a less disruptive track. In addition to its initial points, the paper describes a reforming step that could have been (and still could be) taken by FASB.

To see the CFW from this perspective, the author has rejected the idea that it is primarily an integrated accounting theory and has adopted the premise that it is a set of political

The author acknowledges the very helpful comments received from Dr. Paul Bahnson (University of Colorado at Boulder), Dr. Susan Belden and Dr. Margaret Gagne (University of Colorado at Colorado Springs), and Dr. Andrew Rosman (University of Connecticut at Storrs).

Paul B. W. Miller, "The Conceptual Framework as Reformation and Counterreformation," *Accounting Horizons*. Reprinted by permission of the American Accounting Association.

[1]See: Dale Gerboth, "The Conceptual Framework: Not Definitions But Professional Values," *Accounting Horizons,* September 1987, pp. 1–8; Loyd Heath, "The Conceptual Framework as Literature," *Accounting Horizons,* June 1988, pp. 100–104; Paul Miller, "The Conceptual Framework: Myths and Realities," *Journal of Accountancy,* March 1985, pp. 62–71; Paul Miller and Rodney Redding, "The Conceptual Framework Project," Chapter 5, *The FASB: The People, the Process, and the Politics* (Second Edition), Richard D. Irwin, Inc., 1988, pp. 108–133; David Solomons, "The FASB's Conceptual Framework: An Evaluation," *Journal of Accountancy,* June 1986, pp. 114–124; and Robert Sprouse, "Developing a Conceptual Framework for Financial Reporting," *Accounting Horizons,* December 1988, pp. 121–127.

declarations expressed in the form of an accounting theory. By viewing the CFW from this perspective, readers will be able to more readily and effectively:

- Comprehend events that have occurred and are occurring in financial reporting and standards setting,
- Anticipate and adapt to future changes in reporting practices,
- Participate in the standards setting process,
- Apply (or not apply) the CFW to practice problems,
- Teach others about financial reporting, and
- Learn about financial reporting.

WHAT IS REFORMATION?

This paper uses the term "reformation" to connote that the CFW was a movement toward significant change in the *status quo* without abandoning the structure or central goals of the financial reporting system. This word describes the attitude of the participants more faithfully than the term "revolution," which suggests a concerted effort to reject all features of the existing system to pursue a new political order. Accordingly, the term "counterreformation" was chosen to describe those who acted to protect their power under the *status quo*. Despite the word choices, it should be understood that the reformation's supporters have sought major changes and the counterreformation's proponents have used their power to try to keep existing principles in place.

THE CFW REFORMATION AND COUNTERREFORMATION

The CFW reformation and counterreformation can be explained by examining the major events in the project in chronological order. Seven steps are described below.

1. TAKING IT FROM THE TOP

The first step toward reformation occurred in designing the project to lead to an authoritative set of deductive concepts. This top-down strategy began with the objectives and then moved down to identify concepts, with the ultimate goal of prescribing specific practices based on the preceding conclusions.

While there have been many efforts to define cohesive theoretical structures for financial reporting, the two most immediate predecessors to the CFW are perhaps the best developed and accepted, and are useful for describing the reformation. Even though the Accounting Principles Board had the authority to change practice and its Statement No. 4 (APBS 4) started at the top by identifying objectives for accounting, this quote shows that there was no intent to use it to accomplish any reforms[2]:

[2]Accounting Principles Board, "Basic Concepts and Accounting Principles Underlying Financial Statements of Business Enterprises," *Statement No. 4,* American Institute of Certified Public Accountants, 1970.

> The Statement is primarily descriptive, not prescriptive. It identifies and organizes ideas that for the most part are already accepted. (par 3)

In undertaking its efforts, the Trueblood Study Group produced prescriptive concepts but did not have a mandate for going beyond the objectives.[3] Of course, it did not have authority either to bring about changes in generally accepted accounting principles (GAAP) or to force standards setters to pursue those objectives.

In contrast, FASB was in the political position in the 1970s to prepare the way for reform because of its uniquely granted authority and its announced intent to not only identify deductive concepts but also abide by them in setting standards. The preface to Statement of Financial Accounting Concepts No. 1 (SFAC 1) made this claim[4]:

> This is the first in a series of Statements of Financial Accounting Concepts. The purpose of the series is to set forth fundamentals on which financial accounting and reporting standards will be based. More specifically, Statements of Financial Accounting Concepts are intended to establish the objectives and concepts that the Financial Accounting Standards Board will use in developing standards of financial accounting and reporting. (emphasis added)

Combining this explicit commitment with the decision to establish prescriptive concepts means that FASB created an environment in which major changes could take place.

2. Users First

The next opportunity to create reform was in the choice of the objectives for financial reporting expressed in SFAC 1. The primary objective chosen by the Board was:

> Financial reporting should provide information that is useful to present and potential investors and creditors and other users in making rational investment, credit, and similar decisions. (par. 34)

The determination that accounting information should be useful certainly did not reform accounting theory; however, it was a political reform because it made decision usefulness the primary test for determining which of several competing practices should be generally acceptable. Evidence of the controversy created by what may now seem to be a self-evident goal is found in Armstrong's report that only 37 percent of the responses to the discussion memorandum on the objectives supported this user orientation.[5]

This objective makes it inappropriate for FASB to determine that a practice ought to be acceptable simply because it is widely applied or supported by a majority of its constituents. Instead, there should be a reasonable basis for believing that the information is indeed useful instead of merely being widely used or prepared.

---

[3]"Objectives of Financial Statements," *Report of the Study Group on the Objectives of Financial Statements,* AICPA, October 1973.

[4]FASB, "Objectives of Financial Reporting by Business Enterprises," *Statement of Financial Accounting Concepts No. 1,* November 1978.

[5]Armstrong, Marshall, "The Politics of Setting Accounting Standards," *Journal of Accountancy,* February 1977, p. 77.

The change implied by this objective can be illustrated through the analogy of determining the nutritional value of fast food by (1) observing whether a lot of people eat it or (2) comparing its contents with established nutritional standards. The results of the two tests might coincide, but divergence is more likely because many variables besides good nutrition affect consumers' choices, including not only their tastes and habits but also the goals of those who prepare fast food. Analogously, an accounting practice may have attained (or retained) acceptability because users are accustomed to receiving statements prepared with it, because auditors find the costs and risks of auditing the application of the practice to be satisfactory, or because corporate accountants find cost advantages in preparing the statements or prefer the image projected by them. However, a systematic analysis of the practice might show that it actually does not produce information useful for making rational decisions. Conversely, another analysis might show that some currently unacceptable practice will produce decision useful information. Because of its commitment to decision usefulness, FASB should reject the first practice despite its popularity and should adopt the second in order to take advantage of its ability to support better decisions.

In political terms, this objective promotes the interests of users to the highest priority. That is, it constrains FASB to ensure that users' interests are not left unsatisfied in favor of the interests of other constituents. This step was a reform because the priority had previously belonged to auditors subsequent to the giving of standards setting authority to that profession by the Securities and Exchange Commission (SEC) in Accounting Series Release No. 4 (ASR 4).[6,7] This specific (albeit relatively weak) authority resided first in the Committee on Accounting Procedure and then in the Accounting Principles Board, both of which were part of the American Institute of Certified Public Accountants (AICPA). Although creating FASB moved standards setting outside the AICPA, the Board's initial structure (including its governance, funding, and membership) may have allowed auditors to remain as the priority group with their statement-preparing clients not far below. It is interesting to note that the reforming shift in priorities accomplished by SFAC 1 came shortly after several organizational modifications in 1977 opened the Board's deliberations to the public, reduced the AICPA's influence over governance, and removed the requirement that at least four Board members had to be Certified Public Accountants.

3. WHAT DO USERS NEED?

The next step in the project was the issuance of SFAC 2 on the properties of useful information.[8] Reform continued because the chosen qualities create decision usefulness instead of usefulness for meeting auditors' needs. As before, the change was more political than conceptual.

---

[6]SEC "Administrative Policy on Financial Statements," *Accounting Series Release No. 4,* April 25, 1938.

[7]One reviewer asserted that the SEC's intent was to promote users' interests and that the auditing profession was the most suitable group to turn to for assistance. In any case, giving standards setting power to auditors allowed their own needs to be put first. It is the author's view that many GAAP (especially pre-FASB) constitute resolutions of issues on the basis of auditing concerns instead of decision usefulness.

[8]FASB, "Qualitative Characteristics of Accounting Information," *Statement of Financial Accounting Concepts No. 2,* May 1980.

In conducting examinations, auditors focus on processes used by their clients in preparing financial statements and on the inputs entered into those processes. In effect, they conclude that the output (the statements) presents fairly if it has been prepared in accordance with GAAP. In contrast, the CFW looks first at the output and concludes that the statements are useful only if the information in them has relevance, reliability, and comparability. In turn, principles should be generally accepted only if they produce information that has those characteristics.

This change potentially creates more risk for auditors because practices that produce user-oriented qualities may not be as documentable as present GAAP. The most obvious examples lie in measurement principles because market-based valuations are apparently relevant and verifiable but are not documented by invoices. The change to decision usefulness also would be disturbing to those preparers who would use GAAP to obscure or otherwise retain control over potentially useful information rather than reveal it.

4. Assets and Liabilities Are Important

The next phase of the CFW reformation was equally political, and its outcome has already affected accounting practices. The pivotal issue was the question of what the elements of the financial statements should be, or, in other words, what decision useful information should be about. Three familiar views were identified in the 1976 Discussion Memorandum published by FASB.[9]

The revenue/expense view considers the primary phenomenon of interest to be "management performance" (also called "financial performance," or simply "performance"). The key element is earnings, and the income statement has highest priority. This view is the main rationale for matching and leads to having debit and credit balances on the balance sheet that are not real assets and liabilities. Evidence of the acceptability of this view is found in these extracts from definitions provided in the descriptive APBS 4:

> *Assets* . . . include **certain deferred charges that are not resources** but that are recognized and measured in conformity with generally accepted accounting principles.
>
> *Liabilities* . . . include **certain deferred credits that are not obligations** but that are recognized and measured in conformity with generally accepted accounting principles. (par. 132, emphasis added)

Specific practices consistent with this view are LIFO, the deferral approach to income taxes, and depreciation accomplished through systematic allocation. It also tends to favor historical cost as the relevant attribute of the elements.

The asset/liability view focuses on what the entity owns and owes, and income occurs if there are more net assets at the end of a time period than at the beginning, after adjusting for owners' contributions and distributions. The balance sheet should include only real assets and liabilities, with equity as the residual. The equally important income statement should show all changes in assets and liabilities not related to owner transactions. The relevant attribute suggested by the asset/liability view is current value.[10]

---

[9]FASB, "An Analysis of Issues Related to [the] Conceptual Framework for Financial Accounting and Reporting: Elements of Financial Statements and Their Measurement," *Discussion Memorandum,* December 2, 1976, par. 32–68.

[10]Because of the emotions that arose later in the project, the FASB staff adopted the term "current exchange price" instead of "current value" to avoid the subjectivity connoted by the word "value." It also allowed the Board to avoid the controversial choice between entry and exit values.

The nonarticulation view skates between the other two by embracing a balance sheet limited to real assets and liabilities while accepting a performance-based income statement. The effects of all changes in assets and liabilities are recognized for the balance sheet, but some are not reported on the income statement because they are not produced by management performance. One example of nonarticulation is found in Statement of Financial Accounting Standards No. 12 (SFAS 12), which requires an investor to recognize decreases in long-term investment values below cost on the balance sheet but not the income statement.[11]

The reform in SFAC 3 is that the Board voted unanimously to embrace the asset/liability view.[12] The two key elements were defined in SFAC 3 without the circular references to GAAP seen in APBS 4:

> Assets are probable future economic benefits obtained or controlled by a particular entity as a result of past transactions or events. (par. 19)
>
> Liabilities are probable future sacrifices of economic benefits arising from present obligations of a particular entity to transfer assets or provide services to other entities in the future as a result of past transactions or events. (par. 28)

All the other elements, including comprehensive income, were defined in terms of these two. Earnings were not identified as an element and were left undefined.

With this choice, FASB set the stage for the end of matching as justification for many longstanding practices, including systematic depreciation and other allocations. Its effects are already apparent in the Board's standards that demonstrate initial concern with measuring assets and liabilities, and then assigning changes in those measures to the income statement. Consider these examples:

SFAS 76 A borrower derecognizes assets and liabilities from its balance sheet when an in-substance defeasance takes place, with the difference going to the income statement as a gain or loss, even though management has not performed in the classical sense by actually paying off the loan.[13]

SFAS 87 Fundamentally, pension expense is the change in the market value of the pension liability (caused by service and revaluation for interest), net of the change in the current market value of the plan assets (adjusted for contributions and benefits).[14]

SFAS 96 Income tax expense is the sum of the cash paid and the changes in the actual and deferred tax liabilities; thus, the income statement gets the change in the liability, rather than the balance sheet getting the unpaid portion of the independently calculated tax expense.[15]

---

[11] FASB, "Accounting for Certain Marketable Securities," *Statement of Financial Accounting Standards No. 12,* December 1975.

[12] FASB, "Elements of Financial Statements of Business Enterprises," *Statement of Financial Accounting Concepts No. 3,* December 1980.

[13] FASB, "Extinguishment of Debt," *Statement of Financial Accounting Standards No. 76,* November 1983.

[14] FASB, "Employers' Accounting for Pensions," *Statement of Financial Accounting Standards No. 87,* December 1985. Although this basic measure is modified by other components for prior service costs, smoothing, and transition, footnote information allows users to get back to the basic asset/liability measure.

[15] FASB, "Accounting for Income Taxes," *Statement of Financial Accounting Standards No. 96,* December 1987.

Retrospectively, it is clear that this part of the reformation did not suddenly begin with SFAC 3. Rather, it can be said that SFAC 3 more explicitly described views that had been applied in earlier standards. For example, SFAS 2 was defended on the basis that it was difficult to determine whether research and development expenditures produced an asset.[16] SFAS 5 eliminated deferred credit items, like self-insurance reserves, that were not real liabilities.[17] And, the treatment of leases under SFAS 13 clearly demonstrates FASB's concern with assets and liabilities.[18]

A convincing proof that SFAC 3 implied significant reform is found in Board member John March's dissent to SFAC 5, which cites his strong objection to choosing comprehensive income over earnings as the most fundamental income measure.[19] In light of the fact that March had voted for SFAC 3, perhaps he, like others, failed to initially comprehend its profundity.

5. Staking a Claim in Uncharted Territory

The next stage of the CFW anchored FASB's jurisdiction over the essentially unregulated area of accounting by nonbusiness organizations. Whereas authority over accounting by public business enterprises was firmly established by ASR 150, no similar sanction for nonbusiness had been granted because no parallel government agency exists.[20] Thus, it behooved the Board to establish that it was indeed the authoritative body in this area.

SFAC 4 advanced reform by asserting that financial statements for nonbusiness organizations ought to be useful to those who receive them.[21] Like SFAC 1, this step promoted statement users' interests above those of preparers and auditors.

6. Up Against the Counterreformation

The counterreformation made its appearance known during the recognition and measurement phase of the CFW project. It was led by representatives from the preparer constituency, particularly members of the Financial Executives Institute, and was supported by three Board members.[22]

---

[16]FASB, "Accounting for Research and Development Costs," *Statement of Financial Accounting Standards No. 2,* October 1974.

[17]FASB, "Accounting for Contingencies," *Statement of Financial Accounting Standards No. 5,* March 1975.

[18]FASB, "Accounting for Leases," *Statement of Financial Accounting Standards No. 13,* November 1976.

[19]FASB, "Recognition and Measurement in Financial Statements of Business Enterprises," *Statement of Financial Accounting Concepts No. 5,* December 1984.

[20]SEC, "Statement of Policy on the Establishment and Improvement of Accounting Principles and Standards," *Accounting Series Release No. 150,* December 20, 1973.

[21]FASB, "Objectives of Financial Reporting by Nonbusiness Organizations," *Statement of Financial Accounting Concepts No. 4,* December 1980.

[22]Initially, this group of Board members included Frank Block, March, and Robert Morgan. In 1983, Morgan was replaced by Victor Brown, who displayed the same general interest in maintaining the *status quo.*

As this phase unfolded, it became apparent that many preparers and these Board members had grown uncomfortable with the drift toward the ultimate reform of using current value as the measurement attribute for the primary financial statements. An early sign of the counter-reformation was an initial debate of whether recognition and measurement concepts should be approached separately.[23] Because doing so would have postponed dealing with the attribute issue, the separation strategy appealed to those who preferred keeping the *status quo* in place as long as they could. However, the Board ultimately determined that separation was not feasible. It was reasoned that if a change in an element is a recognizable event (as implied by SFAC 3), it is necessary to know which attribute to examine in order to determine if a change occurred.

Stalemate occurred in October 1982 when Chairman Donald Kirk declined joining with either of the two groups of three Board members who supported or opposed major reform.[24] This deadlock eventually led to the so-called Viet Nam solution[25] in which a subcommittee of Board members developed a draft statement intended to be acceptable to all.[26] SFAC 5 was based largely on this draft and essentially does nothing more than repeat the main ideas of the preceding concepts statements. Specifically, its central proposition was that relevant and reliable measures of elements should be recognized in financial statements (par. 63).

SFAC 5 did propose one potentially significant reform when it asserted that there ought to be separate statements of comprehensive income and earnings (par. 30–32). However, the Board has not created a specific agenda project to pursue this policy and has consistently failed to consider implementing it in any standards setting project. Thus, SFAC 5 did not add much to the reformation.

In contrast, the counterreformation was helped in two ways. First, the Board agreed that:

> Information based on current prices should be recognized if it is sufficiently relevant and reliable to justify the costs involved and **more relevant** than alternative information. (par. 90, emphasis added)

By creating this higher threshold for acceptability, FASB made it more difficult to accomplish the change to current value that the reformation had been headed toward. A more significant political gain for the counterreformation is found in this phrase from the introduction to SFAC 5:

> The recognition criteria and guidance in this Statement are generally consistent with current practice and do not imply radical change. Nor do they foreclose the possibility of future changes in practice. The Board **intends** future change to occur in the gradual, evolutionary way that has characterized past change. (par. 2, emphasis added)

By using the word "intends," the Board members effectively committed themselves to stopping reform and declared themselves accountable for failing to do so. On the other hand, if a

---

[23]Another view of this issue and its significance is presented in Robert Sprouse, "Developing a Conceptual Framework for Financial Reporting," *Accounting Horizons,* December 1988, p. 125.

[24]The three members who generally advocated reporting more current value information were David Mosso, Robert Sprouse, and Ralph Walters.

[25]Paul Miller, "The Conceptual Framework: Myths and Realities," *Journal of Accountancy,* March 1985, p. 71.

[26]The subcommittee consisted of Brown, Sprouse, and Walters.

word like "expects" had been used, the door clearly would have been left open for pursuing reform if the political situation were to become more supportive.

On balance, then, the reform movement lost much momentum when it reached this phase; however, the next step shows that it was not yet finished.

7. Counterreformation Turned Back

The last completed phase of the CFW produced SFAC 6, which expands SFAC 2 and supersedes SFAC 3 to encompass not-for-profit qualitative characteristics and elements.[27] (By 1985, the Board determined that nonbusiness entities should be called "not-for-profit" to avoid offending their managers.[28])

This phase presented an opportunity for the counterreformation to negate the previous steps by abandoning the user orientation of the objectives and characteristics and the asset/liability view of the elements. However, there was not enough power to achieve a return to the pre-reformation *status quo,* and the reform movement succeeded in holding on to its territory. The initial pieces of the framework remain in place, and still constrain FASB to put users' interests at the highest priority, certainly above those of auditors and preparers.

Prognosis for the Reformation

The preceding pages have demonstrated how the CFW contains the seeds of reformation and show that the fruit of the changes are already apparent in the Board's output. As a sign of things that might have been, the 1987 Exposure Draft on financial instruments disclosure was another step toward getting more current value information publicly disclosed.[29] However, the response from its constituents discouraged the Board from proceeding with the full proposal, and SFAS 105 omitted the current value disclosures.[30]

Additional evidence of the counterreformation's continuing existence is found in recent political activity involving very high level members of the preparer and auditor constituencies. Because of the issues raised, it appears that a goal of the activity is to diminish the Board's independence and change the direction and pace of its process. The most notable discussions occurred in several private meetings in 1988. Those attending were members of the Business Roundtable, FASB, and the Financial Accounting Foundation (FAF), the managing partners of seven of the then Big Eight auditing firms, and the chief accountant and the commissioners of the SEC. One result of this activity was a proposal submitted by the Roundtable to Ray Groves, chairman of a Special Advisory Committee to the FAF trustees, which suggested the

---

[27]FASB, "Elements of Financial Statements," *Statement of Financial Accounting Concepts No. 6,* December 1985.

[28]Paul Miller and Rodney Redding, *The FASB: The People, the Process, and the Politics* (Second Edition), Richard D. Irwin, Inc., 1988, p. 119.

[29]FASB, "Disclosures about Financial Instruments," *Proposed Statement of Financial Accounting Standards,* November 30, 1987.

[30]FASB, "Disclosure of Information about Financial Instruments with Off-Balance-Sheet Risk and Financial Instruments with Concentrations of Credit Risk," *Statement of Financial Accounting Standards No. 105,* March 1990.

creation of a "Financial Accounting Standards Oversight Committee" that would control and approve actions taken by both FASB and the SEC.[31]

Evidence of political support for keeping the reformation alive came in a letter from Congressman John Dingell to SEC chairman David Ruder in which he defended FASB's processes and approaches to dealing with the issues.[32] More evidence exists in Ruder's flat rejection of the Oversight Committee proposal.[33] What remains to be seen is the effect on FASB of the FAF trustees' acceptance of several Groves Committee recommendations in 1989, including a new internal "Oversight Committee."[34] Early in 1990, the Groves report had also led to considering a change from a simple majority (4–3) voting rule for the Board to a supermajority (5–2).[35]

It is the author's speculation that there is considerable power behind both the reformation and counterreformation, with a slight edge to the former, such that the likely outcome will be that some change in practice will occur, but only after FASB overcomes substantial opposition and endures prolonged deliberations.

AN ALTERNATIVE BEGINNING

With hindsight, it can be seen that reformation would have been assisted (and FASB's deliberative processes altered) if the Board had selected a different primary objective in SFAC 1. Specifically, FASB could have endorsed the objective of promoting the efficiency of the capital markets in allocating scarce resources by providing information useful for rational decisions.

It is not argued here that the Board at the time should have adopted this alternative because such an assertion would be expecting far too much in light of the state of accounting thought and the political environment in the 1970s.[36] Nonetheless, it may very well be in the present Board's interest to explicitly adopt the alternative now in order to align itself with the main justification for securities regulation. Doing so will help legitimize the authority conferred upon it by the SEC.[37] It would also clarify the purposes of the Board's due process and solidify its Congressional and regulatory support.

---

[31]John S. Reed, Chairman, Accounting Principles Task Force of the Business Roundtable, Letter to Ray J. Groves, Chairman and Chief Executive Officer, Ernst & Whinney, September 22, 1988.

[32]John D. Dingell, U.S. House of Representatives, Letter to David S. Ruder, Chairman, Securities and Exchange Commission, August 26, 1988. Also see, "Dingell Backs FASB in 'Roundtable' Fight," *Accounting Today,* September 26, 1988, pp. 1, 36.

[33]David S. Ruder, Chairman, Securities and Exchange Commission, Letter to John S. Reed, Chairman, Accounting Principles Task Force of the Business Roundtable, October 24, 1988. Also see, David S. Ruder, "Remarks Before the AICPA Sixteenth National Conference on Current SEC Developments," SEC News Release, January 10, 1989.

[34]Financial Accounting Foundation, *Report of Special Advisory Group to the Board of Trustees,* March 1989. Also see: FAF, "Trustees Adopt Special Advisory Group Recommendations Re: FASB," Press Release dated June 15, 1989.

[35]Structure Committee, Financial Accounting Foundation, *Report on the Financial Accounting Standards Board (FASB) Voting Procedures,* October 1989.

[36]As reported in Philip L. Defliese, "The Search for a New Conceptual Framework of Accounting," *Journal of Accountancy,* July 1977, p. 63, this alternative was actually presented to the Board by Ernst & Ernst.

[37]To be effective, the Board would have to not only adopt the objective but also establish a public commitment to actually implement it and then maintain the political will to fulfill that commitment. Acting otherwise would reduce the adoption to lip service.

One rationale that has been presented in support of market regulation is that the entire economy is likely to be better off if the capital markets are more efficient.[38] A supporting rationale is that the markets should be more efficient if they are perceived to be fair and otherwise free of fraud.[39] By committing to this objective, FASB would explicitly add the public to its constituent list and would place the economy's needs at the highest priority. The current objective of providing useful information would still be important, but would clearly be only a means of achieving the new primary objective instead of an end in itself.[40]

A commitment to this new objective also might profoundly affect FASB's processes. To explain, the current primary objective makes it virtually imperative for the Board to demonstrate that a proposed new standard will actually help users. In order to do so, the Board needs to develop clear support from the user constituency. However, sophisticated (and thereby influential) users are not likely to be forthcoming with demands for additional public information that would replace private information available to them at an advantageous cost. Because users get rich by finding inefficient resource allocations, it is inappropriate for FASB to expect them to sacrifice their comparative advantage by supporting efforts to turn private information into public disclosures.

Implications of the Market Objective

If FASB were to commit to this market objective, one result would be that users would come under the regulatory umbrella with other market participants in the sense that they would be forced to change their behavior for the benefit of a larger public interest. That is, regulatory pursuit of market efficiency has already compelled preparers to disclose information that they would rather not disclose and has caused auditors to audit information that they might not choose to audit. By increasing the amount of useful public information, standards consistent with the market objective would spur users to compete more aggressively for new sources of private information. In turn, this competition should help bring about a more efficient allocation of scarce resources.

Another result would be relief for FASB from dependence on user support and from embarrassment when users do not participate in its processes. Their absence would no longer be awkward because no one would expect them to act contrary to their interests.

A third result would be that FASB would be free to search for solutions that would provide useful public information, even if no users ask for or admit using it. Thus, the Board and

[38]As used here, the sense of the word "rationale" is that the reason is stated publicly even though the underlying motivations may indeed be different. Thus, for example, even a captured regulatory process will be defended with a "rationale" that supports the public interest. For commentary on regulation in accounting, see, for example, Tom Dyckman, "Credibility and the Formulation of Accounting Standards under the Financial Accounting Standards Board," *Journal of Accounting Literature,* Vol. 7, 1988, pp. 1–30. Of course, determining whether stated or unstated regulatory goals are suitable is a matter of policy making, which includes but goes well beyond logical analysis. Because the rationale presented here seem to be consistent with existing regulatory policies, it is worth examining their implications for the present structure, even if their optimality or mere suitability cannot be proven.

[39]See: K. Fred Skousen, *An Introduction to the SEC* (Fifth Edition), South Western, 1990, p. 8.

[40]Perhaps ironically, the summary of SFAC 1 says that, "Financial reporting is not an end in itself but is intended to provide information that is useful in making business and economic decisions."

the SEC could pursue new requirements without having to gather support from the constituents they are charged with regulating.

A fourth result would be a trend toward standards that require reporting more information in nontraditional formats. Given a healthy respect for the markets' abilities to process complex information quickly, FASB could reconsider its focus on financial statements as the dominant medium and could give up the traditional view that only one attribute of only one set of phenomena is relevant and reliably measured. For example, there would no longer be an issue of "cost vs. current value." Instead, there would be separate issues of whether cost is useful and whether current value is useful.

In effect, the commitment to reaching this objective would cause the final test of acceptability to be whether a new standard will be likely to cause new useful information to be made public. This change would cause the Board's processes to stop being what often appears to be the development of sufficient power to overcome opposition. Instead, they would be designed to develop logical or otherwise persuasive arguments about the probable usefulness of new information. Although the change would certainly not eliminate political debate, it would focus attention on the issue of usefulness rather than palatability.

In order to help these reforms to be accomplished, the FAF trustees, the SEC, and Congress will need to act in such a way as to maintain the Board's independence and thereby shelter it from attacks by dissatisfied and powerful regulated groups.

CONCLUSION

From the perspective developed here, the CFW can be seen to have paved the way for a reformation based on views that had been gaining influence despite being contrary to previously dominant practices. The reformation can be characterized as elevating users' interests through the objective of financial reporting and the criteria for identifying useful information. There also was reform in the selection of assets and liabilities as the fundamental elements of financial statements. Later, momentum was lost when FASB did not have sufficient political will to face down the counterreformation and endorse expanded use of current values in the recognition and measurement phase of the project.

In retrospect, the CFW may not have begun high enough to facilitate accomplishing the regulatory goal of developing economically efficient capital markets. Perhaps the FASB could have avoided (and still can avoid) many of its conceptual, technical, and political difficulties by adopting this goal as the primary objective for financial reporting and then living up to a commitment to its implementation. If it were to be adopted, there could be substantial reforms in the nature and quantities of information included in financial reports because the FASB and SEC will have been freed of the impossible tasks of accomplishing change by winning approval from the same groups that they are charged with regulating and that have so successfully led the counterreformation.

I-D2

LIMITATIONS ON THE VALUE OF THE CONCEPTUAL FRAMEWORK IN EVALUATING EXTANT ACCOUNTING STANDARDS

Lane A. Daley and Terry Tranter

The Conceptual Framework Project (CFP) of the Financial Accounting Standards Board (FASB) has produced six Statements of Financial Accounting Concepts (SFAC) which were designed to provide basic guidance in the development of accounting and financial reporting standards. Recently, several authors have suggested that previously issued Statements of Financial Accounting Standards (SFAS) should be re-examined in light of the CFP. According to these authors, reporting standards that are inconsistent with the SFAC *may* need to be re-evaluated and brought into conformity with the ideas set forth in the Concepts Statements.

For example, Foran and Foran correctly identify the accounting requirements of SFAS No. 12 as being inconsistent with the tenets contained in the CFP.[1] However, we believe that there is a missing element in these analyses, one that makes it unlikely that such analyses will prove useful in modifying accounting principles. While it is true that SFAS No. 12 does not represent a good application of accounting theory as set forth in the CFP, neither did it represent good accounting theory as it existed when SFAS No. 12 was adopted.

Lane A. Daley and Terry Tranter, "Limitations on the Value of the Conceptual Framework in Evaluating Extant Accounting Standards," *Accounting Horizons*. Reprinted by permission of the American Accounting Association.

[1]Nancy J. Foran and Michael F. Foran, "SFAS No. 12 and the Conceptual Framework," *Accounting Horizons*, December, 1987, pp. 43–50.

While comparative analyses in the spirit of Foran and Foran are useful in identifying deviations from the tenets contained in the CFP, the purpose of this article is to point out why such analyses have only limited value. We believe that the reason some SFASs do not conform to the tenets set forth in the CFP is not because of deficiencies in the pronouncements themselves. Rather, we argue that the Conceptual Framework unrealistically ignores the significant role that economic and political pressures play in development of accounting standards. Furthermore, we argue that such pressures are an appropriate means for groups in society who are affected by the establishment of accounting regulations to be heard.

Through an analysis of the development of several accounting and reporting standards we call into question the applicability of the concept of neutrality as defined in SFAC No. 2. We believe this particular characteristic, which the FASB put forth as a desirable characteristic for accounting standards to have, is at the heart of the shortcomings of the CFP. While there may be many lines of attack on the conceptual framework, we focus on the setting in which accounting standards are designed, and demonstrate that under those conditions it is impossible for accounting standards to be "neutral." This result stems from the fact that accounting standards are social policies without Pareto optimal solutions. As such, a political process must be imposed to resolve conflicts for such social policies. As long as the Concepts Statements ignore the compromises necessary to establish accounting principles in a political environment, SFASs will consistently deviate from the tenets contained in the SFAC.

We go on to demonstrate that the FASB's position in considering cost/benefit tradeoffs in setting accounting policy is the antithesis of the neutrality which they espouse as a characteristic of accounting data. Following this analysis we re-examine the development of several accounting and reporting standards in light of the economic and social forces present at the time these standards evolved and suggest that re-examination of these issues is not likely to result in any greater conformance to the SFACs than is presently observed. We focus on four reporting standards for our analysis. First, we re-examine SFAS No. 12 in light of the work of Foran and Foran. Following this, two other accounting issues which have also been assailed as "bad accounting" are also examined: 1) accounting for troubled debt restructuring and 2) accounting for the investment tax credit. Finally, we turn our attention to the recently released SFAS No. 87 on employer accounting for defined benefit pension plans.

Our purpose in examining these issues is to provide several empirical examples of the recurring problem that incompleteness of our present theory of accounting creates. In addition, the set of standards we examine were chosen to highlight the observation that the problems inherent in the conceptual framework were present before the existence of the CFP (the ITC issue), during the deliberations which went into the Conceptual Framework (SFAS No. 12 and 15), and still exist following the completion of the CFP (SFAS No. 87). Thus the problems we identify are not simply a one-time, or short term set of issues.

ACCOUNTING STANDARDS SETTING AS REGULATION

Setting forth rules that govern the form and content of information which is disseminated from business organizations to the public is a form of regulation. In our society, we have (at least de facto) endorsed the concept that the private market for information will not provide information in an efficient and satisfactory manner. Thus, for at least five decades, we have adopted some form of regulation for this information transfer.

Regulation implies that no Pareto-optimal solution exists to the allocation of information and the incurring of cost for its generation. We take as given that the private information markets have not been able to unambiguously resolve questions of: 1) how much information should be produced, 2) what type of information should be produced, and 3) who should bear the cost of information production. In turn, a regulatory system has been developed to make these choices in the interests of society. At present, this regulatory process is a mix of public and quasi-private organizations from Congress, to the SEC, to the FASB and other private sector groups such as the AICPA.

In developing public policy, Congress must consider the costs and benefits of each policy proposed. Rarely does everyone in the country demand a single policy. Public policy is primarily designed to resolve issues which the private sector cannot. Definition of property rights, allocation of wealth in the economy, and other issues all fall into this domain. However, one key characteristic of this process is making tradeoffs between different segments of society. Imposing costs on some and bequeathing benefits on others. Some social welfare function is being maximized, but through a political process which responds to both economic and social forces.

Accounting standards are really no different from other social policies. Different segments of society (indeed each individual in society) may have different preferences for how much and what type of information they desire about the operations of various businesses. How much they demand is a function of how the cost of developing the information is shared as well as how many other people also have the information. In setting accounting standards, the FASB (or its predecessors) trade off the costs imposed on some segment of society with the benefits reaped by another.

Those with the most to lose have the greatest incentive to oppose the imposition of new standards. When there are few or no proponents for change and significant opposition, proposed new standards do not get implemented. When proponents are many and the benefits appear very significant, even vocal opposition by those affected may not prevent the emergence of a new standard, but it may alter its character so as to find an acceptable political tradeoff between the groups which will benefit and those which will lose.

ACCOUNTING STANDARDS AS SOCIAL POLICY AND THE ROLE OF NEUTRALITY

The FASB appeared to show some appreciation for this social choice problem in SFAC No. 1. In addition, there is a clear indication in SFAC No. 2, that in formulating accounting policy a pervasive constraint is that the benefits of any policy must outweigh the costs. It is important to note, that if these costs and benefits can be translated into dollars, then the private marketplace should be able to resolve the issue of information production. It is when these costs and benefits cannot be translated into dollars, but must be assessed as effects on individual utility that a major role for regulation emerges to tradeoff individual utility effects for the betterment of society as a whole.

In the same statement in which the FASB embraced the notion of cost/benefit tradeoffs for the good of society, it also defined the primary qualities which financial statement information is to possess. Of particular interest in this paper is the quality of reliability. In their definition of the concept of reliability as a primary quality of financial information, the FASB appears to have mistakenly included the concept of neutrality as a desired characteristic of reliability. Neutrality is a characteristic in which the primary concern in formulating or implementing standards is the relevance and reliability of the information that results, not the effect that the new rule may have on a particular sub-sector of the economy. It is defined as "absence in reported information of bias intended to attain a predetermined result or to induce a particular mode of behavior."[2] It appears inconsistent to argue that standard setters can simultaneously take into consideration the costs and benefits associated with a particular accounting standard and then ignore the consequences these costs and benefits have on the behavior of actors in the economy.

If the imposition of costs and the existence of benefits is a pervasive constraint, how is it possible that any accounting standard could be developed which does not have a desire to create a predetermined result of allocating costs and benefits? How can this not result in a predictable mode of behavior by those affected? Neutrality appears to be an appeal to a concept of "true accounting standards" which, when discovered, will clearly be preferred by all because they represent "good accounting."

Alternatively, we argue that there is no concept of "good accounting" which is universal. In fact, what is good accounting to one person is an abomination to another. Good accounting does not exist in the absence of the economic motivation of an actor in the economy. Accounting is a continually evolving social policy which changes as the forces in the economy change. Failure to recognize this feature of accounting standards has often resulted in arguments regarding the proper disclosure of a particular transaction appealing to some notion of "good accounting" when it is actually an argument about the economic consequences to the various players involved.

There is nothing inappropriate about arguing for economic self-interest. The regulatory setting is designed as a political forum for bringing those self-interests to light and resolving allocation problems which arise where private markets are unable to solve such problems. However, to understand the implications of accounting policy and intelligently make choices among alternatives, it is essential that our theory of accounting not focus on neutrality, but in fact reject it altogether as an archaic and unworkable notion.

This observation does not imply that setting forth definitions and objectives is not a useful process. In fact, it may pave the way for obtaining additional consistency and trust in the political process by which accounting standards are developed. We applaud the efforts of the FASB in attempting to reach a consensus regarding the various parts of the conceptual framework. What we question is the role of neutrality and the process of re-examination of existing accounting standards while adopting the FASB's notion of neutrality.

To make our point more emphatically, we offer the following three accounting standards as evidence of situations in which the accounting standard setting bodies of the day either considered the economic consequences of a proposed standard and dampened these effects by political compromise, or failed to appreciate the nature of the social choice being considered and reaped the consequences. In the cases of accounting for marketable equity securities and troubled debt restructuring, conflicts between the FASB and other bodies charged with regulation of economic activity in the insurance and banking sectors gave rise to political compromise. In the last case we discuss, that of accounting for the investment tax credit, the political process was brought to bear without the involvement of specific regulators.

---

[2]Financial Accounting Standards Board, *Statement of Financial Accounting Concepts No. 2, Qualitative Characteristics of Accounting Information,* Stamford, CT, May, 1980, p. xvi.

ACCOUNTING FOR MARKETABLE EQUITY SECURITIES

SFAS No. 12 required that the lower of cost or market (LCM) valuation be applied to marketable equity securities in a manner that was very different from the way LCM had been applied to inventories. The major differences were threefold: 1) the level of analysis was limited only to the aggregate portfolio not individual securities, 2) the portion of any write-down charged to income was limited to the write-down of only the current portfolio with any write-down of the non-current portfolio being charged to a special owners' equity account, and 3) any write-down of marketable securities was to be considered temporary and thus recoverable unless the decline in value was considered permanent. In applying LCM to inventories the level of analysis can be individual items, groups of items, or the inventory as a whole at the discretion of the accountant. Any write-downs of inventory are immediately charged to income regardless of the classification of the inventory on the balance sheet. Lastly, the write-down of inventory is permanent.

The limited write-downs and recovery required by SFAS No. 12 is also inconsistent with the accounting for foreign currency transactions and futures contracts as specified in SFAS No. 52 and SFAS No. 80, respectively. Both these standards require recording of assets at market value with changes in value flowing directly to income for the period.

The effects of the unique accounting treatment afforded marketable equity securities are twofold. First, write-downs are less likely to be required since using the entire portfolio produces fewer and smaller write-downs than an item-by-item approach. Second, volatility of earnings will be reduced because only recoveries of past losses will be recognized rather than the full change in the values of the portfolios, and earnings effects can be eliminated entirely by treating the entire portfolio as non-current.

The reason that SFAS No. 12 required that marketable equity securities be treated differently from inventories, and the reason that SFAS No. 12 has not been brought into conformity with the conceptual framework or other accounting standards can best be viewed as a response to outside pressure groups. Horngren summarized the nature of the outside forces impinging on both the FASB and its predecessor, the Accounting Principles Board (APB).[3]

Originally, following three years of deliberations, the APB was going to issue an exposure draft on marketable equity securities, having narrowed its preferences to either flow-through or spreading of gains and losses over several years. In September, 1971, an exposure draft was issued favoring the flow-through method. The insurance industry bitterly opposed the method and persuaded the Securities and Exchange Commission (SEC) to oppose flow-through.

As a result, the APB reconsidered the topic in October and changed its preferences to either a two statement approach, or spreading. The APB voted for the two statement approach although there was also strong support for spreading. However, in December, the APB was informed that fire and casualty insurers also opposed the spreading method, and the SEC would not impose any solution on an industry that opposed it so adamantly.

The APB then discussed either the two statement approach or modification of current practice whereby companies would use market values in the balance sheet, realized gains and losses in the income statement, and unrealized gains and losses in stockholders' equity. However, the fire and casualty insurers also vigorously opposed the two statement method.

---

[3]Charles Horngren, "The Marketing of Accounting Standards," *Journal of Accountancy,* October, 1973, p. 63.

As Horngren put it, "The APB's feasible alternatives changed in response to the likelihood of acceptability."[4] As the APB was winding down its business it presented the SEC with a summary of its deliberations in March, 1972. The report did not contain any preferred solution.

Consequently, in 1974, when the FASB picked up the topic of marketable securities, it clearly faced a dilemma. The Dow Jones Industrial Average at the time had fallen by approximately one-third since 1972. The FASB needed a way to reflect the effects on investors of the decreased values of equity securities, without running afoul of the insurance industry and the SEC. The earlier exposure draft and deliberations of the APB had exhausted all the theoretically sound alternatives. What the FASB was forced to do was develop a workable compromise.

While SFAS No. 12 is inconsistent with the conceptual framework and some other areas of accounting, it represented an effort by the FASB to balance two competing needs. It had to reflect the declines in market prices of stock without creating an unacceptable effect on the financial statements of an important pressure group, the insurance industry. The existence of the conceptual framework would have been of no help to the FASB in 1973, and would be of doubtful value in overcoming similar objections from the insurance industry today.

While accounting theory, as delineated in the conceptual framework, may dictate the valuation of marketable equity securities using market prices in order to provide the most relevant and reliable presentation of the economic value of such assets, the alteration of the measurement and reporting system for insurance companies changes the rules of the game in that regulated industry. In turn, this has potential economic consequences which this sector of the economy would rather avoid. It is the FASB's job to decide when the negative effects such changes in the measurement rules have on some subset of society are outweighed by the benefits to other parts of society. Presumably, if the FASB does its job poorly, it will be replaced by some other form of regulatory body to make these choices.

This process of weighing costs and benefits on differing sectors of our society is not neutral. It cannot be. In the case of marketable equity securities the decision was clearly that the interests of the insurance industry outweighed the general benefits to financial statement users of moving to flow-through accounting, even though this method has much support in the conceptual framework. This is neither a "good" nor a "bad" accounting practice in and of itself. What should trigger a re-examination of this accounting practice is not the existence of the conceptual framework, but a reassessment of the relative costs and benefits to the various sectors of our society which are affected by this reporting standard.

It is in this observation that we differ from Foran and Foran's conclusion that SFAS No. 12 needs to be amended to become consistent with the conceptual framework. We see no evidence presented to date to suggest that the insurance industry would view such a change as any less costly today than in 1974, nor do we observe any evidence that the benefits to other members of society are larger than they were in 1974. Thus we find no merit to the argument that a re-examination is necessary.

ACCOUNTING FOR TROUBLED DEBT RESTRUCTURING

Another often cited example of similar inconsistencies is SFAS No. 15, *Accounting by Debtors and Creditors for Troubled Debt Restructuring*. In this case the pressure group was not the insurance

[4]Ibid., p. 63.

industry, but the financial community. The underlying events which led the FASB to consider the issue of accounting for troubled debt restructuring was the collapse of the real estate investment trusts and the near bankruptcy of several major cities such as New York and Cleveland. Banks found themselves holding large loan portfolios swollen with distressed loans.[5]

The FASB again faced a situation in which an accounting solution which minimized the impact on a major industry's earnings was desired. *Business Week* reported that the banks had indicated they would be willing to restructure loans if the restructuring did not affect earnings immediately. In addition, the Comptroller of the Currency expressed concern that "the immediate write-down required for restructuring debt would significantly reduce bank capital, and result in turn in a reduction of banks capacity and willingness to lend."[6] Similarly the SEC did not require that banks write down their holdings of New York City securities.

The FASB's discussion memorandum on troubled debt contained five possible approaches, four of which involved some form of current value accounting. The final solution advocated a, "much 'softer' position to debt restructurings than implied in its memorandum."[7] Specifically, the final ruling required immediate write-down only when assets or equity interests are swapped, or when the terms are modified in such a way that future cash flows are less than the carrying amount of the creditors' receivables. However, most restructurings require only disclosure with no immediate write-downs because the modification of terms is done in such a way as to insure that the cash flows exceed the carrying amount of the creditors' receivable, thereby qualifying for prospective recognition.

SFAS No. 15 deviates from the Generally Accepted Accounting Standards in place when it was adopted. The receivables and payables following a troubled debt restructuring accomplished through a modification of terms (reduced periodic interest payments or postponed due dates) are treated prospectively as long as future cash flows exceed the carrying amount of the receivable or payable at the time of the restructuring. Although these modifications result in a decrease in the value of the receivables and payables, they are accounted for under SFAS No. 15 at a new, lower rate of interest.

If the above restructurings had been treated as exchanges in which new receivables were created, APB Opinion No. 21, *Accounting for Receivables and Payables,* would have required that the receivables be written down to their present value by discounting the future cash flows at the market rate of interest. By determining that the restructurings accomplished through a modification of terms represents a continuation of the original receivables rather than exchange transactions, SFAS No. 15 did not require the write-down of receivables. Consequently, firms can carry receivables, which have interest rates (and fair values) substantially below the market value, at their face value. By contrast, other assets such as inventory, marketable securities, plant and equipment, and intangibles, must be written down to their fair market value when permanent declines occur. The reason for this apparent inconsistency arises directly from the FASB's desire to minimize the effect of debt restructurings on creditors' earnings.

The case of troubled debt restructuring is another example of a situation in which the FASB was in the position of making social choices regarding reporting standards in an arena

[5]*Business Week* reported that 65–70 percent of loans from banks to REITs were in a distressed situation. Reported in Lawrence Phillips "Accounting for Debt Restructurings," July, 1977, p. 23.

[6]Response to the FASB Discussion Memorandum Related to Accounting by Debtors and Creditors When Debt is Restructured, Comptroller of the Currency, August 17, 1976, as reported in Phillips, p. 23.

[7]Ibid., p. 26.

where other social choice bodies, such as the Comptroller of the Currency, were already involved. Accounting theory as it existed then, and as it exists now, did not alter the reality that if write-downs were required, the effect on the book value of bank equities would be substantial. While it is economically clear that these effects had already occurred, the bank regulators appear to have been concerned about the representation (or communication) of this reality to the general public through direct write-off of the losses.

The FASB again was forced to compromise in this situation for political reasons. In effect, the accounting treatment selected by the FASB was anything but "neutral" in that it specifically altered a policy of discounting to achieve a compromise of both political and economic proportions. Again our point is not that this compromise is "bad," but that accounting theory as it exists insists on ignoring this force which is at work in the standard-setting environment. In particular, by espousing the concept of "neutrality" the conceptual framework errs seriously in appearing to be naive regarding its own function in society.

In both of the situations discussed above, the accounting standard eventually approved was designed to present a more positive picture of the earnings streams of the insurance industry or the banking industry, during a period of unexpected volatility. In both cases, the industries were regulated by federal government agencies and several state agencies as well. These situations represent conflicts with other public policy-setting agencies. The outgrowth of these conflicts was that the FASB found it necessary to step back from imposing accounting and reporting standards which might have been consistent with the conceptual framework in order to avoid conflict with other social policies being executed by a branch of the federal government. However, it is not only cases within regulated industries where this problem arises.

ACCOUNTING FOR THE INVESTMENT TAX CREDIT

A similar political compromise existed when the APB attempted to set standards for the treatment of the investment tax credit (ITC). After the investment tax credit was created by the Revenue Act of 1962, the APB studied the issue and supported the deferral method, explicitly rejecting the flow-through method, in APB Opinion (APBO) No. 2.

Since the overwhelming majority of firms affected by this requirement had already adopted the flow-through method, there was widespread dissatisfaction with APBO No. 2. Under heavy lobbying the SEC announced that because of this diversity of opinion, both the deferral method and the flow-through methods would be acceptable in reports submitted to the Commission. Finding itself at odds with the SEC, the APB reversed itself with APBO No. 4, stating that while it preferred the deferral method, the flow-through method was also acceptable GAAP.

Congress suspended the ITC in 1966, only to reinstate it in 1967. At that time the APB was considering the issue of accounting for income taxes. The APB included a provision in the exposure draft requiring that the deferral method be used for the investment tax credit. Firms again raised objections to this provision and APBO No. 11 was issued without requiring the deferral method for the ITC.

Congress again abolished the ITC in 1967, only to restore it in 1971. In anticipation of the Revenue Act of 1971, the APB convinced the SEC to support its position on the deferral method. The APB issued another exposure draft proposing the mandated use of the deferral method. Facing the loss of the desired accounting treatment, and unable to turn to the SEC for help, firms directly lobbied Congress. They argued that equipment purchases would increase if the benefits of the credit were reflected immediately in the earnings of firms taking advantage of the ITC. Congress accepted this argument and inserted a provision in the Revenue Act of 1971 stating that "no taxpayer shall be required, without his consent, to use for purposes of his financial reports, any particular method of accounting for the tax credit."

In the case of the ITC, the accounting standard-setting body ran afoul of first the SEC, and then later Congress. Congress ended up taking over the task of accounting standard-setting as a "court of higher standing" in the social policy setting process. This is a case where apparently the social costs of imposing the policy championed by the APB outweighed the social benefits to financial statement users and the political process found resolution by seeking a public policy setting body more closely tied to, and empowered by, the populace. Examining which of the alternative accounting procedures is more consistent with some societal subgroups' definition of "good" accounting, which is what the conceptual framework represents, will not alter the political realities.

EMPLOYERS' ACCOUNTING FOR DEFINED BENEFIT PENSION PLANS

The last example of standard setting which is inconsistent with the Conceptual Framework, but easily understandable in light of the political process by which reporting standards are formulated is SFAS No. 87, *Employers' Accounting for Pensions*. This standard took several years to develop and was unique in that the FASB issued a document entitled "Preliminary Views" in 1984, prior to the formal development of its Exposure Draft, which was issued in 1985. While the preliminary views document was not intended to have the same status as an exposure draft, it did set forth a proposed method for accounting for defined benefit plans and was issued on a majority vote of the FASB. As originally formulated, the preliminary views represented a major change from the accounting requirements of APB Opinion No. 8, which was the previous standard in this area. The preliminary views proposed two basic changes: 1) the method of measurement for periodic pension expense to be recognized by sponsors of defined benefit plans, and 2) a major change in the manner of reporting the size and effect the pension obligation had on the sponsoring firm's balance sheet. Our focus is on the latter of these issues.

The draft recommended that the projected benefit obligation be reported as a liability in the sponsoring firm's balance sheet, along with the assets presently in the pension trust. Offsetting was allowed, such that the net pension liability or asset would be reported. Various forms of valuation allowances as well as the creation of a pension intangible asset which would be recognized in the balance sheet were proposed to deal with such issues as actuarial gains and losses and the effects of amendments to the plan. The measurement rules for determining the periodic expense arose directly from the measurement of the projected benefit obligation, the plan assets, and the various valuation allowances and pension intangible assets.

Since the expense measure was driven by changes in the valuation of assets and liabilities recognized by the sponsoring firm, the original exposure draft presented a reporting requirement which was consonant with the Conceptual Framework. SFAC No. 2 defines an expense as an element of the financial statements representing "outflows or other using up of assets or incurrences of liabilities (or a combination of both) from delivering or producing goods, rendering services, or carrying out other activities that constitute the entity's ongoing major or central operations."[8] SFAC No. 5 defines one of the criteria for recognition of any element as the necessity that it have a relevant attribute which can be measured with sufficient reliability. The original exposure draft presented a proposition that the pension obligation could be measured with sufficient reliability to provide a basis for recognition in the financial statements, and by implication, this measurement was sufficiently reliable to predict expense recognition as well.

While this initial proposal was consistent with the Conceptual Framework, it failed to appreciate the political fallout which would ensue as firms began to evaluate what effect the "capitalization" of the previously unrecorded pension obligation and assets would have on their financial statements. *Barron's* reported considerable opposition to the new rule.[9] Prior to the public meetings on the preliminary views, *Barron's* reports: "When the five-day public hearings open on the FASB idea . . . the overwhelming weight of the testimony is certain to be negative. Indeed, some not so veiled threats have been voiced that the FASB's existence is at stake if it refuses to back down" (p. 15). To highlight the strength of the response, John E. Powers, senior vice-president of Eagle-Picher Industries was quoted as saying, "we will refuse to recognize it (the pension liability) and will encourage all of our peers to do likewise" (p. 46). A spokes-person for Arthur Young and Co. stated, "They (the FASB) may be walking off a plank if they ignore the opposition. If they're going to be a viable force, they have to respond. If you accept the idea that they will be influenced by the response of their constituency, they ought to make some changes."

As a result of this opposition, the FASB developed an exposure draft for the new pension standard which deviated significantly from the Conceptual Framework, but did resolve the major points of contention raised by opposition forces to the preliminary views. In the exposure draft, immediate recognition of the projected benefit obligation was not required. Instead, the obligation, plan assets, and other valuation allowances and intangible assets relating to the defined benefit plan were moved off-balance-sheet. Pension expense was still to be measured by the changes in these elements, but the elements themselves were not reliably enough estimated to warrant recognition in the financial statements. This position is in violation of the Conceptual Framework. The same measurements which are unreliable enough to warrant nonrecognition of the pension assets and liabilities are reliable enough to predicate expense recognition.

This is not the end of the problem. The FASB included a minimum liability provision in the exposure draft which was based not on the projected benefit obligation, but rather the accumulated benefit obligation. This measure of the obligation does not include forecasts of future salary changes, and is an approximation to the termination liability required under ERISA for firms covered by that legislation.[10] When the accumulated benefit obligation is underfunded, the underfunded portion represents a minimum liability which must be disclosed

---

[8]Financial Accounting Standards Board, *Statement of Financial Accounting Concepts No. 6, Elements of Financial Statements,* Stamford, CT, December, 1985, p. 30.

[9]*Barron's,* "The Great Accountancy Shoot Out: New FASB Proposal Triggers a Bitter Fight," by Floyd Norris, January 9, 1984, p. 15.

[10]The ERISA termination liability is not computed using the same actuarial assumptions. However, at termination ERISA requires all accumulated, unvested benefits to be immediately vested. Thus the termination liability and the unfunded accumulated benefit obligation both focus on the actuarial value of all benefits accumulated to date. In this sense, the unfunded accumulated benefit obligation is an approximation of the termination liability a sponsoring firm would face if it elected to terminate a ERISA covered plan.

in the balance sheet of the sponsor. By taking this position, the FASB is implicitly arguing that the reliability of this measure is sufficient to warrant recognition, and to be consistent with the Conceptual Framework, would have had to motivate the recognition of pension expense based on this measure of the pension obligation.

In the final analysis, SFAS No. 87 is inconsistent with the Conceptual Framework, which was fully developed and in place by the time the final standard was instituted. There is ample evidence that the reason for the design of this standard, and its apparent inconsistency with the Conceptual Framework, has to do with the response of a social policy setting board to the economic and political realities of social policy regulation in a democratic society. The FASB managed to enhance the information set available to financial statement users regarding the status of defined benefit pension plans, and find a political compromise with affected parties as to how this information should be relayed to users. This compromise is not indicative of "bad accounting." Rather it is indicative of the FASB recognizing the real cost/benefit issues at the heart of the problem. Neutrality is nowhere in sight.

CONCLUSION

In this paper we set out to provide an argument for why analyses of the inconsistencies between instituted accounting standards and the conceptual framework are not very useful. In particular, we argued that the inclusion of the quality of neutrality as a desired characteristic of accounting standards is a mistake. Our point was that in selecting accounting standards the economic effects on sub-sectors of the economy must and should be taken into consideration. These effects are both positive and negative. At present it is the opinion of members of our society that these effects cannot be left for resolution solely by private market forces, as evidenced by the decision to regulate through Congress, the SEC, and the FASB. Given that this is the case, all regulatory agencies must tradeoff utility effects on various sectors of society and somehow determine a means of judging when one individual's utility should be exchanged for another's. Economics alone cannot resolve this issue, but economic effects are part of the picture and provide insight into why political positions are adopted.

We then examined, in detail, four examples of accounting standards which have been pointed to as being "poor accounting," due to their inconsistencies with the Conceptual Framework. These examples span a period prior to the discussions relating to the Conceptual Framework, a period during which the Conceptual Framework was being forged, and the period after the Conceptual Framework Project was completed. In every case, the same fundamental forces were at work to require that accounting and reporting standards consistent with the Conceptual Framework be ignored in favor of others which resolve the specialized problems of evaluating the cost/benefit tradeoffs present in any social policy regulation situation.

So long as accounting theory, as embodied in the Conceptual Framework and elsewhere, fails to appreciate the role of accounting standards as social policy, we are working with an incomplete theory whose predictions regarding appropriate policy choices will often substantially miss the mark. While identifying the situations in which such deviations occur may be useful, it is inappropriate to base a call for change solely on an inconsistency between actual practice and our presently incomplete theory of accounting standard setting.

I-E

MARKET EFFICIENCY AND ECONOMIC CONSEQUENCES

I-E1

EMH, CMR, AND THE ACCOUNTING PROFESSION

James W. Deitrick and Walter T. Harrison, Jr.

Accountants should be aware of the efficient market hypothesis (EMH) because it has important implications for accounting practice. This article, therefore, identifies EMH-related issues of concern to accountants and brings to light the practical importance of EMH research.

First, some background information about EMH may be needed. The term *efficient market* may be interpreted in different ways. To some, it may mean a market in which resources are allocated to the most efficient entities. This is "allocational efficiency." However, in EMH parlance, the term *efficient* refers to the way information is reflected in security prices and the term *market* refers to the market for securities (e.g., the New York Stock Exchange or the over-the-counter stock market).

In an efficient market, security prices behave as if they fully incorporate all existing information quickly and without bias. This implies that information, old and new, has been impounded into security prices as a result of the analysis and collective wisdom of investors and their advisers. In this context, the term *efficiency* pertains to the securities market as a whole. Efficiency doesn't suggest that every, or any, investor has knowledge of all information. It doesn't mean that all information has been properly presented by a company or correctly interpreted by individual decision makers. Nor does it imply that managers make optimal management decisions. Rather, market efficiency in the context of EMH simply means that security prices reflect the aggregate impact of relevant information in an unbiased way and that the adjustment to new information is very rapid.

James W. Deitrick and Walter T. Harrison, Jr., "EMH, CMR and the Accounting Profession," *Journal of Accountancy,* February 1984, pp. 82–94. Reprinted with permission from the *Journal of Accountancy.*

To accommodate different types of information, EMH has been described in three forms, as follows:

- The "weak form" of market efficiency implies that a security's price at a particular time fully reflects the information contained in its sequence of past prices.
- The "semistrong form" asserts that a security's price fully reflects all publicly available information.
- The "strong form" suggests that a security's price fully reflects all information including information that isn't publicly available, for example, inside information.

Of the three, the semistrong form is of most direct interest to the accounting profession because accountants produce financial statement information that is disclosed publicly.

Numerous studies support the weak and the semistrong forms of EMH. This means that publicly available information alone can't be used to select securities that will yield abnormal returns on average and over long periods of time.[1] This doesn't mean that investors can't earn above-normal rates of return. Over any particular period, some investors will earn abnormal returns by chance, others may correctly identify mispriced securities[2] and some may benefit from inside information. On the other hand, the research evidence shows that the strong form of EMH doesn't hold. Inside information isn't quickly impounded into security prices and, therefore, can be used to develop trading strategies that will yield abnormal returns.

The vast majority of EMH research has been based on the prices of common stocks, as opposed to the prices of preferred stocks, bonds, bank loans or privately placed debt. Therefore, our references to market efficiency are limited to the market for common stocks.

Given that information is quickly impounded into stock prices, it is empirically possible to examine the change in a company's stock price within a "window period" surrounding public release of new information. A window period generally ranges from a date briefly before the release of new information to a date when the company's stock price is believed to fully reflect the new information. Such an investigation reveals what effect, if any, the information had on the stock price. This kind of analysis is called capital market research (CMR).[3]

While EMH describes the pricing mechanism of the securities markets, CMR builds on the EMH foundation to examine actual market responses to various kinds of information. It is natural for companies and their accountants to be curious about how the stock market is likely to react to new disclosures. For example, companies frequently consider how a particular news item will affect their stock prices and whether certain disclosures are likely to confuse investors.

---

[1]A stock or portfolio of stocks is said to have an abnormal stock return if its actual return (i.e., stock price appreciation plus dividends) during a given time period differs from its expected risk-adjusted return.

[2]It is possible to have mispriced securities in an efficient market. For example, the price of a security may not reflect its "true" underlying value because of several possible factors, including the widespread dissemination of false or misleading information about the company (e.g., Equity Funding). Market efficiency doesn't mean that the market is clairvoyant.

[3]Capital market research is based on the premise that security returns are made up of two informational components, one incorporating systematic information about the market as a whole (e.g., news about general political developments and economywide events) and another incorporating company-specific information. By eliminating from a company's stock return the influence of marketwide information, it is possible to focus on the effect of company-specific information.

Many of these concerns are now susceptible to empirical investigation via CMR. Since the late 1960s, CMR studies have examined stock price reaction to a variety of events and disclosures, including annual and quarterly earnings announcements, changes in dividends, forecasted earnings, accounting changes, business combinations, "subject-to" audit opinions and accounting for leases, among many others.

This research, which is based on actual stock price data, has provided some well-established conclusions. Perhaps the most conclusive finding is the importance of accounting income to investors. Numerous studies have found stronger correlations between stock price movements and accounting income than between stock price movements and cash flow. This finding is an important validation of accrual accounting. On the surface, this finding might appear surprising because of analysts' widespread interest in cash flow data and the Financial Accounting Standards Board's belief that financial reporting should help decision makers assess "the amounts, timing, and uncertainty of prospective cash receipts. . . ."[4] However, the FASB also believes that accrual accounting is superior to cash flow accounting as a means of reflecting a company's future cash flow generating ability.

Another interesting finding is that the stock market seems to price securities on the basis of economic reality rather than on cosmetic accounting appearances. This means that two companies that are identical in every way would have the same stock price even though they are using different accounting methods unless their accounting results affect their cash flows. Consequently, although accounting income is important, the CMR evidence suggests that the market does not naively or mechanistically establish prices from accounting income without first examining the company's underlying economic position.

EMH and CMR have brought rigorous, systematic empirical research to important accounting issues. Therefore, accountants can look to CMR for objective evidence that has been developed across many companies and over lengthy time periods. However, EMH and CMR say nothing about the desirability of particular accounting standards or procedures. Because accounting has an impact beyond security prices, accounting policy decisions involve issues of social choice and, to be politically viable, must consider the perspectives of all interested parties.

CMR Studies Commissioned by the FASB and the SEC

The FASB and the Securities and Exchange Commission have commissioned CMR studies to answer practical, real-world questions. To illustrate, companies that were forced to capitalize their leases to comply with FASB Statement no. 13, *Accounting for Leases,*[5] argued that capitalization would result in dire consequences, including downward pressure on their stock prices. To investigate this assertion, the FASB commissioned a CMR study.[6] The FASB also has

[4]Financial Accounting Standards Board Concepts Statement no. 1, *Objectives of Financial Reporting by Business Enterprises* (Stamford: FASB, 1978), par. 37.

[5]FASB Statement no. 13, *Accounting for Leases* (Stamford: FASB, 1976).

[6]FASB Research Report, *The Economic Effects on Lessees of FASB Statement No. 13, Accounting for Leases* (Stamford: FASB, 1981).

commissioned studies of the stock price effects of its Statement no. 8, *Accounting for the Translation of Foreign Currency Transactions and Foreign Currency Financial Statements*[7]; Statement no. 33, *Financial Reporting and Changing Prices*[8]; and Statement no. 19, *Financial Accounting and Reporting by Oil and Gas Producing Companies.*[9] In addition, the SEC commissioned its own study of the stock price effect of FASB Statement no. 19.[10] In these instances the FASB and the SEC presumably identified stock price effects as an important economic consequence of their accounting standards.

Developments in the U.S. during the 1970s, such as the foreign payments scandal, the oil embargo, double-digit inflation and congressional hearings have brought accounting issues before the public as never before. As economic phenomena have become more complex, accounting has grown in importance and lobbying efforts by persons affected by accounting standards have intensified. Thus, it appears that the economic consequences of accounting standards have become a permanent fixture of the standard-setting arena. And CMR is a generally accepted means of measuring economic consequences.

Is EMH Valid?

In the February 1983 *Journal,* an article on EMH by Arthur R. Wyatt was published.[11] Because we regard Wyatt's article as an articulate statement of practitioners' views on EMH, we believe it provides an excellent basis for continuing the dialogue between academicians and practitioners about this important but apparently misunderstood concept. In his article, Wyatt cited four incidents in which companies engaged in seemingly uneconomical transactions that "appear to deny the validity of the EMH."[12] They involve a company's preference for (1) the use of current cost for new items added to its LIFO pool, (2) expensive off-balance-sheet-financing, (3) pooling-of-interests accounting and (4) hedging transactions to reduce its exposure to volatile foreign currency exchange rates. Wyatt asserted that these events are frustrating

---

[7]FASB Statement no. 8, *Accounting for the Translation of Foreign Currency Transactions and Foreign Currency Financial Statements* (Stamford: FASB, 1975). FASB Research Report, *An Empirical Investigation of the Effects of Statement of Financial Accounting Standards No. 8 on Security Return Behavior* (Stamford: FASB, 1981).

[8]FASB Statement no. 33, *Financial Reporting and Changing Prices* (Stamford: FASB, 1979). W. H. Beaver and W. R. Landsman, "The Incremental Information Content of FAS 33 Disclosures" (Working paper, Stanford University, December 1982); and J. W. Bartley and C. M. Boardman, "The Use of SFAS 33 Data to Identify Investment and Takeover Targets" (Working paper, University of Utah, February 1983).

[9]FASB Statement no. 19, *Financial Accounting and Reporting by Oil and Gas Producing Companies* (Stamford: FASB, 1977). T. R. Dyckman and A. J. Smith, "Financial Accounting and Reporting by Oil and Gas Producing Companies: A Study of Information Effects," *Journal of Accounting & Economics,* March 1979, pp. 45–75.

[10]H. Haworth, J. Matthews and C. Tuck, Securities and Exchange Commission Directorate of Economic Policy Research Report, *Full Cost versus Successful Efforts: A Study of a Proposed Accounting Change's Competitive Impact* (Washington, D.C.: SEC, 1978).

[11]Arthur R. Wyatt, "Efficient Market Theory: Its Impact on Accounting," JofA, Feb. 83, pp. 56–65.

[12]Ibid., p. 57.

because the real-world evidence seems to be in conflict with the rigor of EMH. We plan to show that these examples do not indicate a conflict between real-world evidence and EMH and that they have no implications for the validity of the hypothesis.

LIFO EXAMPLE Wyatt's first example concerns the election by companies using LIFO to value new layers of inventory at their current cost rather than at a lower reconstructed cost, which is permitted by the Internal Revenue Service. Wyatt argues that this uneconomical decision, which produces unnecessarily high tax payments, is either a denial of EMH or evidence that management doesn't understand EMH. He reasons that if management believed in EMH, it would adopt the reconstructed base-year cost to obtain the related tax savings.

This example doesn't deny the validity of EMH for two reasons. First, the stock market is either efficient or inefficient; what management believes about EMH is irrelevant. An analogy is the pre-Copernican belief that the earth was the center of the universe. The sun was, of course, the center of the universe regardless of what people thought. It seems to us that Wyatt is confusing allocational efficiency with capital market efficiency in this example.

Second, the election to value new inventory at current cost suggests that managers don't believe in the strong form of EMH. Specifically, managers know it isn't standard reporting practice to disclose the specific costs used to value a new LIFO layer of inventory. Further, they know the stock market won't learn of their uneconomical decision because the decision is inside information. Consequently, they have reason to believe their stock price won't suffer as a result of their pricing choice. In effect, the stock market isn't efficient in the strong form. But this says nothing about the validity of semistrong-form efficiency, which is of primary interest to accountants.

Wyatt's example can be interpreted to suggest that managers both understand and believe in semistrong-form efficiency. This may explain why companies don't disclose all the details of their LIFO election. If managers believe the market isn't semistrong-form efficient, they can disclose all the alternatives, costs and expected benefits without fear of market penalty because, in their view, the market won't impound this information into their stock price. However, companies don't reveal such details in real-world disclosures. We leave the reader to speculate why this is the case.

But, still, why did management make a decision that increased its tax burden? EMH can't answer this question for the reason given above: EMH and management beliefs are logically distinct. Therefore, in addressing the question, "Why did they do it?" we can only conjecture. Possible reasons include the following: (1) the book value effects may help the company secure additional financing at more favorable rates (e.g., due to an improved debt—equity ratio); (2) management's decision provides for a relatively larger amount of retained earnings, which may ease the payment of dividends or reduce the likelihood of a loan covenant violation; (3) management may believe the higher reported earnings will boost their stock price above what it would have been with the alternative method; or (4) management compensation, if based on reported earnings, would be increased. Wyatt mentions the last two possibilities. All four and perhaps others are possible in an efficient market.

While CMR can't tell us why managers behave as they do, it has provided us with clues about stock market reactions to different inventory valuation methods. For instance, companies that use LIFO generally have higher price-earnings ratios than companies that use FIFO, even though FIFO often results in higher reported income. Also, while the findings are somewhat conflicting, there is evidence that companies changing from FIFO to LIFO experience increased stock prices whereas changing to FIFO results in decreased stock prices.[13]

POOLING EXAMPLE In this case, after incurring considerable costs, a company abandoned an economically sound merger because it couldn't be structured as a pooling of interests. Wyatt indicates that the decision to abort the combination was induced by management's belief that purchase accounting would dilute reported earnings and thereby cause the market to lower the price of the company's stock. He asks, "Why do U.S. companies labor so hard to achieve satisfaction with the pooling-of-interests accounting rules when EMH suggests the marketplace won't be fooled by whether the transaction is recorded by the purchase method or by the pooling-of-interests method?"[14] There are many possible answers.

As discussed above in conjunction with the LIFO example, EMH carries no implications about management beliefs. We would argue that, if the market were to discover that a company rejected an economically viable business combination merely for accounting reasons, the market may actually bid down the company's stock price due to decreased confidence in management. But because such information is seldom made public, companies that behave in this way probably suffer no adverse stock price consequences. And since Wyatt's question involved an empirical issue, we can look to a CMR study for an answer. Consistent with the hypothesis that the market isn't fooled by cosmetics, a group of researchers has found that pooling-of-interests accounting does not lead to higher stock prices vis-à-vis purchase accounting.[15] Again, management may have favored pooling for other reasons, such as to increase its own compensation, ease debt covenant restrictions or attempt to fool bankers and other decision makers operating outside of an efficient market.

OFF-BALANCE-SHEET FINANCING EXAMPLE Wyatt raised several questions about companies that use off-balance-sheet financing when apparently less costly financing arrangements are available. Specifically, he asks if the market is fooled by off-balance-sheet lease financing and adds that lessee managers apparently think so. Whether the market is fooled by the accounting treatment is the fundamental issue. The FASB research report entitled *The Economic Effects on Lessees of FASB Statement No. 13, Accounting for Leases,* examined the stock price behavior of lessee companies that were required to capitalize leases formerly treated as operating leases. The report indicated that no significant price adjustments were found. This finding is consistent with an efficient stock market because no new information was provided by capitalization. The pre-Statement no. 13 financial statements generally disclosed sufficient detail in the notes for decision makers to compute the present values of the leases and adjust the financial statements if they so desired.

---

[13]S. Sunder and A. R. Abdel-khalik and J. C. McKeown found positive market reactions to companies that changed to LIFO. W. E. Ricks, on the other hand, found negative reactions. See S. Sunder, "Stock Price and Risk Related to Accounting Changes in Inventory Valuation," *Accounting Review,* April 1975, pp. 305–315; A. R. Abdel-khalik and J. C. McKeown, "Understanding Accounting Changes in an Efficient Market: Evidence of Differential Reaction," *Accounting Review,* October 1978, pp. 851–868; and W. E. Ricks, "The Market's Response to the 1974 LIFO Adoptions," *Journal of Accounting Research,* Autumn 1982, Part I, pp. 367–387.

[14]Wyatt, "Efficient Market Theory," p. 60.

[15]H. Hong, R. S. Kaplan and G. Mandelker, "Pooling vs. Purchase: The Effects of Accounting for Mergers on Stock Prices," *Accounting Review,* January 1978, pp. 31–47.

But why did management elect this "expensive" choice? Again, EMH can't provide the answer. It might have been an attempt to fool a lender whose decision involves a loan committee of, say, three or four persons and thus doesn't benefit from the collective wisdom of a broad aggregate such as the stock market. All management has to do is satisfy one bank to obtain financing. In those situations, the benefits to the company may exceed the higher costs, and the "more expensive" choice may prove to be the economical one.

FOREIGN CURRENCY EXAMPLE Foreign currency translation was the subject of Wyatt's fourth example. Of particular interest were hedging activities to mitigate the volatility in earnings caused by fluctuations in foreign currency exchange rates. These hedging activities could be undertaken for two reasons: to reduce (1) real economic risk or (2) "accounting risk" (i.e., the volatility in reported accounting income).

We believe Wyatt is referring to the FASB Research Report, *An Empirical Investigation of the Effects of Statement of Financial Accounting Standards No. 8 on Security Return Behavior,* which found no significant market reaction to FASB Statement no. 8 disclosures. In this context Wyatt stated, "Many managements ended up with new policies that reduced accounting risks and at the same time, may have reduced economic risks. If, in fact, the stock market is efficient, i.e., isn't fooled by the difference in reported accounting results from adoption of a new hedging policy, the stock market price would remain unaffected. But if the new hedging policy does, in fact, mitigate economic risks as well, and if the stock price remains unchanged, is the market for that stock really efficient?"[16]

We caution against drawing any conclusions about market efficiency from this example for two reasons. First, the point of the example hinges on the word *if.* Second, how could the market know whether hedging activities undertaken to mitigate accounting risk also hedged economic risk? That information would be known only by a handful of company employees, and thus the market couldn't react to such inside information.

WHY SHOULD PRACTICING ACCOUNTANTS BE AWARE OF EMH AND CMR?

We believe accountants should be aware of EMH and CMR because they have important applications to accounting practice. Four such applications follow[17]:

- Counseling clients. CMR results can be used by accountants as a basis for counseling clients. For example, a client contemplating making an accounting change that will increase its reported income for the purpose of supporting its stock price should be informed that such tactics don't fool the market. In fact, downward rather than upward stock price movements are generally associated with companies that make discretionary accounting changes when there is no underlying economic justification (e.g., a switch from accelerated to straight-line depreciation for financial

[16]Wyatt, "Efficient Market Theory," p. 62.

[17]For a more detailed discussion of CMR implications, especially for standard setting, see W. H. Beaver, *Financial Reporting: An Accounting Revolution* (Englewood Cliffs, N.J.: Prentice-Hall, 1981), pp. 163–167.

statement purposes only).[18] One explanation for this result is that the market can see through such attempts to increase earnings artificially or to conceal an underlying negative shift in a company. Also, a client worried about a reduced stock price if it changes to LIFO to get a tax advantage could be advised that the stock market is likely to reward such a decision despite lower reported earnings. These findings are consistent with EMH assertions that the stock market reacts to underlying economic phenomena (e.g., cash flows) rather than to cosmetic accounting appearances.[19]

CMR gives accountants additional evidence and leverage when disagreements arise with clients about the disclosure or nondisclosure of certain information. The research indicates that security prices are affected by numerous sources (e.g., press releases, news conferences, industry publications, the financial press, etc.). Financial statements are but one source of information. Consequently, managers and accountants shouldn't naively believe that stock prices will be affected because of a financial statement disclosure (e.g., a lawsuit) that has already been reported publicly elsewhere. We aren't suggesting that clients will automatically acquiesce to accountants merely because of empirical evidence. We acknowledge that some of these implications of EMH and CMR are hard to sell because they often seem counterintuitive. However, by being well informed about CMR, accountants can assist clients in anticipating the reaction of the stock market to various types of financial disclosures.

- Disclosure. In a semistrong efficient market, publicly available information is impounded into stock prices, regardless of where it is reported. Thus, empirical research demonstrates that the substance of an accounting disclosure is more important than its form or location in the financial report. This means that the resolution of controversial issues such as the capitalization or expensing of a particular cost (e.g., research and development),[20] the question of balance sheet presentation or note disclosure (e.g., unfunded pension liabilities) or the choice of disclosure in a primary financial statement or in a supplementary report (e.g., the effects of inflation) isn't expected to affect security prices unless material economic consequences are based on reported financial statement amounts. As evidence of the market's sophistication in this regard, Moody's Investor Service includes off-balance-sheet pension obligations (disclosed in the notes) when computing its "adjusted debt ratios."[21] Consequently, it seems that both the stock market and the credit-rating agencies don't focus exclusively on the primary financial statements and are able to interpret complex note disclosures. The implication for accounting practice is this:

---

[18] See for example, R. S. Kaplan and R. Roll, "Investor Evaluation of Accounting Information: Some Empirical Evidence," *Journal of Business,* April 1972, pp. 225–257; and W. T. Harrison, Jr., "Different Market Reactions to Discretionary and Non-discretionary Accounting Changes," *Journal of Accounting Research,* Spring 1977, pp. 84–107.

[19] After concluding from a CMR study that the market isn't fooled by accounting techniques, Kaplan and Roll indicated that "earnings manipulation may be fun, but its profitability is doubtful." Kaplan and Roll, "Investor Evaluation," p. 245.

[20] R. L. Vigeland, "The Market Reaction to Statement of Financial Accounting Standards No. 2," *Accounting Review,* April 1981, pp. 309–325.

[21] P. J. Regan, "Credit Ratings and Pension Costs," *Financial Analysts Journal,* March–April 1979, pp. 6–7.

It may be counterproductive to argue with a client over where in the financial statements an item is disclosed. Of greater importance is that the disclosure be adequate.

- EMH and CMR as legal evidence to establish claims for damages. It is common for legal proceedings involving rule 10b-5 lawsuits to examine claims for damages resulting from market transactions in a widely traded security.[22] Often EMH and CMR provide the framework and the quantitative methodology for estimating such damages. The estimation techniques are fairly standard, and we know of specific instances in which an important element of a decision was the damage estimate provided by CMR. Not only is CMR evidence admissible in court but it also can play a key role in damage settlements.[23]
- EMH and CMR and standard-setting. In the standard-setting arena, it is common for the FASB, and to some extent, the SEC, to commission CMR projects. In addition, the American Institute of CPAs auditing standards board recently considered the stock price effects of the subject-to opinion in its deliberations to abolish or retain this type of opinion. Although we don't know the weight given CMR findings in the actual standard-setting process, it is obvious that EMH and CMR aren't being ignored.

What is the implication of this fact for accounting practice? It is this: EMH and CMR are influencing today's accounting and auditing standards. Recently, William H. Beaver critiqued FASB action relative to the five implications of EMH-CMR for standard setting he identified in 1973.[24] In brief, they were

1. "A role of accounting data is to prevent superior returns accruing from inside information and can be achieved by a policy of fuller disclosure.
2. "Accountants much stop acting as if they are the only suppliers of information about the [company]. Instead, the FASB should strive to minimize the total cost of providing information to investors.
3. "The FASB should sponsor a full-scale research program in the areas indicated, so that it may have some evidence of the consequences of their choices among different sets of financial accounting standards.
4. "Financial statements should not be reduced to the level of understanding of the naive investor.
5. "Many reporting issues are capable of a simple disclosure solution and do not warrant an expenditure of FASB time and resources in attempting to resolve them."[25]

---

[22]Rule 10b-5 of the Securities Exchange Act of 1934 is a broad prohibition of "manipulative and deceptive devices" in connection with the purchase on a sale of securities issued under the auspices of the act.

[23]See for example, P. J. Leas, "The Measure of Damages in Rule 10b-5 Cases Involving Actively-Traded Securities," *Stanford Law Review,* January 1974, pp. 371–398.

[24]W. H. Beaver, "What Should Be the FASB's Objectives?" JofA, Aug. 73, pp. 49–56.

[25]W. H. Beaver, "The FASB: The Perspective of an Efficient Market Researcher" (Paper presented at the Eighth Arthur Young Professors' Roundtable, Harriman, N.Y., May 6, 1983), p. 2.

Beaver's conclusion was "I give the FASB full credit for the first four implications and half-credit for the fifth. That is a score of 90% to which I would give a grade of 'A'. . . ."[26] Therefore, it would seem that accountants would want to keep abreast of the factors that are shaping the direction of accounting standards.

SUMMARY AND CONCLUSIONS

EMH and CMR have been a part of the accounting environment since the 1960s. EMH is an aggregate concept describing the relationship between security prices and information. The empirical evidence implies that the stock market is reasonably efficient. In particular, the evidence shows that stock prices are more influenced by the disclosure of real economic events than by cosmetic accounting effects. This implies that the market isn't fooled by differences in accounting techniques that aren't accompanied by economic differences. CMR builds on the EMH foundation to examine the effects of actual accounting disclosures on stock prices. Thus, it helps us understand the economic environment in which we operate.

The issues discussed in this article demonstrate that EMH and CMR are an integral part of the real world of accounting. If Wyatt is correct that few practicing accountants are aware of EMH and even fewer understand it, there is reason for concern. This lack of awareness and understanding can bias perspectives and impair service to clients and to the public. In this vein, Wyatt asks, "What can be done to better educate managers [and accountants] about the ramifications of the hypothesis?"[27] This article is a step toward addressing that question.

[26]Ibid., p. 7.

[27]Wyatt, "Efficient Market Hypothesis," p. 65.

I-E2

ACCOUNTING STANDARDS: THEIR ECONOMIC AND SOCIAL CONSEQUENCES

Victor H. Brown

What weight, if any, should the FASB give to the potential consequences—economic, social, or political—of its actions? This question arises whenever the FASB considers changing accounting practice.

Among those involved and interested in the standard setting process—preparers, users, auditors, and others—there is widespread agreement about three points. The first is that standards of financial accounting and reporting are needed, as is some mechanism for setting these standards. The FASB is the private sector group presently charged with that responsibility. The second is that changing accounting standards will have consequential effects of some sort. Indeed, the very process of changing accounting standards stems from the belief that financial information prepared in accordance with these standards can make a difference in the decisions reached by those using the information. Third, most accept the notion that cost/benefit considerations should enter into setting accounting standards. Changes should be made only when expected benefits exceed anticipated costs.

Victor H. Brown is a member of The Financial Accounting Standards Board.

Expressions of individual views by members of the FASB and its staff are encouraged. The views expressed in this article are those of Victor H. Brown. Official positions of the FASB on accounting matters are determined only after extensive due process and deliberation.

Victor H. Brown, "Accounting Standards: Their Economic and Social Consequences." *Accounting Horizons*. Reprinted by permission of the American Accounting Association.

Beyond these three points, however, there is little agreement to be found. Accounting proposals typically encounter a diversity of response—both within and among constituent groups—concerning both what the economic consequences of a proposal will be and how these consequences should be factored into the proposal finally adopted.

COSTS AND BENEFITS

Among the consequences of changing accounting standards are economic benefits and economic costs. The FASB must constantly be aware of both. This is because one of the precepts that the FASB follows in conducting its activities is to promulgate standards only when the expected benefits exceed perceived costs.

Fully applying this precept implies, at least notionally, the ability to identify all benefits and costs and to put a dollar value on them. Additionally, dollar benefits and costs would be identified in terms of what segments of society would be affected by them. In this way, judgments on standards could be made in light of knowledge about both the aggregate societal cost or benefit of adopting the standards and about the manner in which the costs and benefits would be shared—the wealth distributional effects.

While notionally desirable, the ability to specify and quantify costs and benefits fully does not exist. In an operational sense, the Board cannot make cost/benefit determinations with any degree of precision. This is because both costs and benefits are very difficult to identify and even more difficult to measure.

The FASB has stated that the principal objective or purpose of external general purpose financial reports is to provide information that is useful to present and prospective investors and creditors and other users in making rational investment, credit, and similar decisions. In this view, the benefits of a changed accounting standard result from the increased decision usefulness of the information produced. Decision usefulness is from the primary perspective of present and prospective investors and creditors. Consistent with this view, economic benefits and costs can be assessed from two principal perspectives. One is that of the preparer—the enterprise responsible for issuing the financial statements. The other is that of the users of the information contained in the financial reports—present and prospective investors and creditors.

OUT-OF-POCKET COSTS

The most apparent and most readily identifiable costs of a required accounting change are of an out-of-pocket variety. They initially impact the issuers of financial statements and include:

- costs of collecting, processing and understanding information required by the new standard;
- costs of audit; and
- costs of disseminating information to those who must receive it.

Users also incur costs when standards are changed. These include:

- costs of analyzing, understanding, and interpreting new information; and
- costs of processing excessive information and of rejecting information that is redundant—the diagnosis of redundancy is not without cost.

In addition, out-of-pocket costs are incurred by a number of parties in developing a changed standard. All of those participating in the standard setting process—in researching, developing, debating and promulgating new standards and in commenting on proposed standards—incur out-of-pocket costs.

OTHER ECONOMIC COSTS

From a preparer perspective, costs attending a new standard may include more than just identifiable out-of-pocket costs. Other economic costs may result. Important among them may be increases in the cost or decreases in the availability of capital. Information contained in external financial reports is presumably used by investors and creditors in making investment and lending decisions. Accordingly, changed reporting methods can lead to changed investor and creditor decisions, affecting corporate capital cost and availability.

For this reason, when a new standard is proposed, particularly when it would increase recorded expenses and recorded liabilities, or would increase the volatility of reported earnings, vigorous opposition to the proposal is often expressed by affected enterprises fearing an adverse impact on capital cost and availability. Many such comments have been made in connection with the current FASB proposal to require accruing the cost of other postretirement benefits. Similar comments were heard when the FASB was considering a proposal to require earlier accounting recognition by utilities of the cost of disallowances by public utility regulators and another proposal to require deferred recognition of loan fee income by savings and loan associations.

Another type of economic cost results from ways in which management may respond to a modified external reporting standard. A concern often arises when a standard designed to serve external uses is deemed by management to be inappropriate for measuring internal performance. This can mean that a required standard will have a result which is dysfunctional in terms of management's objectives. If an accounting practice designed for external reporting is adopted for internal purposes, the business may be run on a measurement system not designed to further management objectives or long term corporate profitability. If, on the other hand, separate measurement systems are used for internal and external reporting, the effect can be disorienting. Means must be designed to reconcile the two measures. At a minimum, this is costly.

A similar economic cost may arise if there are cases where accounting standards cause management to behave in uneconomic ways simply to achieve more stability or short run improvement in reported results, or the appearance of greater financial strength. Examples frequently mentioned are uneconomic hedges in foreign exchange markets solely to reduce the volatility of reported earnings, off-balance sheet financing transactions where a more expensive financing alternative is chosen because it does not have to be reported as a liability, and decisions regarding the level of research costs to be incurred which are based on the desire to report a particular earnings figure rather than on the long run economic benefit to a firm.

Another potential economic cost to financial statement preparers arises from adverse competitive effects resulting from required additional disclosures. This has been most frequently cited in relation to business segment disclosures, but it has broader implications as well.

ECONOMIC BENEFITS

Since external financial reports are principally intended for use by present and prospective investors and creditors, the primary benefits of changing accounting standards stem from the enhanced utility of the resulting information to serve these users. While benefits may be qualitatively described in this fashion, identifying and measuring these benefits is a daunting task.

Economic benefits resulting from accounting changes are very rarely, if ever, of a measurable, out-of-pocket variety. Accounting standards are essential to the efficient functioning of the economy because decisions about allocating capital—the capital markets—depend heavily on credible, concise, understandable and widely disclosed financial information. But the benefits resulting from improved standards are difficult to trace. They are of a behavioral, rather than an out-of-pocket, type. Their incidence is diffuse and they accrue broadly to users and preparers of external financial reports. They include:

- improved credibility of financial reports in general resulting in public confidence in financial markets and more efficient allocation of capital resources;
- increased credibility of the individual entity's external financial statements, with resulting improved accessibility to capital markets, possibly at lower capital costs;
- the increased utility the user gains from improved accounting information, including the ability to make better selections from among various investment options; and
- a spur to management efficiency as a result of accountability to shareholders, lenders and others who can make more informed evaluations.

So it is that economic benefits are characterized as serving purposes such as fairness, comparability, the public interest, and other purposes difficult to identify in particular and even more difficult to try to quantify. While diffuse and hard to identify and quantify, these qualities occupy an important place among the characteristics of a competitive economy with free capital markets.

OTHER ECONOMIC CONSEQUENCES

Economic costs and benefits can be assessed from the perspectives of statement preparers and of statement users. But it is often argued that this focus is too narrow. It is argued that economic, social, and political consequences beyond those identifiable from a preparer/user perspective often result and deserve assessment in the standard setting process. In a similar vein, arguments are advanced that public policy considerations, such as fostering domestic economic growth and stability or promoting the competitiveness of the U.S. economy in the global arena, should be factored into standard setting decisions.

At least three factors give rise to these additional concerns about economic and social consequences. First, some consequences represent the aggregate derivative economic or societal impact of actions directly taken by preparers in response to changed accounting standards. Thus, for example, it has been argued that a required change from a cash to an accrual basis in accounting for postretirement health care costs will cause enterprises to curtail their retiree health care plans so as to avoid higher recorded expenses and liabilities. Aggregate employer actions in this direction, it is argued, would have adverse economic and societal consequences. Many employees would find themselves without adequate health care coverage, perhaps forcing governmental action to compensate in some fashion.

As another example, in 1976 and 1977, when the FASB was considering new accounting standards for oil and gas producing activities, a number of companies opined that they would cut back their exploration programs—in some cases by up to 50 percent—if the companies were forced to change from the full cost to the successful efforts method of accounting. This, it was argued, would be an unacceptable national economic and social result, coming as it would at a time of increasing U.S. dependence on imported energy sources. One might question the wisdom of curtailing exploration expenditures because underlying cash flows and economics would be unaffected by the accounting method employed. Nevertheless, it was argued strenuously that some firms attached such importance to the pattern and level of reported earnings that the firms would program their activities to avoid adverse effects on reported earnings.

Assessing these derivative kinds of consequences is very difficult, calling for initially predicting the nature and extent of enterprise behavioral changes in response to changed methods of reporting financial results. Subsequent judgments would then be required of the macroeconomic impact of this modified enterprise behavior.

A second factor giving rise to economic consequence concerns is that the information contained in financial statements is used by a wide variety of parties in addition to present and prospective investors and creditors and for a wide variety of purposes beyond just making investment and lending decisions. Data in external financial statements are widely used to define contracting relationships between the enterprise and other parties. For example, many profit sharing and other compensation arrangements are based on profits as determined for financial reporting purposes. Debt covenants, working capital maintenance agreements, and similar arrangements with capital suppliers often make reference to information as prepared for financial statement purposes. Changing accounting standards can change these contractual relationships in unanticipated ways, either frustrating the initial intent of the contracting parties or necessitating subsequent changes in contract terms.

Financial statement data are often used by regulatory bodies in the discharge of regulatory objectives. In such instances, changing accounting standards will have an economic consequence—it will change regulatory relationships. Concerns are frequently heard that a proposed accounting change will have an effect that is perceived as unfavorable by either the regulator or the regulated enterprise. Thus, for example, financial institution capital requirements may be based on GAAP accounting information. A required accounting change, causing a reduction is reported capital, may place certain enterprises in violation of regulatory capital requirements.

Cost reimbursements from governmental bodies may be based on data as compiled for financial reporting purposes. And in some instances, taxes may be assessed on income as measured for external financial reporting purposes. In such cases, financial reporting changes can have direct cash flow consequences.

Financial statements are used by many parties, including customers, employees, and the public at large, to form opinions about enterprise financial health and performance. Thus, customers may use financial statement data to assess the financial stability of their sources of supply. In formulating wage demands, organized employees may use financial statements to assess employer ability to pay. And the general public may form opinions about companies and industries based on information in published financial reports. For example, public opinion favoring increased price regulation or increased taxation can arise when increasing health care costs are juxtaposed against seemingly high pharmaceutical company earnings, or when, as happened in the decade of the 1970s, dramatic increases in oil industry profits were reported in a period of energy shortage.

A third source of economic consequence concerns stems from the fact that financial accounting standards are not consistent among countries and that companies increasingly compete in a global market. This gives rise to concerns about the impact of accounting standards on U.S. competitiveness, either when changes in U.S. accounting standards are proposed or when U.S. enterprises are perceived to have a competitive disadvantage stemming from financial reporting differences among countries. Thus, it has been argued that requiring U.S. enterprises to record post retirement health care costs on an accrual rather than a cash basis would have a negative impact on U.S. competitiveness. This is because non U.S. enterprises, not having to apply U.S. accounting standards, would not be burdened by the increased reported expenses attending the accounting change. It is further argued that non U.S. countries typically have national health care coverage. Enterprises in these countries bear the costs associated with post retirement health care benefits through taxation rather than through individually established company health care plans. Paying the costs through taxes results in a charge more akin to a pay-as-you-go cost rather than an accrual cost. In either case, U.S. enterprises would record higher expenses than would their competitors overseas. This, it is argued, would be adverse to U.S. competitiveness.

As another example, it is sometimes argued that existing U.S. standards concerning accounting for goodwill, requiring initial balance sheet recognition of purchased goodwill and its subsequent amortization to earnings, penalizes U.S. enterprises in making acquisitions. Foreign companies, not subject to U.S. accounting standards, are not required to amortize goodwill and thus avoid a future penalty to reported earnings. This difference, it is claimed, gives foreign companies a relative advantage in making acquisitions.

IDENTIFICATION AND MEASUREMENT

However desirable it may be, it seems practically impossible even to identify, let alone measure, all of the economic consequences of an accounting change. Much research has been directed to identifying and measuring the consequences of particular accounting standards on an ex post basis. These studies have proven interesting and suggestive, but by no means definitive.

A complete and precise ex post assessment of the consequences of accounting changes is virtually impossible. Even more difficult is the ex ante identification of these consequences. In response to proposed changes, the FASB often receives expressions of concern about potential adverse consequences. These expressions of concern, reflecting apprehension about the unknown and perhaps unknowable, often assume Doomsday proportions. The only thing certain is that actual consequences are virtually never as dire or drastic as at least some of the anticipated concerns would suggest.

Reasons for the inability to identify and measure consequences in any precise sense include the fact that considerations deal with an uncertain future in a complex world where few economic predictions can be made with assurance. The inability also stems from the fact that some consequences are difficult to measure on a strictly economic scale. Some consequences are of a political, social, or moral variety—impossible to measure on a one dimensional economic scale. Thus, even if the wealth distribution effects of an accounting change were known, determining whether these effects are desirable or not requires judgment. This judgment can be characterized more as political, or social, or moral, rather than as exclusively economic.

Of course, the inability fully to describe and quantify potential consequences of a proposed standard does not necessarily argue that consequences should be ignored. The question is how consequence considerations should be factored into the standard setting process.

FASB CONSIDERATION OF CONSEQUENCES

How much weight the FASB should accord consequence considerations is a question with no clear answer. At one extreme is the possibility that consequences should dominate the Board's conclusions. At the other end of the spectrum is the view that conceptual and technical accounting considerations alone should drive accounting standard decisions—with no weight accorded economic consequences. Between these extremes lies a wide range of possible conclusions.

A number of factors argue against the position that only consequences should matter in setting accounting standards. In the first place, the difficulty of determining consequences has already been discussed. Not only would the ability to forecast future behavior be required, but also the conversion into a single dimension of political, economic, social and moral objectives that cannot meaningfully be so transformed. Persons with this ability simply do not exist. Accordingly, standard setters would base their decisions on supposed consequences and seek those accounting solutions most likely to promote popular social, political, or economic goals. Such a process would result in an eclectic and inconsistent collection of accounting standards and practices. New rules would be developed to foster changing political, social, or economic goals. Old rules, set when different needs or priorities were predominant, would become counter productive and would require modification. Accounting standards and practices would be in a state of continual change in response to the shifting political breezes.

Such a situation would call the credibility of financial statements into serious question. Institutionally, there would clearly be no need for the present standard setting structure. The FASB, with members selected because of their interest and expertise in financial reporting, has no unique ability or power to make economic, political, or social judgments concerning the distribution of wealth. If accounting decisions were to be made based on their popularity, or based on the way they promote whatever economic, political, or social goals are currently popular, the FASB would be redundant. Such decisions are political. Politicians can make political decisions better than can accountants.

At the other end of the spectrum is the position that economic consequence considerations should play no part in deciding upon accounting standards. Conceptual and technical accounting considerations alone would determine answers to accounting questions. A comprehensive conceptual framework would initially be developed setting forth agreed financial reporting objectives and the criteria to be followed in attaining those objectives. Accounting questions would be resolved by adopting that solution that best meets the specified objectives and criteria.

Experience suggests that such an approach, relying exclusively on agreed concepts and logic to produce accounting standards, will not prove successful. The Board's experience in working on its conceptual framework project suggests some of the problems.

Extensive efforts to develop an agreed conceptual framework for financial accounting and reporting began anew in 1973 when the FASB was formed after prior efforts by the

Accounting Principles Board had proved unsuccessful. Work extended through 1985 and resulted in six Statements of Financial Accounting Concepts.

These Concept Statements, by establishing parameters within which accounting issues can be addressed, have been helpful in standard setting. But, as developed to date, the conceptual framework deals more with questions to ask than with ultimate solutions. The conceptual framework is not sufficiently definitive to serve as a set of formulas from which solutions to particular accounting problems can readily be derived.

As a consequence, resolving accounting questions is rarely a process of searching for a single correct answer—one which has a unique claim on truth. Accounting is utilitarian in nature. It is an inexact social science in which absolutely right answers are extremely rare.

There are no easy, or demonstrably correct and universally applicable, answers to most of the questions that the Board addresses. This is in part because most problems amenable to clear cut solutions acceptable to all never reach the Board. Matters that the Board is asked to deal with are typically those on which reasonable and informed people have different views. It is not surprising then that among seven Board members, each with his own background and view of the world, there are differences of opinion. Among other matters, these differences of opinion relate to what information is decision useful, what accounting changes will be cost beneficial, what the behavioral impacts of an accounting change will be, and what accounting changes are needed to accommodate to a changing economic environment. These differences of opinion are inevitably reflected in Board member judgments about particular accounting questions. Final accounting standards reflect the culmination of a process, not of discovery of truth, but of discussion, deliberation and agreement among Board members. Final standards reflect a consensus of essentially subjective judgments among at least a majority of seven Board members. Inevitably, these individual subjective judgments reflect the full background of each Board member—not just technical accounting considerations.

The FASB's cost/benefit precept explicitly requires that decisions on accounting standards be based on more than exclusive reliance on conceptual and technical accounting considerations. There is widespread agreement about the appropriateness of this overall cost/benefit constraint. Because accounting is a utilitarian subject whose benefits are described best in terms of the usefulness of the resulting information, it seems reasonable to demand that the perceived increased informational utility resulting from a change at least offset the costs of making the change. Adoption of an accounting standard for the exclusive reason of conceptual or logical consistency when the standard is clearly not cost beneficial would be without economic purpose.

Another reason for not relying exclusively on conceptual and technical accounting considerations relates to the need for general acceptability of accounting standards. The FASB was created to be an instrument of accounting change. But, in any given circumstance, limits exist concerning the acceptable amount, direction, and pace of change. The Board must weigh the identified need for accounting change against the need for a degree of stability in financial reporting.

In an immediate sense, FASB standards derive their authority from the fact that both the SEC and the AICPA consider FASB standards as authoritative for the purpose of preparing financial statements in accordance with generally accepted accounting principles. This authority doubtless accounts for the immediate adoption of FASB standards. But, in a broader sense and on a longer term basis, the authority of FASB statements rests with their being viewed by all segments of a diverse constituency as being useful, cost beneficial, and fairly established. It is in furtherance of this objective that the Board has established its elaborate due process procedure It is also for this reason that the Board has indicated that it will attempt to make accounting changes on an evolutionary rather than a revolutionary basis.

Thus, economic consequences cannot be ignored when standards are set. On the other hand, conceptual, logical and technical accounting considerations are also essential to maintaining and improving existing standards. The real issue is striking a balance between the two.

The FASB has attempted to strike this balance by giving paramount consideration to agreed concept, principles, and logical consistency in setting accounting standards. The answer produced by following this process is presumptively adopted, absent compelling evidence that cost/benefit and economic consequence considerations would make the solution unacceptable.

The fundamental reason for the primacy of conceptual considerations is the importance of neutrality and objectivity to a credible and effective standard setting process. A basic precept followed by the Board is to be objective in its decision making and to ensure, insofar as possible, the neutrality of information resulting from its standards. To be neutral, information must reflect economic activity as faithfully as possible without coloration for the purpose of influencing behavior in any particular direction.

The essence of the notion of neutrality is freedom from bias toward an identified result. Thus, to be neutral, the standard setter must avoid predetermining a desired result and selecting a standard to induce that result.

In the neutrality view, financial accounting and reporting is a system of measurement which should report economic activity as objectively and as faithfully as possible. In this view, just as other measurement systems—academic grading systems, systems of weights and measures, and temperature scales, for example—are expected to be objective and neutral, so also is the financial reporting system. The neutrality notion does not mean that the way information is reported does not have consequences. It does, just as the results produce by any measurement system can cause the user to take certain actions. Neutrality does mean, however, that the selection of the measurement system itself should not be influenced by a desired result. If a measurement system is viewed as not being neutral, or as biased to induce a particular result, resulting information loses credibility. Credibility is enhanced if, both in fact and in perception, reported information is verifiable and can be relied upon faithfully to represent what it purports to represent—provided there is no bias in the selection of what is reported.

A Look at History

A look at history may be useful. Although many might disagree with how it has done so, the Board has clearly factored economic consequence considerations into its standard setting decisions. And it has done so in various ways.

Cost/benefit considerations have been at least partially responsible for some agenda decisions. For example, since its issuance in 1976, Statement 13, dealing with accounting for leases, has been widely criticized as too procedural and complex as well as lacking in conceptual foundation for its specific and detailed rules for segregating leases which should be capitalized from those which should not. The FASB has been urged to readdress the lease accounting subject with a view towards promulgating a new standard which would both have a stronger conceptual basis and be simpler in application. On several occasions the Board considered formally adding a project to reconsider lease accounting to its agenda. So far the Board has decided not to do so. This is in part for cost/benefit reasons. The Board has not become convinced that it would be able to produce a conceptually superior standard which would produce information of sufficiently enhanced usefulness to justify the costs involved both in achieving acceptability of the standard and in effectively implementing the standard.

Sometimes cost/benefit considerations are the reason for issuing a statement. For example, Statement 89 was issued to supersede Statement 33 requiring certain inflation disclosures. Cost/benefit considerations were used to justify this action. A large body of research literature was available about the lack of usefulness of disclosures made pursuant to Statement 33. The Board cited that literature as the basis for rescinding Statement 33. The Board became convinced that the usefulness of the information being provided did not justify a requirement to continue its issuance.

Another example was Statement 104 which amended Statement 95 dealing with cash flow statements. Statement 104 relied on cost/benefit considerations to permit banks, savings institutions, and credit unions to report cash flows on a net rather than gross basis for certain deposit and lending activities.

Sometimes cost/benefit considerations affect decisions concerning specific provisions of accounting standards. For example, in its Exposure Draft on accounting for the costs of post retirement benefits, the Board proposed to require a number of specific disclosures about the obligation to provide post retirement benefits and about the cost of providing those benefits. About two thirds of the commentators on the Exposure Draft opined that the proposed disclosures were too extensive, too complex, and not cost/beneficial. In light of these comments, the Board did reconsider the proposed disclosures and simplified some of them in moving ahead to a final accounting standard.

Sometimes economic consequence considerations temper the basic provisions of an accounting standard. Thus, in its Statement 87, dealing with employer's accounting for pensions, the Board adopted certain provisions concerning the delayed recognition of gains or losses and footnote disclosure of pension assets and liabilities. These provisions were something less than what the Board believed to be conceptually appropriate but were adopted to accommodate constituent concerns about both dramatic changes in balance sheet presentations and undue earnings volatility. In its basis for conclusions, the Board noted that "it believes that it would be conceptually appropriate and preferable to recognize a net pension liability or asset measured as the difference between the projected benefit obligation and plan assets, either without delay in recognition of gains or losses, or perhaps with gains and losses reported currently in comprehensive income but not in earnings. However, it concluded that those approaches would be too great a change from past practice to be adopted at the present time. In light of the differences in respondents' views and the practical considerations noted, the Board concluded that the provisions of this statement as a whole represent an improvement in financial reporting."[1]

Lastly, the Board very commonly factors economic consequence considerations into decisions about the required effective dates of its statements and the transition provisions for adopting new standards. For example, referring again to Statement 87, the Board noted that it "continues to believe that transition is a practical matter and that a major objective of transition is to minimize the cost and to mitigate the disruption involved, to the extent that is

[1]FASB Statement No. 87, *Employer's Accounting for Pensions,* par. 107.

possible without unduly compromising the objective of enhancing the ability of financial statements to provide useful information."[2] Clearly, practicality questions involve considerations of cost/benefit and economic consequences.

CONCLUSIONS

There is no simple answer to the question of how much weight should be accorded economic consequences in formulating accounting standards. While it is clear that these consequences cannot be ignored, considerations of conceptual consistency, neutrality, and objectivity are, or should be paramount in the establishment of standards. The question is not one of whether conceptual or consequence considerations should prevail to the exclusion of the other, but rather what the appropriate balance is that can be struck between the two.

The course that the FASB has followed is one of giving paramount consideration to objectivity, neutrality, and conceptual consistency with agreed accounting objectives and principles. Conclusions reached by following these considerations are adopted, absent compelling evidence about unacceptable consequences. Just when these consequences would be unacceptable is a matter of judgment in each case. Applying the appropriate judgment to achieve the right balance will continue to be a challenging task.

[2]Ibid., par. 256.

PART II

ISSUES IN ACCOUNTING MEASUREMENT AND DISCLOSURE

The papers included in Part II are concerned with issues of measurement and disclosure in financial reporting. Topics are organized into seven lettered sections. Section A addresses the purpose of income measurement and consists of two papers. Gellein (1987) asks whether wealth enhancement (i.e., an increase in net assets or shareholders' equity) is the underlying characteristic of business income. If so, Gellein questions whether such an income concept is suitable also for evaluating the periodic performance of the management of the enterprise. These potentially conflicting roles for income measurement are examined in the context of the Conceptual Framework's asset/liability approach to the determination of comprehensive income. Gellein believes that efforts to measure bottom-line net income in a manner that is indicative of operating performance have little chance of succeeding. He suggests instead the design of a multistep statement of comprehensive income, containing an intermediate line that reflects current management performance.

Thomas (1975) discusses the thorny problem of allocating costs and revenues in income measurement. All such allocations are arbitrary, asserts Thomas, because they can be neither refuted nor verified. Because factors of production interact, generating joint benefits, any attempt to allocate such benefits among the inputs is bound to be unsuccessful. Thomas calls for an end to allocation and recommends two alternatives to accomplish that goal: the use of (1) exit values or (2) cash flow statements.

Section B contains four papers that address issues in the definition and measurement of assets and liabilities. Weil (1990) surveys the treatments of the time value of money in financial reporting, and addresses the following questions: (1) For which assets and liabilities does accounting now prescribe or proscribe discounting? (2) What anomalies in valuing assets and liabilities arise from the failure to discount? (3) Who gains from the current standards? and (4) What reasons are given in the authoritative literature for proscribing discounting? Weil identifies a variety of inconsistencies that have developed in practice and articulates a single set of conceptual criteria consistent with the historical cost model. The current inconsistencies among standards in Weil's view are due largely to exceptional lobbying power on the part of banks and other financial institutions.

Jones (1988) explores new accounting issues that have surfaced with the recent explosion in new types of financial instruments, discusses various problems that the historical cost accounting model fails to resolve, and proposes a possible solution that is compatible with the Conceptual Framework. Jones does not believe that the existing Conceptual Framework justifies a full fair-value model for all financial instruments. Instead, he proposes fair values for financial assets that are held for their ability to be traded—at the lower of cost or recoverable value—for assets that are held for purposes of generating a yield, and he suggests historical cost values for financial liabilities.

Stepp (1985) considers whether deferred taxes should be discounted, given that the FASB has adopted the liability concept of deferred taxes. Those who support discounting say it is a more appropriate measure of the tax liability. Such a liability is not, however, an account payable at a fixed time. Reversals of timing differences will occur in the future, and the economic incentive in deferred taxation is an interest-free loan granted by the government. There are other problems associated with discounting, including the questions of which discount rates to use and what the discount period should be. Stepp concludes that deferred taxes should not be discounted.

King, Ortegren, and King (1990) address the practicality of making the kinds of estimates required to apply the FASB's intended approach to valuing hybrid financial instruments. The FASB's approach is based on the premise that all financial instruments consist of a few "building blocks," or fundamental financial claims, and that the values of hybrid instruments can be disaggregated and assigned to these fundamental components. The authors provide reassuring empirical evidence on the practicality of valuing the debt and equity elements of convertible debt and suggest that the same general approach may be extended to other types of hybrid financial instruments.

In Section C, Scott (1979) argues that the existing basis of classification on the credit side of the balance sheet is deficient. The categories are neither exhaustive nor mutually exclusive. The rationale for the categories of debt and equity is shown to be invalid. Scott proposes a new basis of classification possessed by all items on the credit side of the balance sheet. They represent sources of capital invested in assets. These sources of capital may be validly classified into transitory and standing sources. Transitory sources are commitments to meet future demands on resources from outside the firm, and standing sources of capital are those currently uncommitted to meet such future demands.

Wiseman (1990) and Cheung (1992) debate the appropriate treatment of "option-like" securities (e.g., convertible debentures) in EPS calculations. Wiseman argues that option-like securities issued by the firm do not qualify as residual equity, and that changes in the current values of such securities should be recognized as holding gains and losses by the issuing firms. Because current redemption values for options can be determined, Wiseman asserts that inclusion of such gains and losses in income is more useful than the potential EPS dilution disclosures required by GAAP. Cheung, on the other hand, insists that some of the option-like securities issued by the firm are, in substance, residual equities, and that a meaningful calculation of diluted EPS may be provided based upon the current values of these securities.

Section D contains two papers dealing with post-employment retirement benefits. Miller and Redding (1992) reason that, because the FASB uses a political process to resolve financial reporting issues, the resulting standards will fall short of theoretically sound solutions. SFAS 87 on accounting for pensions is identified as an example of an FASB pronouncement that includes many politically based compromises. The authors use a sample of major U.S. firms and evaluate the effects of political compromises on a variety of key financial statement relationships (e.g., ratio of liabilities to equity, return on stockholder equity). The sampled firms exhibit large differences between theoretically sound measurements and those produced pursuant to SFAS 87.

Thomas and Farmer (1990) evaluate arguments for and against accrual-basis reporting for post-employment retirement benefits other than pensions, usually referred to as OPEBs. The article considers four key questions: (1) Do OPEBs meet the definition of a liability? (2) If so, how should the liability be measured? (3) If measureable, how should the liability be reported? (4) How should the transition to accrual-basis accounting be handled? The discussion of these issues relies upon Conceptual Framework definitions, precedents from earlier standards (especially SFAS 87 for pension benefits), and potential social and economic consequences of changes in OPEB reporting standards.

Section E includes four papers that consider issues in reporting for business combinations and consolidations. Pacter (1992) offers an overview of the issues in the FASB's discussion memorandum (DM) on consolidation policy and procedures. The fundamental issues in the DM are whether and how separate financial statements of two or more affiliated entities should be combined in a single set of consolidated statements. Pacter identifies control versus ownership as probably the most important issue in the DM. Varying views on this issue have led to three different concepts of consolidated financial statements—the economic unit concept, the parent company concept, and the proportionate consolidation concept. As Pacter demonstrates, the three concepts can result in significantly different accounting measurements.

Rosenfield and Rubin (1990) present opposing views on the reporting of minority stockholdings in consolidated financial statements. Three treatments are reflected in current reporting practices. One treatment presents the minority interest as a separate component of liabilities; a second is the presentation of the minority interest between liabilities and equity; and the third treatment presents the minority interest as a separate component of shareholders' equity. The authors suggest that the entity should not present the minority interest in its consolidated financial statements, but disagree on how to accomplish this result.

Bierman (1992) recommends that proportionate consolidation be used for any common stock investment that is material to the investor company. Under this dictate, questions of ownership percentage and control are entirely irrelevant, and there is no need to divide investments into those to be consolidated and those not to be consolidated. Bierman bases his suggestion upon the information needs of financial analysts. All-or-nothing consolidation is demonstrated to show too much debt when consolidation occurs, and too little when it does not occur.

Davis (1991) urges a repeal of accounting standards that permit the pooling-of-interests method of reporting business combinations, which he believes can lead firms to report misleading improvements in earnings. Today few other countries allow poolings. The worldwide trend is to abolish or severely restrict this method of accounting for business combinations. Davis observes that the pooling method is often applied when the economic circumstances indicate that no "true" pooling has occurred.

Section F is devoted to international issues in financial reporting, and consists of two papers. Sundby and Schwieger (1992) highlight areas of major differences between U.S. financial reports and those prepared by firms in various countries with membership in the European Community (EC). The authors note various reporting differences that render comparisons of EC financial statements to those of U.S. companies either difficult or meaningless. Asset write-ups, reserves, liberal definitions, lack of economic substance over form, and expenses listed by class are identified as factors that render any ratio analysis useless if these ratios are compared to U.S. ratios.

Beaver and Wolfson (1984) disagree with the methods of translating foreign operations specified in SFAS 52, which result in the exclusion of translation gains and losses from income. The authors argue that the relationship between interest rates and changes in exchange rates is critical. Countries with relatively high nominal interest rates tend to have weak currencies, implying exchange-rate losses, whereas countries with relatively low interest rates tend to have strong currencies, implying exchange-rate gains. Because translation gains and losses capture at least some of the economic factors behind the systematic relationship between interest rates and exchange rates, excluding them from an analysis of earnings can provide misleading performance measures.

Section G considers two types of expansion in the content of financial reports. Ramanathan (1976), in a piece on social accounting, notes that traditional performance criteria may be in conflict with social priorities and provides an approach to incorporating social effects into the firm's formal performance-measurement system. Ramanathan accepts the notion of a "sound contract," which implies that a set of social performance dimensions can be developed. A definition of socially responsible performance may then lead to methods of performance measurement and evaluation.

Ewer, Nance, and Hamlin (1992) examine the accounting implications of the Federal Clean Air Act as a likely precursor of future environmental laws that will create unconventional business assets and liabilities. The authors focus upon the government's authorization to grant air pollution emission rights—in effect a limited license to pollute—and the eventual creation of a market in which these rights can be sold or traded. After considering the resemblance of these rights to familiar asset categories, such as securities, property, and inventories, the authors conclude that the "new asset" does not fit comfortably into any existing asset classification and that, as a result, it justifies special treatment.

II-A

MEASUREMENT OF INCOME

II-A1

PERIODIC EARNINGS: INCOME OR INDICATOR?

Oscar S. Gellein

Perceptive observers of the standard-setting process for financial reporting are concerned about the persistent confusion with respect to the meaning and nature of business income, as well as about the role of periodic earnings in evaluating enterprise performance. Introduction by the Financial Accounting Standards Board (FASB) of the terms "comprehensive income" and "earnings," without final resolution of their differences, has refocused attention on some enduring issues:

- What is the nature of business income?
- Should periodic income or earnings be measured in a manner deemed suitable for evaluating the performance of the management of an enterprise?
- If periodic earnings is so measured, will it be essentially different in nature from income for the lifetime of the enterprise?

Comments from different elements of the financial community about proposed financial reporting standards indicate both differences of opinion on those issues and uneasiness about the possible consequences, if they are resolved. Above and beyond this confusion is a cloud of public concern about the usefulness and, at times, the reliability of accounting measurements in general, and of periodic income in particular. Attention to some income theory seems in order. One observer has said:

Oscar S. Gellein is a former member of the Financial Accounting Standards Board.

Oscar S. Gellein, "Periodic Earnings: Income? or Indicator?" American Accounting Association: *Accounting Horizons*. Reprinted by permission of the American Accounting Association.

Determination of periodic earnings has been a major focus for many accounting writers and for standard setters since the late 1930's. Despite that focus and the centrality of income to financial reporting, the attention given to the nature of periodic earnings has been sporadic and, quite often, has been confined to description.[1]

THE NATURE OF BUSINESS INCOME

The nature of business income is a good place to start because there appears to be considerable agreement on the matter. The prevailing view is that wealth enhancement or, in accounting terms, net asset increase, is the underlying characteristic of business income. There are diverse views about how to measure wealth enhancement, but near unanimity that an increase in net assets attends accounting income. In 1940, Paton and Littleton said it this way:

> Gains and losses are changes in enterprise assets, not in proprietors' assets or stockholders' assets. Accounting theory, therefore, should explain the concepts of revenue and expense in terms of enterprise asset changes rather than as increases or decreases in proprietors' or stockholders' equities.[2]

Thirty-five years later, income was characterized similarly:

> Income is in some sense the *gain in wealth* from being in business. It is the amount that can be spent without encroaching upon the initial wealth, net assets or capital of the firm.[3]

Despite the long-standing consensus about wealth enhancement, or net asset better-offness, as the underlying characteristic of business income, the FASB encountered significant and strongly expressed opposition to the notion of better-offness presented in a discussion memorandum issued in 1976 on a conceptual framework for financial reporting.[4] That opposition appeared to manifest a concern that adoption of the better-offness idea would result in basic changes, with sweeping consequences, in accrual accounting. That concern remains unresolved.

Accrual accounting has been the focus of financial accounting for almost all of this century. Standard setting for financial reporting, since inception, has sought to improve the results of accrual accounting, especially the measure of periodic income, often referred to as earnings—a term used almost exclusively when referring to per-share results. The term has evolved to connote aspects of enterprise performance for a period. Some observers relate earnings to management performance insofar as it affects enterprise performance.

---

[1] Allan Barton, *An Analysis of Business Income Concepts* (International Centre for Research in Accounting, University of Lancaster, 1975).

[2] W. A. Paton and A. C. Littleton, *An Introduction to Corporate Accounting Standards* (American Accounting Association, 1940).

[3] Barton, 1975, op. cit.

[4] FASB, Discussion Memorandum, *Conceptual Framework for Financial Accounting and Reporting; Elements of Financial Statements and Their Measurement* (FASB, 1976).

That not uncommon perception of earnings for a period (ordinarily a year) probably accounts for the uneasiness about applying a net asset better-offness notion of income to the determination of earnings in the accrual accounting system.

Net asset better-offness is too abstract, by itself, for direct use in determining earnings. W. A. Paton was quoted as having described in 1922 a concept of income that had common acceptance:

> The most conservative criterion of income is the receipt of cash. Cash—meaning thereby any generally recognized medium of exchange—can be used to purchase any desired commodity or service whatsoever, provided the same is available on the market, to retire obligations, to pay taxes, to pay dividends, to liquidate terminable proprietary investments, etc. Cash is the *asset excellent*. The receipt of cash for product, consequently, furnishes the ultimate test of revenue realization. From this standpoint the cash sale and the collection of cash following the so-called credit sale constitute the principal income transactions, the important occasion for entries in the revenue account.[5]

Paton may or may not have intended to be defining income, but he did advance an idea about cash consequences that has had a profound, continuing influence on accrual accounting. Business income is ultimately grounded in cash; increases in wealth with a low probability of fruition in cash are suspect as income. From the beginning of an enterprise through its ultimate liquidation, lifetime income is the difference between the amounts of cash (or cash equivalent) invested in the enterprise by owners and the amounts of cash distributed to owners, sometimes called the cash-to-cash notion of better-offness. The question of whether cash should be adjusted for a change in general price levels is separable from the question of the nature of income, and is not dealt with here.

THE NATURE OF PERIODIC EARNINGS

Uncertainty about the probability of cash consequences imposes constraints on financial reporting. Accrual accounting is the response to those constraints. Its characteristics are well known. They are highlighted here simply to provide a context for considering whether earnings of a period should be viewed as an indicator of enterprise performance that may, or may not, have the same nature as lifetime income. Those characteristics are:

1. *A universe for recording.* The universe of things accounted for is generally limited to financial statement elements arising (a) in transactions—that is, in exchanges between the enterprise and other parties; and (b) in connection with certain events, internal or external to the enterprise, that cause existing assets to shrink or, rarely, to grow; liabilities to arise; and the measure to change. Other things are often excluded from the universe for reasons of uncertainty of measure of cash equivalence or cash consequence.
2. *Financial statement focus.* Things on center stage are assets, liabilities, revenues, expenses, income, and equity (ownership interests), and their articulation in a double-entry system. Those factors combine to show and validate a measure of periodic earnings.

[5]Stephen Gilman, *Accounting Concepts of Profit* (The Ronald Press Company, 1939).

3. *Matching.* The matching of costs with revenues produces a measure of periodic earnings. Matching is based on the thought that (a) often there is a discernible association of cost and revenue, and (b) if there is no discernible association with expected future revenue, there is no basis for deferral; accordingly, the cost is borne by current revenue.
4. *Recognition.* Recognition criteria are used to determine the time for initial recognition of assets and liabilities and the time to record revenue; that is, to record a measure for the asset received that is different from the measure of the asset relinquished in exchange. Extensive efforts have been expended on attempts to formulate a workable guideline for realization of revenue, with mixed success. Recognition criteria are the weakest link in accrual accounting, despite significant recent efforts to clarify and strengthen the criteria.
5. *Cost allocation.* Allocation of cost of long-lived assets to periods is an integral part of matching costs with revenues.
6. *Historical measures.* Historical cost is the measure of nonmonetary assets, ordinarily allocated through matching with revenues during asset life. Impairment criteria are applied to recognize impairment of cost—that is, an adverse cash consequence deemed to be permanent.

EARNINGS—INDICATOR OR INCOME?

Those characteristics of accrual accounting do not address the issue of whether the nature of periodic earnings should be the same as the nature of lifetime income. The view that earnings is different apparently is held by many and has been for many years. The issue can be restated as whether periodic earnings should be an indicator of enterprise performance or a measure of periodic income representing enterprise wealth enhancement during the period, or whether it can fill both roles.

There is a long history, frequently revisited, of standard-setting efforts to change the display of the effects of unusual or extraordinary or nonrecurring happenings. The context has always been a concern about whether the measure or display of earnings is a meaningful and evenhanded indicator of performance. The force tugging on the other side is whether what is represented to be the earnings of the period can be viewed as the income of the period in terms of net asset enhancement.

In the 1940s the opposing views centered on the issue of whether, philosophically, periodic earnings should measure current operating performance or, instead, should be an all-inclusive measure representing an estimated aliquot part of lifetime income. Standard setters, including the Committee on Accounting Procedure, the Accounting Principles Board, and the Financial Accounting Standards Board, have issued more pronouncements dealing with display of the effects of unusual and nonrecurring events than any other subject. Positions taken at various times have tended to erode because of forces stemming from perceptions of abuses, on the one hand, and of unfairness, on the other. That history is not recounted here; it is well known.

At the same time, other manifestations of the persistent controversy about the nature of reported earnings are to be seen in some accounting principles and standards that underlie practice. In short, some financial statement measurements themselves have been affected by the view that earnings is an indicator and, accordingly, that by nature it may not be like lifetime income.

As mentioned previously, the essence of lifetime income is cash realization. Determination of periodic income, however, must deal with uncertainty, since some cash-to-cash cycles are incomplete when the determination of earnings is made. That suggests that periodic earnings will be similar in nature to lifetime income only if assets and liabilities at the end of a period are grounded in cash. But what does that mean? For some assets the carrying amount represents cost, perhaps amortized cost, based on cash (or its equivalent) expended in connection with acquisition. That is a grounding in cash. Other assets await collection of cash. If the carrying amounts of those assets have a high probability of being collected at amounts equalling or exceeding the carrying amount, they are grounded in cash. Similarly, liabilities are grounded in cash if the carrying amount measures a probable outflow of cash (or of assets grounded in cash). If assets and liabilities are grounded in cash, the related revenues and costs will be grounded in cash. If that kind of cost is matched with that kind of revenue, the nature of the resulting measure of periodic earnings will be similar to the nature of income for a lifetime.

Financial Statement Measurements Causing Earnings to Be Different in Nature from Lifetime Income

Two kinds of situations result in financial statement amounts that are not grounded in cash. One kind would ignore certain events that have occurred. Instead of recording them at occurrence, their effects are accounted for in the future. The other kind would account currently for the effects of events that might, or might not, occur in the future.

An example of the first kind is the deferred method of accounting for the tax effects of differences in treatments for financial reporting purposes and income tax purposes. Under that method, changes in tax rates are ignored. As a result, earnings after the change in rates is affected by amounts different from expected cash consequences. Earnings for many years after the change could be affected as reversals of the tax effects occur. It should be noted that the FASB had indicated an intention to proscribe the deferred method before a reduction in federal income tax rates for 1987 seemed likely.

Another example of the first kind of situation is the accounting by the creditor for the effects of a restructured troubled debt of a borrower. The adverse effect of the transaction is ignored in determining earnings of the creditor in the year of the restructuring. Instead, the adverse consequence is applied to future years as the newly scheduled collections are received.

An example of the second kind of situation is the recognition of future changes in general price levels in determining current pension costs in plans where pension benefits are based on final pay levels. Recognition of that kind of possible future consequence breaks the link between earnings and cash. Anticipated changes in future price levels do not meet the test of probable and reasonably predictable cash consequences.

Another example of the second kind of situation was the accounting for so-called self-insurance—which, indeed, is no insurance—before issuance in 1975 of Financial Accounting Standards No. 5, *Accounting for Contingencies*. No insurance does not meet the test of highly probable, predictable cash payments.

EARNINGS VOLATILITY

The unsettled issue of whether periodic earnings is an indicator, rather than a measure of wealth enhancement, feeds controversy about volatility of earnings. Not surprisingly, complaints that a proposed standard of financial reporting would induce improper volatility continue at an increasing rate. In Statement of Financial Accounting Standards No. 87, *Employers' Accounting for Pensions,* for example, eighteen paragraphs (Nos. 173 through 190) are given to describing constituents' concerns about volatility and the Board's conclusions for rejecting or accommodating those concerns.

Those who believe that earnings serve as an indicator see volatility in relation to the role they perceive for earnings. Those perceptions cover a wide range. Among the matters that have been suggested for portrayal by earnings are the following:

- *Enterprise earning power.* That role has a future dimension. Accordingly, it has been suggested that effects of non-recurring events either be separately displayed or omitted from earnings. Some would say that in fulfilling the role, a broadened group of future events should affect currently reported earnings.
- *Enterprise or management performance.* This role suggests that effects of noncontrollable happenings (like so-called acts of God), although recurring, should either be separately displayed or omitted from earnings.
- *Sustainability of income (or of dividends).* This perceived role also suggests separate disclosure or elimination from earnings of the effects of unusual, nonrecurring events. A further implication, however, is that unusual losses might be treated differently from unusual gains.

Those perceived roles lead to different norms for identifying volatility or distortion of earnings. Volatility and distortion are sterile terms if unaccompanied by a norm by which to judge their existence. Accrual accounting, as highlighted earlier, has no built-in mechanism for identifying nondistortion or proper volatility.

Perhaps it is fair to say that as an unstated assumption of accrual accounting, the volatility appropriately reflected in earnings is that which is inherent in the ebb and flow of the operating circumstances of an enterprise. Any exaggeration or suppression of that volatility introduced by accounting alone is improper. That idea is so abstract, by itself, as not to be very helpful in identifying the norm.

Yet nonvolatility as an appropriate element of accrual accounting has long had its supporters. Some twenty years ago, Bevis[6] noted that a nondistortion guideline was needed to supplement the theory of the accrual basis of accounting. He proposed this guideline: "From among systematic and rational methods, use that which tends to minimize distortion of periodic income." Despite the acceleration of expressions of concern about accounting-induced volatility in the last twenty years, little effort has been made to identify the norm from which distortion would be measured in that guideline.

[6]Herman W. Bevis, *Corporate Financial Reporting in a Competitive Economy* (The MacMillan Company, 1965).

SOME OBSERVATIONS, SOME CONCLUSIONS

In the 1940s the first private sector standard-setting body for financial reporting, the Committee on Accounting Procedure, contrasted the all-inclusive and current operating performance views about an income statement. The Committee expressed a leaning toward the all-inclusive view, but left the way open for exclusion of specified kinds of items.

Forty years later, the third standard-setting body, the FASB, left the issue unresolved, and noted further in FASB Statement of Concepts, *Recognition and Measurement in Financial Statements of Business Enterprises,* that the concept of earnings is expected to be subject to the process of gradual change or evolution.

In the intervening forty years, all three standard-setting bodies struggled with the issue of earnings as (a) an indicator or (b) an estimated aliquot part of lifetime income, and with limited success. Several lessons have been learned from that forty years of experience:

- Arbitrary definitions of "extraordinary," "unusual," "infrequent," and "uncontrollable" tend to erode.
- Efforts to make earnings an indicator through measurements affecting reported net income of a period lead to inconsistent treatment of similar things.
- Direct inclusion in equity (ownership interests) of the effects of certain transactions or events results in confusion, as well as inconsistencies.[7]
- As a consequence of such erosion, inconsistencies, and confusion, financial reporting's credibility has suffered.

Credibility of financial reporting is ever so precious, but ever so fragile. Financial reporting has a significant role to play in maintaining an orderly capital market. It has little chance to fulfill the potential of that role without a sustained perception of evenhandedness and fairness—evenhandedness to enterprises seeking capital and fairness to those providing capital. Order and the attending discipline are necessary to sustain a perception of evenhandedness and fairness. A coordinated general theory of accrual accounting can go a long way in providing the necessary order, if that general theory is sufficiently well articulated to assure consistent treatment of similar matters.

BOTTOM-LINE EARNINGS, AN INDICATOR

Efforts to measure bottom-line net income so as to indicate operating performance during the period have little or no chance of succeeding. That kind of an effort has never been tried, or even charted. Further, any move toward financial statement measurements that cause earnings to be different in nature from lifetime income should be halted (see page 62 for examples).

Most observers of financial reporting in the financial community will not believe that earnings or net income reported for a period is only an indicator, rather than a measure of wealth enhancement. Most people believe that to have income is to have more wealth. They know that income enhances their wealth, and that a loss eats into it. They transfer that belief

---

[7]Examples are found in Statement of Financial Accounting Standards No. 12 and 52, *Accounting for Certain Marketable Securities* and *Foreign Currency Translation,* respectively.

to their perception of business income. The belief is so embedded that the risk of continuing the controversy about the nature of bottom-line earnings is intolerable.

As mentioned before, there is nothing in the general theory of accrual accounting that provides the necessary order for heightened general belief in reported periodic earnings. An anchor is needed to provide reasonable assurance that periodic income manifests wealth enhancement.

That anchor is a grounding in cash. Assets and liabilities shown in balance sheets should meet the test of cash grounding, as that notion has been explained in this paper. Matching, recognition criteria, and a grounding in cash for assets and liabilities would then combine to form three sturdy legs undergirding a general theory with considerable operating potential.

EARNINGS AND PERFORMANCE

At the same time, financial accounting should not neglect assessments of performance. Although financial reporting does not provide a net income measure of performance, a great deal can be done to assist in assessing performance. Certain measurements can be made, displayed, and explained in helpful ways. The scope of this paper does not allow for extensive consideration of ways of improving the presentation of information that will be more useful in assessing operating performance. Instead, only a few guidelines are suggested:

- Separating the results of discontinued operations to show income from continuing operations has proved to be useful. The longer-term success of this display depends on whether the constraints on identification of a discontinued business segment are sustained. Nonetheless, a bottom line in the income statement for overall net income and an intermediate line for net income from continuing operations, if applicable, provide a helpful basic structure.
- Efforts to draw workable lines between ordinary and extraordinary, usual and unusual, and frequent and infrequent have been less than wholly successful. Some arbitrary lines have been drawn and then suffered from erosion. Concern with per-share amounts "before" and "after" a defined class of items has been overriding. A different approach may be needed. Nonrecurrence probably is the central consideration in assessing current performance. Each material effect of nonrecurring transactions and events should be described for what it is in the appropriate place in the income statement.
- Direct inclusion in equity of matters not resulting from transactions with owners should be re-examined. Growing disbelief in financial reporting is inevitable if income effects by-pass the income statement. Designation of income as comprehensive has not been helpful. Income has long been viewed in accounting as broad in concept and in use. If the term "comprehensive income" is to be retained, it would be helpful if all items comprising comprehensive income were brought together in one statement.

Financial accounting may have furthered an excessive concern with short-term enterprise performance, to the virtual exclusion of concern with longer-term performance, by focusing on a display geared to emphasis on different classes of earnings per share. A new look at the display might lead to a better balance between short-term and long-term considerations. Eventually, it might even lead to consideration of rate of return on assets as an important indicator of performance.

II-A2

THE FASB AND THE ALLOCATION FALLACY

Arthur L. Thomas

Off to an impressively active start, the Financial Accounting Standards Board has already wrestled with a broad range of accounting issues. Topics on its active agenda or on which it has issued Standards include

1. Accounting for leases.
2. Accounting for research and development costs.
3. Contingencies and future losses.
4. Gains and losses from extinguishment of debt.
5. Interest costs and capitalization.
6. Accounting for pensions.
7. Segment reporting.
8. Business combinations.
9. Interim financial statements.
10. Reporting by development stage entities.
11. Reporting in units of general purchasing power.

I am grateful to Paul Rosenfield for his comments on an earlier draft of this article.

Arthur L. Thomas, "The FASB and the Allocation Fallacy," *The Journal of Accountancy*, November 1975, pp. 65–68.

12. Translation of foreign currency transactions and financial statements.
13. The recommendations of the Trueblood Report.[1]

All these topics involve some kind of *allocation,* which is the assignment of a total to one or more locations or categories. A thesaurus gives "division," "partition," "slicing," "splitting," and "apportionment" as synonyms of "allocation." Accounting's allocations include assignment of a lease's costs to the individual years of its life, assignment of R&D costs to the single year of their expenditure and assignment of long term investment interest to successive annual revenues. All the FASB topics listed above fall into one of the following two classes of allocations, with items 7 through 9 falling into both:

1. The first nine topics require deciding when to recognize revenues, expenses, gains or losses—that is, deciding to what periods they should be assigned. For example, the FASB may eventually specify how to allocate pension costs to successive annual pension expenses.
2. The last seven topics involve ways of preparing financial statements composed mainly of allocated data. For example, this is implicit throughout the Trueblood Report and explicit in its position statement and income statement recommendations.

In fact, almost all of our revenue recognition and matching efforts require allocation.

THE ALLOCATION PROBLEM

The foregoing is background to a problem that we accountants acknowledge, but whose severity we usually misjudge. To use a term from formal logic, recent research indicates that, unfortunately, our allocations must almost always be *incorrigible*—that is to say, they can neither be refuted nor verified.[2] Incorrigibility will be a central concept in this discussion, and it is well to give a few examples even if doing so may initially seem to be a detour.

Let's suppose that someone claims that beings live among us who look and act exactly like humans, but who actually are aliens, seeded on this planet by flying saucers. We ask: do they come equipped with authentic looking birth certificates? Yes. Would tests of their internal structure, chromosomes or the like expose them? No. Could psychiatrists unmask them? No. The horrible thing is that they have such good counterfeit memories that even the aliens themselves don't know their real nature—you may be one yourself.

Such claims are incorrigible, for no experiment could prove either that such aliens exist or that they don't. Here are some other incorrigible claims:

- Charles Dickens may not have been a greater author than Shakespeare, but he was more of a person.
- Our bourbon is mellower.

---

[1]"Objectives of Financial Statements," Report of the Study Group on the Objectives of Financial Statements, Robert M. Trueblood, Chairman (New York: AICPA, October 1973).

[2]Arthur L. Thomas, Studies in Accounting Research No. 9, *The Allocation Problem: Part Two* (American Accounting Association, 1974), hereafter SAR 9.

- The official state flower of Unicornia is the marsh mallow.
- Even if the colonists had lost their war of independence, by now America would be independent of Britain.
- Since I've lost weight, I've become more spiritual.

Now, if our allocations are incorrigible, practicing accountants should be deeply concerned. We attest that financial statements present fairly the positions of companies and the results of their operations. But if both our revenue recognition and matching are founded upon allocations that we can neither refute nor verify, *we have no way of knowing whether these attestations are true.*

Are they incorrigible? I'll begin with matching and for brevity will disregard extraordinary items (and other nonoperating gains and losses), lower-of-cost-or-market writedowns and the like. Our matchings assign costs of a firm's non-monetary inputs (inventories, labor, other services, depreciable assets, etc.) to the expenses of one or more accounting periods, temporarily reporting as assets costs assigned to future periods. We're all familiar with the theory behind these matching assignments: each input's purchase price should be allocated to successive periods in proportion to the contribution it makes to each period's revenues. Academics and most practitioners also know that an equivalent matching theory can be developed around contributions to net cash inflows.

The allocation problem has several dimensions, some of which are subtle. But one is easily described: to match costs with revenues, we must know what the contributions of the firm's individual inputs *are*. Unfortunately, as I'll illustrate below, there's no way that we can know this.

Seeing why this is so requires introducing a final concept, *interaction*. Inputs to a process interact whenever they generate an output different from the total of what they would yield separately. For instance, labor and equipment interact whenever people and machines working together produce more goods than the total of what people could make with their bare hands and machines could make untended. As this example suggests, interaction is extremely common. Almost all of a firm's inputs interact with each other—their failure to do so would ordinarily signal their uselessness.

Surprising as it may seem, it can be proved that whenever inputs interact, calculations of how much total revenue or cash flow has been contributed by any individual input are as meaningless as, say, calculations of the proportion of a worker's services due to any one internal organ: heart, liver or lungs. Thus, despite all textbooks and American Institute of CPAs or FASB releases to the contrary—despite what you've been trained to believe—our attempts to match costs with revenues must almost always fail. The next section tries to demonstrate this.

A SIMPLE EXAMPLE

A complete demonstration, meeting all possible counterarguments, is very lengthy.[3] But a simple example reveals the kernel of the matter. What follows is offered in the same spirit as Robert Sterling's recent illustration in these pages that only price-level-adjusted current-value financial statements are fully relevant and interpretable:

[3]See SAR 9, chapters 1–6, for the attempt.

"A highly simplified case will be considered in this article. The advantages of simplified cases are that they are easily understood by both the reader and the author and they are more easily solved. If we cannot solve the simplified cases, then we can be fairly certain that we also cannot solve the complex cases. Thus, if a particular approach fails to provide a solution for simplified cases, then we can avoid wasting effort by trying that approach on complex cases."[4]

However, instead of Sterling's cash, securities, bread and milk trading economy, I'll describe a production process for bread alone and confine the discussion to strictly physical measures (to avoid complications introduced by monetary valuations).[5] If individual contributions are necessarily incorrigible even in the following example, it's hard to imagine how they could be otherwise in the vastly more complex processes by which business enterprises generate their products, services, revenues and cash flows.

A prospector manufactures sourdough bread by a three-stage process:

1. He makes leaven by mixing flour, sugar and water in a crock, then keeps it in a warm place for about a week (until it bubbles).
2. He makes bread by transferring all but a cup of leaven to a large pot, where he mixes it with soda and additional flour, sugar and water, kneads it slightly and then lets it rise. He digs a shallow pit, fills it with coals from his camp fire, covers the pot, places it in the pit, buries it in hot coals and keeps it there until the bread is baked.
3. He replenishes the leaven (for the next baking) by adding enough flour and water to restore the crock to its original level.

Water, airborne yeasts and wood are free goods here. We accountants would be concerned with the following inputs to this process: flour, sugar, soda, labor, the crock, the pot and a shovel. Finally, part of the flour and sugar leaven for one loaf becomes included in the leaven for the next. The output of each baking is one loaf of bread.

Although its manufacture is simple, the moment we try to calculate the contributions of any individual input to this output we face a dilemma. Each input (except, perhaps, the soda and the shovel) is essential. Therefore, we could plausibly assign all of the output to any individual input. For example, we could assign all of the output to the flour, reasoning that were flour withheld from the process there would be no bread. Yet, we could equally well assign all of the output to the pot, since without it the loaf would have been incinerated.

Having assigned all output to any one input, we've implicitly assigned zero to each other input. But if either all or zero is appropriate for each input, any intermediate allocation will be equally appropriate—say, half the loaf to the flour and a sixth each to the pot, labor and the crock.

I'm unable to prove which of the infinitely many possible ways of allocating the loaf is correct. Therefore, I can't specify the individual contributions of the inputs; instead, all I'm entitled to say is that they generate the loaf jointly. Research shows that other writers on economics and accounting—even efficient-markets investigators—are equally unable to solve this problem. Perhaps the reader can. But until someone does, any contributions calculated for these inputs must be incorrigible:

---

[4]Robert R. Sterling, "Relevant Financial Reporting in an Age of Price Changes," *Journal of Accountancy,* February 75, p. 42.

[5]As a technical point, I've also simplified by discussing only incremental contributions of inputs. See SAR 9, especially pp. 32–40, 47–48 and 141–44, for the parallel problems that arise for their marginal contributions.

1. One can't verify them, because any other calculation is just as good.
2. One can't refute them, because their calculation is just as good as any other.

Therefore, any attempts at matching based on these contributions (say, depreciation of the pot or calculation of a value for the ending leaven inventory) will also be incorrigible. But the sourdough process is so much simpler than the productive processes of business enterprises, that *matching must necessarily be incorrigible for them, too*—unless, again, the reader can show how complications ease the calculations. To generalize, when a company tries to match costs with revenues there's no way either to refute or to verify the results. Instead, all possible ways of matching will be just as good—or bad—as each other.

If it's any consolation, I don't like this conclusion either, and have spent years trying to disprove it. Nor should you accept it without further inquiry. But I urge you at least to suspend disbelief in it (and in what follows) until you've read the detailed research, cited earlier, that backs it up.

And please notice that the difficulty here isn't one of being unable to allocate—there might be some way of getting around that problem. Instead, we're drowned in possible allocations, with no defensible way to choose among them. To be sure, since we must prepare reports, we eventually do pick one set of figures or another. Long before completing our training, we became accustomed to do this with few (if any) pangs. First, we narrow the possibilities by looking to generally accepted accounting principles and then select one of the survivors according to industry custom, apparent advantage to the company, apparent appropriateness of the method to the firm's circumstances or some other plausible rationale. But how can the incorrigible results be useful to decision makers?

Unless you (or someone) can suggest ways in which calculations that can neither be verified nor refuted assist decisions,[6] our allocations of the costs of depreciable assets, inventories, labor and other inputs are irrelevant to investor needs. Indeed, although it's painful to say this, they are mere rituals—solemn nonsense—and our beliefs in them are fallacies. This should trouble all of us, because practitioners spend much time conducting such rituals, and theorists much time elaborating on such fallacies.[7]

The Accounting Principles Board was well aware of this, but, underrating its severity, was satisfied to claim that exact measurements are seldom possible and that allocation often requires informed judgment.[8] With all due respect, acknowledging that few allocations are exact is like replying, "Few animals are ever completely healthy," in response to the statement, "Sir, your cow is dead."

Finally, since what's true of individual inputs also holds for groups of inputs, I'm forced to conclude that our revenue recognition practices are rituals, too. For revenue recognition allocates the firm's *lifetime* output to the groups of inputs that constitute its resources during the individual years of its life. Once again, the details of this appear in SAR 9.

---

[6]Assistance that goes beyond the unsatisfactory, short run utilities is described on pp. 8–9, 40–46, 65–70 and 163–74 of SAR 9.

[7]For examples of the latter, see SAR 9, pp. 94–110, 116–19 and 128–55.

[8]For examples, see APB Statement No. 4, pp. 11, 13–15, 21–22, 46–48 and 102.

THE FASB'S RESPONSIBILITY

What, then, of the FASB? We've seen it worry, or propose to worry, about which allocations are most appropriate for various accounting situations. The FASB should stop doing this. Instead, whenever possible, it should *eliminate* allocations. Such incorrigible figures don't do readers of our reports any real good, and they

1. Cost money.
2. Strain relations between auditors and clients (when they disagree about which incorrigible figures to report).
3. Cause many of the nonuniformity problems that plague us (since allocations are incorrigible, naturally GAAP conflict—there's no way to settle which rules are right).
4. Thereby confuse individual readers, thus violating what the Trueblood Report designates as the basic objective of financial statements.
5. Generally breed distrust in our profession.

When their elimination isn't possible, the FASB should keep allocations unsophisticated (if we must be incorrigible, at least let's be simple), choose allocation rules on expedient, political grounds (ceasing to worry about theory) and be candid about what it's doing. In particular, the FASB should actively

1. Try to convert conventional reporting practices to allocation-free ones. There are two main allocation-free alternatives to conventional accounting: current value reporting and the type of funds statement reporting that defines "funds" as net quick assets.[9] Certainly, Sterling is correct that merely adjusting allocated historical costs for changes in purchasing power serves little purpose: adjusted ritual remains ritual. The same is true of foreign currency translations.

2. Meanwhile, avoid launching any new incorrigible allocations in such areas as interim and segment reports, leases, contingencies, interest and pensions. And eliminate the more flagrantly incorrigible allocations that we now commit. A prime example of the latter (despite its being one of the APB's greatest political triumphs) is tax deferral: we take the difference between an incorrigible book allocation and an incorrigible tax allocation and allocate it, incorrigibly.

In conclusion, I would emphasize that none of these remarks is intended to disparage accounting practitioners. As SAR 9 points out (p. 157), practitioners have honestly believed that allocations are appropriate and have struggled to cope with them, while we academics saddled practitioners with a matching theory that requires such assignments, then failed to provide defensible ways for their calculation. But the hard fact remains that so long as we continue to certify that incorrigible allocations present fairly a firm's financial position and the results of its operations, we're making claims that we just can't back up. Professional responsibility urges that we, and the FASB, cease to tolerate this.

---

[9]See SAR 9, chapter 7.

II-B

MEASUREMENT OF ASSETS AND LIABILITIES

II-B1

ROLE OF THE TIME VALUE OF MONEY IN FINANCIAL REPORTING

Roman L. Weil

This article surveys the treatments of the time value of money in financial reporting. The current treatments appear to some observers to be mutually inconsistent. The Financial Accounting Standards Board (FASB) has convened a Task Force to address the problem of creating a coherent treatment of interest and discounting in accounting. This article addresses the following questions:

A. For which assets and liabilities does accounting now prescribe or proscribe discounting?

B. What financial statement assets and liabilities are anomalous when accounting fails to consider the time value of money?

C. Who gains wealth from the current treatment of these assets and liabilities and who might lose if accounting were to state the items at the expected net present value of the cash flows?

The author thanks Coopers & Lybrand for the research support which made this study possible and the grant corecipient, Sidney Davidson, who collaborated on parts of the foundational work for this study. Coopers & Lybrand does not agree with everything in this article, but has been generous with its intellectual, as well as financial, support. James C. Meehan and John J. McCauley have helped by reading earlier drafts and pointing out errors of both omission and commission. Participants in the Accounting Workshop of the University of Chicago, particularly John Elliott, Laurentius Marais, Abbie Smith, and Thomas Stober, provided illuminating remarks. Katherine Schipper provided a critical and helpful reading.

Roman L. Weil, "Role of the Time Value of Money in Financial Reporting," *The Accounting Review.* Reprinted by permission of the American Accounting Association.

D. What reasons has the authoritative literature given for proscribing discounting? Are those reasons still valid? Why or why not?

I do not argue that GAAP should change the attribute measured in accounting from historical cost to current cost. While current cost accounting would likely incorporate more discounting than GAAP currently uses, I focus on historical cost accounting, as currently promulgated and practiced. Nor do I consider accounting's sometimes inconsistent *timing* in recognizing events. Sometimes, such as for some pension obligations, discounted amounts are disclosed in notes to financial statements. I focus only on items appearing in the financial statements.

Readers of this article know that over long-enough time spans, income is cash in less cash out. Accounting's not discounting when it should or discounting when it should not affects the timing of income recognition, but not the ultimate amount. It should not be necessary to argue that users of financial statements are interested in periodic measurement, not ultimate results. The interim flows are of course reflected in the interim income statements. The adjustments required to reflect those amounts are reported on the balance sheet. For convenience of exposition, this analysis focuses on the balance sheet.

MEANING OF DISCOUNTING

As I use the phrase, *discounting in accounting* means using a measurement technique which takes into account the value of money over time. It recognizes that the timing of a cash flow affects its value. The discounting calculation usually takes the following form:

$$PV = F \times (1 + r)^{-t}$$

where

F is a future cash flow which occurs t periods from the valuation date;

PV represents the present value on the valuation date of F discounted at the interest rate r;

r is the interest or discount rate appropriate for the borrower for periods counted by t.

Historical cost accounting sets r, the "interest rate appropriate for the borrower," when the firm first records the asset or liability.[1] It does not change, unless the firm revalues the balance sheet item because of new information.[2]

[1]The methods of accounting for all long-term monetary assets and liabilities are conceptually and procedurally identical. Accounting initially records the asset (liability) at the present value of the future contractual payments using the interest appropriate for the borrower on the date the loan begins. Call this rate the *historical interest rate.* At any subsequent interest accrual or interest payment date, accounting computes Interest Revenue (Expense) by multiplying the book value of the asset (liability), including previously accrued interest, times the historical interest rate. The amount of this interest increases the asset (liability) account. The amount of cash payment, if any, reduces the amount in the asset (liability) account.

[2]Accounting does not usually treat the change in interest rates alone, however, as new information sufficient to cause revaluation. An exception is the revaluation of a portfolio of marketable securities whose market value has dropped below cost because of an increase in interest rates.

While loan contracts usually specify an interest rate, market forces will use the interest rate currently appropriate for the borrower, not an "interest rate" specified in the contract, in setting the market value of a series of cash flows. As the Accounting Principles Board said in *APB Opinion No. 21*[3]:

> The prevailing rates for similar instruments of issuers with similar credit ratings will normally help determine the appropriate interest rate for determining the present value of a specific note at its date of issuance. . . . [T]he rate used for valuation purposes will normally be at least equal to the rate at which the debtor can obtain financing of a similar nature from other sources at the date of the transaction. The objective is to approximate the rate which would have resulted if an independent lender had negotiated a similar transaction under comparable terms and conditions. . . .

DISCOUNTING IN GENERALLY ACCEPTED ACCOUNTING PRINCIPLES: PRESCRIBED AND PROSCRIBED

The Appendix lists all GAAP mentions of discounting and the items where discounting might arise in GAAP. A blank in the "discounting treatment" column means that the reference mentions discounting, but there is no specific item requiring a decision about whether to discount.

A difficulty arises in interpreting silence on the subject of discounting in a given pronouncement. Some accountants interpret silence to mean, "do not discount the item,"[4] while others appear to believe that GAAP forbid discounting where they do not specifically require it. This presentation is more literal: if GAAP do not forbid discounting in a given situation and I believe the situation satisfies the criteria for discounting discussed below, then the Appendix states that the accounting may, but need not, use discounting. An example follows.

Example The requirement of *SFAS No. 5* for the accrual of a loss contingency does not mention discounting. Assume, to make a clear-cut example, that the firm has lost a lawsuit. The plaintiff has won damages of $1 million and the losing firm's debt rate is ten percent. The Court has tentatively trebled those damages under a novel reading of RICO. It further rules that post-judgment interest will not accrue between the dates of judgment and decision on the appeal. The firm is confident it will have to pay $1 million two years hence without post-judgment interest, but it believes the trebling will not withstand appeal. Thus, the firm expects to pay $1 million two years hence, which has a present value of $826,445 (= $1,000,000 $\div$ 1.10^{-2}), at a discount rate of 10 percent.[5] Many, even most, accountants would have accrued the undiscounted amount of $1 million as a loss contingency by the end of the period

[3]Paragraph 13, 1971.

[4]I can provide only anecdotal evidence based on conversations with practicing accountants to support this statement.

[5]See J. M. Patell, R. L. Weil, and M. A. Wolfson, "Accumulating Damages in Litigation: The Roles of Uncertainty and Interest Rates," *The Journal of Legal Studies,* 11, 3 (June 1982), 341–364, for a discussion of why the defendant's debt rate is appropriate for discounting in these circumstances.

when the firm lost the lawsuit, or even earlier. GAAP would, I believe, allow discounting the expected payment, recording an initial obligation of $826,445. Not all accountants would record the discounted amount. Some might even judge discounting improper because neither *SFAS No. 5* nor its *Interpretation No. 14* explicitly mentions discounting.[6]

Discounting Not Allowed in GAAP

GAAP specifically *forbids* discounting in only a few instances:

Deferred income taxes,[7]

Convertible bond debt,[8]

Liabilities (sometimes called "deferred revenues" or "deferred credits") for amounts received for goods or services the firm will provide in the future,[9] and

Contractual payments made or receipts collected under troubled debt restructurings.[10]

Discounting Required in GAAP

GAAP specifically *requires* discounting for the following items:

Deferred compensation payments,[11]

Noncurrent accounts/notes payable and long-term debt,[12]

Monetary assets and liabilities (contractual obligations to pay fixed amounts on fixed or determinable dates),[13]

Minimum lease payments and receivables,[14]

Fees to be received from film licenses,[15]

---

[6]I have observed some Big 6 accounting firms calling for discounting of estimated liabilities for worker's compensation claims, while other accountants believe such discounting improper because GAAP do not specifically require it.

[7]*APB Opinion No. 10,* paragraph 6 and *SFAS No. 96,* paragraph 6.b.

[8]The rule in paragraph 12 of *APB Opinion No. 14* says only that "no portion of the proceeds from the issuance of the types of convertible debt securities described [above] should be accounted for as attributable to the conversion feature." This rule is equivalent, however, to prohibiting discounting of the contractual promises of nominal dollars at the interest rate appropriate for the borrower at the time of the borrowing.

[9]*APB Opinion No. 21,* paragraph 3.b.

[10]*SFAS No. 15,* paragraphs 16–18 and 30–32.

[11]*APB Opinion No. 12,* paragraph 6, footnote 1.

[12]*APB Opinion No. 16,* paragraph 88.g.

[13]*APB Opinion No. 21,* paragraphs 11 and 12. *APB Opinion No. 17,* paragraph 25 (in the valuation of intangibles). *APB Opinion No. 26,* paragraphs 3.c (in the recording of liabilities incurred to retire debt issued previously).

[14]*SFAS No. 13,* paragraphs 10, 17, and 18.

[15]*SFAS No. 53,* paragraph 9.

Insurance company policy benefits (net of future premiums) for long-duration contracts or premium deficiencies,[16]

Various activities and holdings of a mortgage-banking enterprise,[17]

Profit computations on sales of improvements to real estate,[18]

Disclosures of future cash flows from oil and gas,[19]

Service costs components of pension costs and projected benefit obligations,[20]

Future payments for employee termination benefits,[21]

In defining "recoverable amount" and "value in use" for current cost disclosures,[22]

Future cash flows from abandoned plant in computing book value of the new asset the firm will record,[23]

Loan origination fees,[24]

Phase-in plans with indirect disallowances for regulated companies,[25] and

Investment contracts.[26]

ANOMALOUS RESULTS FROM FAILURE TO CONSIDER THE TIME VALUE OF MONEY

My discussion of anomalous results follows from my assumption that the accounting for a balance sheet item on a nominal, that is non-discounted, basis is incorrect in historical cost accounting when the item satisfies the following criteria:

1. The item represents a claim to, or an obligation to pay, an amount the firm can estimate with reasonable precision;

[16] *SFAS No. 60,* paragraphs 10, 21, and 35.

[17] *SFAS No. 65,* paragraphs 6, 18, and 26.

[18] *SFAS No. 66,* paragraph 39.

[19] *SFAS No. 69,* paragraph 30.

[20] *SFAS No. 87,* paragraph 16.

[21] *SFAS No. 88,* paragraphs 15.

[22] *SFAS No. 89,* paragraphs 29 and 44.

[23] *SFAS No. 90,* paragraphs 3.b, 6.b, 7, 39, and 51.

[24] *SFAS No. 91,* paragraphs 16 and 18.

[25] *SFAS No. 92,* paragraphs 23 and 24.

[26] *SFAS No. 97,* paragraphs 16, 22–25.

2. The firm will collect or pay the amount more than one year after the balance sheet date[27];
3. a. The claim or obligation arises from other than an executory contract[28]; or
   b. The firm has revalued the balance sheet item because of new information.[29]

In addition, the analysis views a discounted amount as incorrectly computed unless the discounting uses the interest rate the borrower would pay at the time it incurs the obligation for a loan with characteristics roughly equal in amounts and timing of future cash payments (the borrower's debt rate).[30] A later section discusses the practicalities of choosing an interest rate.

ANOMALY: CONVERTIBLE BOND DEBT

Convertible bond debt, as defined in *APB Opinion No. 14,* paragraph 3, "generally" includes "an interest rate which is lower than the issuer could establish for nonconvertible debt. . . ." Part of the issue proceeds from convertible bond debt represents the present value of future cash payments. Part represents the economic value inherent in the option to convert the bonds into common or preferred shares at a stated rate.

Opinion No. 14, 1969, changed the rules of *Opinion No. 10,* 1966. In *Opinion No. 10,* the APB recognized that part of the value of a convertible bond resulted from the holder's option to convert and had called for separating the two components. In *Opinion 14,* the APB acknowledged that separate accounting for the option and the debt would lead to implied debt costs which some issuers would not regard as "an acceptable cost of financing."[31] *Opinion 14*

[27]This criterion results from considerations of materiality, not from a theory. I believe that if the discount rate were to become high enough to make the difference between nominal and discounted amounts material, GAAP would require discounting even for items due within one year of the balance sheet date.

[28]An "executory contract" is an exchange of mere promises. This condition is another way of stating one of the FASB's essential characteristics for an item to be a liability: "the transaction or other event obligating the entity has already happened." See *Statement of Financial Accounting Concepts No. 6,* paragraph 36.

[29]It's an open question whether the changing of interest rates alone should signal a revaluation of balance sheet items. GAAP are inconsistent in this regard. GAAP do not, for example, revalue bond liabilities for interest rate changes after initial issue. GAAP do allow, in practice—at least according to practicing accountants who have informed this discussion—a liability recorded under SFAS 5 to change as a function of changes in interest rate assumptions.

Historical cost accounting does not change the discount rate as market rates change. Historical cost accounting principles suggest, at least to this writer, that balance sheet revaluations should not occur merely because of changes in market interest rates.

[30]Some readers have suggested that when a financial institution receives cash, such as an insurance premium, in return for future payments, such as those contingent on the insured's loss, then the appropriate discount rate be the incremental investment rate available to the holder of the cash. I view this issue as moot, for the moment at least. If the obligation were discounted, then the discount would need to be credited somewhere, presumably to revenue or unearned revenue. This article does not challenge current GAAP's dictum that a firm will not recognize revenue or gain when it receives cash before it renders services, so the credit will not be to revenue. The account Unearned Revenue appears on the balance sheet in the same section as the liability for the advance payment, so crediting Unearned Revenue with the discount affects merely the labeling in the liability section.

[31]*APB Opinion No. 14,* paragraph 8.

requires accounting that understates interest expense of those who issue convertible debt and understates their contributed capital.[32]

In 1969, when the APB issued *Opinion 14,* options to purchase securities did not trade as widely as they do today. Perhaps now accounting can more easily comprehend the anomaly caused by stating convertible debt on the balance sheet of the borrower at original issue proceeds.[33]

WHO BENEFITS FROM THE REQUIRED REPORTING FOR CONVERTIBLE BONDS? Two beneficiaries of the required reporting appear:

1. Firms issuing convertible debt, which get to show lower interest expense (at the cost of showing higher leverage ratios[34]) than if they issued the same bonds without the convertibility feature, and
2. Auditors of firms issuing convertible debt, who need not judge management's estimate of the incremental borrowing rate of the identical issuer who issues nonconvertible debt.[35]

ANOMALY: TROUBLED DEBT RESTRUCTURINGS[36]

The aspect of a troubled debt restructuring pertinent for this discussion is that the lender makes concessions to a borrower in financial difficulty that the lender would not otherwise consider. The lender judges that it will be better off making concessions rather than trying to enforce the original agreement.

Take a simple example. Assume a firm borrows \$10,000, agreeing to repay \$11,000 in one year (implying an interest rate of ten percent). Just after origination, the borrower experiences a major uninsured fire loss. The lender decides not to force bankruptcy (which would require awaiting the outcome of the court proceeding) and agrees to accept a restructuring. The restructuring requires the borrower to pay \$11,000, not in one year as originally planned, but in five years.

Generally accepted accounting principles for troubled debt restructurings cover two conceptually different cases:

[32]Some view the accounting issue as being governed by the inseparability of the debt and the conversion option. Because, the argument goes, the holder cannot separate the two features, one must account for them as a single item, shown as debt. Paragraph 7 of *APB Opinion No. 14* argues the point of inseparability, but it does not indicate why inseparability of the financial instrument implies inseparability of the accounting for the instrument.

[33]A thorough airing of this issue will recognize that callable debt, too, is incorrectly accounted for in GAAP in light of the lessons of modern financial economics. The call feature has a value (to the issuer, cost to the buyer) separate from the contractual payments. This value can, in principle, be separately accounted for.

[34]Current GAAP results in higher debt/equity ratios than would result from separating the convertibility feature from the straight-debt feature.

[35]Since 1969, other GAAP pronouncements, such as those on leases, have required the auditor to estimate an incremental borrowing rate.

[36]I have adapted the description here from S. Davidson, L. J. Hanouille, C. P. Stickney, and R. L. Weil, *Intermediate Accounting: An Introduction to Concepts, Methods, and Uses,* 4th ed., Hinsdale, IL: The Dryden Press, 1985, 821–827.

1. the borrower gives the lender assets or equities to settle the debt, or
2. the borrower agrees to pay cash to the lender, but in lesser amounts or at later times, or both, than originally planned.

Only the second of these ignores the time value of money.

Continuing with the illustration above, assume that after the fire, the borrowing firm's borrowing rate increases to 15 percent per year (from 10 percent per year). Then the present value of the lender's expected repayments decreases from \$10,000 to \$5,469 (= \$11,000 × .49718). If one believes that the restructuring is an arm's-length transaction, then the fire and restructuring have together resulted in a lender's loss (and a borrower's gain) of \$4,531 (= \$10,000 − \$5,469). The criteria stated above lead to a conclusion that troubled debt restructurings require discounting. The FASB, of course, thought otherwise. It provided justification for its view in *SFAS No. 15.*[37]

> The Board found persuasive the arguments that a creditor in a troubled debt restructuring is interested in protecting its unrecovered investment . . . and, if possible, obtaining a return. To the creditor, therefore, the effect of a restructuring that provides for a recovery of the investment is to reduce the rate of return (the effective interest rate) between the restructuring and maturity. . . .
>
> [T]he Statement is based solidly on the need to consider the effect of interest. Indeed, the Board's conclusion is that a troubled debt restructuring affects primarily the effective interest rate and results in no loss or gain as long as the effective rate does not fall below zero.

In the sentences just quoted, by *effective interest rate* the FASB means the internal rate of return on a series of cash flows. It does not mean the interest rate referred to in paragraph 13 of *APB Opinion No. 21,* quoted above. In *Opinion No. 21,* the APB recognized the importance of future cash flows and market rates of interest, not of amounts designated by the parties as principal or interest. For troubled debt restructurings, the Board has chosen to view the amount of principal, the recorded investment, as fixed and independent of the interest rate earned on that investment.

As discussed further below, the FASB does not view modification of debt terms as an exchange requiring accounting recognition. I believe, however, that the renegotiation leading to a troubled debt restructuring is an arm's-length transaction, although the lender may not be as free to bargain with its current borrower as it would with someone who had not yet borrowed. The troubled loans occurred in the past and the losses are sunk costs. The forward-looking lender has negotiated the best deal it could under the circumstances. No one coerced it. When a business engages in a transaction voluntarily, historical cost accounting typically records the transaction.

A similar anomaly arises in the accounting for banks' non-performing loans. In a non-performing loan, the borrower is not now paying interest and the accountant judges the borrower will likely not pay it. When a bank holds a non-performing loan, accounting stops the accrual of interest on the loan, but does not write down the loan asset to the present value of future cash receipts.

[37]Paragraphs 147 and 148.

WHO BENEFITS FROM THE REQUIRED (NON)-DISCOUNTING OF TROUBLED DEBT RESTRUCTURINGS? The lenders who agree to troubled debt restructurings benefit from the required accounting: their assets and income are higher in the periods immediately following the restructuring than if the accounting recognized the economic substance of the restructuring.

At the time the FASB was considering this subject, many bank loans involving large amounts were in default. Bankers told the FASB that if they had to report losses on debt restructurings, then they would not engage in them. The banks agreed that the accounting for the restructuring does not change the reality of economic loss. Bank regulations look to historical cost accounting books, not necessarily at the economic substance of transactions. So, whether the historical cost records show loss would therefore matter because of regulators' behavior. While I criticize the FASB for its pronouncement on this subject, it is easy to see how the regulation of banks and their importance in our economy may have led to the actual result. The fault, if any, lies in bank regulators' choice of regulatory accounting principles.

ANOMALY: DEFERRED INCOME TAXES

In 1966, the APB said about discounting deferred income taxes[38]

> One of the questions now being considered is whether certain long-term tax allocation accounts should be determined on a discounted basis as recommended in [*Accounting Research Study No. 9,* "Interperiod Allocation of Corporate Income Taxes"]. . . . Pending further consideration of this subject and the broader aspects of discounting as it is related to financial accounting in general and until the Board reaches a conclusion on this subject, it is the Board's opinion that . . . deferred taxes should not be accounted for on a discounted basis.

In 1967, the APB said[39] "The Board's opinion . . . [quoted in the preceding paragraph] continues in effect pending further study of the broader aspects of discounting. . . ."

In 1971, the APB said[40]

> In paragraph 6 of *APB Opinion No. 10,* Omnibus—1966, the Board concluded that deferred income taxes should not be accounted for on a discounted (present value) basis. That conclusion is not modified by this Opinion.

Note that by 1971, the Board omits the reference to "pending further study," which had qualified its conclusions in 1966 and 1967.

In 1987, the APB said[41]

> Conceptual issues, such as whether discounting income taxes is appropriate, and implementation issues associated with discounting income taxes are numerous and complex. . . . The Board decided not to consider those issues at this time.

[38]*APB Opinion No. 10,* paragraph 6.

[39]*APB Opinion No. 11,* paragraph 3.

[40]*APB Opinion No. 21,* footnote 3, referred to in paragraph 4.

[41]*SFAS No. 96* paragraph 172.

> Board members who favor that decision do so for a number of reasons. Some . . . oppose discounting because of the complexity. . . . Other[s] believe that discounting should be addressed in a broader context than just accounting for income taxes.

Simultaneously, the FASB, for the first time, labeled as a liability the balance sheet credit balance for deferred taxes. It reasoned that the deferred tax items have the characteristics of liabilities—non-avoidable obligation to transfer assets at a reasonably specific future time and the transaction obligating the entity has already happened.[42]

Before 1987, accounting referred to the balance sheet item for deferred taxes as a "deferred credit" (or charge).[43] Some observers suggest that this approach viewed book/tax timing differences as amounts currently saved, therefore requiring no discounting. But in 1987 the FASB recognized the deferred tax items as liabilities. The method required for computing the amount at each balance sheet date involves constructing a schedule of reversals of temporary differences, year by year. In light of the changes, the only barrier to discounting these amounts is to choose the discount rate. Because taxes are a senior claim on a firm's assets, the correct discount rate is the firm's first-line borrowing rate. Not discounting deferred taxes implies a discount rate of zero, which I think is wrong.

WHO BENEFITS FROM THE REQUIRED ACCOUNTING FOR DEFERRED INCOME TAXES? Firms with large deferred income tax liabilities have the larger liabilities, smaller income amounts in early years, smaller owners' equity accounts, and larger debt-equity ratios resulting from the non-discounting. Accountants benefit from not having to audit management's estimate of the correct discount rate.

ANOMALY: DEPOSITS, SUCH AS THOSE IN LIEU OF TAXES

Consider a firm making (or receiving) a cash deposit, expecting to get (pay) it back, dollar for dollar. Such a firm records the asset (or liability) at the amount of cash paid (or received). *APB Opinion 21* requires this accounting,[44] no matter how much time will elapse before the depositor receives return of the cash. The required accounting overstates assets of the paying firm and liabilities of the receiving firm, relative to the economic benefit or burden of the payment. The paying firm never explicitly recognizes the economic loss from giving up control of cash. The receiving firm never explicitly recognizes the benefit from having interest-free use of cash. Material amounts of advance deposits not repaid for many years are rare in practice, which might explain accounting's failure to mention discounting for the item.

Example One extreme example appeared at the Emerging Issues Task Force (EITF) in 1988.[45] The Revenue Act of 1987 allows partnerships and S Corporations to retain their

---

[42] *Ibid.*, paragraphs 83–89.

[43] *APB Opinion No. 11,* paragraph 56.

[44] Paragraph 3.c.

[45] *EITF Issue 88–4,* "Classification of Payment Made to IRS to Retain Fiscal Year," prepared by Price Waterhouse and disposed of by the EITF at its meeting on January 28, 1988.

fiscal years, provided they make a single-payment annual deposit which approximates the income tax the partners would have paid on the short-period income had the entity switched to the calendar year. Each year, the entity adjusts the amount of the deposit based on the entity's prior year's income, making further payment or receiving a refund. Thus, a going concern expecting to be stable or growing in profitability, has made a deposit of cash that it will not get back soon.

The EITF considered three treatments of the deposit:

1. Record the payment as an expense;
2. Record the payment as a deposit (an asset);
3. Record the payment as a debit to owners' equity accounts.

It adopted the second option and gave little consideration to the first. It gave none to discounting the asset even when the firm can reasonably estimate the timing of refund.[46] The first, rejected, alternative reflects the economic substance when the firm expects not to receive the payment until much time has elapsed. The second, adopted, alternative would reflect the economic substance when the firm anticipates receiving a refund, provided the firm recorded the asset at its present value. The firm would charge the difference between cash payment and the present value of refund to income in the period when it pays the cash[47] and amortize the discount to income over the life of the deposit, just as with a single-payment note.

WHO BENEFITS FROM THE (NON)-DISCOUNTING OF DEPOSITS. The firm making the deposit can show larger assets and larger income than it would if it were to record as asset only the present value of the asset representing the right to receive return of the deposit. (All, or nearly all, of the public accounting members of the EITF are thus able to show higher income than would result from a discounting treatment.[48]) A firm receiving a deposit shows larger liabilities and smaller income than under a discounting treatment. Accountants benefit from not having to audit management's estimate of the time until expected return of the deposit or the appropriate discount rate.

ANOMALY: PRODUCT WARRANTIES

When a firm makes sales under a warranty agreement, it can neither identify the specific customers who will receive warranty benefits nor ascertain the amounts of their claims. In some firms, experience provides information for estimating both the likely proportion of customers who will make claims and their probable amounts. In such a case, the firm must debit expense and credit an estimated liability for the cost expected to fulfill the warranty promises.

---

[46]Although the EITF minutes do not provide evidence for this version of its history, I attended the meeting and observed the deliberation. Some view the tax deposit as the flip side of deferred tax liabilities, where the discounting issue has been specifically deferred by the FASB. The EITF, at least, did not discuss this point on January 28, 1988.

[47]If the firm is a going concern, expecting to be stable or growing in profitability indefinitely, then the present value of the refund is zero and the accounting would charge the entire deposit to expense.

[48]No one at the EITF meeting on January 28, 1988, raised any issue that those voting on this issue were taking a position that affected their own financial statements.

Now, GAAP does not discount the amounts for warranty costs, overstating liabilities and understating owners' equity.

WHO BENEFITS FROM THE REQUIRED (NON)-DISCOUNTING OF PRODUCT WARRANTIES? Only the accountant, saved the judgment of checking management's estimates—both of the future cash flows and of the correct discount rate—benefits. The firm giving the warranties reports expenses earlier in larger amounts than discounting would entail.

ANOMALY: PLANT ASSET WRITE-DOWNS

A firm acquires property, plant, and equipment because the present value of the future cash inflows (or savings of outflows) exceeds its cost. When the firm acquires property, it records the property at cost and bases future depreciation charges on that cost.

Now, assume that, after acquiring the property, the firm reduces the estimate of expected future cash flows. Before *SFAS No. 90* (which applies only to regulated industries), accounting delayed recognizing this diminution in expected cash flows. In current GAAP, a write down occurs only when the estimated future cash flows sum to less than the net book value of the item. Then, the usual accounting writes down the asset to the summed expected future cash flows.

As recently as *SFAS No. 86* (1985), the FASB decided not to require write-down of balance sheet assets unless the book value exceeds the summed *undiscounted* future net cash flows from the asset. The Statement, which treats capitalized computer software costs, does not specifically mention discounting. Accounting appears to allow discounting in this computation, although most accountants in practice would not discount and some might judge discounting prohibited.

While I do not try to state the conditions under which plant write-downs *should* occur, I find anomalous, however, the ignoring of the time value of money when such write-downs *do* occur. The accountant has re-estimated future cash flows (and found their sum less than book value). Rather than merely sum those numbers, one can sum the present values of those numbers. If the firm does not write the property down to the present value of its future cash flows, then the operating statements reflecting use of that property will distort results. The operating statement will show lower rates of return for the property than the firm earns on its current investments.

Writing in 1963, Davidson[49] adapted an example presented by Green and Sorter[50] to illustrate the point:

> A machine now owned by a firm has a book value of $5,000, nominal resale value and a remaining estimated life of 5 years. It is capable of producing a given quantity of product at an annual out-of-pocket cost of $1,600. A new machine has been developed which costs $5,000 and will also last 5 years but which is capable of turning out the same quantity of product at a yearly out-of-pocket cost of only $1,000. Clearly it is not worthwhile to replace the existing machine with

---

[49] S. Davidson, "The Day of Reckoning: Accounting Theory and Management Analysis," *Journal of Accounting Research,* I, 2(Autumn 1963), 117–126. The quotation is taken from page 120.

[50] D. Green, Jr. and G. H. Sorter, "Accounting for Obsolescence—A Proposal," *The Accounting Review,* XXXIV, 3(July 1959), 433–441.

> a new machine costing $5,000 in order to realize the five annual cost savings of $600 each. However, it is equally clear that a firm newly entering this field would select the new model rather than the old. . . . [I]n years following the correct decision not to replace, income reported by the firm is lower than it would have been had the incorrect decision been made. . . . [R]eported depreciation in the two cases would be the same since undepreciated cost of the old asset and purchase price of the new are the same and both have five years of service remaining. Out-of-pocket operating costs with the old equipment would be higher. As a result, operating income reported with the old equipment would be less than that shown if the replacement had been made. Sound managerial analysis would lead to the correct decision not to replace, but the pay-off for the correct decision would be lower reported earnings. A more appropriate accounting treatment, in my opinion, would write down the old asset to a point which indicates its operating inferiority to the new asset. A nonoperating loss would be recognized at the time of the replacement analysis. In this way depreciation charges for the old asset in later years would be lower and its annual reported income would be no lower than with the new asset. . . .

While Davidson did not discuss the amount of the write-down called for in his second paragraph, the write-down would be such that future rates of returns for the old asset will equal those of the new asset. The initial book value to achieve that goal is the net present value of the cash flows from operating the old asset. The discount rate is the internal rate of return earned from an investment in the new asset, assuming there were no old one. In *SFAS No. 89,*[51] the FASB defined "value in use" of an asset as

> The amount determined by discounting the future cash flows (including the ultimate proceeds of disposal) expected to be derived from use of an asset at an appropriate rate that allows for the risk of the activities concerned.

The amount, value in use, is the correct book value after it has been written down for partial obsolescence, so one computes the writedown by subtracting the "value in use" from book value before write down.

Testing for technological obsolescence of each piece of machinery or equipment would be expensive, likely not cost-effective. Still, GAAP could establish the principle of write down for obsolescence, and let the usual criteria for materiality govern its practical implementation.

WHO BENEFITS FROM THE REQUIRED (NON)-REPORTING OF PLANT WRITE DOWNS? Two beneficiaries of the required reporting appear:

1. Firms which do not have to write down plant until the future cash flows have diminished to such an extent that write-down becomes necessary under current GAAP can delay reporting losses,[52] and

---

[51]Paragraph 44.

[52]But as noted above, these firms show lower rates of return because of the inflated asset base.

2. Auditors who can delay the judgment of checking management's estimates both of the future cash flows (at least until their amounts come close to book value) and of the correct discount rate.

ANOMALY: NEGATIVE SALVAGE VALUES

The estimated costs for dismantling plant assets several decades after they begin operations can exceed in nominal dollars the summed cash flows from operating the asset. Accounting has not required that management discount these future costs when it constructs the original depreciation schedules.

Example A firm signs an agreement with an electric utility to provide coal; the utility will pay all operating costs of mining coal, dollar for dollar, plus $10 million in cash today for this privilege. At the time of completing the agreement, the firm's investment in the coal mine, based on its historical cost net of depletion, is $1 million. The firm estimates that it will abandon the depleted coal mine, ten years hence and spend an estimated $15 million to return the site to its natural state.

Although this deal results in an accounting loss of $6 million: $10 million in revenues less $16 (= $1 + $15) million in costs, it makes economic sense so long as the firm's cost of capital exceeds 5 percent. For example, at a 12 percent discount rate, the present value of the site-cleanup costs is $4.83 (= $15 × .32197) million. The economic profit is about $4.2 (= $10.0 − $1.0 − $4.8) million.[53]

The accounting for such a deal is unsettled. Many accountants would, today, record the signing of this agreement by recognizing a $6 million loss. This leads, I believe, to an anomalous result. Under current GAAP, the firm would probably structure the deal to avoid this accounting result. It could, for example, ask that the utility pay $5.2 million today and $15 million in ten years, instead of $10 million today. This alternate payment schedule, discounted at 12 percent, has a present value of $10 million.[54]

An accounting unable to recognize the present value of the site-cleanup costs at the time the firm makes the agreement cannot report the project as profitable.[55]

WHO BENEFITS FROM THE (NON)-DISCOUNTING OF NEGATIVE SALVAGE VALUE? Only the accountant, saved the judgment of checking management's estimates—both of the future cash flows and of the correct discount rate—benefits. The firm loses the ability to report

---

[53]Some readers have suggested that if accounting were such that the firm recognizes a $4.2 million profit based on discounting clean-up costs at 12 percent, management would take steps to protect this profit from subsequent interest rate changes. Management could use asset securitization techniques, for example. Whether accounting's use of discounting would indeed encourage management to protect economic profits that have become accounting profits can be answered only by observing behavior after such a change. Whether such management steps is a good or a bad thing remains an open question.

[54]For simplicity, I have used 12 percent as the discount rate in both parts of this example. In the first part, the discount rate is the mine owner's borrowing rate. In the second, it is the utility's.

[55]The long-term income of the firm does not, of course, change as a result of accounting's failure to report income from this particular project. The firm that undertakes the profitable project will report larger future investment income or smaller future interest expense than had it avoided the project.

the economic substance of the transaction and the investor incurs additional cost to understand the report.

SUMMARY: WHO BENEFITS FROM FAILURE TO DISCOUNT?

This review of GAAP has identified the following anomalies resulting from GAAP's failure to require discounting:[56]

1. convertible bond debt,
2. troubled debt restructurings,
3. deferred income taxes,
4. deposits,
5. product warranties,
6. plant asset write-downs, and
7. negative salvage value.

In every case, the accountant need not make judgmental estimates—and the auditor need not confirm those estimates. Research has been unable to identify other groups who systematically gain from the current configuration of GAAP or who would systematically lose from its change.

The current system of rewards and punishments treats accountants' liability for misestimates asymmetrically. Make good estimates and break even (avoid liability); make bad estimates and sometimes lose, perhaps large amounts. One can understand accountants' reluctance to inject increased use of estimates in the basic accounting model. If auditors believe that fees would adequately compensate them for taking the risks of making judgments of this sort, then one cannot conclude that auditors are benefitted by accounting's current failure to require discounting in the enumerated settings.

POLITICS OF THE TIME VALUE OF MONEY. Raymond Lauver brought to my attention the following notion. Seldom, if ever, in the history of setting GAAP have banks lost an argument on an issue about which they have lobbied strongly.[57] The history of the treatment of the time value of money is consistent with this notion even though the notion does not explain all the anomalies. The notion itself requires explanation: why do banks, as opposed to other industries, have such lobbying clout that they alone can overwhelm the promulgators. In any event, financial institutions seem less likely to prevail in anti-economic arguments in the future which will follow the savings and loan crisis of the last few years. Indeed it may be argued that the banks were caught in their own trap as the failure of financial statements of

---

[56]Analysis suggests that each of these seven satisfies each of the three criteria discussed earlier for an item to be discounted.

[57]The current treatment—not revaluing loan assets to reflect the time value of money—gives banks opportunity to manipulate income and capital by the timing of transactions. The accounting issue may be more an issue of market value accounting than one of consistent treatment of the time value of money, although the GAAP treatment of troubled debt restructurings clearly is pertinent to this issue. For a discussion of market value accounting in the context of banks, see W. H. Beaver, S. Datar, and M. A. Wolfson, "The Role of Market Value Accounting in the Regulation of Insured Depository Institutions," in Barth, Brumbaugh, and Stiglitz, editors, *Reform of Deposit Insurance and the Regulation of Depository Institutions in the 1990s: Setting the Agenda,* Ballinger, Inc., forthcoming.

borrowers to reflect economic losses on a timely basis contributed to the credit losses suffered by financial institutions.

EDUCATION AND THE TIME VALUE OF MONEY. During the time (approximately 1945–1980) when promulgating bodies issued most accounting principles described in this article, mature practicing accounting professionals appear not to have fully comprehended the arithmetic of compound interest. The literature contains analysis using the word *complex* in discussions of the issues. We can sympathize with promulgators who cannot persuade a constituency which does not understand.

The generation of professionals who found compound interest to be complex is no longer in command. The current generation seems comfortable with compound interest arithmetic. Some even see how it can be simpler than the alternative. Consider, for example, the straight-line amortization method of bond premium and discount. Moreover, a profession which has learned to deal with the complexities of leveraged lease transactions (requirement promulgated in 1976) and interest rate hedges or swaps can comprehend compound interest computations.

REASONS STATED IN GAAP FOR EXPLICIT REQUIREMENTS NOT TO DISCOUNT

Earlier discussion identified only four places where GAAP explicitly prohibits discounting. Here, I review these four and the reasons GAAP provides for nondiscounting.

1. Deferred Income Taxes

   APB Opinion No. 10, paragraph 6, prohibited discounting "[p]ending further consideration of this subject and the broader aspects of discounting as it is related to financial accounting in general. . . ." After more than 20 years with no further consideration nor analysis, maybe now is the time to act.

2. Convertible Bond Debt

   In *APB Opinion No. 14,* the APB did not explicitly prohibit the discounting of the straight-debt portion of the combined debt/option financial instrument. Its sole justification, in paragraph 12, was that

> no portion of the proceeds from the issuance . . . should be accounted for as attributable to the conversion feature. . . . [T]he Board places greater weight on the inseparability of the debt and the conversion option . . . and less weight on practical difficulties.

Opinion 14 contained this dissent:

> while the debt obligation and the conversion feature coexist in a hybrid instrument, such fact is not a logical reason for failing to account separately for their individual values.

The reasoning of the dissent remains as valid today as in 1969 or in 1966 (when the APB in its Omnibus *Opinion No. 10*) separated the debt and equity portions of the convertible bond. The 1969 action by the APB did require separate accounting treatment for the debt and equity portions of debt issued with detachable warrants. As my colleague Sidney Davidson says, this may be the only time that GAAP raised perforations to the level of an accounting principle.

3. Liabilities to Provide Goods or Services

APB *Opinion No. 21* gives no explicit reasons for the required nondiscounting of obligations to provide goods and services. There is probably an implicit assumption that the amounts and timing of future cash flows are sufficiently uncertain to preclude discounting.

Even if the amounts and timing of future cash flows were certain, discounting the obligation would leave an unallocated credit balance. Is that credit revenue? No—accounting has never allowed a firm to record earnings for the receipt of cash before the rendering of services. Therefore, recording the obligation at less than the amount of cash received results in the recording of a liability.

Consider a simplified example. A firm receives $100 cash today to provide services two years hence. The services will cost $80 to deliver. At a discount rate of 10 percent per year, the future value of $100 two years hence is $121. To use present value computations for the obligation while not recognizing earnings before the firm renders service, accounting must make the following journal entry:

Dr.	Cash	100.00	
Dr.	Discount on Service Obligation	21.00	
	Cr. Service Obligation		121.00

Over the two-year period before the firm performs the services, it will reduce the discount to zero, amortizing the amounts to expense, using the effective interest method. When the firm performs the services, the Service Obligation, net of its contra, would have increased to $121. The firm then recognizes earnings of $41 (= $121 − $80). When compared to current GAAP, the effect is to increase reported expense during the holding period and to increase reported earnings in the performance period.

4. Troubled Debt Restructurings

Paragraph 137 of *SFAS No. 15* states the case for discounting the debt instruments using a current interest rate at the time of restructuring. The argument stands on the foundation that a restructuring results from an exchange transaction. The FASB responded to this argument in paragraph 145 by saying,

> The Board concluded that since a troubled debt restructuring involving modifications of terms of debt does not involve transfers of resources or obligations (paragraph 77), restructured debt should continue to be accounted for in the existing accounting framework, on the basis of the recorded investment. . . .

The FASB's nondiscounting treatment rests on the foundation that such modification does *not* result from an exchange.[58] This appears to be an excuse, not a reason. If the FASB concluded that the modification exchanged one set of terms for another, the reasoning would be as

[58]In paragraph 151 of *SFAS No. 15,* the FASB states that it believed it had achieved consistency of its views with received accounting doctrine (GAAP promulgated as of that time) because "modifications of terms of continuing debt are different in substance from exchanges of resources or obligations. . . ."

valid. Note, for example, that GAAP recognize the decline in market value of a portfolio of marketable equity securities. To support the case for lower of cost or market for equity securities, some argue that the method is conservative. Then, the argument proceeds, because conservatism is an overriding principle in the historical cost accounting model, using lower of cost or market is correct in GAAP. This reasoning applies equally to the accounting by the holder of troubled debt instruments.

CHOOSING AN INTEREST RATE

I have suggested that the rate appropriate for discounting is an estimate of the rate the market would use to value a financial instrument issued by the firm making the promises. This is not the same as the rate the firm incurs when it raises funds—its average cost of capital—or the rate the firm uses in making its capital budgeting decisions for projects of average risk for the firm.

The cost of capital for a specific investment is an opportunity cost, the rate the firm could earn on other investments of comparable risk. Firms often measure a firm-wide cost of capital by computing the weighted-average cost of all the liabilities and owners' equity in the balance sheet. The resulting number is not the firm's cost of capital; it is a measurement of the cost of capital of the average project of the firm. Each project has its own cost of capital—the rate of return required to induce the firm to undertake it. In this sense, the appropriate discount rate for a given stream of expected cash flows is *its* cost of capital, but this may or may not equal the measured cost of capital just described.

If accounting requires discounting in situations meeting the criteria outlined at the beginning of this discussion, the accountant must sometimes estimate a discount rate. Consider, for example, deferred taxes or liabilities for future deliveries of goods and services. Accountants could spend much energy trying to approximate the theoretically correct rate, identified in *APB Opinion No. 21*[59] as "the rate which would have resulted if an independent lender had negotiated a similar transaction under comparable terms and conditions."

Not to discount is to use a zero discount rate. This misses the mark. GAAP could specify that accountants use some arbitrary rate, for example ten percent, in all circumstances where discounting is appropriate. To be conservative, the rule might be to use a high discount rate, say 15 percent, for asset valuations and a low discount rate, say 10 percent, for liability valuations.

While this proposed surrogate for the correct rate is arbitrary, GAAP has used arbitrary cut-offs before. Consider, for example, the maximum amortization period for intangibles (40 years), the presumed cut-off ("burden of proof" ownership test) for the equity method (20 percent), and the coupon rate where accounting judges a convertible bond to be a common stock equivalent (two-thirds of the prime rate at the date of bond issued).[60]

Exhibit 1 shows some effects of using an approximate discount rate, rather than zero. Refer to the panel for the "correct" discount rate of 12 percent per year and the five-year row. Note that using a ten percent rate errs by less than ten percent of the correct amount. In contrast, not discounting (using a zero percent discount rate) errs by over 75 percent of the correct amount.

---

[59] *APB Opinion No. 21,* paragraph 13.

[60] *SFAS No. 55* (1982), which substituted the AAA bond yield for the bank prime rate, subsequently amended this test.

EXHIBIT 1

Illustrations of Approximations to Correct Present Values from Using Varying Interest Rates

Present Values of $1,000 Due in 2, 5, and 10 Years at Various Interest Rates

	Discount Rate Used				
Years to Payment	**0%**	**5%**	**10%**	**12%**	**15%**
2	$1,000	$907	$826	$797	$756
5	1,000	784	621	567	497
10	1,000	614	386	322	247

Errors in Present Value from Using Incorrect Discount Rate [See Note]

Assuming 5 Percent Is Correct Discount Rate

	Discount Rate Used				
Years to Payment	**0%**	**5%**	**10%**	**12%**	**15%**
2	10.3%	0.0%	−8.9%	−12.1%	−16.6%
5	27.6	0.0	−20.8	−27.6	−36.5
10	62.9	0.0	−37.2	−47.6	−59.7

Assuming 12 Percent Is Correct Discount Rate

	Discount Rate Used				
Years to Payment	**0%**	**5%**	**10%**	**12%**	**15%**
2	25.4%	13.8%	3.7%	0.0%	−5.1%
5	76.2	38.1	9.4	0.0	−12.4
10	210.6	90.7	19.7	0.0	−23.2

Assuming 15 Percent Is Correct Discount Rate

	Discount Rate Used				
Years to Payment	**0%**	**5%**	**10%**	**12%**	**15%**
2	32.3%	20.0%	9.3%	5.4%	0.0%
5	101.1	57.6	24.9	14.1	0.0
10	304.6	148.4	56.0	30.3	0.0

Note: Error is defined as the number one subtracted from the computed number divided by the correct number. For example, in the 12% panel, 2-year row, 10% column, the number 3.7% is $826/$797 − 1.

CONFORMING THE INTEREST RATE TO THE TREATMENT OF RISING PRICES

Sometimes, the amount of an obligation discharged in the future depends on uncertain future prices, as in the cases of negative salvage values and product warranty obligations, discussed above. When the accountant makes estimates of future payments for specific goods and services, will those estimates be based on expected future costs or on current costs for equivalent goods and services? The correct discount rate will depend on the choice.[61] If forecasts of future cash flows involve nominal (that is, actual) dollar amounts, then the discount rate should include anticipated general inflation. If forecasts involve real dollar cash flows, then discount using a rate that excludes anticipated inflation. Some accountants argue that if the firm bases the expected future cost on today's costs, without escalation, then discounting is not necessary. Conversely, moreover, they argue that when the expected future costs contain escalation for inflation, not to discount is wrong.

Mere general inflation, without change in relative prices, removes the need to forecast the rate of anticipated inflation because the effects of general inflation and anticipated inflation would cancel each other. Mere general inflation without change in relative prices is unlikely. The accountant will, therefore, have to estimate the increase in the specific costs at issue as well as the general inflation part of interest rates. The accountant cannot assume that future general inflation and future increases in specific costs at issue will cancel.

CONCLUSION

The review and analysis here suggest that accounting treats discounting haphazardly, that inconsistencies have arisen in practice, and that a single conceptual set of criteria consistent with the historical cost accounting model exists to achieve coherence in historical cost accounting for amounts of cash paid or collected in the future. One might wonder why the FASB's conceptual framework has not been more successful in dealing with these issues. When the FASB first began, in 1978, to issue *Statements of Financial Accounting Concepts,* it explicitly stated that the new concepts would not by themselves overturn an existing accounting pronouncement.[62] Because the anomalies reported here arise in particular pronouncements no general *Concepts* statement could correct them.

I believe that the current state of accounting for the time value of money is due to exceptional lobbying power on the part of banks and other financial institutions and the apparent discomfort of many accountants with compound interest arithmetic. The savings and loan crisis seems to be reducing the clout of the banking industry while the accounting profession is becoming more comfortable with compound interest. The Task Force on Interest Methods is likely to find a more benign environment than it would have found even five years ago.

[61]Market interest rates reflect three separate phenomena: (1) a pure or real rate reflecting the productive capability of capital assets, (2) a risk factor reflecting the likelihood of default of the specific borrower, and (3) a premium reflecting inflation expected to occur over the life of the loan. Some would say that interest rates include a fourth factor: a premium for liquidity, so that all else equal, loans for short periods of time carry lower rates than those for longer periods.

[62]See the unnumbered paragraphs, particularly the fourth one, preceding the Table of Contents of *SFAC No. 1* (1978).

APPENDIX

Required, Permitted, Prohibited Uses and Other Mentions of Discounting in Authoritative Pronouncements

Date and Pronouncement	Discounting Treatment	Item
12/66 APB Opinion No. 10 paragraph 6	No	Deferred income taxes.
12/67 APB Opinion No. 11 paragraph 3	No	Deferred income taxes.
12/67 APB Opinion No. 12 paragraph 6, fnt. 1	Must	Accrue costs by end of active employment for deferred compensation payments equal to their present value.
3/69 APB Opinion No. 14 paragraph 12	No	Convertible bond debt.[63]
8/70 APB Opinion No. 16 paragraph 88.g	Must	Accounts and notes payable, long-term debt, and other claims payable acquired in business combination.
paragraph 88.i	Must	Other liabilities and commitments, including leases, contracts, and plant closing costs acquired in business combination.
8/70 APB Opinion No. 17 paragraph 25	Must	Discount to present value liabilities incurred in acquiring intangible assets.
8/71 APB Opinion No. 21 paragraph 3.a–f	No	Receivable and payables to be settled within one year; amounts received currently for goods or services to be provided in the future[64]; security deposits; cash lending activities of financial institutions; transactions where interest rates are affected by tax attributes or legal restrictions imposed by governmental regulations.
paragraph 4	Not required	Obligations assumed in connection with sales such as product warranties.
paragraphs 11 & 12	Must	Receivables representing contractual right to receive money or payables representing contractual obligations to pay money on fixed or determinable dates (when rights or privileges have been exchanged).

(continued)

[63]Because the debt must be booked originally at the cash proceeds received, rather than at the present value of the cash payments promised discounted at the borrower's current borrowing rate, discounting is effectively prohibited, although no specific words directly prohibiting discounting actually appear in the statement.

[64]Note that AICPA Accounting Interpretation of APB *Opinion No. 21,* June 1972, allows nondiscounting even when cash must be repaid in the event goods or services are not delivered.

APPENDIX (CONTINUED)

10/72 APB Opinion No. 26 paragraph 3.c	Must	Discount to present value liabilities issued to retire outstanding debt.
3/75 FASB Stmnt. No. 5	May[65]	Loss contingencies.
11/76 FASB Stmnt. No. 13 paragraph 5(1)		Defines "incremental borrowing rate" as "the rate that . . . the lessee would have incurred to borrow over a similar term the funds necessary to purchase the leased asset."
paragraph 10	Must	Minimum lease payments by lessee, subject to fair market value of leased property.
paragraph 17	Must	Minimum lease receivables and unguaranteed residual value of lessor in sales-type lease to compute unearned income from lease.
paragraph 18	Must	Minimum lease receivables and unguaranteed residual value of lessor in direct financing lease to compute unearned income from lease.
6/77 FASB Stmnt. No. 15 paragraphs 16, 17 & 18	No	Contractual payments to be made by a debtor under a troubled debt restructuring.[66]
paragraphs 30, 31 & 32	No	Contractual collections to be received by a creditor under a troubled debt restructuring.
12/77 FASB Stmnt. No. 19 Dissent		Two dissenters argue that discounted cash flow methods are sufficiently reliable to be used for oil/gas reserve disclosures.
9/79 FASB Stmnt. No. 33 paragraph 63b	Must	Future cash flows from using and then disposing of an asset in computing "recoverable amount" in computing current costs of asset.
12/79 FASB Tech. Bull. 79-12 paragraph 3		Allows the use of a secured borrowing rate as the incremental borrowing rate for a lessee.
9/80 FASB Stmnt. No. 38 paragraph 5a	May; must[67]	Preacquisition contingencies recorded at "fair value," presumably requiring discounting.

[65] *SFAS No. 5* is silent on the amounts to be accrued. *FASB Interpretation No. 14,* 1976, addresses the amounts, but does not mention discounting. It seems likely that some accountants would not discount and others would. Informal surveys indicate that accountants tend to discount when the difference between nominal and discounting is material.

[66] Rather, the book value of the debt is left as is, and future accounting is based on the internal rate of return given that book value and the future contractual cash flows.

[67] The item must be recorded at "fair value," which cannot, in an economic sense, be much different from discounted present value. Still, discounting is not explicitly required.

APPENDIX (CONTINUED)

10/80 FASB Stmnt. No. 39 paragraph 48	Silent[68]	Says, "A measurement that reflects the net present value of the cash flows from an asset, if it has sufficient reliability, may provide a useful basis for the assessment of overall enterprise performance."
FASB Stmnt. No. 40 paragraph 23		Says, ". . . The second approach [estimating the net present value of cash flows to be derived from the asset] would depend on estimates of the discount rate,. . . . Even if quantities were estimatable with acceptability, future prices and costs would be highly uncertain. . . . Accordingly, the Board was not satisfied that fair value would meet the minimum standards of reliability appropriate to inclusion in financial reporting."
3/81 FASB Stmnt. No. 45 paragraph 7	Silent	Portion of initial franchise fees deferred to cover costs of future services.[69]
3/81 FASB Stmnt. No. 47 paragraph 8	May; need not	Unconditional purchase obligations, such as throughput contracts or take-or-pay contracts.[70]
6/81 FASB Stmnt. No. 48 paragraph 7	May[71]	Revenues and costs of goods sold when right of return exists and amounts can be estimated with reasonable precision and returns will occur more than one year hence.
12/81 FASB Stmnt. No. 53 paragraph 9	Must	Discount to present value the future license fees for a film in computing the sales price of the film.

(continued)

[68]The opinion paragraphs of this statement make no reference to discounting, but the background material included in Appendix C of the statement contain the mention of discounting cited next.

[69]The amounts deferred should provide for a reasonable future profit, which, presumably includes a reasonable rate of return on investment. The statement, then, appears to call for discounting, but accountants seem not to interpret the rule this way in practice.

[70]Note that this item is merely disclosed, not recorded as a balance sheet liability.

[71]Paragraph 7 refers to *SFAS No. 5* for guidance on computation of amounts. As noted above, *SFAS No. 5* is silent on the amounts to be accrued. *FASB Interpretation No. 14,* 1976, addresses the amounts, but does not mention discounting. It seems likely that most accountants would not discount, but that the existing rules would allow it.

APPENDIX (CONTINUED)

6/82 FASB Stmnt. No. 60 paragraphs 10 & 21	Must	Estimated future insurance policy benefits less estimated future premiums to be collected from policy holders. Interest rate choice described in paragraph 22.
paragraph 18	Silent	Liability for unpaid claims.
paragraph 20	May	Claims adjustment expense for short-duration contracts.[72]
paragraph 35	Must	Premium deficiency.
6/82 FASB Stmnt. No. 63 paragraph 4	May	Broadcast license agreements; discussion in paragraphs 24–31.
9/82 FASB Stmnt. No. 65 paragraph 6	Must	Mortgage-backed securities transferred to investment account.
paragraph 18	Must	Compute discounted present value of servicing revenues over estimated future servicing costs and use net as lower bound on asset carrying value.
paragraph 26	Must	Stand-by commitments fees amortized to revenue using interest method, if practicable, during loan period.
10/82 FASB Stmnt. No. 66 paragraph 39	Must	Use present value computations in computing profits on sale of improvements to real estate.
paragraph 57	May	Use an interest rate less than the appropriate rate in discounting to present value an installment receivable on sale of real estate.
11/82 FASB Stmnt. No. 69 paragraph 30	Must	Use 10 percent discount rate in computing standardized measure of discounted future cash flows to be disclosed.
12/82 FASB Stmnt. No. 71 paragraph 20	Need not	Discount costs to be recovered by regulated enterprise when costs are to be recovered without return on investment and the costs would ordinarily be expenses in financial reporting.
paragraph 75	Need not	Discount costs to present value when rate regulation promises return of investment, but not return on investment.
8/83 FASB Stmnt. No. 74 (Later superseded) paragraph 2	Must	Discount to present value termination benefits offered to employees that are accepted under a program that lasts for a short time.

[72]Paragraph 20 is silent, but paragraph 60.d indicates that these costs may be discounted like those in paragraph 18.

APPENDIX (CONTINUED)

3/85 FASB Stmnt. No. 85 paragraph 3	Must	Consider yield to maturity in judging whether convertible securities are common stock equivalents.
3/85 FASB Tech. Bull. 85-2 paragraph 2, fnt. 5		Computes the "expected residual interest" in collateral of a collateralized mortgage obligation as the "present value of all amounts expected to revert to the issuer. . . ."
8/85 FASB Stmnt. No. 86 paragraph 10	Need not[73]	Discount to present value in computing net realizable value of software assets when comparing that amount to book value in judging need for write-down.
12/85 FASB Stmnt. No. 87 paragraph 16	Must	Discount to present value in computing service cost component of pension cost.
paragraph 16	Must	In computing projecting benefit obligation.
12/85 FASB Stmnt. No. 88 paragraph 15	Must	Discount to present value future payments for termination benefits.
12/86 FASB Stmnt. No. 89 paragraph 29		Defines "recoverable amount" in terms of "current worth" of net cash flows to be received from an asset.
paragraph 44		Defines "value in use" as discounted present value of future cash flows using a rate that allows for the risk of the activities involved.
12/86 FASB Stmnt. No. 90 paragraph 3.b	Must	Discount to present value expected future cash flows from plant being abandoned in computing book value of new asset being recorded. Must use incremental borrowing rate.
paragraph 6.b	Must	Use compound interest amortization of asset.
paragraph 7	Must	Reduce carrying value when return on investment has been disallowed; seems to require present value methods.[74]

(continued)

[73]This is another example where the pronouncement is silent. The user might judge, therefore, that discounting, because it makes sense here, is allowed.

[74]Others appear to read this paragraph differently. Here is the critical language:

> If part of the cost is explicitly, but indirectly, disallowed (for example, *by an explicit disallowance of return on investment on a portion of the plant*), *an equivalent amount of the cost shall be deducted* from the reported cost of the plant and recognized as a loss. [emphasis added]

Assume a plant is on the books for \$100 and had been expected to earn the firm's cost of capital, say 10 percent, and the return of 10 percent is disallowed. If the cost is recovered equally over five years at the rate of \$20 per year, then the present value of those payments, discounted at 10 percent, is \$75.82 (= 3.79079 × \$20). Paragraph 7 appears to require a write-down to \$75.82, which seems to be a requirement that the amounts be discounted.

APPENDIX (CONTINUED)

paragraph 39 & paragraph 51		Abandoned plant is essentially monetary, requiring discounting treatment & paragraph 47 following APB Opinion No. 21.
12/86 FASB Stmnt. No. 91		
paragraph 16	Must	Use interest method for loan origination fees when loans are purchased.
paragraph 18	Must	Use interest method for loan origination fees.
paragraph 58	May	Anticipate projected prepayments in applying interest method.
12/86 FASB Tech. Bull. 86-2		
paragraph 4		Mentions present value in valuing liabilities assumed as part of recorded cost of an interest in a leased asset's residual value.
8/87 FASB Stmnt. No. 92		
paragraphs 23 & 24	Must	Use discounting for phase-in plan that includes indirect disallowance.
12/87 FASB Stmnt. No. 96		
paragraph 6.b	May not	Discount deferred tax liabilities; refers to paragraph 6 of APB Opinion No. 10.
12/87 FASB Stmnt. No. 97		
paragraph 16	Must	Use interest method for investment contracts.
paragraphs 22–25	Must	Use compound interest amortization of capitalized acquisition costs.
3/90 FASB Stmnt. No. 105		
paragraph 8		Acknowledges the definition of discounting used elsewhere in accounting and in this article.

REFERENCES

Abramowicz, Ken, "Deferred Income Taxes: Why Aren't They Discounted?" D. R. Scott Memorial Lectures in Accountancy, XVI, 1987, pp. 45–54.

Aggarwal, Raj and Charles H. Gibson, *Discounting in Financial Accounting and Reporting,* Morristown, New Jersey: Financial Executives Research Foundation, 1989.

AICPA, Task Force on Discounting Applications of the Accounting Standards Division, "The Use of Discounting in Financial Reporting for Monetary Items with Uncertain Terms Other than Those Covered by Existing Authoritative Literature," New York: AICPA, Issues Paper dated September 9, 1987.

AICPA, Task Force on Impairment of Value of the Accounting Standards Division, "Accounting for the Inability to Fully Recover the Carrying Amounts of Long Lived Assets," New York: AICPA, Issues Paper dated July 15, 1980.

Bierman, Harold, Jr., "Deferred Taxes, Income and the 1986 Tax Reform Act," *Financial Analysts Journal,* 43, 3(May/June 1987), 72–73.

Chrystie, Thomas L. and Frank J. Fabozzi, *Left Hand Financing,* Homewood, IL: Dow Jones-Irwin, 1983.

Davidson, S. and R. L. Weil, "Deferred Taxes," *Journal of Accountancy,* 161, 3(March 1986), pp. 42–45.

Fetters, Michael L., Ph.D., CPA (Professor, Division of Accounting, Babson College) and John Leslie Livingstone, Ph.D., CPA (Professor and Chairman, Division of Accounting, Babson College), "How to Improve the Credibility of Financial Reporting? Reduce the Inconsistency Between GAAP Pronouncements," 1987.

Findlay, M. C. and E. E. Williams, "Opportunity Cost, Discounting, and Deferred Tax Liabilities: A Final Note," *Journal of Business Finance & Accounting,* 12, 2(Summer 1985), 183–185.

——— and ———, "Discounting Deferred Tax Liabilities: A Reply," *Journal of Business Finance & Accounting,* 8, 4(1981), 593–597.

Ijiri, Yuji, "*Historical Cost Accounting and its Rationality,*" Research Monograph Number 1, The Canadian Certified General Accountants' Research Foundation 1981, Price Printing Limited.

———, "*Recognition of Contractual Rights and Obligations: An Exploratory Study of Conceptual Issues,*" Research Report, High Ridge Park, Stamford, CT: Financial Accounting Standards Board of the Financial Accounting Foundation, December 1980.

Jeter, D. C. and P. K. Chaney, "A Financial Statement Analysis Approach to Deferred Taxes," *Accounting Horizons,* 2, 4(December 1988), 41–49.

Milburn, J. Alex, *Incorporating the Time Value of Money Within Financial Accounting,* Toronto: Canadian Institute of Chartered Accountants, 1988.

Nurnberg, Hugo, "Discounting Deferred Tax Liabilities," *The Accounting Review,* XLVII, 4(October 1972), 655–665.

Rayburn, Frank R., "Discounting of Deferred Income Taxes: An Argument for Reconsideration," *Accounting Horizons,* 1, 1(March 1987), 43–49.

Stepp, James O., "Deferred Taxes: The Discounting Controversy," *Journal of Accountancy,* 160, 5(November 1985), 98–108.

Sterling, Robert R., *An Essay on Recognition,*" Sydney, Australia: The University of Sydney Accounting Research Center, 1985.

Williams, Edward E. and M. Chapman Findlay III, "Discounting Deferred Tax Liabilities: Some Clarifying Comments," *Journal of Business Finance & Accounting,* Spring 1975, 121–133.

Wolk, Harry I., Lynn K. Saubert and Frank M. Tiernan, "A Further Note on Discounting Deferred Taxes," *Journal of Business Finance & Accounting,* 11, 2(Summer 1984), 253–255, Basil Blackwell.

II-B2

FINANCIAL INSTRUMENTS: HISTORICAL COST VERSUS FAIR VALUE

Jeffrey C. Jones

There has been no lack of criticism by elected officials, regulators, accounting standards-setters, and practicing accountants of present generally accepted accounting principles for financial instruments. With the recent explosion in new types of financial instruments, new accounting issues have surfaced; examination of these issues points out inherent inconsistencies in the current accounting model. The increase in the number and complexity of transactions designed to take advantage of the current inconsistencies in accounting literature has caused some to question whether the current accounting model for financial instruments is valid.

This article:

- Explores the issues involved with determining an appropriate measurement basis for financial instruments.

Jeffrey C. Jones, CPA, is a Professional Accounting Fellow in the Office of the Chief Accountant of the SEC. His responsibilities include the study of accounting and disclosure issues and concepts, participating in the development of SEC releases on financial reporting matters, and evaluating current reporting by registrants.

Jeffrey C. Jones, "Financial Instruments: Historical Cost Versus Fair Value." *The CPA Journal.* Reprinted with permission from *The CPA Journal,* August 1988, copyright 1988.

See also: "New and Innovative Financial Instruments" by Donald E. Brooks and Bhaskar Bhave, *The CPA Journal,* July and August 1987.

The SEC, as a matter of policy, disclaims responsibility for articles written by its employees. The views herein are those of the author and do not necessarily reflect the views of the Commissioner or of other members of the staff.

- Discusses some of the problems that the current model fails to resolve and the issues which must be addressed in conjunction with any change in the measurement basis of financial instruments.
- Discusses a possible solution which is compatible with the conceptual framework for financial accounting established by the FASB.

THE FINANCIAL INSTRUMENTS PROJECT

Many accountants are concerned that present accounting principles, consisting primarily of a historical cost measurement basis for financial instruments, does not faithfully represent the economic realities of today's complex instruments, nor the financial position and results of operations of financial institutions whose balance sheets consist almost entirely of such instruments. In their view, the present standards fail to provide a consistent, workable framework for preparers and auditors of financial statements to use in deciding the appropriate accounting for the complex transactions and instruments. Today's markets demand these transactions and instruments, and indeed many are structured to take advantage of the "opportunities" provided by present standards. The response from the standard-setting bodies has been to deal with these issues on a transaction-specific or industry-specific basis without, thus far, formulating any broad concepts.

As a result, and partially at the urging of the SEC, the FASB has added a major project to its agenda entitled, "Financial Instruments and Off Balance Sheet Financing." This project is one of the most complex ever undertaken by the FASB and could have the most far reaching impact on financial institutions of any standard-setting efforts to date. The Bureau of National Affairs has said that it is "probably the largest in scope in FASB history." A FASB member called it "the most important and possibly most pervasive" project the FASB has undertaken.[1]

The first phase of the project, dealing with disclosures, has resulted in the release of an Exposure Draft. While this is an important and perhaps controversial first step, this article will discuss the issues dealing with recognition and measurement of financial instruments.

The need for such a project is manifested by the fact that over half of the issues addressed by the FASB's Emerging Issues Task Force ("EITF") to date have dealt with financial instruments or financial institutions. Although each issue has been unique, for purposes of the project the FASB staff broadly categorized the issues into two major questions:

- How should financial instruments be measured?
- How should the relationship between particular instruments affect their recognition and measurement in balance sheets?

Various individuals would define financial instruments differently. For purposes of this article, however, the term financial instruments will be confined to monetary assets and liabilities.

[1]"FASB will add large project on financial instruments and off-balance-sheet financing," Washington Financial Reports, May 26, 1986, 892–893.

PRESENT GAAP

An analysis of the current accounting model is necessary to understand the problems which have surfaced. The present system of accounting for financial assets and liabilities is generally the same as that for other assets and liabilities; paragraph 69 of FASB Concepts Statement No. 5 describes it as a "transaction-based system." Under this system, assets and liabilities are recorded based on their historical exchange prices. Subsequent changes in the fair value of the assets and liabilities generally do not affect their carrying value unless an exchange has occurred. However, the assets and liabilities so recorded are sometimes adjusted for subsequent events and factors which are not the result of a subsequent exchange of assets or liabilities. For example, a financial asset whose recoverability is in doubt is reduced to current market value or net realizable value. Certain reporting entities, including mutual funds, broker-dealers, investment companies, and pension plans, carry all such instruments at current market value.

For financial institutions, amortized historical cost is generally used for those instruments for which the institution has the intent and ability to hold to maturity. Market value is used for those which are designated at their acquisition as trading portfolio securities as it is for speculative futures contracts or those that otherwise fail to meet the hedge criteria. For those instruments which are not trading securities, but for which the institution does not have the ability and intent to hold to maturity, lower of cost or market is used. Thus, for a financial institution, amortized historical cost is the model which is used as the carrying value for most of its assets and liabilities. Trading portfolios are rare in savings and loans, and generally do not represent a significant portion of the assets of most banks.

An alternative to the current model is the utilization of fair value. Given the measurement problems inherent in full current value or fair value financial statements, as well as the pervasive nature of such a change, it must be presumed that a move to full current value or fair value financial statements is one that will not and can not be made in the foreseeable future. However, the concerns with the carrying values of financial instruments must be addressed in a timely manner. Accordingly, proposed solutions must fit within the current conceptual framework. Fair value for financial instruments only may be consistent with the conceptual framework.

ACCOUNTING PROBLEMS CAUSED BY CURRENT MODEL

Two fundamental issues common to many financial instrument transactions are: 1) whether sale accounting or borrowing treatment is appropriate when financial assets are converted to cash; and 2) whether financial liabilities should be considered settled or extinguished in certain circumstances.

Questions regarding sale vs. financing have arisen partially as a result of the increased ability to securitize, monetize, or liquify and thereby make tradeable almost any financial asset. Tax-exempt bonds, home mortgages, commercial real estate loans, installment loans, consumer credit card loans, automobile loans, lease obligations, and other such traditional loans which financial institutions previously held to maturity are now being converted, in whole or in components, to cash. The conversion to cash is often accompanied by some type of recourse to, or continuing involvement by, the "seller." The emergence of these new markets enhances financial institutions' ability to convert assets to cash. At the same time, the current accounting model provides them with an ability to get the best of both worlds: structure the transaction as a borrowing for accounting purposes if sale accounting would result in a loss, and structure the transaction as a sale if there is an unrealized gain in the asset or if there is a concern as to the level of debt to be reported on the balance sheet.

An example of the inconsistencies in the accounting literature and the resulting ability to structure the form of transactions to achieve a desired accounting result is shown by a comparison of FASB Statement No. 77, "Reporting by Transferors for Transfers of Receivables with Recourse," with FASB Technical Bulletin No. 85-2, "Accounting for Collateralized Mortgage Obligations (CMOs)." FASB Statement No. 77, allows for sale treatment by sellers of receivables who retain all of the credit risk associated with such receivables if certain conditions are met concerning the ability to estimate the effect of the recourse provisions, the surrender of control by the transferor, and the lack of a transferee put option.

On the other hand, in FASB Technical Bulletin No. 85-2 the FASB concluded that CMOs should be presumed to be borrowings. The technical bulletin prescribes certain conditions which must be met to overcome such presumption and account for a CMO as a sale. Such conditions, if present, indicate a relinquishment by the issuer of all future economic benefits and all risks in the underlying collateral. The FASB concluded that Statement No. 77 does not apply to CMOs since it applies only to those transactions which purport to be sales. Since a CMO does not purport to be a sale, then it is presumed to be a borrowing. However, the inconsistencies in this position appear obvious: in a sale of receivables with recourse, the transferor retains all of the credit risk and may still account for the transaction as a sale and recognize any unrealized changes in the fair value of the assets. In a CMO, the issuer retains none of the risk in the underlying assets, however, if the issuer retains more than a "trifling" portion of the benefits of owning the assets; the transaction is accounted for as a borrowing. Therefore, the form of the transaction is the primary determinant of the accounting.

Although a reconsideration of these pronouncements will be part of the FASB's project, fair value accounting for financial instruments would remove some of the motivations to take advantage of these inconsistencies. If the assets in question were already carried at their fair value, questions would still exist as to whether debt should be reported on the balance sheet, but the motivation by the institution to either avoid recognition of a previously unrealized loss or cause the recognition of a previously unrealized gain in the asset would disappear.

Financial Liabilities

A further example of the limitations of the historical cost model is the propensity of enterprises to structure transactions to recognize, or avoid recognition of, unrealized gains and losses inherent in liabilities, as well as to reduce debt on the balance sheet. The subject of debt extinguishment is one which accountants have struggled with for many years. The SEC itself has taken a particular interest in the subject, as evidenced by the issuance of FRR No. 3, its subsequent rescission and issuance of FRR No. 15.

APB Opinion No. 26 requires that the extinguishment of debt for an amount different than the debt's carrying value be accounted for as a gain or loss in earnings, which is reported as an extraordinary item if material in the aggregate, in accordance with FASB Statement No. 4. APB Opinion 26 defined extinguishment in paragraph 3(a) as the "reacquisition of any form of debt security or instrument . . ."

The environment which generally results in gain recognition on extinguishment of debt is that in which an enterprise's debt carries a rate lower than what the current market is demanding. In such a situation, companies are motivated to account for the removal of debt from the balance sheet as an extinguishment. Conversely, if the financial liabilities carry an interest rate higher than current market, an extinguishment will most likely result in a loss and companies are motivated to reduce their borrowing cost and avoid reporting such loss.

In the early 1980s, almost 10 years after the issuance of APB Opinion 26, interest rates were at historically high levels, and most borrowers which had issued debt in previous periods had inherent gains in such debt. Partially in response to transactions motivated by desires to account for debt as if it were extinguished, the FASB issued Statement No. 76, "Extinguishment of Debt," in November 1983.

Currently, however, rates have fallen from their previous high levels and many entities who had issued debt in the high interest rate environment find themselves with higher debt cost than that which the current market would require. Such entities are motivated to lower their overall borrowing cost, but are concerned with the income statement impact of extinguishing debt at a loss. Therefore, many transactions are designed to fail the FASB Statement No. 76 criteria for extinguishment, while allowing the entity to achieve its objective of reducing its overall borrowing cost.

These transactions may take the form of "debt modifications." For example, if the debt has call provisions, the debtor may agree to modify the terms to remove the call feature in exchange for a fee. The amount of the fee is roughly equal to the present value of the difference between the debt's stated rate and the current market rate, adjusted for the time period remaining to the first call date, during which time the debt holder(s) would have received the higher rate anyway. The original debt instrument is unchanged; the debtor has not paid the creditor, is not relieved of its obligations, and is not legally released. Yet, it is clear that the debtor has, in substance, extinguished the old debt and issued new, noncallable debt at a total cost which is less than the cost of the old debt.

The EITF is presently attempting to determine the criteria necessary to consider debt extinguished when the debtor and creditor agree to a modification of debt terms, but in which the same debtor/creditor relationship remains. Although no consensus has been reached, a practical approach based on an analysis of the impact of the modification on the present value of the cash flows associated with the debt has been proposed. It appears that most EITF members believe such a practical approach is conceptually appealing; however, they are concerned that such an approach would lead to accounting for debt as extinguished in cases where the narrow criteria established in FASB Statement No. 76 have not been met.

A change in the historical cost model for financial liabilities to recognize the inherent changes in the value of such liabilities prior to their extinguishment would obviate some of the necessity of defining when an exchange involving the redemption or extinguishment of debt has occurred. Clearly, questions would remain as to when debt should be removed from the balance sheet, and the reconsideration of Statement No. 76 in that context is, I believe, welcome. However, the motivations to either extinguish debt or modify debt without extinguishment accounting, based on the resulting impact on earnings, would no longer be a factor in the structuring of transactions.

AN ANALYSIS OF ISSUES ASSOCIATED WITH FAIR VALUE

Because so many of the issues surrounding financial instruments would be solved by fair value accounting for such instruments, such an approach has appeal. But there are problems with a total fair value ("mark-to-market") model.

The issues which must be addressed when considering fair value accounting can be broadly categorized as those dealing with (i) recognition, (ii) relevance, and (iii) measurability. Paragraph 88 of FASB Concepts Statement No. 5 concludes, in part, "[o]nce an asset or a liability is recognized, it continues to be measured at the amount initially recognized until an event that changes the asset or liability or its amount occurs and meets the recognition criteria." Included in the recognition criteria as stated in paragraph 63 is "measurability—[the item] has a relevant attribute measurable with sufficient reliability" and "relevance—the information about it is capable of making a difference in user decisions."

RECOGNITION

Recognition in the financial statements of changes in the fair value of financial instruments is based on the concept that the increase or decrease in the value of the instrument is realizable by the enterprise. FASB Concepts Statement No. 5 concludes, in paragraph 83, in part:

> Revenues and gains of an enterprise during a period are generally measured by the exchange values of the assets (goods or services) or liabilities involved, and recognition involves consideration of two factors, 1) being realized or realizable and 2) being earned, with sometimes one and sometimes the other being the more important consideration.

Paragraph 85 further states, in part:

> Expenses and losses are generally recognized when an entity's economic benefits are used up in delivering or producing goods, rendering services, or other activities that constitute its ongoing major or central operations or when previously recognized assets are expected to provide reduced or no further benefits.

It is clear that when the fair value of a financial instrument changes due to movements in interest rates or other factors subsequent to its initial recording, an event has occurred. It is also apparent that today's financial instruments are realizable to a far greater extent than financial instruments have historically been. Shouldn't enterprises acknowledge such economic events and record their effects in the financial statements?

RELEVANCE

Some would say that the answer is "not necessarily." A fundamental recognition criteria is that the information has relevance to the user of the financial statements. Changes in the fair values of financial instruments are not necessarily any more relevant to the user than are changes in the fair values of other assets, including nonmonetary assets.

For example, financial assets whose function is to provide a return to the enterprise and which the enterprise will likely recover at maturity have as their relevant attributes the cost, maturity value, and yield to the enterprise on a period to period basis if such assets are held to maturity. Subsequent market changes do not necessarily affect the enterprise. Certainly, if the enterprise does not dispose of the asset while its fair value is below its cost, then such reduction in value does not affect the enterprise if it is held to maturity or its value "recovers" prior to ultimate disposition.

One of the objectives of financial reporting is to provide information that is useful to potential users. Paragraph 25 of FASB Concepts Statement No. 1 states, in part:

> "Potential users of financial information most directly concerned with a particular business enterprise are generally interested in its ability to generate favorable cash flows because their decisions relate to amounts, timing and uncertainties of expected cash flows."

If the change in the value of the asset or liability will not affect the enterprise's cash flows, then such change may not be relevant to users to the extent necessary to justify a change in the measurement attribute of such asset or liability. Of course, the value is relevant to users, and the disclosure phase of the FASB's current project will attempt to require that such information be provided.

On the other hand, assets whose purpose is to generate profit for an enterprise via their sale have, as their relevant attribute, the amount of cash into which they could be converted. Changes in the fair value of such assets affect the amount of cash realizable by the enterprise at a point in time, and thus such changes may be deemed to be relevant.

The question therefore becomes one of distinguishing between assets held for their yield, and assets held for their value. Amortized cost is appropriate for the former, but a departure from such model for the latter would probably better present the enterprise's financial position and would properly reflect in income the effects on the enterprise of the economic events that caused a change in their value. To some extent, financial institutions already make this distinction by designating certain assets as trading portfolio assets. However, it is clear that many assets that are not so designated are, in substance, trading portfolio assets due to the frequency with which Financial institutions purchase and sell them. For example, many thrifts consistently "churn" their portfolios of morgage-backed securities. One could argue that such enterprises should apply FASB Statement No. 65, "Accounting for Certain Mortgage Banking Activities," and carry the securities at the lower of cost or market. Such treatment is called for by paragraph 4, which requires lower of cost or market accounting for "mortgage loans and mortgage-backed securities held for sale." In practice, however, it appears that few thrifts apply Statement No. 65 either because they believe that the scope of the standard does not apply or because the assets in question are not "held for sale." Such thrifts argue that the assets are sold only at points in time when their fair value exceeds their carrying value; otherwise the assets are held. Thus, the carrying value is recoverable either through normal principal reductions to maturity or through sale at an amount at least equal to the carrying value.

MEASURABILITY

If a change in the measurement attribute of financial instruments is made, the issue of the measurability of whatever attribute is chosen will be critical. The recognition of unrealized gains is currently limited to circumstances such as futures contracts not accounted for as hedges, trading portfolio assets, certain specialized enterprises such as pension plans, investment companies and broker-dealers, and measurement of pension plan assets under FASB Statement No. 87. In arriving at the conclusion that futures contracts not qualifying as hedges should be carried at market value, the FASB put a great deal of weight on the fact that the contracts are traded on regulated futures exchanges and that there is daily cash settlement of gains and losses. Such features do not exist for other financial instruments. In addition, in concluding that the fair value of pension plan assets provides the most relevant information, the FASB, in paragraph 118 of Statement No. 87 noted that, ". . . most pension assets are invested in marketable securities and are priced regularly for investment management purposes."

Questions could arise as to what methods would be considered acceptable in estimating fair value for financial instruments not traded or quoted on exchanges. Currently, many savings and loans are having to face such a question in attempting to value large tracts of real estate which are obtained via foreclosure on commercial mortgage loans. Under the current accounting model, such a transaction is considered an exchange, and therefore, as required by FASB Statement No. 15 and recently reiterated by the SEC in FRR No. 28, the fair value of the collateral received provides the exchange price. Many times, however, active markets do not exist for such real estate, and therefore the institution must look to the opinion of experts such as real estate appraisers to determine the appropriate exchange price. Two or more appraisers may disagree on such basic factors used in estimating the value as highest and best use and appropriate total discount rate to be applied to the estimated cash flows. The result is that a large amount of analysis and judgment is required to determine the appropriate value for financial reporting purposes. Although the same degree of diversity is not likely to exist for financial reporting purposes when valuing financial instruments as it is when valuing real estate, a certain degree of diversity is likely, particularly for delinquent loans for which foreclosure is not yet probable. Thus, the cost of preparation of financial information as well as the degree of possible misstatement of recorded balances due to differences in judgment will increase if all financial instruments must be carried at their fair value.

If fair value is deemed appropriate, questions as to consistency with other types of assets will surely be raised. In December 1975, the FASB issued Statement No. 12, "Accounting for Certain Marketable Securities," and it is interesting to note the reasons for rejecting market value as the appropriate carrying value for marketable equity securities. Paragraph 29(a) states:

> The Board excluded from its consideration market value alone as the determinant of carrying value. Consideration of that alternative would raise pervasive issues concerning the valuation of other types of assets, including the concept of historic cost versus current or realizable value. The Board concluded that it could not examine these conceptual issues in a project of such limited scope.

It would appear that the same pervasive issues would be as relevant today as they were in 1975. Assuming that a major shift in the conceptual framework to current or fair value for the entire balance sheet is unlikely, a move to fair value as the appropriate determinant of carrying value for financial instruments could only be made if a logical explanation is made as to why financial instruments are different, conceptually, than other assets and liabilities. A move to fair value for only some assets and liabilities might raise significant concerns as to the credibility of financial reporting.

A Possible Solution

I believe that a possible solution to the problems discussed would be to accept initially the FASB's conceptual framework as a boundary within which any change must fit. In spite of existing criticism of the conceptual framework, it is, I believe, naive to think that the FASB will propose any solutions contrary to such framework. Within such a framework, I believe that the issues should be analyzed in steps.

The first step in such a process would be to establish criteria for distinguishing financial assets held for long-term investment from those held for speculation, (i.e., those that the enterprise intends to recover by selling them). A starting place might be to conclude that all instruments which are traded on recognized exchanges carry a presumption that they are trading assets. In other words, the ability to easily trade the assets creates the presumption that the enterprise is holding such assets to invest in their trading values. Such a presumption could only be overcome by demonstrated intent not to trade such securities prior to their maturity. On the other hand, loans to individual borrowers (which are not securitized) would carry a presumption that the enterprise's intent in owning such assets is for investment purposes. Again, such presumption can be overcome by a history of trading such assets. Further, at any point that it becomes probable that the enterprise will sell the assets in question, then their character would change. It is conceivable that some financial institutions would be required to classify substantially all of their assets as trading assets. For example, to protect against interest rate risk, many newly chartered savings and loans fully intend to sell all loans which are ordinated and use the proceeds to invest in new loans which will subsequently be sold. Such enterprises would classify all of their assets as trading assets.

The second step would be to determine the measurement attribute for those assets designated as trading assets. Although many or all of the assets so designated could be exchange traded and therefore have a readily determinable fair value, many may have a value which can only be determined by independent appraisal or subjective analysis of cash flows. In spite of such difficulties, fair value may be the most relevant attribute and such consideration could override objections based on the measurement difficulty.

Finally, the question of whether to adjust the carrying value of financial liabilities is an integral part of any change in the model. Absent a move to current value statements, it would appear difficult to conclude that all financial liabilities should be carried at the amount at which they could be settled by the enterprise. Such a conclusion would apply to reporting entities in all industries, many of which have not been affected by any of the financial instrument abuses. It would also unnecessarily distort income and cause unusual fluctuations and aberrations from period to period. Therefore, three choices remain.

> *First,* the conclusion could be that only financial institutions must carry liabilities at their settlement amounts since their balance sheets primarily consist of financial instruments and the effect of changes in interest rates on the entire enterprise should be reflected in the period of change. A problem with this approach is the question of consistency and comparability among enterprises in different industries.
>
> *Second,* it could be that only those financial liabilities which funded the acquisition of financial assets should be carried at their settlement amounts. However, this position would require a change from concepts expressed by the FASB in both Statement No. 34 and Statement No. 80; as stated in paragraph 50 of Statement No. 34, "association of sources and uses of funds is primarily subjective."
>
> *Third,* it would be to have the historical cost (proceeds) model remain operative for financial liabilities. Although enterprises actively manage their financial liabilities, these are not, unlike certain assets, incurred with the intent of profiting by settling them at amounts different than their face.

CONCLUSION

The FASB has decided to undertake a project related to financial instruments since it is clearly an area where guidance is needed. The first step has been taken by proposing additional disclosures of financial instruments. However, very significant conceptual questions related to, in some cases, the basic framework of financial accounting must be answered. If the issues related to the appropriate carrying value of financial instruments can be answered in a manner which is consistent with the conceptual framework, and maintains relevance, reliability, and consistency, then a step will have been taken in the direction of improving the usefulness of financial statements of enterprises which issue, own, or trade in financial instruments.

I do not believe that a full fair value model for all financial instruments can be justified when measured against the existing conceptual framework. I believe, however, that if a presumption exists that certain financial assets are held for their ability to be traded, such assets should be carried at their fair values. If assets are held for purposes of generating a yield, then the current method of accounting for such assets at lower of cost or recoverable value remains appropriate. Finally, it is my view that it would be inappropriate at this time to change the measurement basis for financial liabilities. I have detailed herein only one possible solution; many others exist. However, it is time to start down a path in this area, and see if it provides a workable solution.

II-B3

DEFERRED TAXES: THE DISCOUNTING CONTROVERSY

James O. Stepp

Should deferred taxes be discounted? Although much attention has been directed to this question, the proscription against discounting has been in place since Accounting Principles Board Opinion no. 10, *Omnibus Opinion—1966.*

The Financial Accounting Standards Board has been reconsidering the accounting for income taxes, and its timetable indicates that an exposure draft is imminent. Discounting was a principal concern of the August 29, 1983, discussion memorandum, but the subject won't be addressed in the exposure draft. The board may consider discounting of deferred taxes in the future, but it isn't currently on the agenda. The American Institute of CPAs accounting standards executive committee (AcSEC) has established a task force to study the broad issue of discounting, including its potential application to deferred taxes, and initial discussion by AcSEC is expected in the near future.

An examination of the conceptual difficulties and implementation problems in discounting deferred taxes offers strong arguments against a change in policy. First, though, a look at the conceptual basis of deferred taxes expected in the exposure draft seems in order.

The Comprehensive Liability Framework

Deferred taxes are provided to reflect timing differences between financial accounting and taxable income originating in the current or prior periods and not yet reversed at the balance sheet date.

James O. Stepp, "Deferred Taxes: The Discounting Controversy," *Journal of Accountancy,* November 1985, pp. 98–105.

One of the major issues the FASB had to consider in its income taxes project was the conceptual basis for providing deferred taxes. Three different approaches were proposed—liability, deferred and net of tax—as well as combinations of these methods. The FASB settled on the liability method, under which the deferred tax credit represents a liability for taxes payable on realization of the carrying value of assets (liabilities) because of their lower (higher) tax bases.

Another significant issue was whether allocation should be partial or comprehensive. Under the form of partial allocation most widely understood, deferred taxes wouldn't be provided for reversals of timing differences expected to be replaced by new, originating differences from similar transactions. Although partial allocation generally is considered a subset of the liability method, the FASB has decided that comprehensive allocation should be followed.

Given the FASB's tentative conclusion that deferred taxes should be provided under the comprehensive liability approach, it is now much easier to focus on the discounting issue. Indeed, it seems that the strongest arguments for discounting can be made under this approach.

The deferred method merely defers the past tax effects of timing differences, focusing on past cash flows, whereas the liability method attempts to measure future tax cash flows. Although the net-of-tax method can look to either past or future tax cash flows, it is usually proposed in the context of past tax cash flows.

Similarly, partial allocation dissipates, if not the arguments for discounting, the fervor with which they are advanced. Partial allocation generally would serve to reduce the deferred tax liability considerably, and further reductions for discounting would entail computational complexity with little effect.

CONCEPTUAL DIFFICULTIES

Increasingly, the time value of money is reflected both in structuring transactions and in the accounting for them. The high interest rates of recent years have underscored the fact that a dollar today is worth more than a dollar several years in the future. Following the adoption in 1971 of APB Opinion no. 21, *Interest on Receivables and Payables,* the prevailing presumption has been that liabilities should be measured and recorded at present values. If deferred taxes represent amounts payable in future periods, why shouldn't such amounts be recorded at their present values?

Advocates of discounting argue that present value is clearly a more meaningful measure of the deferred tax liability. In addition, they assert, deferred taxes and taxes currently payable should be reflected differently—that is, the amount of deferred taxes should be smaller as the length of the discount period increases, and the charge to income for $1 of tax currently payable should be higher than the charge to income for $1 of tax payable in the future.

It should be noted, however, that frequently there is a considerable difference between deferred taxes and liabilities on which interest imputation is required by Opinion no. 21. Timing differences can be distinguished between (1) those reflected first in financial reporting income and subsequently in taxable income and (2) those reflected first in taxable income. Indeed, many respondents to the discussion memorandum found this distinction compelling and recommended the liability method for the former timing differences and the deferred or net-of-tax method for the latter.

For timing differences first reflected in financial reporting income—for example, gross profit on installment sales—there is a future tax cash flow that can be predicted to occur on reversal when the timing difference is reflected in taxable income. When the timing difference is first reflected in taxable income, however, the tax cash flow has already occurred, and the future reversal of the timing difference is accomplished by its reflection in financial reporting income. Included in this group of timing differences is accelerated tax depreciation, which, in a macroeconomic sense, is clearly the most important source of timing differences.

For depreciation, actual tax cash flows follow the allocation method prescribed or elected for tax purposes, but a different allocation, deemed better to reflect the benefit of the capital asset's use in operations, is used for financial reporting. Deferred taxes, in this case, are provided to reflect the absence of an actual tax deduction in the future periods when the cost of the capital asset is "recovered" by financial reporting depreciation.

Reversal entails an actual tax cash flow only in the sense that taxable income derived from use of the asset won't be reduced by tax depreciation equal to financial reporting depreciation. The timing of reversal of the deferred tax liability will change if the depreciation methods or lives used for financial reporting depreciation are changed.

Clearly, the deferred tax liability represents a future tax cash flow only in a limited sense.

Moreover, unlike the Opinion no. 21 liabilities, deferred tax liabilities aren't fixed sums payable at fixed dates, and arguments for discounting are weaker as a result. As for payment dates, reversals of certain timing differences may depend on future events, and for certain timing differences the occurrence of reversals can be determined only by arbitrary ordering. The amount and timing of the tax payable on reversal of timing differences will depend on the tax rates enacted for future periods and the taxpayer's tax position, including taxable income or loss, carry-back availability, and available credits and carry-forwards.

Another distinction is that the transactions covered by the opinion are negotiated between buyer and seller or borrower and lender, and the interest rate used to impute interest is that presumably implicit in the negotiation, that is, the market rate at that time. By contrast, the ability to generate timing differences that defer income taxes by entering into specified types of transactions isn't a result of negotiation but of availability of provisions of the tax law. Such provisions aren't directly affected by changes in the market interest rate and are available on the same basis to all taxpayers regardless of their creditworthiness.

The most important timing differences represent economic incentives—the temporary deferral of tax payments—that the government provides for specific transactions. The "discount" on the deferred taxes (the difference between the gross amount of the deferred tax liability for reversing timing differences and the present value of that gross tax) arguably measures the amount of the economic incentives. Proponents of discounting believe that it would provide useful information by reflecting directly the availability and use of these incentives.

But the economic incentive that timing differences provide is an interest-free loan from the government, and not discounting reflects this. When deferred taxes are recorded gross in the balance sheet, the benefit of timing differences is reflected as it is realized as the absence of interest on deferred tax balances. This is the measure of the subsidy that the government has provided, and it shouldn't be anticipated by discounting.

The most important timing difference incentive is accelerated tax depreciation. For recording depreciation in financial statements such interest methods as sinking fund and annuity, methods that credit early operating periods with an interest equivalent for funds invested in the capital asset, are precluded by generally accepted accounting principles. The depreciation assigned to periods of use doesn't reflect the fact that funds may have been invested in the asset for many years before "recovery" by depreciation.

In these circumstances there is no compelling reason to adopt an accounting technique (discounting) to reflect the fact that the tax depreciation from the same asset acquisition may serve to defer cash outflow for taxes.

The dichotomy between financial statement depreciation and discounting deferred taxes arising from tax depreciation is perhaps sharpest when the question raised by discounting the deferred taxes is considered: Should the benefit provided by the government's economic incentive be reflected in income immediately or, rather, be spread over the life of the asset as a type of subsidy or cost reduction? This is the same question that has made the accounting for the investment tax credit controversial since its enactment in 1962. The Revenue Act of 1971 effectively precludes those who set accounting standards from prescribing either the flow-through or the deferral method of accounting for the investment tax credit, and the FASB has elected not to deal with the issue.

Because the "discount" on the deferred taxes measures the benefit that the government's economic incentive has made available, its treatment as a subsidy would result in its amortization over the life of the property. Under this approach, deferred taxes would be reduced by the "discount," and the "discount," representing the subsidy, would also be reflected separately as a deferred credit. The aggregate "discount" would be accreted by charge to income on an interest method over the period to payment of the deferred taxes and would be credited to income over the life of the fixed asset as an adjustment of depreciation. This approach would complicate the accounting, and the resulting effect on income would only be the difference between two spreading patterns.

The sidebar on pages 104–105 compares the effects of not discounting and discounting, and the two approaches to the "discount" arising from accelerated tax depreciation are illustrated.

IMPLEMENTATION PROBLEMS

In addition to its conceptual shortcomings, discounting would create serious implementation problems. One of the FASB's primary objectives in reconsidering income taxes was simplification, and it is probably the complexity and increased computations required by discounting, more than conceptual considerations, that caused the FASB to defer indefinitely its consideration of discounting. Among other considerations, implementation of discounting would require largely arbitrary rules for choosing the rate and the period.

DISCOUNT RATE

A number of questions would arise in any attempt to select the discount rate:

1. Should an investment or a borrowing rate be used?

   In most discounting applications in accounting, a borrowing rate is used. In recording a specific debt instrument, for example, interest imputation ascribes to the debt the current market interest rate applicable to the debtor's credit rating, the maturity of the debt, its priority and the collateral securing it. This is the typical approach to discounting other types of liabilities.

By contrast, the discounting concept used in accounting for pension obligations under APB Opinion no. 8, *Accounting for the Cost of Pension Plans,* is an investment rate, which embodies a funding and growth or accumulation concept.

It can be argued that an investment rate is more relevant than a borrowing rate in discounting deferred taxes because the "borrowing" from the government doesn't arise through direct negotiations and, therefore, the creditworthiness of the debtor isn't relevant. On the other hand, use of a borrowing rate could be based on the premise that, absent the deferred taxes, additional borrowing would have been required.

2. Should a pretax or an aftertax rate be used?

   Presumably, the discount rate should be an aftertax rate. Accretion of a discounted deferred tax liability would have to accumulate aftertax dollars.

3. Should a company-specific or an external rate be used?

   Valid conceptual arguments can be made for using a company's specific rate in discounting deferred taxes. But if a borrowing rate is used, an anomalous result of using a company's specific rate is that the benefit of discounting deferred taxes would be greater for less established, less profitable, higher risk companies. The lower the taxpayer's credit rating, the lower the recorded deferred tax liability.

   If an investment rate is used, the investment possibilities attributable to such funds would include

   - Investment in capital assets.
   - Research and development activities.
   - Investment in equity or interest-bearing securities.

   Use of a company's specific investment rate would entail practical difficulties in measurement and verification (for example, in determining the use and related return for incremental funds). Use of an external rate would avoid the subjectivity inherent in a company-specific rate.

4. Should a single rate or multiple rates be used?

   Because yields available or demanded in interest markets depend on maturities, rates should vary for different discount periods. Although a certain amount of grouping and imprecision would be acceptable, a number of discount rates could be required to reflect adequately the different "maturities" of the deferred taxes.

   It is likely that the FASB would require the use of external, aftertax, risk-free investment rates.

DISCOUNT PERIOD

Determining the discount period would involve considerable mechanics. The cumulative timing differences at the balance sheet date would have to be scheduled by the expected year of reversal. This requirement would go well beyond the information about the period of reversal of timing differences required by the liability method.

In applying the liability method, information about specific reversal periods will be important only when (1) rate changes have been enacted to take effect in some future period, therefore applying to some but not all reversals, or (2) carryforwards exist and it must be determined whether reversals will occur within or beyond the carryforward periods.

In an article in the September 1984 *Journal of Accountancy,* "Accounting for Income Taxes: Predicting Timing Difference Reversals," Barry Robbins and Steven Swyers discuss three categories of timing differences:

1. Reversal isn't dependent on future events (or the occurrence and timing of the future event is highly predictable), and either origination or reversal takes place within a single, discrete period. Examples are gross profit on installment sales and deferred gain on sale-leasebacks.
2. Reversal isn't dependent on future events, but both origination and reversal take place over several periods. Although the reversals follow a predetermined schedule, the association of specific originations with specific reversals requires the selection of an arbitrary ordering, such as Fifo, Lifo or average. The primary example is depreciation, for example, the straight-line method for financial reporting and accelerated methods and shorter recovery periods for tax.
3. Reversal depends on future events, and predicting the period of reversal may be difficult and estimates may be subject to change over time. Examples include depreciation or amortization related to operating levels (for example, intangible drilling costs in the oil and gas industry), revenue recognition on long-term construction contracts, and warranty reserves.

Obviously, when timing differences fall into the third category, imprecision, subjective judgments and frequent revision of the reversal period used in the discounting computation are likely. Calculating the reversal periods for the second category of timing differences would entail substantial computations.

In considering the discount period for reversal of cumulative timing differences at the balance sheet date, there is a conceptual position similar to the form of partial allocation already described. Under this approach, the discount period would be extended by future originations scheduled or predicted to occur to offset the reversals. Prediction of continuing rollover of deferred taxes by future originations could extend the discount period indefinitely and, accordingly, minimize the discounted amount of deferred taxes.

OTHER PROBLEMS

Adoption of any discounting methodology would raise another question: Should there be a comprehensive recalculation at each balance sheet date using the discount rate determined by conditions at that date, or should "discount" on deferred taxes be established separately for each period of origination and worked forward using the discount rate assigned in the period of origination? The latter approach is the typical accounting for liabilities in the historical cost framework: The original interest rate is used regardless of subsequent changes in market interest rates.

Tracking discounted deferred taxes by year of origination probably would be impractical, however, and recalculation is more consistent with the liability method, in which the deferred tax amount is revalued to reflect tax rate changes. Given the frequency and magnitude of interest rate changes, a comprehensive recalculation at each balance sheet date could give rise to considerable volatility in reported numbers and therefore in reported income.

Assuming comprehensive recalculation, a number of factors would change the amount of "discount" applied to reduce deferred tax balances in a given period:

- New tax rates that would change the "principal," the gross amount of deferred taxes payable.
- The "discount" on new, originating differences (and possibly the "discount" applicable to scheduled or predicted future originations).
- Changes in the discount rate(s) applied.
- Accretion of "discount" on deferred taxes previously provided (there would be a question whether this amount should be shown in the tax provision or in interest expense, possibly eligible for capitalization under FASB Statement no. 34, *Capitalization of Interest Cost*).
- Changes in estimated periods of reversals (for example, changes resulting from changed amortization methods or lives for capital assets or by reserve estimate changes or additions to the full-cost pool for intangible drilling costs).

Several of these changes could interact to affect the change in the amount of "discount" in a given year, and it is unlikely that any specific effect could be isolated.

Special consideration would have to be given to timing differences arising from transactions in which discounting is integral to pretax accounting. Examples are pensions, direct financing leases and capital leases. The accounting literature for these transactions establishes the interest rate used in pretax accounting. Across-the-board application of discounting to all deferred tax balances would apply a different interest rate to the tax effects.

Separate discounting calculations would have to be made for each taxing jurisdiction, and a different discount rate (or a series of rates) would have to be selected for each foreign jurisdiction.

The effects of discounting would have to be reflected in interim periods as well as in the annual computation. Short-cut methods possibly could be devised for interim calculations. For example, the change in the amount of "discount" for the year could be estimated and considered part of the annual effective tax rate. But this would entail predictions of the interest rate to be used in the year-end computation. More important, it would be conceptually at odds with the basic discounting technique that charges annual periods for the benefit of having the use of funds interest free, such charges varying with the amount of funds available, the time period of their availability and the applicable rate.

The alternative—a discrete approach to discounting in interim periods—isn't attractive either. The discrete assignment of the effects of timing differences to interim periods would be arbitrary at best. For example, should the excess tax over financial reporting depreciation for the year be assumed to occur one-fourth in each quarter? Should that related to the current year's additions be reflected as the additions are placed in service? Or should originations be deemed to occur when they affect taxes payable (for example, on quarterly prepayment dates)?

It is important to note that if changes, especially discount rate changes, are reflected by catch-up adjustments for comprehensive recalculations, at interim dates, of the amount of "discount," interim provisions could be subjected to severe volatility.

THE QUESTION IN CONTEXT

Should deferred taxes be discounted? It would at first appear, given the time value of money in an environment of high interest rates, that the obvious answer is yes. But a consideration of the nature of deferred tax liabilities produces compelling arguments for not discounting.

Regardless of conceptual appeal, discounting would add considerably to the complexity of tax computation. The routine bookkeeping made possible by the advent of computers might indicate that discounting deferred taxes is an idea whose time has come. But in recent years increasing concern about standards overload has been expressed, and there is a demand, especially from small businesses and small CPA firms, for simpler standards. Consideration of the arbitrary rules and mechanical problems involved makes it clear that deferred taxes should not be discounted.

WITH AND WITHOUT DISCOUNTING: A COMPARISON OF EFFECTS

A comparison of the effects of not discounting and discounting is illustrated in the accompanying table by a hypothetical transaction in which a fixed asset is purchased for $1,000 in cash in year 1 and depreciated straight line over 10 years for financial reporting.

The following additional assumptions are made:

- The entire cost of the asset is deductible in the year of acquisition (an unrealistic assumption for a U.S. taxpayer but one made for the sake of simplicity).
- A tax rate of 50 percent is effective in the year of acquisition and doesn't change over the 10-year period.
- The tax effects for a specific year are deemed to occur at the fiscal year-end date.
- An aftertax discount rate of 6 percent is appropriate throughout the 10-year period.

Absent discounting, deferred taxes of $450 are provided at the end of year 1 because $100 of depreciation will be recorded for the purpose of financial reporting in each of the nine years 2 through 10 without any actual tax deductions available in these years. Beginning in year 2, the deferred tax balance is reduced annually by the $50 tax effect of reversing depreciation differences. Without discounting, the benefit of the accelerated tax depreciation is reflected simply as the absence of an interest charge on the deferred tax liability.

In discounting, the present value of the reversing deferred taxes of $50 in each of the years 2 through 10 is computed to be $340 at the end of year 1. The difference between gross deferred taxes and present value is $110 at the end of year 1; this is the measurement of the benefit of the accelerated tax depreciation. Starting in year 2, the deferred tax balance is reduced by the annual $50 reversal but is also increased by the interest shown in column G at the assumed 6 percent rate.

In this hypothetical example, all the cash flows (ignoring those that will be generated by use of the asset in operations) appear in columns A and C. The taxpayer expends $1,000 and obtains a related $500 tax reduction in year 1. Columns B and F illustrate that, without discounting, depreciation and its tax effects are spread in the same pattern over the 10-year period. Discounting deferred taxes would recognize that the tax reduction is actually availed of

	A	B	C	D	E	F
				WITHOUT DISCOUNTING		
				Deferred Taxes		
Year	Expenditure for Asset	Depreciation	Taxes Payable	Provision	Balance	Net Tax (Benefit)
1	$1,000	$ 100	$(500)	$450	$450	$ (50)
2		100		(50)	400	(50)
3		100		(50)	350	(50)
4		100		(50)	300	(50)
5		100		(50)	250	(50)
6		100		(50)	200	(50)
7		100		(50)	150	(50)
8		100		(50)	100	(50)
9		100		(50)	50	(50)
10		100		(50)	0	(50)
	$1,000	$1,000	$(500)	$ 0		$(500)

before its reflection in income; yet no recognition is given to the fact that the cash disbursement for the fixed asset is made in advance of its charge to income as depreciation.

Columns K and L illustrate the effects on income if discounting is adopted and should be compared with column F. Column K reflects the effects of discounting if the entire benefit of accelerated tax depreciation is reflected in the year it is deducted on the tax return. The net tax benefit in year 1 comprises the $50 tax effect of financial reporting depreciation and the $110 "discount" on the deferred tax liability; in subsequent years the net tax benefit comprises the $50 tax effect of financial reporting depreciation reduced by interest on the deferred tax balance.

Column L reflects the effects of discounting if the $110 benefit of accelerated tax depreciation is considered a type of subsidy—a reduction in the cost of the fixed asset—and is spread in the same pattern (straight line over 10 years) as financial reporting depreciation. The net tax benefit comprises the $50 tax effect of financial reporting depreciation, increased by the $11 annual amortization of the subsidy, reduced (beginning in year 2) by interest on the deferred tax balance.

G	H	J	K	L
WITH DISCOUNTING				
	Deferred Taxes		Net Tax (Benefit)	
Discount and Accretion	Provision	Balance	Immediate Recognition	Subsidy Treatment
$(110)	$340	$340	$(160)	$ (61)
20	(30)	310	(30)	(41)
19	(31)	279	(31)	(42)
17	(33)	246	(33)	(44)
15	(35)	211	(35)	(46)
13	(37)	174	(37)	(48)
10	(40)	134	(40)	(51)
8	(42)	92	(42)	(53)
5	(45)	47	(45)	(56)
3	(47)	0	(47)	(58)
$ 0	$ 0		$(500)	$(500)

II-B4

A REASSESSMENT OF THE ALLOCATION OF CONVERTIBLE DEBT PROCEEDS AND THE IMPLICATIONS FOR OTHER HYBRID FINANCIAL INSTRUMENTS

Thomas E. King, Alan K. Ortegren, and Robin M. King

As the use of convertible bonds increased dramatically in the 1960s, a question arose as to how to account for the issuance of such securities. Many argued that a convertible bond consists of two bundled securities, a straight bond and an option to acquire stock. Acceptance of this view implies that the issuer's accounting treatment recognize both features of the security and allocate the issue proceeds partially to debt and partially to equity. The Accounting Principles Board (APB), however, chose to require, in *APBO 14,*[1] that no portion of the proceeds of convertible debt be attributed to the equity or conversion feature of the debt. At the time considerable controversy surrounded the issue, and, in retrospect, the arguments presented by the APB to support its position seem less than convincing.

This concern again has come to the forefront as new types of hybrid securities have appeared in recent years. With many of these securities, the question is whether the proceeds of

Thomas E. King, Alan K. Ortegren, and Robin M. King, "A Reassessment of the Allocation of Convertible Debt Proceeds and the Implications for Other Hybrid Financial Instruments," *Accounting Horizons.* Reprinted by permission of the American Accounting Association.

[1]Accounting Principles Board Opinion No. 14, "Accounting for Convertible Debt And Debt Issued with Stock Purchase Warrants" (AICPA, March 1969).

issuance are associated with debt, equity, or a combination of the two. When related to both debt and equity, the question is how the issue amount is to be allocated between the two. The Financial Accounting Standards Board's (FASB) financial instruments project is intended to address accounting and reporting issues created by these nontraditional securities. New attention to hybrid securities is needed because the approach taken by the APB more than 20 years ago seems unable to capture the substance of these securities.

This article re-examines accounting for the proceeds of convertible bond issues and assesses the practicality of estimating price differentials attributed to different features of a hybrid instrument in a real trade setting. The results of this study are relevant to accounting for traditional convertible bonds, normally issued at prices significantly in excess of their straight debt values (i.e., at lower coupon rates and yields than straight debt), and the newer hybrid securities. Evidence provided by this study bears directly on the practicality of making the kinds of estimates needed to apply the FASB's stated approach to dealing with hybrid financial instruments.

THE IMPORTANCE OF HYBRID FINANCIAL INSTRUMENTS

Financial reporting issues related to company financing are among the most important facing the accounting profession today. The accounting literature and the popular financial press contain many articles about off-balance sheet financing, hidden debt, dilution of earnings, and other problems associated with new approaches to financing. Keeping abreast of the new financial instruments and understanding their nature have become increasingly difficult.[2] Examples of new financial instruments include asset-backed securities (such as those collateralized by mortgages or credit card receivables), traditional bonds split so that interest and principal sell separately (e.g., STRIPS, CATS), and puttable stock. King and Ortegren[3] discuss one type of hybrid security, the adjustable rate convertible note, and demonstrate some of the difficulties in accounting for this and similar securities using currently acceptable procedures.

Interestingly, an unintended result of *APBO 14* is the creation of new hybrid securities specifically designed around the opinion's requirements; i.e., they are designed to comply in form with *APBO 14* while avoiding the spirit of its requirements. One example is the adjustable rate convertible note. Another is the "synthetic" convertible, discussed in a later section. *APBO 14* therefore bears partial responsibility for the explosion in number and diversity of financial instruments.

One indication of the magnitude of the problems related to financial instruments is that the FASB's Emerging Issues Task Force has focused on issues concerning financial instruments, financial institutions, or off-balance sheet financing in almost half of the more than 200 items it has considered since its formation in 1984.[4] Thus, the FASB's project dealing with financial instruments is quite timely and is viewed in the profession as one of far-reaching importance.

---

[2]For a description of some new financial instruments, see R. Sanborn and M. Atchison, "A CPA's Field Guide to New Financial Instruments," *Journal of Accountancy* (October 1985), pp. 165–172; and T. Rollins, D. Stout, and D. O'Mara, "The New Financial Instruments," *Management Accounting* (March 1990), pp. 35–41.

[3]T. King and A. Ortegren, "Accounting for Hybrid Securities: The Case of Adjustable Rate Convertible Notes," *The Accounting Review* (July 1988), pp. 522–535.

[4]C. Woods III and H. Bullen, "An Overview of the FASB's Financial Instruments Project," *Journal of Accountancy* (November 1989), p. 43.

THE FASB'S FINANCIAL INSTRUMENTS PROJECT

The FASB's financial instruments project is divided into three related phases:

- Disclosure
- Recognition and measurement
- Distinguishing between liabilities and equity

The FASB undertook phase three of the project largely in response to problems of applying *APBO 14* to new financial instruments that cloud the distinction between debt and equity. These innovative financial instruments and relatively recent changes in the financial markets also "have raised fundamental questions about the adequacy of current accounting standards for *traditional* instruments."[5]

In attempting to resolve issues associated with accounting for both traditional and new hybrid financial instruments in phases two and three of the project, the FASB adopted a "fundamental financial instrument approach."

> The approach is based on the premise that all financial instruments are made up from a few "building blocks"—fundamental financial instruments—and that resolving the accounting issues related to those building block instruments will help resolve the accounting issues related to the other instruments. . . .[6]

In applying this building block approach, the FASB intends to deal with such questions as:

> How should a compound financial instrument (such as convertible debt) with both liability and equity fundamental components be accounted for? Should the entire instrument be accounted for in the aggregate as either a liability or equity or should the instrument be broken into its fundamental components for financial reporting purposes?[7]

Consistent with the direction of the FASB's project, this study follows a building block approach and deals specifically with the feasibility of dividing hybrid financial instruments into their component fundamental instruments. Further, as recognized by the FASB, this approach applies to both new and traditional financial instruments. Although the focus in this study is on traditional convertible bonds, the fundamental financial instrument approach leads to identification of certain basic instruments that can be combined and configured in different ways to form hybrid financial instruments. This approach, therefore, is a general approach to dealing with all types of financial instruments.

THE STANCE OF THE APB

APBO 10 required that, upon issuance of convertible bonds or bonds with stock warrants, "the portion of the proceeds attributable to the conversion feature or the warrants should be

[5]Ibid.

[6]Financial Accounting Standards Board, Financial Accounting Series, *Status Report* (January 8, 1990), p. 5.

[7]Woods and Bullen, op. cit., p. 47.

accounted for as paid-in capital."[8] In determining the amount of proceeds attributable to the conversion feature or warrants, *APBO 10* indicated that the amount assigned to equity would be the difference between the issue price of the debt and the estimated price at which the debt would have been issued without the equity feature.

A short time later, the APB issued *APBO 12,* suspending the accounting treatment for convertible debt required by *APBO 10.* The APB noted that, based on their observations and comments received, convertible securities "raise difficult estimation and other problems."[9] After further study the APB issued *APBO 14,* stipulating that no portion of the proceeds from the issuance of convertible debt should be assigned to the conversion feature of the securities. Five of the 18 members of the APB dissented from this requirement.

Interestingly, *APBO 14* gave a conceptual reason for abandoning the debt/equity allocation requirement of *APBO 10* in addition to the practical estimation problems. The principal rationale identified in *APBO 14* for treating all proceeds from the issuance of convertible debt as attributable to the debt was the "inseparability of the debt and conversion option." Practical estimation difficulties were identified only as a secondary consideration.

THE INSEPARABILITY ARGUMENT

The validity of the "inseparability argument" has been questioned from the beginning. Within *APBO 14* itself, the dissenting views included examples of generally accepted accounting treatments of "separate accounting recognition for disparate features of single instruments."[10] The literature includes additional arguments and examples indicating the inappropriateness of ignoring the value associated with the conversion feature simply because the debt and conversion feature could not be separately traded.[11] Casting further doubt on the viability of the inseparability argument, *APBO 14* itself concluded that "when convertible debt is issued at a substantial premium, there is a presumption that such premium represents paid-in capital."[12] This provision suggests that the failure to separately recognize conversion features was not a matter of inseparability but rather one of materiality. This, in turn, implies that the major reason for the APB's position in *APBO 14* was its original concern over measuring the value of the conversion feature.

An additional flaw in the approach of *APBO 14* is the failure to differentiate between two possible causes of a substantial premium. A substantial premium when a convertible debt security is issued could be due to a conversion feature with a significant value unto itself, a nominal interest rate set significantly above the prevailing market rate for the instrument, or some combination of the two. By not distinguishing between these two sources of a substantial

[8]Accounting Principles Board Opinion No. 10, "Omnibus Opinion—1966" (AICPA, December 1966), para. 8.

[9]Accounting Principles Board Opinion No. 12, "Omnibus Opinion—1967" (AICPA, December 1967), para. 11.

[10]APB Opinion No. 14, para. 9.

[11]See, for example, A. Ford, "Should Cost be Assigned to Conversion Value?" *The Accounting Review* (October 1969), pp. 818–822; A. Ford, "Why Cost Should be Assigned to Conversion Value—A Critique of APB Opinion No. 14," *The New York Certified Public Accountant* (October 1970), pp. 826–829; and L. Imdieke and J. Weygandt, "Classification of Convertible Debt," *The Accounting Review* (October 1969), pp. 798–805.

[12]APB Opinion No. 14, para. 18.

premium, *APBO 14* allows for a significant premium caused by a high nominal interest rate to be assigned to equity.

PRACTICAL PROBLEMS OF ALLOCATION

The traditional argument against accounting for any issue proceeds attributable to the conversion feature as equity flows from the practical problems of assigning a subjective value to the conversion feature. Brigham[13] provides a theoretical model for determining the portion of the proceeds from convertible bonds associated with the debt, with the residual value assignable to the conversion feature. Brigham's model identifies the present value of a pure debt instrument through the use of a "market rate of interest on equivalent risk, pure debt issues." The difference between this value of a pure debt instrument and the total issue proceeds is residually assigned to the conversion feature, precisely the approach required in the superseded *APBO 10.*

Imdieke and Weygandt[14] discuss the problems of actually measuring conversion value in practice. After pointing out the existence of models to estimate the value of the conversion feature and noting the lack of consistency between these models, Imdieke and Weygandt call for further research on whether assessments of conversion value can be made with reasonable accuracy.

Allocations of convertible bond issue amounts should be possible by estimating the straight-debt value (the price at which the securities would sell without the conversion feature) of convertible securities. Discussions with professional bond traders and underwriters indicate that they regularly make the kinds of valuations needed for an accounting allocation of the issue price of convertible bonds. Moreover, pricing by different bond traders is expected to be relatively homogeneous, otherwise those traders consistently far "off the market" would soon be out of business.

FORM OVER SUBSTANCE

The requirements of *APBO 14* seem to emphasize the form of a financial instrument at the expense of substance. As an example, a hybrid security known as a "synthetic" convertible bond enables companies to issue what is essentially convertible debt and at the same time skirt the major requirement of *APBO 14.* A synthetic convertible is a nonconvertible bond with detachable stock warrants and certain other characteristics. According to *APBO 14:*

> the portion of the proceeds of debt securities issued with detachable stock purchase warrants which is allocable to the warrants should be accounted for as paid-in-capital . . . The same accounting treatment applies to issues of debt securities (issued with detachable warrants) which may be surrendered in settlement of the exercise price of the warrant.[15]

---

[13]E. Brigham, "An Analysis of Convertible Debentures: Theory and Some Empirical Evidence," *Journal of Finance* (March 1966), pp. 35–54.

[14]L. Imdieke and J. Weygandt, "Accounting For That Imputed Discount Factor," *Journal of Accountancy* (June 1970), pp. 54–58.

[15]APB Opinion No. 14, para. 16.

Therefore, the proceeds from the issuance of synthetic convertibles are appropriately allocated between debt and equity.

The additional features of the nonconvertible bond that make it equivalent to a convertible are that (1) the bond may be tendered at face value as payment for the stock upon exercise of the warrants and (2) the nominal interest rate on the bond is low enough that the value of the bond is straight debt (without the warrants) is well below its face amount. These features virtually assure that, if the warrants are exercised, the bonds will be tendered in payment.

The form of these securities is such that under *APBO 14* the proceeds from issuance must be accounted for partially as debt and partially as equity. In substance, however, these securities are equivalent to convertible bonds; exercise of the warrants, with the accompanying issuance of stock, most assuredly results in the tendering (conversion) of the bonds. *APBO 14,* therefore, effectively requires that securities nearly identical in substance be accounted for in significantly different ways.[16]

ASSESSING THE VALUE OF SPECIAL DEBT FEATURES

The research reported next examines two aspects of the practicality of assessing the value of conversion and other features of debt. First, the study considers whether estimates of conversion feature values presently are being made in practice. Second, the study deals with the reliability of such estimates.

ASSESSING THE VALUE OF CONVERSION FEATURES IN PRACTICE

Discussions with 11 bond traders and underwriters indicated that finance professionals currently do estimate price or yield differentials associated with specific features or characteristics of debt securities and assign these differentials to the securities when issuing or trading those securities.[17] The general approach for pricing corporate bonds is to determine the yield for U.S. Treasury securities of similar maturity and then to adjust for differences in risk and other characteristics. Major differences include bond ratings, conversion features, debt seniority and collateral, sinking fund requirements, and call protection.

The first part of this study provides additional evidence regarding whether finance professionals currently make assessments of the price or yield associated with convertible debt issues as if the issues were nonconvertible. This part of the study involved a mail survey of 29 convertible bond underwriters. Where King and Ortegren focused mainly on bond traders, this survey solicited underwriters (1) to see if they price bonds using the same approach as traders and (2) because they are responsible for pricing the bonds at original issue.

A relatively small sample of underwriters was used for two reasons. First, the results of this portion of the study were meant only to add to the evidence already provided by King and

[16]While application of *APBO 14* results in different accounting treatments for the two instruments, the guidelines in *APBO 15,* "Earnings Per Share" (AICPA, May 1969), para. 43, specify that, for purposes of computing earnings per share, securities not specifically dealt with in the opinion "should be dealt with in accordance with their substance." As synthetic convertibles are not mentioned directly in *APBO 15,* they presumably should be treated in the same way as convertible securities when computing earnings per share.

[17]King and Ortegren, pp. 530–531.

TABLE 1

Results of Survey of Bond Underwriters

Question	Yes	No
1. Prior to the issuance of convertible debt, do you and your clients normally consider the issuance of nonconvertible debt as an alternative?	11	1
2. When considering the issuance of convertible debt, do you normally estimate the yield (effective interest rate) that would be required to issue the debt if it were nonconvertible?	12	0
3. When establishing an issue price for convertible debt, do you base the price (or yield) on the price (or yield) of other securities (e.g., Treasuries) and adjust for differences in ratings and features (e.g., convertible, call protection, sinking fund requirements)?	11	1

Ortegren. Second, there are relatively few underwriters of convertible securities compared with the number of underwriters in general.

Twelve responses were received. In addition to their yes or no responses, 5 respondents provided clarifying comments. The survey results are reported in Table 1; nearly all respondents answered yes to the three questions asked. The clarifying comments accompanying the one dissenting response to Question 1 indicated that the respondent's firm normally considers straight equity as an alternative to convertible debt, but does estimate a straight-debt rate as a basis for pricing convertibles. The clarifying comments explaining the one "no" response to Question 3 focused on computation of the conversion premium and are not inconsistent with a "yes" response.

These results indicate that convertible bond underwriters currently do estimate the yields or prices associated with convertible debt as if the debt were nonconvertible, and that these estimates are used in making important financing decisions. The results also indicate that these underwriters use a "building block" approach to estimate the price or yield of convertible securities from a benchmark security, with adjustments for differences between the securities, such as convertibility, rating, and seniority.

THE RELIABILITY OF ESTIMATES OF THE VALUE OF CONVERSION PREMIUMS

The fact that convertible bond underwriters and their clients make financing decisions based on estimates of conversion premiums (or yield differences) implies that such an approach could be used to assist accountants in accounting for the proceeds of convertible debt issues. The standard for measuring the ability to estimate the value of conversion premiums should be whether agreement exists among those making the estimates. Value at a particular point in time represents a consensus among those in the market and is based on knowledge and expectations at that point in time. For accountants, the relevant question is whether a consensus can be reached as to the value of a conversion premium when a convertible security is issued. Once a security is traded in the market, this consensus on value is evidenced by the market price. Apparently underwriters have been reasonably successful in estimating the value of conversion premiums because nearly all convertible bonds are issued at par value or a price very near to par value.[18]

EVIDENCE REGARDING THE ABILITY TO ACHIEVE A CONSENSUS AS TO VALUE

Although the current successful use of estimates of conversion premiums can be observed in practice, this study provides some additional evidence that a reasonable consensus can be achieved when adjusting bond prices and yields for differences in features and characteristics. An experiment was designed in which traders at firms making a market in a nonconvertible issue of a company with a convertible issue outstanding were asked what price they would quote for the convertible bonds if the bonds were nonconvertible. This was done in a real trade setting by a professional bond trader, although the question was hypothetical. All quotes solicited for the study for an individual bond were obtained within a few minutes of each other.

Bond traders rather than underwriters were used in the study because individual underwriters possess detailed knowledge about securities they underwrite, but not generally about those underwritten by others. Thus, unless underwriters were placed in an artificial situation, only one subject per bond would be available for the study, precluding any assessment of consensus. On the other hand, a number of traders often make a market in a particular security and work with that security on a regular basis, providing a number of subjects for each bond. The evidence provided by King and Ortegren and by the survey of underwriters in this study indicates that bond traders and underwriters employ similar or identical models for pricing convertible debt instruments (excluding convertible bonds trading primarily off the value of the underlying stock).

The experimental design included the following conditions:

1. There had to be both convertible and nonconvertible bonds outstanding for each company used. Different approaches often are used in pricing convertible and nonconvertible bonds in the after-markets, and the same individuals do not normally trade both convertibles and nonconvertibles. In this experiment, nonconvertible traders were asked to price the convertible bonds as if the bonds were nonconvertible.
2. For each security, there had to be at least 5 market-makers. Because some market-makers were expected not to participate, a consensus would be hard to establish with a lesser number.
3. The firms selected for the study could not have nonconvertible bonds listed on an exchange. Listed prices might allow traders to make assessments of the value of the hypothetical securities that were biased by the quoted prices of the firms' nonconvertible bonds.
4. The bonds could not be nearing maturity, they had to be trading with interest (i.e., not in default on interest payments), the company could not be in bankruptcy, nor

[18]Underwriters generally attempt to issue corporate bonds at par (except zero coupon bonds). See F. Fabozzi and F. Zarb, *Handbook of Financial Markets* (Homewood, Illinois: Dow Jones-Irwin, 1981), p. 255; and D. Kieso and J. Weygandt, *Intermediate Accounting,* Sixth Edition (New York: John Wiley & Sons, 1989), p. 627.

TABLE 2

Estimates of the Debt Value of Convertible Bonds

Bond Issuer	Nominal Rate and Maturity	Moody's Bond Rating	Price Estimates	Bid Variation as % of Low Bid	Bid Variation as % of Face Value
MCI Communications	7.75% 2003	BA3	65 64 62, 62	4.8	3.0
Midlantic Banks, Inc.	8.25% 2010	A2	78 77 75.5	3.3	2.5

could there be other obvious abnormalities that might significantly affect the company's bond prices.

Only two companies met all of the conditions, partly because there often are only a few market-makers for bonds that are not heavily traded. Those bonds that are heavily traded often are listed on an exchange.

Table 2 shows the price quotes obtained for the two issues in this part of the study; the price variation is less than 5 percent. Even though the evidence generated is limited because of the strict requirements placed on the bond issues that could be included in the study, it does indicate achievement of a reasonable consensus as to the value of the debt and equity portions of convertible debt. Generalizing from a sample of two securities and quotes from seven traders should be done with care; however, the results do conform to the overall pattern established by other evidence.

A TEST OF CONSENSUS WITH RESPECT TO BOND VALUATION

Difficulties associated with a direct test of whether consensus could be achieved in valuing conversion premiums led to a more indirect approach that focused on a somewhat broader issue. Bond underwriters and traders value a bond by (1) considering all features of the bond and (2) adjusting the price or yield for each of the relevant features or characteristics. A convertible bond trades in a fashion similar to a nonconvertible bond (but with a yield difference) as long as the bond's straight debt value is significantly above the value of the stock into which the bond is convertible. Convertibility is just one of many features considered when valuing the bond. Each relevant feature may cause the underwriter or trader to incrementally increase or decrease the estimate of the appropriate price or yield for that bond. For example, a trader bidding on a corporate bond might base the bid on the relevant-maturity Treasury security, increase the yield (decrease the price) for the lower rating of the corporate and for a call feature, and decrease the yield (increase the price) for a sinking fund provision.

Existence of a conversion feature is one additional element to be considered along with other features in valuing a bond. *APBO 14* indicates that adjustments for features other than the conversion privilege also may be needed because nonconvertible bonds often have different restrictions and characteristics than convertibles.[19] Thus, the broader question is whether a general consensus among individuals valuing convertible bonds can be reached when valuing various convertibles with different ratings and features. In other words, can finance professionals agree as to the value attributable to the various features and characteristics that are found in convertible bonds?

To test this question, an experiment was conducted in which corporate bond market-makers were asked to bid on convertible bonds. The bids of the different traders were compared for each bond to determine the extent to which the traders agreed with one another in their bidding. Because the bonds used in the experiment were selling at prices well in excess of the equivalent stock values—the bonds were not trading off the stock values—the traders were expected to estimate both the debt value of the bonds and the value of the various additional features, including the conversion option, and provide total valuations in the form of bids.

The experiment was conducted by a professional bond trader in a real trade setting; the market-makers from whom bids were solicited were not aware that an experiment was being conducted. All bids on a particular issue were solicited within a few minutes of one another, as would be done in a real trade situation.

Corporate bonds for the study were selected from those listed in both the National Daily Quotation Service (Bond Section) and Moody's Bond Record. Only bonds with at least eight market-makers were included in the experiment. A higher limit for the minimum number of market-makers was set than in the previous section because bids (a commitment to buy at a particular price) were solicited in this part of the study rather than quotes (general levels with no commitment). Therefore, some market-makers were expected to "pass" rather than bid, passes often having to do with that trader's inventory position. In addition, not all market-makers in a particular issue were asked to bid. Traders often establish working relationships with particular market-makers and may avoid dealing with certain other market-makers for some reason. Bids were solicited from at least five market-makers for each security; the selection of specific market-makers from whom to solicit bids for each security was left to the trader.

Only bonds not listed on an exchange nor included in the NASDAQ (National Association of Securities Dealers Automated Quotation) system for over-the-counter securities and only bonds trading with interest and not nearing maturity were selected. Bond listings and automated quotes were viewed as having the potential for reducing the variability of bids because market-makers would have knowledge of other bids. Unusual situations were excluded because the aim of the study was to focus on the valuation of bond features and not upon assessments of the impact of unusual occurrences. Further, the bonds selected had to be trading at prices well in excess of the equivalent stock prices.

A total of six bond issues were found to be suitable for the study. The relatively small number of usable bonds resulted primarily from the need for a sufficient number of bids for each bond issue so that the degree of consensus could be assessed while ensuring that traders were unable to use electronically shared information in the determination of those bids.

As indicated in Table 3, the six bond issues used in the study carried Moody's bond ratings ranging from BAA3 to B3. The issues also reflected a range of relationships between the value of the convertible bonds and the value of the equivalent shares into which those bonds were convertible (see Price of Equivalent Shares in Table 3).

---

[19]APB Opinion No. 14, para. 8.

TABLE 3

Bids on Selected Convertible Bonds

Bond Issuer	Nominal Rate and Maturity	Moody's Bond Rating	Bids	Price of Equivalent Shares*	Bid Variation as % of Low Bid	Bid Variation as % of Face Value
America West Air	7.5% 2011	B2	59.5, 59.5 59.125 59, 59 58.5 Pass	500	1.7	1.0
Convex Computer Corp.	6.0% 2012	B3	63.5, 63.5, 63.5 63 Pass, Pass	339	.8	.5
Costco Wholesale Corp.	7.25% 2011	B3	97 96.25 96 Pass, Pass	792	1.0	1.0
Hechinger Corp.	5.5% 2012	BAA3	90.25 90 89.5 89 Pass, Pass, Pass	638	1.4	1.3
Nortek Inc.	7.5% 2006	B1	64, 64, 64, 64 63	265	1.6	1.0
Tri-Star Pictures, Inc. (Columbia Pictures Entertainment, Inc.)	7.125% 2006	B2	88 87.75 87.5 87 86 80** Pass	672	2.3	2.0

*This column represents the market value of the equivalent shares for a $1,000 face value bond on the day bids were solicited for the bonds. A comparison of the value of equivalent shares to the value of a $1,000 bond can be accomplished by multiplying the amounts in the Bids column by ten.

**See footnote 20

The bids received for each bond issue in the study are shown in Table 3, as is the variation (high bid minus low bid) for each bond, both as a percentage of the low bid and as a percentage of the par value of the bond. The variation of bids as a percentage of the low bid ranges from .8% to 2.3%, and the variation of bids as a percentage of the face value of the bonds ranges from .5% to 2%.[20] While no attempt was made to define or test for statistical significance of the variability of bids under virtually any measure of materiality used in accounting, the variations found would be considered not material.

[20]The analysis excludes one bid received for the bonds of Tri-Star Pictures. As can be seen from Table 3, one bid (80) differed from the others by a considerable margin. This bid was provided by a market-maker who stated that the normal trader specializing in that issue was absent that day and he was not very familiar with the issue. In the opinion of the trader soliciting the bids, the substitute market-maker bid well off the market, a method sometimes used by traders to pass.

The results of this experiment are not conclusive evidence that finance professionals agree in their estimates of the values of conversion premiums. Given, however, that valuation of the straight-debt component of a convertible security is very mechanistic, little variability would be expected in the valuation of this component of a convertible security.[21] Thus, the small amount of bid variability over the several securities in the study implies a lack of variability in estimates of individual features of the securities.

SUMMARY, CONCLUSIONS, AND IMPLICATIONS

The results of this study provide insight into (1) the practicality of the fundamental financial instrument approach identified by the FASB as the appropriate means of accounting for new hybrid financial instruments and (2) the question of whether the *APBO 14* guidelines for accounting for traditional convertible debt securities should be restructured to conform with the APB's original position in *APBO 10.*

APBO 14 presented two reasons for requiring that all proceeds of convertible bond issues be accounted for as debt. The first reason given was the inseparability of the constituent components. This argument was not well supported in the opinion or in the literature. Because *APBO 14* requires that when the equity element of a convertible debt issue is significant it should be recognized, materiality seems to be the issue, not inseparability. The major reason for not apportioning some amount to the conversion feature of convertible debt, seems to relate to the practical problems of making such an allocation.

While the practical difficulties of estimating the value of a conversion option may have been a barrier at the time *APBO 14* was issued, accounting and finance professionals now have had more than twenty years of experience in dealing with convertible securities and, to a lesser extent, other types of hybrid financial instruments. Clearly those estimates are being made currently. Evidence presented in this study supports previous findings and shows that finance professionals do estimate the prices (or yields) of convertible bonds as if they were nonconvertible and then value the conversion feature. These estimates are apparently suitable for decisions involving many millions of dollars and should prove satisfactory for the accounting allocations originally required by *APBO 10.*

This study also provides evidence that different finance professionals assessing the same debt features independently can achieve a consensus as to the value of the debt. Currently, even though there is agreement that a conversion option has value, accountants assign it a value of zero. While there is no way of determining the "true value" of a particular debt feature such as a conversion option, agreement among finance professionals should provide a better estimate than accounting for the feature as if it had no value.

In sum, the study provided several pieces of evidence collectively favoring the feasibility of estimating the portion of the proceeds of convertible debt issues attributable to the conversion feature. This evidence supports the notion of accounting for hybrid financial instruments according to the economic substance of the instruments by dealing with each of the key elements individually instead of classifying an entire instrument as either debt or equity. The approach reported herein may help resolve the issues currently before the FASB involving hybrid financial instruments.

---

[21] M. Stephens, "Inseparability and the Valuation of Convertible Bonds," *Journal of Accountancy* (August 1971), p. 57.

II-C

MEASUREMENT OF SHAREHOLDER EQUITY AND E.P.S.

II-C1

OWNERS' EQUITY: THE ANACHRONISTIC ELEMENT

Richard A. Scott

One of the most deep-seated and incontrovertible concepts embraced by accounting theory is that of "owners' equity." It is a concept that seems to be held universally, there being little attention directed specifically to its critical evaluation in the accounting literature. The FASB *Conceptual Framework* Discussion Memorandum [1976, par. 187–191] presents the element of owners' equity in a way that makes it appear closed to discussion from the outset, except for how it is affected by income determination. Elsewhere in the literature, the concept is also generally accepted as a truism. Owners' equity is a subset of the extant classification system employed in accounting. It is not, however, a part of the only conceivable basis for classification and so its validity, as well as that of the system of which it is a subset, ought to be scrutinized and evaluated.

In the sections that follow, an analysis of the process of constructing and employing classification systems will be undertaken. The conditions that should be met by this process are stated as principles of division, nomenclature, and definition. The concept of equity, and particularly owners' equity, is then examined in light of the tenets of classification and typology theory. Finally, a proposal is offered for a different classification scheme.

Richard A. Scott is Associate Professor of Accounting, McIntire School of Commerce, University of Virginia.

Richard A. Scott, "Owners' Equity, the Anachronistic Element," American Accounting Association, *The Accounting Review,* Vol. LIV, No. 4, October 1979. Reprinted by permission of the American Accounting Association.

CLASSIFICATION AND CATEGORIES

Even though the process of classification and the use of categories is pervasive in accounting, there has been less effort devoted to their systematic analysis and theoretical rationalization than in many other disciplines. An abundant literature on this topic exists in anthropology [Washburn, 1963], biology [Blackwelder, 1967; Simpson, 1967], logic [Searles, 1968], and the social sciences [Hempel, 1963]. There are theories and principles *apropos* to accounting that can be borrowed to its advantage. A synthesis follows.

The subjects with which we work and that are to be classified are discrete, objective events or units. They are known as transactions in accounting and specimens in the natural sciences. Each object that is a candidate for classification is unique; in a sense, every single object is somehow different from every other. Were there no facets of objects that correspond to those of other objects, classification would not be possible. It is the correspondence of some feature, attribute, or property between objects that permits grouping and makes possible the ensuing generalizations of description and prediction. An objective of description is to indicate the relationship, by kind and degree, between groups or classes. That, in turn, implies the creation of at least two, and possibly several coordinate categories, each forming an enclosure for objects with a correspondent attribute. The attribute that demarcates and distinguishes one coordinate category from another is known as its *differentia*. Thus, a particular attribute serves both to unite some objects as well as to segregate those allied objects from other congregations.

If all objects were strictly viewed as being unique, it would be difficult to attach significance to their observation or measurement. They take on far more significance when comprehended as the constituency of a population that is related by some common feature and identified as belonging to a category. Because of the multiplicity of characteristics possessed by objects, it is possible to divide a population into subsets based upon a commonality of still other characteristics and for which lower-order categories are then created. This is accomplished by specifying additional attributes to that which initially established the higher-order category. A lower-order category, therefore, is based upon and implies population members that possess both a correspondent attribute that makes them part of the higher-order population, and a *differentia* attribute that distinguishes them from those members in the other lower-order category.

A hierarchic system of categories is formed by expanding the number of specified, identifying characteristics that a population to be classified must possess. The more extensive the specification of characteristics, the narrower in scope a category becomes and the more exactingly described is its member population. And so descriptive power is enhanced. At one extreme, each object could be classified in a category based on all of its characteristics. One category for every single object would result, providing information virtually devoid of its power of generalization. At the other extreme, were only a single category established for all objects, it would be so lacking in its power of specificity as to be virtually devoid of informational value.

Exactly what constitutes an optimum number of categories, and how are the characteristics selected that will serve to distinguish population members? The selection of distinguishing attributes hinges on how the information is to be employed. Any one of a number of different attributes possessed by an object may be chosen to serve in some special inquiry. Soil possesses a pH factor that is of importance to a farmer, a mineral content that is of importance to a metallurgist, and a weight-bearing capacity that is of importance to an architect. User needs and interests determine which characteristic or attribute of an object is to be identified. Similarly, the number of categories in a system is a function of the nature and objective of the activity that brought about observation of classifiable objects in the first place, subject to the requirements of *systematic fruitfulness* and *parsimony*. Categories will be fruitful if they facilitate sound descriptive generalization and serve well in the process of prediction. The fewest meaningful or significant major categories possible should be created to cover the greatest number of observations if the mandate for parsimony is to be fulfilled. The structure of a classification system is not inviolable, however. Change can create the need for a different system or basis of classification; change in the form of new knowledge, differing circumstances, phylogeny of population members, *etc.*

Certain principles apply to categorization in addition to those of systematic fruitfulness and parsimony:

1. Categories must be exhaustive, or comprehensive. Each and every member of a population can be classified in one of the categories that have been established. All of the sub-categories add to the total of the next highest order of class. Ideally, then, there ought to be no objects left over, or incapable of being classified.
2. Each object ought to be classified in only one category. Coordinate categories should be mutually exclusive.
3. A coordinate category should be differentiated on the basis of a single characteristic, or *fundamentum divisionis*. The basis of division should be explicitly stated and of central importance to the purposes of the activity.

As an example, biologists have devised a classification system for the animal kingdom [Collingwood, 1965, p. 30]. The principal category exhaustively includes all animals and will not include any vegetables or minerals. Articulating subcategories (subphylum) further divide certain animal members in accordance with whether they have a spinal column into vertebrates (with backbone) and invertebrates (without backbone).

NOMENCLATURE AND DEFINITION

A concomitant aspect of division, or category creation, is their designation with appropriate nomenclature. There are certain principles that apply to nomenclature and the definition of terms, or titles used in classification systems. Clearly a category must have an appelation, or descriptive label for identification, differentiation, and analytical purposes. These designative titles, or terms, have semantic implications that are important to accounting theory. In addition, the designative terms used to label categories must be defined as a corollary aspect of a classification system. Let us examine the requirements for category titles and title definitions in that order.

Linguistic rules require that terms have the same meaning for both parties, sender and receiver, and that they operate as a referent to the thing or concept being portrayed by a category. In other words, ideally, the content of a category ought to be unambiguously revealed to the message participants by its title. Class terms and common nouns (*e.g.*, man, horse, accounts payable) have two types of meaning: connotative and denotative. The *denotation* of a term is all of the specific objects, class members, or actual things to which the term applies and the class of these objects constitutes its extension. For example, "owners' equity" denotes all members of the class: capital stock, additional-paid-in-capital, and retained earnings. These members in turn constitute an extension of the term "owners' equity." The denotative capacity of a term relates to the principle of classification requiring that all categories should be exhaustive.

A term also has a *connotative* value. It captures and identifies that set of essential characteristics or attributes that hold for all the members of a class. These essential, defining characteristics are a term's intensional meaning. Because terms or titles have this trait, category labels can be expected to refer to the characteristics that are the basis for correspondence and differentia of member populations. It appears reasonable to ask that category titles employed in accounting be consistent with their class or population by expressing the distinguishing attributes of the class and exhaustively extend to all of its members.

A category label, despite its connotative and denotative meanings, should be explicitly defined. Definition of the designation given to a category ought to comply with rules of definition. These rules are outlined by Searles [1968, pp. 47–49]:

1. It should state the essential attributes or characteristics (correspondent and differentia) of the population that is to be classified in the category.
2. It should be exactly equivalent to the class of objects being defined: neither too broad nor too narrow.
3. It should not contain the name or label of the category being defined.
4. It should not be negative when it can be affirmative.
5. It should not be expressed in ambiguous, obscure, or figurative language.

ACCOUNTING CLASSIFICATION

Classification in accounting can be readily observed in: (a) data collection, (b) account posting, and (c) financial statement preparation. Classification and the use of categories takes place at other levels and in other accounting activities, but those just enumerated are particularly relevant to our discussion.

Data collection involves two concurrent aspects: observation of a unit to identify its distinguishing attribute for purposes of categorization, and, secondly, measurement of the magnitude of that attribute. It is useful in analysis to maintain a conceptual distinction between the two phases of attribute identification and attribute measurement that take place in accounting data collection. For example, a problem of measurement may exist even though a "correct" attribute has been identified, and, conversely, a measurement may be "correct" but the attribute identified is inappropriate. In both cases, the outcome is flawed; the explanation for the imperfect outcome, however, is quite different.

Summarization of data takes place and is eventually recorded in accounts, which are themselves categories. Accounts are then employed—as is, or upon further aggregation with other similar accounts—to construct financial statements. Financial statements can also be conceived as sets of categories with each statement containing its own compartments such as assets, owners' equity, operating expenses, *etc.* It is financial statement categories, and in particular the credit side of a balance sheet, that are the subject of what follows.

The categories of "owners' equity," "liabilities," and their sum, the balance sheet credit side—a category in itself—will be made subject to the principles of division (categories), nomenclature, and definition discussed earlier and evaluated accordingly. The law has been a significant influence in the evolution of accounting, especially for owners' equity. This analysis proceeds with an awareness of the role of law but also recognizes the desirability of evaluation according to precepts of theoretical propriety. Accounting theory and practice already reflect departures from strictly legal considerations, as, for example, in the case of consolidated financial statements, the recording of executory contracts such as capital leases, and the realization of revenue prior to or after the passage of title (precious metals; cash receipts basis). Nor would it seem a reasonable proposition that because of law, theoretical inquiry should either cease or remain within limits imposed on the accounting discipline by legal prescriptions.

THE BALANCE SHEET CREDIT SIDE

A balance sheet is demarcated into a debit side where assets and contra assets are classified, and a credit side where other real accounts are classified. The discriminate segregation of items into one side or another, and the dollar equality of the two sides, establish the idea that these are categories. As a category, the balance sheet credit side is subject to the principles of division, nomenclature, and definition. The credit side itself is divided into sub-categories which are also subject to the same principles. Furthermore, because measurement aggregations as well as attribute groupings are involved, it should be expected that the attributes are not only capable of being measured but that the measurements have some logical association with assets.

It is fairly common, in practice as well as in the literature, to observe the credit side of a balance sheet without a label identifying what this category is. "Liabilities and Owners' Equity" does not identify the credit side itself, only its two major sub-categories. The sub-category titles do not make it clear which is the correspondent attribute and which the differentia. Paton [1922, C. 2, 3, and 4] recognized these requirements and identified the credit side as "equities" (the correspondent attribute). He also called attention [p. 54n] to a practice of the day which was to denominate the entire credit side of a balance sheet as "liabilities." In the absence of consistent, widespread use of a category title, we could look to definitions or explanations of what the balance sheet credit side represents. However, a more efficient mode of analysis can be undertaken by drawing on some of the ideas developed earlier.

The two major sub-categories, liabilities and owners' equity, ought to be based upon a single characteristic or attribute which they share in common, because they are subordinate components of the principal category, the balance sheet credit side. That correspondent characteristic should be the *fundamentum divisionis* that is possessed by all members. In addition, the two major sub-categories should be demarcated by differentia—attributes exclusive to the populations of each. The connotative meaning of each category's title should indicate its differentia and correspondent characteristics and can serve as a point of departure. In short, by analyzing the sub-categories of liabilities and owners' equity and evaluating them with the standards for division, nomenclature, and definition, we can simultaneously draw conclusions regarding the balance sheet credit side category.

OWNERS' EQUITY

In the literature of accounting, owners' equity is usually described as being a representation of owner rights or claims. It is also viewed as a residual interest [FASB, 1976, par. 187; AICPA,

1970, par. 132], the "residual" being a result of regarding it as a difference between the categories "assets" and "liabilities." An "interest" is a legal share, a right or a claim. The balance sheet credit side has also been described [AAA, 1957, p. 7] as being made up of creditor equities (interests, claims) and shareholder equities (interests, residual claims) in the same way as Paton had described it [1922, p. 53]. We can explore the validity of "equity" as the attribute jointly possessed by all members classified in the balance sheet credit side, and owner versus creditor as designations of the attributes that serve to demarcate that side into its two major divisions.

Claims and rights are essentially equivalents, both being legal concepts. Black [1957, p. 313] describes a claim as being "legal capability to require a positive or negative act of another person." Kohler [1963, p. 86] defines "claim" as a demand under law. He also equates claim with equity, which in turn is defined by him as a right or claim to assets. If owners' equity is equivalent to the rights or claims of owners, then those rights should not only be subject to quantification but they should also be linked with assets both in amount and through logical association. These requirements would seem to be implied by the fact that a variety of individual "owners' equity" accounts are created and the magnitude of each is measured, throughout which accountants purposively and painstakingly maintain a balance between assets and "equities." As a case in point the rights of shareholders will be examined, although by the time this paper is finished, it will be apparent that the conclusions drawn extend to all legal forms of business ownership.

The rights of shareholders have been enumerated (see Figure 1) by Dewing [1953] and grouped accordingly as rights to management, rights to the corporate property, and rights to pass on changes in the original contract. Rights to pass on changes in the original contract (C), and to management (A) are neither reducible to quantitative values in any objective way, nor are they logically correlated with assets in a manner that would justify a proposition such as the basic accounting equation. For example, one would be hard-pressed to substantiate that "X" number of dollars in shareholders' equity is a measure of the right to demand financial statements, to elect directors, or to pass on changes in the bylaws or charter. Furthermore, as a practical matter, the value of most of these rights is questionable. Of the rights to management, all but the election of directors are seldom exercised, and the election of directors is of dubious significance. Voting is for a single slate of directors that is submitted by a nominating committee often dominated by the directors themselves, a number of whom may be members of executive management. The vote is either for or against, is seldom cumulative, and is frequently exercised by proxy. Changes in the original contract are uncommon. The scope of allowable corporate activities is ordinarily stated in broad terms to provide for change or expansion without shareholder consent. Many capital stock issues do not contain a preemptive right (C4), and even when present it often has been voluntarily surrendered.

Nor is shareholders' equity an expression and valuation of rights to corporate property (B). The right to dividends is not classified as shareholders' equity. Once a dividend is declared, it is a terminable obligation of the firm, and is classified as a liability. The right to share in liquidating proceeds from sale of the firm's assets after settlement of all liabilities, is contrary to an assumption of the going concern as expressed in the postulate of continuity [Moonitz, 1961, pp. 38–41]. It would be incongruous to report on a right which, it is assumed, will not be exercised. Even where exercise is the intention, valuation of such a right certainly would not be based on acquisition costs of assets, but rather on liquidation values. Obviously, no attempt is being made to measure this possibility in contemporary general-purpose financial statements.

FIGURE 1

Shareholder Rights

A. Rights to Management
   1. To elect directors. (Certain state statutes also vest in the shareholders the right to elect certain officers.)
   2. To inspect certain books—and in most jurisdictions, to demand financial statements.
   3. To approve or disapprove of certain extraordinary transactions, such as the sale or mortgage of important corporate property.
   4. To review, in general, the fiduciary action of directors by a plenary power of removal or action in equity for abuse of the discretionary power of the directors.

B. Rights to the Corporate Property
   1. To receive dividends when, as and if declared by the directors.
   2. To receive a proportionate share of the corporate property, when the corporation is wound up, or its property sold or exchanged.

C. Rights to Pass on Changes of the Original Contract
   1. To pass on changes in the purposes for which the corporation was organized.
   2. To pass on changes in the charter.
   3. To pass on changes in the bylaws.
   4. To subscribe to all subsequent issues of stock, subject to restrictions by state statutes or the provisions of corporate charter.

Source: Dewing [1953, p. 106].

An additional right absent from Dewing's list is the legal right of a shareholder to take his certificate and transfer it at his pleasure. This right is an abstraction which is perhaps reducible to valuation by reference to current market values for the shares, but market values are equal to book values only by sheer coincidence. It is doubtful in any case that the market price of shares would relate solely to this single right.

The idea that the shareholders' equity category and its associated valuation is a representation of shareholder rights has no substance. Rights are either abstractions that defy objective valuation, or are valued only by reference to amounts obtainable on liquidation, or in the market transfer of shares. The latter valuations are either contradictory to the basis of valuation for a going concern, or are irrelevant to accounting for the entity. Lastly, rights and claims are invoked by shareholders when they turn to the courts for redress. That is an occurrence that is neither in keeping with the usual, expected course of events, nor is it consonant with assumptions of enterprise continuity.

Equity has an additional connotation to that of rights or claims. It is also held by Black [1957, p. 634] to be "the amount or value of a property above the total liens or charges." It is a concept of wealth which is commonly used in conjunction with real property ownership [Boykin, 1975, p. 49], or life insurance policies [Levy, 1968, p. 180]. In both cases, reference is made to the current amount of resources that could be obtained upon liquidation of those assets. When applied to corporate shareholders, the concept of residual wealth can be interpreted in different ways. One might base such a measure on either the market value of outstanding shares or the liquidation value of net assets. Quite obviously, neither of the two possibilities is germane to the issue at hand since the former is irrelevant to measurements about the corporate accounting entity and the latter is a contradiction of the going concern assumption.

There is a third concept of the residual wealth of shareholders. In theory, if the net assets of an entity reflected the discounted present value of all future net cash flows, owners' equity would represent the shareholders' residual wealth. However, the historical cost model and current cost models are based upon entry price valuations of net assets. The discounted present value of future cash flows is an exit price basis of valuation. Conceptually the two are different, and consequently it would be theoretically incorrect to contend that an entry price valuation model will generally reflect shareholder residual wealth. Furthermore, the discounted present value of future cash flows from recorded net assets will not equal the same sort of measure of present value for the entire entity. And finally, it is generally conceded that a present value model of the firm is not yet capable of being implemented. It is apparent that shareholders' residual wealth is not portrayed in the traditional balance sheet. There are additional flaws in the received rationale attending owners' equity that have to do with it as a category within a system of categories. They will be discussed in the next section, where "liabilities" will be analyzed.

LIABILITIES

We are immediately confronted with a question: Is this category "creditor equities" or "owner liabilities?" The title is ambiguous; it does not clearly indicate the essential attributes of the population (correspondent *and* differentia), and it is not equivalent to the class of objects being classified, as we will soon see. Moonitz [1960] called attention to the disparity between a legal definition of liability and what was implied by accounting practice. Although he did not suggest that the category label be changed, it is apparent that the meaning he attached to the title is not confined by law but instead is an economic concept concerned with commitments ("obligations") to future resource outflows.

The meaning of liability in the law is either very broad and general, or quite specific, being tantamount to debt. The former interpretation—an obligation to do, pay, or make something good—goes beyond the boundaries of accounting and economic affairs. The notion of debt, in turn, is too restrictive to explain the variety of balances that are classified as liabilities but are not unconditional promises to pay a fixed or determinable sum at a specified time, including interest. Persistent efforts to describe this category as liabilities, which is basically a legal concept, have led to conflicts in the past that were very difficult to resolve and which raised questions about the "fruitfulness" of such a category. For example, the recording of executory contracts such as capital leases and unfunded pension cost liabilities was resisted on the ground that they were not liabilities or "legal debt." But they were commitments taken on by the firm that would call for resources in the future, and that, in the final analysis, was a more important and relevant consideration than legal status. Rather than holding out this category as a representation of liabilities, can it be held to be creditor equities? If so, it would corroborate the proposition that the credit side of a balance sheet represents claims or rights.

It is difficult to conceive of creditors having any claims or rights with respect to the debtor firm other than those afforded by the courts. Legal rights are those which give the creditor an ability to demand that the terms of a contract be fulfilled, or to receive indemnification for damages suffered because of non-performance. However, in the usual course of events, especially when operating under the assumption of a going-concern, a firm will virtually always discharge its obligations without creditors having to invoke their legal rights. It would seem reasonable to believe that financial statements purport to communicate something more than that which is highly unlikely to occur.

In addition, the notion of rights or claims has returned us full-circle to a legal basis for classification essentially equivalent to "liability." We have already pointed out that financial statements customarily include accounts such as capital lease contracts payable and unfunded pension costs payable, which are not rights, claims, or legal liabilities. The same is true of estimated warranty costs, deferred profit on certain installment sales, and deferred investment tax credits, among others. A principle of logic stipulated by Werkmeister [1968, p. 168] states that, "what is true universally, *i.e., what is true of each and every member of a given class, is true of any given member of that class.*" This condition is also cited as a necessary property of a rational classification system by an American Accounting Association committee [1977, p. 77]. It is illogical to contend that all species in a category, such as claims, are claims, when in fact some are not. It is not only the category label that is deficient—be it liabilities, claims, rights, or equities—the category itself fails the criterion of being exhaustive.

The category also suffers from another shortcoming. Lazarsfeld and Barton [1951, p. 157] explain that, "In an articulated set of categories those on each step must be exhaustive and mutually exclusive." Because owners' equity and liabilities are coordinate categories, this requirement pertains to both with equal force. A cursory examination of balance sheets is sufficient to reveal items, seemingly adrift in a "no-man's land" between liabilities and owners' equity, such as Minority Interest, Deferred Income Taxes, and Deferred Investment-Tax Credits. Is the Excess of Unallocated Book Value Over Cost arising out of a bargain purchase business combination a liability or an element of owners' equity? Although accountants are disposed to claim that they are concerned more with economic substance than legal form, it is likely that a bond in perpetuity would be classified as a liability. By the same token, convertible debentures with underlying shares whose market price has risen well beyond their conversion price threshold would remain in the liabilities category along with other terminable obligations, and preferred shares with a mandatory retirement provision would be excluded because they are legally members of the "ownership equity" group. Distinctions such as these do not rest on substantive differences but rather on legal technicalities which inordinately stretch the boundaries of common sense. In large measure, this shortcoming is a fault of a classification system based on equities and liabilities, categories which are not exhaustive and not mutually exclusive.

A RECOUNTING

From the preceding analysis of the balance sheet credit side and its major sub-divisions, the following conclusions can be drawn:

1. The attributes presumed to characterize the categories in question are legal qualities. It is very questionable that in the course of observing transactions an analysis is made of whether a change has occurred in the asserted legal rights of shareholders: rights to manage; rights to pass on changes in the original contract, or; rights to corporate property upon liquidation. It is dubious that accounts, or the categories of which they are a part, could portray qualities such as these.

2. Legal qualities (attributes) are abstractions that do not lend themselves to measurement in dollar terms.
3. There are members being classified that cannot be explained as possessing the attribute of "equity of creditors" (*e.g.,* warranty cost, certain executory contracts). Therefore, the category being identified by the title is not exhaustive, and the title itself fails in denotating class members.
4. The categories of liabilities and owners' equity are neither exhaustive nor mutually exclusive. Balance sheets are readily observable which contain credit side members that are not in either category (*e.g.,* deferred credits, minority interest) or that are factitiously classified (*e.g.,* preferred stock with mandatory retirement provision, convertible bonds with prices that make conversion almost inevitable).
5. A representation of equities would be irrelevant to the accounting entity as a going concern since legal claims and rights are not resorted to under normal circumstances. Furthermore, even if that were what was being presented, the basis of valuation would logically be some form of liquidation price, not entry prices.

Principally because of these reasons, it is concluded that owners' equity and liabilities (and equities in total) are not valid bases of classification. An alternative basis will now be proposed.

A DIFFERENT CLASSIFICATION BASIS

Several writers [Marple, 1962, pp. 57–60; Goldberg, 1965, p. 171] have posited that a balance sheet can be viewed as a reflection of economic resources or capital (intangible as well as tangible) and the sources of capital. The balance sheet is not only a financial statement but a category as well. It is a category whose correspondent characteristic is resources, with subdivisions that reflect the composition (debit side) and sources of capital (credit side). Paton [1922, pp. 44, 76] referred to equities as "sources of funds" and "investments." Only assets that accountants are able to record are comprehended by the term "economic resources." The entry process that takes place when assets are initially acquired identifies the asset and its source. Subsequent events and decisions may bring about substitutions and shifts in both the composition of assets as well the sources of capital, but the basic nature of neither is thereby altered.

It is understood, therefore, that the sources of capital presented on a balance sheet are not necessarily the original providers of capital to the firm. Capital obtained originally from customers or creditors for example, may be committed for conveyance to the government or employees. Although the latter parties did not supply the capital originally, we may attribute to their willingness to forego immediate collection, credit for the firm holding more in assets than would otherwise be the case. There is no intention to purport that all of the various sources are either original suppliers or original creators of capital. The entity has assets (capital) because sources have furnished them directly, or suspended temporarily their prerogative to withdraw them. Nor is it intended to suggest that the *specific* assets presented on a balance sheet came from any particular source, or even from these reported sources for that matter. For example, a specific asset may have been secured with proceeds from sale of another asset.

"Sources of capital" is a classification basis for the credit side of a balance sheet that is rational, consistent, exhaustive, and which clearly identifies the common characteristic shared by all included accounts. Furthermore, it is linked with assets (capital) both in amount and through logical association. Note, also, that this basis of classification relates directly to the entity unlike "owners' equity" which incongruously attempts to make a representation about another, outside entity (shareholders). How it may be divided into mutually exclusive categories will be demonstrated shortly.

Many accounts are evident and self-explanatory sources of capital. This is apparent in the case of trade credit, notes, bonds, mortgages, lease contracts, customer deposits, donations, capital stock, and retained earnings. Others are not and therefore call for some further explanation. At first glance dividends payable may not appear to be a source of capital because they are born out of a declaration by the Board of Directors. If we rephrase the wording of the account to "profits awaiting distribution to shareholders," the source of capital becomes clearly evident. Estimated product warranty costs arise when product sales are recorded and it is recognized that there will be a future use of resources to carry out repair services. In setting product price, a factor is taken into consideration to provide for repair services so that revenues are, in part, resources obtained in advance from customers for fulfillment of warranty contracts. Therefore, the presence of a warranty sold in conjunction with a product results in capital being obtained by the firm. Similarly, because income taxes are passed on to customers, taxes payable can also be identified with that source.

Accrued liabilities and employee withholdings have been labeled by Hunt *et al.* [1971, pp. 203–8] as "spontaneous," or "self-generating" sources of credit. These liabilities would call for immediate payment were it not for institutionalized procedures established for the sake of economical collection and payment of obligations. In theory, payment of taxes, salaries, interest, and fees could be required daily instead of at longer intervals. The expense and effort necessary to accomplish this kind of arrangement would be inordinate. Consequently, the designated recipients of these resources, by leaving them with the firm pending payment are, in essence, sources of capital. The reasoning underlying a liability for an adverse legal judgment is correspondingly based upon the court's deference in collecting the decreed amount.

How all accounts on the credit side of a balance sheet are alike has been explained. This category can now be defined.

> **Sources of Capital:** A designation accorded the credit side of a balance sheet. It is a category that portrays the entity's acquisition of capital in past transactions which is now invested or held in various asset forms, and the magnitude thereof.

We may now inquire into how some accounts are different from others in order to move on to a new set of mutually exclusive categories.

A NEW DIVISION

Of the several characteristics that are possessed by different sources of capital, the one which seems to be of paramount interest to financial statement users is whether or not, as the firm now views it, they will be settled by conveying assets. The conveyance of assets is a critical event. Ordinarily, it will be accomplished in the form of cash, and so provision must be made for an appropriate alteration in the composition of assets. Then assets have to be obtained to replace those liquidated and disbursed, or a contraction of operating levels must take place. This theme is keynoted in the FASB *Statement of Concepts* on objectives of financial reporting [1978, par. 37]. The extent to which sources of capital are transitory or not is relevant to many users of financial information. Some sources are transitory while others are not, in the sense that an entity has recognized and made commitments[1] to a future outflow of resources as a consequence of past events or transactions.

Fundamentally, in reporting liabilities an entity is recognizing that a critical, interrelated series of asset transformations, cash flows, and refinancing-reinvestment activities will have to take place which requires careful balancing and timing. At the heart of these cyclical phases in a corporation's life are asset flows. Conversely, some sources of capital do not impose the same sort of exigencies. They are standing sources of capital devoted to an investment in resources which are not now committed to a future outflow. It is cognizance of the permanence, or lack of permanence of sources of capital which can serve as the basis for demarcating a balance sheet credit side into two mutually exclusive categories. These categories will be referred to hereafter as "Transitory Sources of Capital" (TSC) and "Standing Sources of Capital" (SSC). The basic accounting equation thus becomes:

$$\text{(Assets) } A = SC \qquad \text{and} \qquad SC = TSC + SSC$$

Transitory Sources of Capital

Those items which are customarily classified as liabilities are for the most part terminable obligations, and therefore should be classified as Transitory Sources of Capital. Liabilities which are unconditional promises to pay or deliver a sum certain are included as are obligations of estimated amount even when the other party is not specifically known. A necessary proviso is that all obligations are from past transactions [Cf. Moonitz, 1960]. In addition to liabilities, other accounts representing a source of capital which is transitory would be classified in this category. An issue of preferred shares that will be retired either because of a mandatory provision in the contract, or because the firm intends to exercise an optional call provision, is an example of such an item. Other items which are now conventionally reported as liabilities—often because it is difficult to reason that they are components of "owners' equity"—would be classified in the Standing Sources of Capital category. We can now explicitly define the basis of this category as follows:

> **Transitory Sources of Capital:** A designation accorded one of the two coordinate divisions of the category, Sources of Capital. It represents an entity's commitment, and the magnitude thereof, to satisfy future demands on resources that are certain, or highly likely to occur (subject to close estimation) resulting from past transactions.

Standing Sources of Capital

In contrast to those sources that are transitory, the remaining items are characterized as being uncommitted to meet future demands on resources coming from outside the firm. They consist of an assortment of items which represent standing sources of capital invested in recorded assets, whether or not they are owner sources. Standing Sources of Capital does not mean that there is a permanent and inviolable source of capital which will never be encroached upon. It

[1]The Committee on External Reporting [AAA, 1969, p. 98] took the position that a balance sheet is a source of information on "stocks of resources" and "resource commitments."

can be diminished by reason of future losses, distributions of future dividends in excess of profits, or other disinvestments. However, it is not now earmarked as a source which will result in an outflow of resources and as such is intrinsically different from Transitory Sources of Capital. Numbered among the constituents of the Standing Sources of Capital group are: contributions by majority and minority shareholders, except for those cases where repayment is anticipated; donations; warrants capitalized as outstanding or because they expired; retained earnings; convertible bonds when conversion is anticipated and probable; the excess of unallocated book value over cost; bonds in perpetuity; and holding gains or losses.[2]

Treasury shares carried as a contra to the shareholders' capital account can be interpreted as an amount of capital returned to a particular source. A more consistent application of the sources of capital concept would be to treat the shares as if they had been formally retired by an appropriate reduction of accounts. By the same token, a deficit should be reported as a reduction of the total sources of capital to indicate the extent to which resources obtained by the entity have been depleted due to unprofitable activities.

A technical problem arises out of the convention of capitalizing retained earnings when stock dividends and certain split-ups (which are essentially stock dividends) are effected. In these cases, an amount is deducted from retained earnings and added to the capital stock, and possibly to the additional-paid-in-capital accounts. This aberrant transfer distorts the valuation of each of the respective source-of-capital accounts. Presenting each of the paid-in capital accounts as being comprised of two elements, that actually paid in and that transferred in, would allow us to preserve the integrity of source valuations. In conclusion, a definition can be stated as follows:

> **Standing Sources of Capital:** A designation accorded the second of two coordinate divisions of the category, Sources of Capital. It represents the source and magnitude of capital arising out of past transactions that is presently uncommitted to the settlement of obligations and, therefore, is devoted to a standing investment in assets.

CONCLUSION

The existing basis of classification for the credit side of a balance sheet and for its sub-categories is deficient. It is not exhaustive nor are the articulating categories mutually exclusive. Owners' equity is incapable of being satisfactorily explained, and its measurement is an enigma. The rationale offered to explain what this category represents is contradictory, internally inconsistent with other aspects of accounting theory, and invalid. An entirely new basis of categorization is needed that is founded on principles of classification and which is consonant with a coherent accounting theory for modern-day entities. The one which is developed here is rooted in a pervasive characteristic possessed by all credit-balance items on the credit side of a balance sheet—they represent sources of capital invested in recorded assets of an entity. An important distinction between these various sources of capital provides the basis for their demarcation into Standing Sources and Transitory Sources of Capital.

[2]The author takes no position in this paper on the question of whether holding gains are determinants of income. It is simply recognized that some accounting models consider them to be capital adjustments, and provision has to be made for such an account.

REFERENCES

American Accounting Association, Committee on Accounting Concepts and Standards, *Accounting and Reporting Standards for Corporate Financial Statements* (AAA, 1957).

American Accounting Association, Committee on External Reporting, "An Evaluation of External Reporting Practices," *The Accounting Review* (Supplement, 1969), pp. 79, 123.

American Accounting Association, Committee on International Accounting Operations and Education. "Report of the Committee on International Accounting Operations and Education," *The Accounting Review* (Supplement, 1977), pp. 67, 132.

American Institute of Certified Public Accountants, "Basic Concepts and Accounting Principles Underlying Financial Statements of Business Enterprises," *Statement of the Accounting Principles Board No. 4* (AICPA, October, 1970).

Black, H. C., *Black's Law Dictionary* (West Publishing Co., 1957).

Blackwelder, R. E., *Taxonomy, A Text and Reference Book* (John Wiley & Sons, Inc., 1967).

Boykin, J. H., *Mortgage Loan Underwriting* (Mortgage Bankers Association of America, 1975).

Collingwood, R. G., *An Essay on Philosophical Method* (Oxford University Press, 1965).

Dewing, A. S., *The Financial Policy of Corporations* (The Ronald Press Company, 1953).

Financial Accounting Standards Board, *Conceptual Framework for Financial Accounting and Reporting: Elements of Financial Statements and Their Measurement* (FASB, December 2, 1976).

Financial Accounting Standards Board, "Objectives of Financial Reporting by Business Enterprises," *Statement of Financial Accounting Concepts No. 1* (November, 1978).

Goldberg, L., *An Inquiry Into The Nature of Accounting* (American Accounting Association, 1965).

Hempel, C. G., "Typological Methods in the Social Sciences," in M. Natanson, editor, *Philosophy of the Social Sciences* (Random House, 1963).

Hunt, P., C. M. Williams, and G. Donaldson, *Basic Business Finance* (Richard D. Irwin, Inc., 1971).

Kohler, E. L., *A Dictionary for Accountants* (Prentice-Hall, Inc., 1963).

Lazarsfeld, P. F. and A. H. Barton, "Qualitative Measurement in the Social Sciences: Classification, Typologies, and Indices," in D. Lerner and H. D. Lasswell, editors, *The Policy Sciences* (Stanford University Press, 1951).

Levy, M. H., *A Handbook of Personal Insurance Terminology* (Farnsworth Publishing Company, Inc., 1968).

Marple, R. P., "The Balance Sheet—Capital Sources and Composition," *The Journal of Accountancy* (November 1962), pp. 57–60.

Moonitz, M., "The Changing Concept of Liabilities," *The Journal of Accountancy* (May 1960), pp. 41–46.

———, "The Basic Postulates of Accounting," *AICPA Accounting Research Study No. 1* (AICPA, 1961).

Paton, W. A., *Accounting Theory* (New York: The Ronald Press Company, 1922), reissued by Scholars Book Company, in 1973.

Searles, H. L., *Logic and Scientific Methods,* Third Edition (The Ronald Press Company, 1968).

Simpson, G. G., *Principles of Animal Taxonomy* (Columbia University Press, 1967).

Sprouse, R. T., "The Balance Sheet—Embodiment of the Most Fundamental Elements of Accounting Theory," in W. E. Stone, editor, *Foundations of Accounting Theory* (University of Florida Press, 1971).

Washburn, S. L., editor, *Classification and Human Evolution* (Aldine Publishing Company, 1963).

Werkmeister, W. H., *The Basis and Structure of Knowledge* (Greenwood Press, Publishers, 1968).

II-C2

HOLDING LOSS/GAIN AS AN ALTERNATIVE TO EPS DILUTION

Donald E. Wiseman

This article presents current value accounting as an alternative to the EPS dilution reporting of APB Opinion No. 15 [1969].[1] Specifically, it argues that information produced by current value accounting for corporate-issued securities options, a generic classification used by this article, is superior to the EPS dilution information produced by current GAAP. "Corporate-issued securities options" should be understood to include conversion options, employee stock options, stock appreciation rights, stock purchase warrants and any other corporate-issued contract that is a call or a put on another security[2] or its asset value. Accepting the proposed accounting would mean that the generic term "corporate-issued securities option"

Donald E. Wiseman, "Holding Loss/Gain as an Alternative to EPS Dilution." *Accounting Horizons,* December 1990, pp. 18–34. Reprinted by permission of the American Accounting Association.

[1]American Institute of Certified Public Accountants, Accounting Principles Board, "Earnings per Share," *Opinion No. 15* (1969).

[2]What constitutes a "security" is discussed later in this article. It includes a variety of contracts other than common stock. It could include compensation contracts not generally defined as securities, or it could include a security's "value equivalent" for those options redeemable by payment of cash or other asset based on the callable security's market value.

would replace "dilutive security," and accounting for holding gains and losses would replace EPS dilution reporting.[3]

The current value accounting alternative proposed by this article responds to recent calls in the literature for *major* change in EPS dilution reporting.[4] Indeed, most articles on this subject over the last 20 years have only sought to refine the measurement and/or disclosure of EPS dilution.[5] However, acceptance of the EPS dilution reporting mode may well be changing, as indicated by discussion memoranda forthcoming from the FASB task force on financial instruments.[6] That task force has been working for several years on "new and unusual" financial instruments, including those described by this article as corporate-issued securities options. *Tentative* conclusions by the FASB would seem to correspond with *essential* conclusions in this article. One in particular should be noted: options are to be regarded as a "fundamental security" distinct from equity contracts. In addition, the discussion memoranda promise to address the feasibility of current value accounting for options, using models and other valuation techniques; and they will discuss the merits of accounting for the elements of convertibles separately—the option component separately from the bond (or preferred) component.[7]

These emerging authoritative viewpoints—or, at least, the discussion of them—suggest the real possibility of a current value alternative to the EPS dilution reporting that is now GAAP. The prospects for such change will no doubt turn on responses to these three questions:

1. Are corporate-issued securities options classifiable as *non-residual* equity contracts? If they are not, they would not be susceptible to the sort of current value accounting that would produce holding gains and losses.
2. Are appropriate current values readily available for corporate-issued securities options? If they are not, current value accounting would not be operational.
3. Is information of a holding gain/loss nature superior to EPS dilution information? If it is not, there would be little reason to change the EPS dilution reporting mode.

[3]This article assumes that GAAP will continue to trend toward being an eclectic, multi-paradigm phenomenon. Thus this article has no reservations about applying current value accounting in an *ad hoc* fashion. Presently, current value accounting (or elements thereof) is found in GAAP for inventories, investments, pensions, stock appreciation rights, and others. The accounting proposed herein for corporate-issued securities options could be argued to parallel the current-exit value accounting advocated by Friedman (footnote 41, below) for liabilities as part of an overall current-exit value system.

[4]See Lola W. Dudley, "A Critical Look at EPS," *Journal of Accountancy* (August, 1985), pp. 102–111; and David R. Mautz, Jr. and Thomas Jeffery Hogan, "Earnings per Share Reporting: Time for an Overhaul?" *Accounting Horizons* (September, 1989), pp. 21–27.

[5]Perhaps the one exception to this would be Knutson (1970) who saw the problem in terms of income distribution. See Peter H. Knutson, "Income Distribution: The Key to Earnings per Share," *The Accounting Review* (January, 1970), pp. 55–68. Examples of those which accept the EPS dilution mode are Benzion Barlev, "Contingent Equity and The Dilutive Effect on EPS," *The Accounting Review* (April, 1983), pp. 385–393; Robert L. Vigeland, "Dilution of Earnings per Share in an Option Pricing Framework," *The Accounting Review* (April, 1982), pp. 348–357, and Mautz and Hogan (September 1989) *loc. cit.*

[6]Clifford C. Woods and Halsey G. Bullen, "An Overview of the FASB's Financial Instruments Project," *Journal of Accountancy* (November, 1989), pp. 43–47.

[7]Halsey G. Bullen, Robert C. Wilkins and Clifford C. Woods III, "The Fundamental Financial Instrument Approach," *Journal of Accountancy* (November, 1989), pp. 71–78.

This article will address these three questions in order. It can be said at this point that positive responses to all three are possible, but it is the persuasiveness of the responses that will determine the prospects for the current value accounting alternative.

CORPORATE-ISSUED SECURITIES OPTIONS—NON-RESIDUAL EQUITY?

As to the question of their equity nature, this section argues that corporate-issued securities options are *non*-residual equity contracts. They may have features of both debt and equity, in varying degrees, but these options do not qualify as residual equity contracts in the same sense that common shares do. This conclusion is essential to this article for two reasons. Hundreds of thousands of accountants have been trained since the latter 1960s to view options as "dilutive securities," a term which arguably pre-judges their outcome or at least distorts the reporting of their conditional nature. Indeed a leading intermediate accounting textbook has a chapter entitled, "Dilutive Securities and Earnings per Share Calculations."[8] In short, a substantial vested interest exists in the accounting community in the dilutive security jargon and the GAAP associated with it. Secondly, corporate-issued securities options must be non-residual in nature if current value accounting is to be applicable to them. That is because residual equity is, by definition, what remains; it is a residuum; it is the dependent variable. It is the one element in a current value accounting system that cannot be found by direct reference to current values in the marketplace or elsewhere. Therefore, to establish the *non*-residual nature of corporate-issued securities options and to encourage accountants to rethink the EPS dilution jargon and associated GAAP, these two assertions will be examined: (1) corporate-issued securities options are taxonomically distinct[9] from common (residual) equity and (2) the official rationale which underlies GAAP and prescribes EPS dilution reporting is flawed.

DISTINCT, NON-RESIDUAL NATURE

If the term "specific equities" can be used to include liabilities and all other *non*-residual equities, then *residual* equity as conventionally understood is the dependent variable in this basic accounting equation: ASSETS minus SPECIFIC EQUITIES equals RESIDUAL EQUITY. As the current values of specific equities increase or decrease, the opposite change registers on the residual equity.

Corporate-issued securities options qualify as one of the "specific equities." They are capital raising contracts which must be redeemed. They are distinguished from other "specific equities" by their option-like nature. To the option issuer, the option is a capital raising contract which is *conditionally* redeemable by paying another security to the holder of the option—or in some cases by paying asset value equivalent to that of the callable security. The put version of the option allows the option holder to put a security to the corporate issuer at a set price.

---

[8]Specifically this is Chapter 17 in Kieso/Weygandt's *Intermediate Accounting* (6th Edition, 1989). Weygandt apparently bases this classification on his "management intent" perception of corporate-issued options. See Leroy Imdieke and Jerry J. Weygandt. "Classification of Convertible Debt," *The Accounting Review* (October, 1969), pp. 798–805.

[9]"Taxonomy" refers to the science of classification or, as used here, refers to the process of systematically distinguishing corporate-issued options from other capital raising instruments.

The conditional nature of the option means that future redemption may be accomplished by the transfer of a wide range of values, depending on the value of the security (or its cash equivalent) that is transferred at exercise to the option holder; indeed "redemption" may be accomplished by the transfer of no value at all if the option lapses unexercised. That is the nature of the conditionality.

Options may take on some characteristics of the securities for which they constitute a call or put. For example, the current value of the option may fluctuate to one degree or another in sympathy with the current value of the callable security. But all corporate-issued options will still have certain non-residual equity features: they are a conditional obligation to pay out valuable securities; these obligations arise from past transactions; these obligations would be concluded by future transactions that would pay out valuable securities (an asset to the recipient); these obligations, unlike common, are closed-ended contracts; and these obligations literally do not have the bundle of rights generally accorded to the callable security. And, again, if a change in the value of the option holder's equity has the opposite effect on the common equity, it is difficult to argue that both have the same claim on the corporation's wealth.

Call them distinct hybrids; call them distinct amphibians; call them distinct combinations or mixtures—the point is, they are *distinct*. In that regard, they are a *tertium quid*—neither debt nor equity. They are a class of security unto themselves. They have their own beginning and their own ending. They are a subspecies of "specific equity." Or, in the language of the FASB's task force on financial instruments, the option is a "fundamental instrument."[10] And, again, note that options are taxonomically distinguished from all other specific equities by one feature: They are conditionally redeemable by exchange with another class of security—or its equivalent in asset value.

Of course, if corporate-issued options are pre-judged to be deferred residual equity contracts, they might be expected to be characterized as dilutive securities. Under this assumption, the eventual issuance price of the "deferred" common is set when the *option* is issued; it is the sum of the option's exercise price and the value of the option when it is issued. That sum typically is well below the prevailing price of the common when the option later is exercised, assuming it is exercised. But this pre-judging of options to be deferred equity is open to serious dispute. Indeed, Lewellan and Racette, after a lengthy study, conclude that the deferred equity jargon is "arrant nonsense," part of the "folklore of finance."[11] The deferred equity jargon may describe what financial management hopes to accomplish, but it hardly defines objectively the conditional nature of the option obligation. Indeed, it could be argued that the most successful convertible bonds—as properly judged by the immediate impact on present shareholders—are those which are never expected to be converted.

Just as the "book value" approach to accounting for conversion of preferreds and debentures assumes the deferred equity ("arrant nonsense") perception of the conversion option, the "market value" approach to accounting for conversion views the conversion option as conceptually independent and susceptible to current value accounting. The gain or loss on conversion is by and large the holding gain or loss on the conversion option.

---

[10]Bullen, Wilkens, and Woods, *op cit.*, p. 73.

[11]Wilbur G. Lewellan and George A. Racette, "Convertible Debt Financing," *Journal of Financial and Quantitative Analysis* (December, 1973), pp. 777–92.

In further support of the proposed accounting, the term "corporate-issued securities option" is more appropriately subsuming; that is, it classifies better the array of corporate-issued securities options. The dilutive security term is limited to options which are calls on the common of the issuer, such as, conversion options, stock purchase warrants, employee stock options, stock appreciation rights, contingent payment contracts, and others. But the term corporate-issued securities options also includes calls on the issuer's bonds, usually allowing conversion from a shorter to a longer maturity. It would also include puts on the issuer's bonds which are used by institutional investors especially during periods of rising interest rates. Another variety of puts on bonds would be warrants which allow the holder to purchase a share of common for a specified sum payable in cash or in the par amount of the associated debenture, regardless of the debenture's market value. Calls on preferreds and calls on calls are possible, for example, as with a convertible debenture that is convertible into preferreds which, in turn, are convertible into common. Also, corporations write calls on securities held as investments, as with so-called hybrid convertibles; and corporations can write options "naked," that is, where the underlying securities are not owned or otherwise controlled by the writer.

In a taxonomy sense, then, all of these contracts are corporate obligations distinguishable by a common feature: all are conditionally redeemable by payment of a specified security or in some cases by payment of assets of equivalent value. The value of the option will be a function of the current and prospective value of the callable/putable security, its volatility, and the terms of the option contract; but the distinguishing feature in all cases will be the option's redeemability by another security (or equivalent value) under certain conditions. Conditions may render the option valueless but it is still distinguished by the conditionality of its redemption potential. Corporate-issued securities options, it seems fair to conclude, are distinct and *non*-residual equity contracts. As such, they should be susceptible to current value accounting, if current values are available.

NATURE OF OFFICIAL SUPPORT FOR EPS DILUTION

It is appropriate, if not necessary, for an article which proposes a wholesale change in GAAP to challenge the official rationale that underlies that GAAP. Also, it would be appropriate to note any evolution in the nature of that support. And so, this sub-section presents a brief, critical review of official support for EPS dilution.

THE ACCOUNTING PRINCIPLES BOARD The initial codification of EPS dilution into GAAP was in December, 1966, specifically, paragraph 33 of APB Opinion 9.[12] That paragraph was in response to a threat by the Securities and Exchange Commission six months earlier that it (the SEC) would require "full dilution" reporting if appropriate accounting standards to

[12]American Institute of Certified Public Accountants, Accounting Principles Board, "Computation and Reporting of Earnings Per Share," *Opinion No. 9* (1966). It would be very difficult to construe anything in ARB 49, "Earnings per Share," 1958, as a sanctioning of EPS dilution reporting. Indeed, a careful reading of ARB 49 reveals that the *supplementary* disclosure of the dilutive effect of new shares on current EPS is recommended only when the redemption of outstanding securities by the new common issue is, for all practical purposes, a *fait accompli*.

protect the investor did not materialize.[13] The SEC was alarmed by the flood of convertibles being used to finance the extraordinary merger activity of the 1960s and in particular by the hidden deterioration in the quality of earnings per share reported to investors. To express its alarm, the SEC had adopted the dilution jargon of security analysts and investment advisors in the 1960s; but those groups would not have had a usable definition of that jargon, even if such definition had been sought by the SEC. The dilution concept is just too complex.[14]

But once the dilution concept had been accepted as part of official accounting dogma in the 1960s, the standard setters had to somehow standardize the measurement and disclosure of EPS dilution. In theory, the APB might have satisfied the SEC by promulgating current value accounting for corporate-issued securities options, disclosing holding gains and losses on those contracts as proposed by this article. But that was not a viable alternative in the 1960s. Current values for all corporate-issued options would not have been available in an acceptable manner in the 1960s, that is, prior to the development of certain option pricing models in the next decade (as discussed in the next section of this article). Also, the extensive discussion of current value accounting in the 1970s had not yet occurred and, obviously, would not have been available to help persuade the SEC, the APB, and accountants generally, who overwhelmingly saw current value accounting as a threat to the realization principle and to historical cost accounting.

In May, 1969, the very lengthy Opinion 15, dealing almost exclusively with the measurement and disclosure of EPS dilution, replaced paragraph 33 of Opinion 9. It was influenced substantially by powerful vested interests—investment bankers and large law firms in this case—who had belatedly awakened to the significance of APB Opinions 9 and 10, especially as they affected the issuance of convertibles.[15] They did not protest the potential dilution concept, only the manner in which it was determined. In fact, it has been argued that they succeeded in turning the dilution concept to their own ends by causing the central "common stock equivalency" concept of Opinion 15 to become virtually meaningless.[16] In particular, the conversion terms of convertibles could be set in such a way that the "two-thirds" rule would disqualify the convertible at issuance and thereafter from the primary EPS calculation. The Chairman of the APB at that time, Leroy Layton, noted that after discussion with interested groups the Board "had to

[13] *Business Week* reported that the SEC, about mid-year 1966, sent a letter to the investment banking community, asking for comments on a proposed ruling that might require companies that issue certain convertible securities to report earnings per share based on full conversion into common. The SEC opposed convertibles that had the effect of increasing earnings per share. The inference was clear: If the APB didn't act, the SEC surely would. *Business Week,* "A Relic of the 1920s Returns" (August 13, 1966), p. 84.

[14] Tritschler (1971) reviewed several notions of dilution in the finance literature and concluded that what constitutes dilution is not self-evident. He termed the Opinion 15 version of dilution naive and ill-defined. Charles A. Tritschler, "Dilution and Counter Dilution in Reporting for Deferred Equity," *Accounting and Business Research* (Autumn, 1971), pp. 274–283.

[15] Based on information in "Cloud Over Convertible Debenture," *Business Week* (October 7, 1967), pp. 143 and 148, and on Leonard Savoie, "Controversy Over Accounting Principles Board Opinions," *Journal of Accountancy* (January, 1968), pp. 37–41.

[16] Frank T. Weston in his dissent, as a Board member, to Opinion 15. In that time frame, he had done extensive publishing and speaking on the subject, for example, "Reporting Earnings per Share," *Financial Analysts Journal* (July-August, 1967), pp. 45–53, and (with Sidney Davidson) "What Will Accounting Changes Do To Earnings?" *Financial Analysts Journal* (Sept-Oct, 1968), pp. 59–66.

include some *arbitrary rule making* and we hope there will not be many more like this."[17] (Emphasis added.)

Little can be inferred from the APB's treatment of the dilution concept (1966–1972), including discussions accompanying the Opinions, that would suggest that a seriously considered theoretical rationale underlies the EPS dilution reporting that is current GAAP. Only the deferred equity notion and the so-called inseparability of the conversion option are cited as supporting rationales. There may have been little time, or perhaps little inclination, on the part of standard setters for a discussion of the varied concepts of dilution. Apparently, they were busy "putting out a fire," a fire that was started by the SEC and later re-ignited by special interests.

THE FINANCIAL ACCOUNTING STANDARDS BOARD The FASB's publication of Standard 12 (1975)[18] could be regarded as the first endorsement by a standard setting body (in this country) for current value accounting for options, albeit these were options held as assets and the prescribed accounting was asymmetrical because of its lower of cost or market rule. The publication of Interpretation 28 (1978)[19] could also be regarded as a kind of endorsement for current value accounting for the SAR option, inasmuch as it required the option obligation to be adjusted periodically to market value; but again this was not full fledged current value accounting because the complementary entry was not to holding gain or loss, but rather to compensation expense. Nevertheless, these forays into current value accounting do begin to suggest a willingness to experiment with current value accounting for securities options.

But later pronouncements in the conceptual framework discussion—especially the elements statements—did not suggest much of a change by the FASB of the 1960s perceptions of corporate-issued options. At the discussion memorandum stage for FAC 3 the FASB was apparently puzzled about the taxonomical position of warrants, options, and convertibles; they were termed anomalous securities and hybrid securities because they were deemed to have features of both debt and equity.[20] Several years later, based on the final draft of FAC 3 (1980),[21] the FASB had resolved the classification problem, at least for the time being, by simply stating that convertibles posed only a problem for the application of the basic definitions of debt and equity. And warrants were equity, pure and simple: they "entirely lack the characteristics of liabilities."[22] This unqualified assertion about the intrinsic nature of warrants—even though

[17]Reported in a news note "APB Chairman Urges Support for Board," *Journal of Accountancy* (June, 1969), pp. 12–13.

[18]Financial Accounting Standards Board, "Accounting for Certain Marketable Securities," *Statement of Financial Accounting Standards No. 12* (1975).

[19]Financial Accounting Standards Board, "Accounting for Stock Appreciation Rights and Other Variable Stock Option or Award Plans," *Interpretation No. 28* (1978).

[20]Financial Accounting Standards Board, *FASB Discussion Memorandum,* "Conceptual Framework for Financial Accounting and Reporting: Elements of Financial Statements and Their Measurement" (December 2, 1976), esp. paragraph 193.

[21]Financial Accounting Standards Board, "Elements of Financial Statements of Business Enterprises," *Statement of Financial Accounting Concepts No. 3* (1980).

[22]*Ibid.,* especially paragraph 254.

they satisfy most of the characteristics of a liability as specified by FAC 3[23]—indicated the FASB's intention at that time not to pursue a further break-down of the basic elements, debt and equity.

FAC 6 (1985),[24] which revises FAC 3, also does not distinguish different kinds of equity. Equity is defined in the FAC 6 emphasis as what remains after liabilities are subtracted from assets. All contracts which do not meet the definition of a liability are, by definition, equity. Thus the FASB's concept of equity is residual in nature, but it is quite distinct from residual (common) equity as generally understood. Subtract residual (common) equity from the FASB's gross definition of equity, and the remainder is all *non*-residual equity interests. Indeed, increase the value of a *non*-residual equity contract, as by current value accounting, and there will be a complementary decrease in the value of residual equity. Inadvertently, the FASB in Concepts 6, with its gross definition of equity, may have drawn attention to the two major subsets of equity which it chose not to define.

The FASB in the 1984–85 period did offer the tentative conclusion, in its stock compensation plan project, that companies should recognize an expense for the fair value of incentive stock options and that periodic estimates of options' fair values should be charged to expense ratably from the date of grant with final expense measured when options vest. This is, again, another form of current value accounting but, as noted above for SARs, the complementary entry is to compensation expense, not to holding gain or loss. The FASB's concern was not with the financial instrument.

The 1990s may bring dramatic changes. Discussion memoranda will be forthcoming from the FASB task force on financial instruments and they will discuss such questions as: should a stock purchase warrant or employee stock option that "obligates an enterprise to issue its own stock at a fixed price rather than to transfer its assets qualify as a liability on the balance sheet?" Or should a convertible "be broken into its fundamental components for financial reporting purposes?"[25] The FASB has already responded to task force efforts by tentatively identifying six "fundamental financial instruments," among them the "option."[26] "Equity instruments" were another one of the "six fundamental financial instruments." This represents quite a change from FAC 6 in which the FASB confirmed without qualification that options were equity contracts.

In conclusion, the supporting rationale underlying current GAAP on EPS dilution was generated in the late 1960s and there is good evidence to suggest that what was driving Opinion 15 at that time was political accommodation and operational feasibility, not sound theory. Certainly, the current value accounting proposed by this article should not be precluded by the slim theoretical rationale underlying the EPS dilution concept in Opinion 15. Indeed,

[23]The three characteristics of a liability are (1) probable future sacrifices of economic benefits, (2) arising from present obligations of a particular entity to transfer assets or provide services to other entities in the future, (3) as a result of past transactions or events. The option is a conditional obligation of one entity to another to transfer economic benefits, as the result of a past transaction (i.e., the transaction which originated the option obligation).

[24]Financial Accounting Standards Board, "Elements of Financial Statements: A Replacement of Financial Concepts Statement No. 3," *Statement of Financial Accounting Concepts No. 6* (1985).

[25]Woods and Bullen, *op. cit.* p. 47.

[26]Bullen, Wilkins, and Woods, *op. cit.,* p. 73.

there is now some reason to suggest that the FASB may be close to redefining corporate-issued options in such a way that they will be amenable to the current value accounting proposed by this article.

CURRENT REDEMPTION VALUES—HOW AVAILABLE ARE THEY?

Current redemption values for corporate-issued securities options must be available if the proposed current value accounting system is to operate. This section examines that availability.

It would be difficult to include all possible corporate-issued options in this discussion. Nonetheless, this process is greatly facilitated when certain premises are understood to underlie the valuation bases. First, current redemption value is the objective. It is the price that should remove the option obligation from the corporate capital structure. It is a plausible, "as if," value. It should be sufficient within a reasonable period of time to redeem an entire issue of options, as with a successful investment banking operation. Although current redemption value as used by this accounting system anticipates the payment of one security for another (the option), the current value of the redeeming security can also be understood to be its cash value at the time of redemption.

Although it would seem that the option holder in this setting would be in an enviable bargaining position, indeed one from which he could exercise a "short squeeze" and insist on extraordinary premiums to give up his option position, this could be easily finessed by the option issuer. That is, it is just as reasonable to assume that the corporate issuer could go into the market and purchase the securities callable by the option holder in an appropriate amount (discussed later), then place these securities in a hedge fund managed by a third party until the options are exercised or until the next statement of financial position is issued. Or the issuer possibly could issue securities directly to the fund at the going market price. This finessing hedge operation would be similar to an in-substance defeasance.

Also, options can be classified in such a fashion that generalization about the availability of current redemption values is facilitated. This section will look at three major categories of options.

1. *Callable Options.* These are primarily conversion options and non-detachable warrants which are callable by the issuer as part of the callability of the combined securities package (the "convertible"). Or perhaps the option itself is callable.
2. *Non-Callable Options.* These are primarily stock purchase warrants, certain closely held convertibles, employee stock options, stock appreciation rights, and contingent payment contracts which are not callable by the issuer. They can be further sub-classified as those with market values and those with modeled values.
3. *All Other Options.* These are options with unusual terms—stepped up or stepped down exercise prices, unusual exercise periods, and such.

CALLABLE OPTIONS

The availability of current redemption prices for callable options such as conversion options and non-detachable warrants is best understood in the context of a chart (see Figure No. 1). There are three possible prices, depending on circumstances: market price, call price, or conversion

FIGURE 1

Price Relationships between Convertible Security and Associated Common Shares

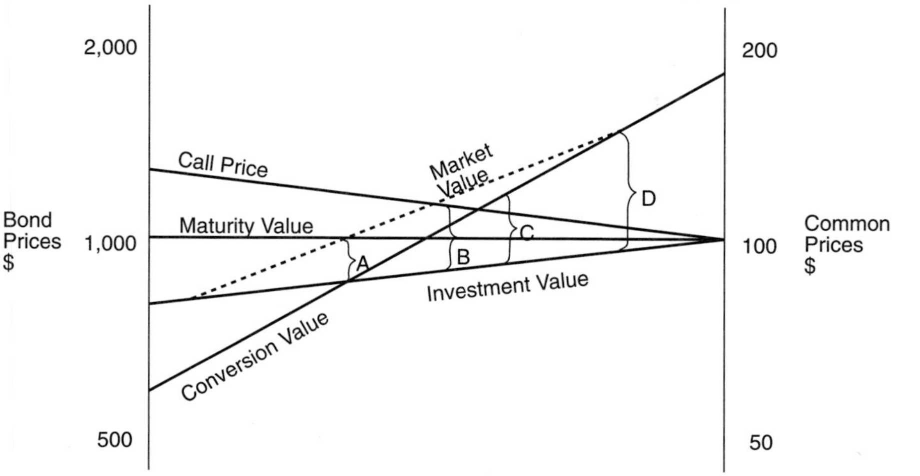

price. The call price would be appropriate when it is below market but above conversion price, as with Bracket B. The issuer can dictate this price by calling the convertible. The conversion price would be appropriate when it is below market but above call price, as with Bracket C. The issuer can force this price by, once again, calling the convertible. The market price would be appropriate when it is below call but above conversion price, as with Bracket A; or market would be appropriate when it coincides with conversion price, as with Bracket D.

The investment value of the bond was subtracted from the combined securities value in all cases above to arrive at the value of the option. The investment value of the bond element of the contract could be determined by discounting expected cash payments on that bond at market rates for similar contracts that do not contain a conversion option.

NON-CALLABLE OPTIONS

Current redemption values for non-callable options can be classified as those with a market basis and those with a modeled basis.

MARKET-BASED CURRENT REDEMPTION VALUES Stock purchase warrants are probably the only corporate-issued option which trades directly on a well developed secondary market. Those values should suffice, again, having in mind the finessing hedge discussion (above). Another possibility would be a convertible which trades on a market but has no call privilege. The discussion in the preceding section would indicate that market value of the option, as a residual of the bond's investment value and the convertible's market value, would be appropriate.

MODEL-BASED CURRENT REDEMPTION VALUES Market values are not available for many, non-callable corporate-issued options. Thus current redemption values must be inferred by using option pricing models. The ideal model would have as much of a market basis as possible and would involve as little human judgment as possible. Further, it would assume a finessing hedge operation, described above as the appropriate counter to the likely short squeeze position taken by the option holder in a redemption operation.

The Black-Scholes (1973) option pricing model[27] is all of these things. It assumes that a perfect hedge can be maintained by being "long the stock (i.e., owning) and short the associated option." That is the same as the finessing hedge operation that would purchase the callable stock to blunt a short squeeze maneuver in a redemption procedure. Note that writing/issuing an option is comparable to short selling that option: in each case the option must be redeemed—or the position closed—at some later date by delivering the value of the option to another party. The option writer/issuer or the short seller wins if the option's price declines; he loses if the option's price increases.

A number of articles have proposed the usefulness of Black-Scholes option prices in accounting contexts.[28] For some time now, Black-Scholes normative option values have been used by operators on the organized exchanges. With hand-held, programmed calculators they can quickly determine prices and hedge ratios. Investment houses routinely generate lists of options that conform to parameters specified by clients, including percent deviations from theoretical values as determined by the Black-Scholes option pricing model. Also, software is routinely used in college investments classes to generate Black-Scholes option values.

The Black-Scholes model produces a concave curve relationship between the option and its associated stock, as indicated by the dashed line on Figure 2. That line is similar in shape to the relationship drawn by many other option pricing models,[29] but the Black-Scholes model is distinct in that it uses only variables which are directly observable in the marketplace. All variables, excepting the variance of the stock's rate of return, can be observed by reference to market information at the effective date of valuation; and the variance can be estimated by reference to market information over some time period. But judgment could be required as to which time period. For example, weekly stock prices over the last year is a possibility. Standard setters could stipulate the procedure for determining variance, perhaps requiring the use of variances provided by a financial institution.

Some empirical tests tend to confirm the validity of the Black-Scholes option prices, and some tend to challenge it.[30] Noreen and Wolfson,[31] for example, conclude that Black-Scholes

[27]Fischer Black and Myron Scholes, "The Pricing of Options and Corporate Liabilities," *Journal of Political Economy* (May-June, 1973), pp. 637–54.

[28]Examples are: Jerry J. Weygandt, "Valuation of Stock Option Contracts," *The Accounting Review* (January, 1977), pp. 40–51; John S. Hughes, "Toward a Contract Basis of Valuation in Accounting," *The Accounting Review* (October, 1978), pp. 882–94; Robert L. Vigeland, "Dilution of Earnings per Share in an Option Pricing Framework," *The Accounting Review* (April, 1982), p. 348.

[29]To see these curves for a variety of models, refer to: John P. Shelton, "The Relation and Price of a Warrant to the Price of Its Associated Stock," *Financial Analysis Journal* (May-June, 1967), pp. 143–151.

[30]Fischer Black and Myron Scholes, "The Valuation of Option Contracts and a Test of Market Efficiency," *Journal of Finance* (May, 1972); James D. Macbeth and Larry J. Merville, "An Empirical Examination of the Black-Scholes Call Option Pricing Model," *Journal of Finance* (December, 1979).

[31]Eric Noreen and Mark Wolfson, "Equilibrium Warrant Pricing Models and Accounting for Executive Stock Options," *Journal of Accounting Research* (Autumn, 1981), pp. 384–398.

FIGURE 2

Generic Corporate-Issued Call Option and Associated Common-Price Relationships

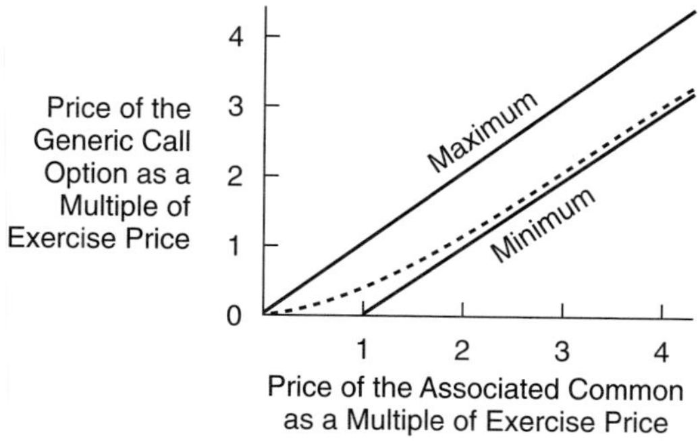

values can be used "with caution" as surrogates for the (unknowable) market value of executive stock options. They concluded this after studying a sample of warrants which they argue were similar to the non-trading options. But it must be noted again that the proposed current value accounting system is not based on market values; rather it uses market values (where available) as surrogates for current redemption values. Market values and redemption values, of course, do not necessarily equate. But market values can at least be presumed to be objectively based exchange values; and the assumption of the possibility of a finessing hedge operation does make them reasonable redemption values.

The possibility that Black-Scholes values might overstate somewhat the "market values" of employee stock options (Noreen and Wolfson) does not mean that the modeled value is unacceptable as a current redemption value; indeed, it could be a better estimate of the equilibrium value of the option at the hypothetical point of redemption. Certainly, the modeled value would be far more relevant than the zero value that GAAP presently places on most employee stock options; moreover, holding gains and losses based on modeled values would no doubt reflect rather well the variations in option redemption value from period to period. And again, it bears repeating, the concave curve in Figure 1 is similar in shape to the curves produced by many other option pricing models. The Black-Scholes curve, however, requires virtually no human judgment.

The assumptions underlying the Black-Scholes option pricing model may seem limiting—no penalties for short sales; no transaction costs or taxes; stock prices behaving as a continuous-time random walk, log-normally distributed with constant variance for rates of return; constant risk-free interest rate; no dividends on stock; exercise of call only at terminal date of contract. However, in his review article on option valuation, Smith states: "subsequent modifications of the basic Black-Scholes model by Merton and others show that the analysis is quite robust with respect to relaxation of the basic assumptions under which the model is derived. No single assumption seems crucial to the analysis."[32]

[32]C. W. Smith, Jr., "Option Pricing: A Review," *Journal of Financial Economics* (January/March, 1976), pp. 3–51.

The Black-Scholes option value also determines the number of shares to be purchased into the hypothetically possible finessing hedge fund. At the point where its slope (or hedge ratio) is .5, one share of stock will hedge two options. Or, a $.25 increase (decrease) of two options would be roughly offset by the $.50 decrease (increase) of one share of common. If the stock's price is $20 per share and the option's price is $7, then the net investment in that hedge position will be $6, or $20 − $14. The Black-Scholes model assumes that the net investment will earn at the risk-free rate and that arbitragers in an efficient market will eliminate excess returns. The proper hedge ratio at any point in time can be determined. Note that the hedge ratio will change as the securities' values change on the dotted curve (Figure 2). Also, the line itself will shift downward as the option's maturity date approaches. Thus, the number of shares in the finessing hedge would require continuous adjustment. Granting this prospect, the finessing hedge would still successfully circumvent any short squeeze pressures attendant to option redemptions; and the Black-Scholes option price (the slope of the dotted line) at any financial reporting date would establish an appropriate finessing hedge ratio at that point in time. It is only necessary that the *assumption of the possibility* of a finessing hedge operation be valid.

OTHER OPTIONS

The valuation techniques discussed thus far would cover all options that might be found in most capital structures of corporations required to do this sort of accounting. But the exceptional option should also be susceptible to the current value accounting proposed by this article. This article will not attempt to categorize appropriate current redemption value procedures for all exceptional options; that is the subject for another article. However, the accountant specializing in this area should rather quickly develop the judgment as to which contractual terms are accommodated by the Black-Scholes model, especially when keeping in mind the valuation principles and premises outlined above. For example, when attempting to determine the redemption values for an option with stepped-up exercise prices, the accountant may have to view the option as a series of options with different exercise prices and maturity dates, perhaps taking an average of that series. Regarding calls and puts on bonds (please see brief descriptions on page 224), the accountant might contrast the market value of the subject bond with the market value of a bond similar in all regards excepting the option.

THE AVAILABILITY OF CURRENT REDEMPTION VALUES—CONCLUSION

When implementing current value accounting for a firm's outstanding options, the procedure for determining current redemption values could be generalized as follows:

1. Separate options in terms of callability, that is, callability by the issuer.
2. If options are callable, use conversion (exercise) value if it is above call value. This assumes forced conversion by the issuer. Market value and conversion value could coincide in this setting. If conversion value is below call value, then use the lower of call value or market value. This is illustrated by Figure No. 1.
3. If options are not callable, assume the possibility of a "finessing hedge" operation. Then use the higher of market-based value (if available, especially as with warrants) or modeled value, using the Black-Scholes option pricing model.

4. For the unusual option, not included above, use some appropriate valuation base for redemption value, as suggested above. In an extreme case, an outside consultant might be required.

For all but a relatively few corporate-issued options, it seems fair to conclude, current redemption values are available in a reliable fashion—with acceptable verifiability and outstanding representational faithfulness. Even in exceptional cases where the valuation basis described in #2 and #3 above do not seem to apply, objective bases are probably available to the accountant. Certainly, the valuation problem, such as it is, should not preclude the current value accounting system proposed by this article.

INFORMATION USEFULNESS: HOLDING GAIN/LOSS VERSUS EPS DILUTION

Is the information content in holding gains and losses demonstrably more useful than that in EPS dilution? It should be, that is, in order to conclude that current value accounting is the preferred reporting mode. Therefore, this section will examine the relative usefulnesses of these two reporting modes in terms of (1) how each impacts income determination, (2) how each conforms to the "qualitative characteristics" guidelines in FAC 2[33] and (3) how each provides relevant information in a specific decision-making context.

INCOME DETERMINATION: CUMULATIVE VERSUS PERIODIC INFORMATION

This segment will assume that a theoretically acceptable and operational method for generating EPS dilution information does exist. Indeed, this author has constructed such a model based on the same current value information used for the holding gain/loss model proposed by this article.[34] In brief, it measures the dilution (anti-dilution) that results from using options rather than the associated common stock to raise capital. It subscribes to the notion, rejected earlier by this article, that options are a form of residual equity. This segment also assumes that income determination—accrual-based profit information—is among the major concerns of users of financial reports.

Income is a period concept. It occurs over some time period, and time periods repeat themselves, in series. But EPS dilution is not a period concept. To illustrate, consider the EPS of HYPO Incorporated over the first four years of its operation. (The discussion which follows is summarized in Table 1.) Earnings per share the first year is $5.00 Dilution per share is reported at $1.00, resulting in a $4.00 primary EPS figure. Assume further that HYPO's earnings and capital structure remain constant over the next three years, but market conditions change, causing dilution to change. If dilution per share is reported at $.75 in Year #2, primary EPS

---

[33]Financial Accounting Standards Board, "Qualitative Characteristics of Accounting Information," *Statement of Financial Accounting Concepts No. 2* (1980).

[34]Donald E. Wiseman, "Two Exit-Price Alternatives to Dual EPS Reporting," Midwest Business Administration Association, Chicago, Illinois: Twentieth Annual Meeting (April, 1984), pp. 1–21.

TABLE 1

Comparison of Hypo Corp's EPS over a Four-Year Period—Dilution Basis and Gain/Loss Basis

	Year #1	Year #2	Year #3	Year #4	Total
Operating EPS	$5.00	$5.00	$5.00	$5.00	$20.00
Dilution per share	(1.00)	(0.75)	(0.25)	0.00	N/A
Diluted EPS	4.00	4.25	4.75	5.00	$17.00
Loss/Gain per share	(1.00)	0.25	0.50	0.25	-0-
EPS after holding gain/loss	4.00	5.25	5.50	5.25	$20.00

would be reported at $4.25. But the $.25 year-to-year *decrease* in EPS dilution from Year #1 to Year #2 would not be reported specifically on the income statement. By the same token, if market conditions in Year #3 cause dilution per share to be reported at $.25 per share, EPS would be reported at $4.75. Again, the $.50 *decrease* in EPS dilution would not be reported specifically on the income statement. Finally, if market conditions cause zero dilution or anti-dilution in Year #4, EPS would be reported at $5.00. The $.25 *decrease* in EPS dilution again would not be reported specifically on the income statement. In short, EPS dilution is disclosed as an amount that has cumulated, typically, over more than one period. And so, based on diluted EPS information, HYPO's EPS trend—$4.00/$4.25/$4.75/$5.00—improved steadily over the four-year period. However, the market looked through that "growth" trend to HYPO's flat operating results, or so the declining market value for its common would imply.

Continue with the HYPO case but assume now that the increases and decreases in EPS dilution are reported as periodic holding losses and gains. The EPS trend noted above—$4.00/$4.25/$4.75/$5.00—would now change to $4.00/$5.25/$5.50/$5.25. That is, in Year #1 the period holding loss due to the increase in the options' redemption value would have been $1.00 per share. Then in Year #2, the year-to-year decrease in the options' redemption value would be reported as a $.25 holding gain. Similarly the holding gains for Years #3 and #4 would be $.50 and $.25 respectively.

The latter trend superimposes the *periodic* effects of using option contracts on HYPO's flat earnings trend for operations. Total EPS over the four-year period is $20, which is consistent with the four-year total of operating income—$5.00 per share each year for four years, and the fact that holding gains and losses have offset each other over the same four years. However, when cumulative EPS *dilution* is reported each period, total EPS is only $17, distorting the total amount of earnings as well as the trend of earnings for the four-year period.

Thus, potential EPS dilution is a cumulative amount that can reflect the results of more than one accounting period. Subtracting that amount periodically from EPS would be comparable to using the unrealized holding gain or loss reported in a valuation account on the balance sheet to arrive at net income each period.

Thus it follows that the periodic information provided by current value accounting would allocate the economic effects of events or circumstances to appropriate time periods, *both in net income and EPS terms.* Also, if the cumulative effect of using currently outstanding options is required, current value accounting provides that information in a valuation account on the face of the balance sheet.

Holding gains and losses, contrary to EPS dilution information, provide the information that is required to disclose "comprehensive income" as that concept is defined in FAC 6[35]:

> Comprehensive income is the change in equity of a business enterprise during a period from transactions and *other events and circumstances from nonowner sources.* It includes all changes in equity during a period except those resulting from investments by owners and distributions to owners. (Emphasis added.) [Paragraph 70]

The italicized portion of the definition above deserves special attention. Holding gains and losses on corporate-issued securities options are caused by "other events and circumstances." They are indeed from "nonowner sources," or *non*-residual sources, as argued at length earlier in this paper. If the FASB's conceptual framework had distinguished between residual (common) equity and other equity in its definition of basic elements, it might have avoided some of the confusion as to appropriate accounting for the corporate-issued option.

CONFORMANCE TO "QUALITATIVE CHARACTERISTICS" GUIDELINES

Dudley (1985)[36] evaluated the usefulness of EPS dilution information produced by current GAAP in terms of how well it conforms to the "qualitative characteristics" guidelines for accounting information as presented in FAC 2. Information must be useful, primarily to investors, but also to an array of other constituencies. To be useful, it must be understandable. That requires relevancy and reliability (the "primary" characteristics); and it should also have comparability and therefore consistency. Relevancy implies timeliness and predictive value or feedback value or both. Reliability implies representational faithfulness, verifiability, and neutrality.

As to relevancy, Dudley cites the arbitrariness and implausibility of Opinion 15's implementation rules as *prima facie* evidence of irrelevancy; then she cites numerous studies and tests that demonstrate an absence of "predictive value." As to reliability, Dudley notes the absence of "representational faithfulness," concluding that PEPS (primary EPS) and FDEPS (Fully diluted EPS) produced by Opinion 15 represent "neither current conditions nor realistic expectations about future conditions." The one acceptable qualitative characteristic is verifiability. However, "comparability" is lacking, especially because of the common stock equivalency rule which may require similar convertibles to be treated quite differently. And "understandability" is limited by the complexity, arbitrariness, and inconsistency of implementation rules.

Others have arrived at similar conclusions after systematic analyses, including Mautz and Hogan (1989)[37] and the present author.[38] Without further analysis, this article accepts these conclusions. The balance of this section will apply the FAC 2 "qualitative characteristics" criteria to holding gain/loss information as proposed by this article.

---

[35]Financial Accounting Standards Board, "Elements of Financial Statements: A Replacement of Financial Concepts Statement No. 3," *Statement of Financial Accounting Concepts No. 6* (1985).

[36]Dudley, *op. cit.*

[37]Mautz and Hogan, *op. cit.*

[38]Donald E Wiseman, *The Financial Reporting of Conditional Ownership,* Ph.D. dissertation, The University of Michigan, 1971.

Understandability Holding gains and losses associated with options are probably understood, instinctively and logically, by the great majority of statement readers. In any event, the concept of gain and loss on options is readily explained. The gains and losses of the private option writer is a good reference point. An increase in redemption value is a loss, and vice versa. This is true whether gains and losses are realized or unrealized. Also, whereas EPS dilution (and anti-dilution) can be an amount cumulated over more than one period, as discussed in the preceding section, the holding gains and losses which result from events and circumstances of a particular period are allocated to that particular period when determining net income (per share and in total). Cumulative holding gains and losses at the close of the period are reported on the balance sheet in a valuation account.

Understandable as holding gains and losses are, most statement readers would have to take on faith the redemption values that are produced by models and used in the current value accounting system. But the widespread acceptance of those modeled values in the financial world should help promote that faith. Understanding that acceptance by sophisticated professionals might have to substitute for understanding the model per se, although anyone who chose to, of course, would be welcome to analyze the logic underlying the Black-Scholes model.

It is certainly arguable that the understandability of an option's cost in gain/loss terms contributes to its usefulness vis-a-vis EPS dilution. Gain/loss information translates readily to percentage terms—the universal reference for determining and comparing the cost of most financial instruments. To say, for example, that options used as bonus compensation for executives cost the firm $.17 in EPS dilution terms last year conveys information, but of limited value. A two for one stock split, for example, would cut that cost in half. Contrast this with information that states that a particular option had a cost last year of 45 percent based on the increase in redemption value. "Forty-five percent" is a readily understandable concept which can be compared to costs of other capital instruments. To illustrate further, note that the annualized percentage cost of a conversion option called by Boeing in 1967 was 695 percent.[39] It was attached to a 5.5% debenture that was outstanding for 277 days. The increase in the value of the associated common over that same time period was 124 percent. Percentages are the customary mode of understanding the costs of these contracts, certainly in a manner that allows for comparisons. Also, as difficult as EPS dilution may be to understand, EPS anti-dilution would be even more confounding.

Relevancy Current value accounting as proposed by this article would make no effort to predict exercise of options, as does Opinion 15. Rather, it discloses the periodic and cumulative loss (or gain) of corporate decisions to use options. It provides that information for both individual options and options as a whole. This loss (or gain) is easily translated to percentage terms. A continuous record of this sort of information could supply "feedback" that would assist prediction about future management behavior. Also, unrealized gains or losses disclosed on the face of the balance sheet provide a basis for evaluating potential cash (or cash equivalent) flows related to all outstanding options; indeed, the balance in the valuation account is the maximum impact on income that could be caused by exercise initiated by option holders and/or by redemption initiated by option issuers at a particular point in time.

[39]Calculated by determining the option's values at issuance and termination (determined by subtracting the investment value of the bond component from the convertible's market value) and then converting the percentage increase in the option's value to an annualized basis.

The relevancy of the proposed gain/loss information is not compromised by the assumptions underlying the procedures used to generate current redemption values. If the assumption of an in-substance defeasance or finessing hedge operation were to seem improbable because of a large number of outstanding options, which is the reason for the arbitrary 20 percent rule which modifies the implausible treasury stock assumption of Opinion 15, it would be plausible to assume an issuance of common shares at the going market value with the funds therefrom to be used to re-purchase those same shares and place them in a hedge fund controlled by an outside party. Or just assume that the common was issued directly to the hedge fund at the going market price. It is only necessary that these maneuvers be theoretically possible to justify the use of the current redemption values described earlier in this article.

If the current value accounting mode defines relevancy in terms of information which realistically reflects current conditions, at a point in time and over an accounting period, then it should be noted that the proposed accounting does just that. It provides current redemption values which should be the focus of concern for any writer/issuer of options. This point is made more specifically in the concluding section of this usefulness discussion.

Reliability Verifiability and representational faithfulness are the prime ingredients of reliability. Verifiability, based on the preceding discussion of the availability of option values, should be a strong feature of the proposed accounting system. Only a relatively few complex options should not fit into the valuation references described for callable and non-callable options. And valuation procedures for those relative few probably would be susceptible to reasonable assumptions as to what constitutes redemption value. Verifiability for these few options could be achieved by FASB stipulation, if that were deemed essential in a new accounting standard.

The proposed system has representational faithfulness in that it provides exactly what it purports to provide—current redemption values. Again, it is only necessary that the finessing hedge assumption be reasonable, which the preceding discussion has supported at some length.

As to the neutrality of information, it would be difficult to argue that holding gain/loss information favors one group over another. It may make management more accountable, but that hardly constitutes a bias. More likely it would remove a special group advantage.[40]

Other Qualitative Characteristics Current redemption values should provide information that has good comparability over time and among firms. The determinants of redemption value are based on what is reasonable under a certain set of circumstances. Valuation techniques are uniformly applied. Current redemption value can be market value, call value, conversion value, or a modeled value, but among firms which are actively traded there should seldom be any question as to which of these values applies. Also, the benefits of the proposed system should far exceed its cost. Only modeled values should require any special effort (excepting the very unusual cases). It should be noted again that college classes in investments presently are using software to generate Black-Scholes option prices and, as mentioned above, floor operators on options exchanges use hand-held calculators that are programmed to generate Black-Scholes option prices. Indeed, the proposed current value accounting system should

[40]There is a very substantial literature on managers' incentives to choose accounting methods under bonus plans. See, e.g., Ross L. Watts and Jerold F. Zimmerman, "Positive Accounting Theory: A Ten Year Perspective," *The Accounting Review* (January, 1990), pp. 131–156.

not require as much time to implement as is currently the case with the complex and arbitrary rules of Opinion 15 and sequelae GAAP. And, finally, materiality should not be a consideration (e.g., the three percent rule of Opinion 15), because the cost/benefit of a given option may not seem material for the firm as a whole and yet it could reflect on management's performance of its stewardship function.

In conclusion, when evaluated against the qualitative characteristics of FAC 2, a strong argument exists for the superior usefulness of information reported as holding gains and losses. This contrasts with EPS dilution information produced by Opinion 15 which is severely limited as to understandability, relevance, comparability and representational faithfulness. Neutrality, as was argued above, is also compromised by the input into Opinion 15 in the late 1960s by vested interest groups, as evidenced by the two-thirds rule which determines common stock equivalency for convertibles. Verifiability is the one strong point for Opinion 15. Holding gains and losses, on the contrary, are concluded to have all of the desired qualitative characteristics, with only some small concern for the verifiability of certain complex options.

USEFULNESS IN A MORE SPECIFIC CONTEXT

A theoretical justification for the proposed accounting could be found in the current exit value accounting rationale, especially as it has been extended to liabilities by Friedman.[41] He concluded that information based on current redemption values (exit values) was more relevant than historical cost information when evaluating the use of debt to expand a wheat trader's operations.[42] He assumed that the trader used zero-coupon bonds (although not by that name). Quite arguably, then, zero bonds and corporate-issued options are similar with regard to the measurement of their costs; that is, both would compare successive current values over some relevant time span to determine cost.

Since each investor or other user of information will choose his own method of projecting the future, "we are left with gathering evidence about the past." The past success of management (i.e., trader) would be indicated by its demonstrated ability to have foretold prices on both the wheat market and the bond market. In short, investors look to management's past performance as a clue to its future performance. Regarding cost of capital information, the investor would like to know if management's past use of debt cost more or less than the return on the assets financed by the debt. That same reasoning can be extended to the use of option capital.

But, of course, the information required to evaluate a wheat trader operation can be argued to over-simplify investors' needs for information when earnings operations are more complex. Nonetheless, Friedman's analysis is similar to a capital budgeting audit that would compare capital costs over time with asset earning power over the same time period to evaluate management's performance. Only if the cost of option capital is first computed individually can it then be included as part of the mix of financial costs. In short, current redemption values provide the information required to determine option cost. EPS dilution information does not.

---

[41]Laurence Friedman summarized the literature on this in "Exit-Price Liabilities: An Analysis of Alternatives," *The Accounting Review* (October, 1978), pp. 805–809. He extended and supported the arguments of Ronald Ma, "On Chambers' Second Thoughts," *Abacus* (December, 1974), and Errol Iselin, "Chambers on Accounting Theory," *The Accounting Review* (April, 1968), pp. 231–38.

[42]Friedman used Robert Sterling's so-called "wheat trader" model to make his argument. Robert R. Sterling, *Theory of the Measurement of Enterprise Income* (The University Press of Kansas, 1970).

Investors' information needs where options are concerned would seem to go beyond those specified by Friedman for zero-bonds. In addition to financing assets, option capital can be used as an incentive—e.g., to motivate employees in the firm and to motivate investors in the capital markets—which over time could have an impact on earning power. But to evaluate the success of such incentives, the investor would again require cost information. Just because the investor may have to speculate about the *benefits* of incentive plans (unlike what happens to the price of wheat over an accounting period) does not mean that he should also have to speculate about the cost of those plans. This seems especially applicable when the very managements being evaluated by investors may well have had a significant role in designing and granting stock options to themselves. In this context, the current cost of option capital appears to be the best way for revealing in a timely way how much options are costing. Large losses to option holders would be revealed as gains to common shareholders. And *vice versa*. Also, the cost of a particular conversion option incentive ("sweetener") would be revealed.

In sum, Friedman's extension of current exit value accounting to liabilities to allow an evaluation of the wheat trader's decision-making as to assets and financing, would seem to apply just as well to an evaluation of management's use of option capital. In fact, the major objection to Friedman's analysis, namely, that investors are primarily concerned with the maturity values of liabilities, simply does not apply to corporate-issued securities options.[43]

Cost information disclosed in EPS dilution (anti-dilution) terms, however, just is not relevant in this context, even assuming its calculation could be sound. It provides no basis for comparison with asset returns or for evaluation of incentive plans. Dilution (anti-dilution) is in per share terms and it is a cumulative (non periodic) concept. It cannot be used readily in the calculation of the overall cost of capital.

CONCLUSION

This article concludes as follows: current value accounting for corporate-issued options is possible; holding gain/loss information is better than potential EPS dilution information; and current value accounting for options should replace Opinion 15. These conclusions follow from analyses which demonstrate that options are classifiable as non-residual equity contracts (specific equities), that current redemption values for options are available in an operational manner, and that holding gain/loss information is more useful than potential EPS dilution information.

Options are non-residual equity contracts largely because they do not qualify as residual equity contracts; moreover, as to their GAAP treatment as pre-residual equity contracts, no compelling theoretical rationale accompanied the introduction of the EPS dilution concept into GAAP. As to the availability of current redemption values, they can be demonstrated to be available for virtually all options in the forms of market values, call values, conversion values, or modeled values, as dictated by circumstances; furthermore these values can be demonstrated to qualify as redemption values because of the plausibility of a finessing hedge operation. And,

---

[43]Chambers, uncharacteristically, emphasized the importance of the maturity values of debt in financial reports. Raymond J. Chambers, *Accounting, Evaluation and Economic Behavior* (Prentice-Hall, Inc., 1966); "Second Thoughts on Continuously Contemporary Accounting," *Abacus* (September, 1970); and "Third Thoughts," *Abacus* (December, 1974), pp. 129–37.

finally, gain/loss information is more useful because, contrary to EPS dilution, it contributes to the determination of comprehensive income (FAC 6); because it embodies better the "qualitative characteristics" guidelines prescribed by FAC 2 for useful information; and because it is clearly more relevant to decision-making in the context of a specific model.

Key conclusions of this article—specifically, the independent nature of the option contract and the possibility of current value accounting for options—may anticipate forthcoming discussion memoranda by the FASB task force on financial instruments.

II-C3

AN OPTION-THEORETIC ARGUMENT FAVORING EPS DILUTION OVER HOLDING GAIN/LOSS

Joseph K. Cheung

In the December 1990 issue of this journal, Donald E. Wiseman took an extreme position regarding the treatment of option-like securities in EPS calculations.[1] In sharp contrast to existing practice, he advocated that the concept of EPS dilution be abandoned in favor of reflecting the earnings effects of *all* option-like securities issued by the firm as holding gains or losses. Mr. Wiseman based his view on three claims: none of the option-like securities issued by the firm is residual equity; current values of such securities are readily available; and the resulting EPS is more useful information. This note aims to balance Mr. Wiseman's view by making a case for EPS dilution. It argues that certain option-like securities issued by the firm are in substance residual equity and that current value, information of these securities, if available, can be used to compute diluted EPS meaningfully.

Joseph K. Cheung, "An Option-Theoretic Argument Favoring EPS Dilution over Holding Gain/Loss," *Accounting Horizons*. Reprinted by permission of the American Accounting Association.

[1]Donald E. Wiseman, "Holding Gain/Loss as an Alternative to EPS Dilution," *Accounting Horizons* (December 1990), pp. 18–34.

EQUITY CHARACTERISTICS OF CERTAIN OPTION-LIKE SECURITIES

Option-like financial instruments issued by a firm fall into three categories.[2] Put options issued obligate the firm to transfer assets at some point with some probability. Examples are guarantees of the debts of others and the put option in a puttable preferred stock. Clearly, these are liabilities of the firm. Call options underwritten by the firm also are liabilities of the firm to the extent that they too obligate the firm to transfer assets with some probability. Examples are call options on interest rates or on foreign currencies. Finally, there are call options underwritten by the firm that do not obligate the firm to transfer assets at all. Examples are employee stock options and stock purchase warrants; upon the exercise of these securities, the firm only needs to issue common stock. What is argued here is that this last category of option-like securities are essentially residual equity, which contradicts Mr. Wiseman's position that all such securities are non-residual equity.[3]

To be sure, securities such as employee stock options differ from the firm's common stock in a number of ways: they usually have fixed maturity dates; their holders are not entitled to dividends; and they confer no voting rights. On balance, however, these distinguishing features of employee stock options are dominated in importance by the securities' equity characteristics. Existing practice clearly lends support to this view. Under existing practice, no losses are recorded from the exercise of employee stock options, although such a transaction appears to be an unfavorable exchange from the standpoint of the existing stockholders. This reflects the thinking that employee stock options are an equity investment in the firm and that the firm's gains and losses result from transactions other than those with its owners.[4]

A rationale behind this existing practice is given by the current conceptual framework of financial reporting, where the characteristics of residual equity are discussed in detail. According to FASB *Concepts Statement No. 6*,[5] one of the essential characteristics of residual equity is that the transfer of assets to the shareholders is discretionary. Although employee stock options and similar securities are "closed-ended" contracts that must be redeemed, according to Mr. Wiseman, their redemption does not obligate the issuing firm to transfer assets. Thus *some* of the option-like securities issued by the firm meet this criterion of the conceptual framework as residual equity. Current reception of this argument is overwhelming, as evidenced by practitioners' reaction to the question whether the obligation to issue stock is a liability or an equity.[6]

---

[2]Based on the definition in FASB, "Disclosure of Information about Financial Instruments with Off-Balance-Sheet Risk and Financial Instruments with Concentrations of Credit Risk," *Statement of Financial Accounting Standards No. 105* (1990), financial instruments include not only equity or option-like securities, but also contractual rights and obligations such as receivables and guarantees.

[3]Mr. Wiseman also grouped non-residual equities with liabilities, calling them "specific equities" collectively. Wiseman, op. cit., p. 19.

[4]A well received application of the latter is the accounting for treasury stock transactions.

[5]In particular, see paragraph 61 of FASB, "Elements of Financial Statements: A Replacement of Financial Concepts Statement No. 3," *Statement of Financial Accounting Concepts No. 6* (1985).

[6]This reaction is based on approximately 100 comment letters and a two-day public hearing on the discussion memorandum, "Distinguishing between Liability and Equity Instruments and Accounting for Instruments with Characteristics of Both," and is summarized in "Highlights of Financial Reporting Issues," FASB *Status Report,* May 31, 1991, p. 5.

Apart from relying on this entrenched argument, which is largely derived definitionally, one can also reason that an employee stock option is a residual interest by ascertaining the security's economic substance in terms of its payoff profile. This note suggests an "upper bound" test as follows. A firm's residual equity is analogous to a call option on the firm's assets, with an exercise price equal to the maturity value of the firm's debt.[7] Now the payoff profile of a call option has no upper bound. Thus, an essential characteristic of an equity instrument is that its payoff has no upper bound, such payoff being tied to the earning potential of the firm's assets. On the other hand, the payoff profiles of other financial claims issued by the firm all have an upper bound specified either contractually or otherwise, regardless of the earning potential of the firm's assets.

To illustrate an application of this upper bound test, consider once again the classification of employee stock options. Employee stock options are call options on the firm's residual equity, so they are in effect compound call options—options whose payoffs are options—on the firm's assets. Hence, their payoffs are tied to the earning potential of the firm's assets and have no upper bound. Therefore, employee stock options pass the upper bound test for being equity instruments. Note that this compound option characterization of employee stock options is consistent with Mr. Wiseman's "dependent variable" characterization. Under this dependent variable notion, the value of residual equity depends on everything else in the accounting equation. Employee stock options derive their value from the firm's common stock, not the other way around. In fact, options and warrants have price elasticities that are greater than one,[8] meaning that their prices are highly sensitive to those of the underlying stock. Therefore, employee stock options are also a "dependent variable," thus meeting Mr. Wiseman's criterion for being residual equity.

SHORTCOMINGS OF THE HOLDING GAIN/LOSS APPROACH

Because of their equity nature, securities such as employee stock options affect the firm's economic balance sheet by diluting the firm's equity. Unlike the hypothetical EPS dilution under existing practice, however, this dilution is *actual*—the market value of the firm's equity shares is diluted.[9] Hence, EPS dilution also has a practical appeal because it coincides with how the market accounts for the impact of securities such as employee stock options on the firm's equity. Moreover, in keeping with the actual dilution of the firm's equity, the appropriate EPS dilution should be based on the current values of the dilutive securities. That is, the EPS denominator should be increased by the number of common shares equivalent in current value to the dilutive option-like securities outstanding.[10]

---

[7]This observation was originally made by Fischer Black and Myron Scholes in their seminal article, "The Pricing of Options and Corporate Liabilities," *Journal of Political Economy* (May-June 1973), pp. 637–659, and has become a standard notion in the theory of finance.

[8]For example, see John Cox and Mark Rubinstein, *Options Markets* (Prentice-Hall, 1985), p. 229.

[9]This dilution of the market value of the firm's equity has been documented by Raymond King in "The Effect of Convertible Bond Equity Values on Dilution and Leverage," *The Accounting Review* (July 1984), pp. 419–31.

[10]Clearly, this suggests that the current practice of EPS dilution is defective. As pointed out in Raymond King, op. cit., p. 425, this defect is due to the fact that, under existing rules for calculating EPS, either full dilution or no dilution is assumed, corresponding to full conversion and no conversion, respectively, of potentially dilutive securities outstanding.

A shortcoming of the holding gain/loss approach is that it ignores the actual dilution of equity by option-like securities that are effectively residual equity. This shortcoming is especially obvious when the current values of the option-like securities remain unchanged between two dates. In such a case, EPS under the holding gain/loss approach fails to reflect the outstanding option-like securities altogether, despite the securities' actual dilution of the market value of the common stock. As a result, the price-earnings ratio is distorted. A numerical example can help illustrate this point.

Suppose Firm A has 2,000 common shares outstanding and grants 600 stock options to its employees at *Date 1.* These stock options will expire in four years, each option entitling the holder to buy one share of common stock for $1 at any time prior to the maturity date. Suppose the stock options are valued at a total of $1,056, or $1.76 per unit. Immediately after the stock options are granted, the firm's common stock drops from $2.958 to $2.43 a share. Because the stock options are deep-in-the-money,[11] it is almost certain that they will be exercised. Hence they are constructively common stock. Based on this information, these stock options are equivalent in current value to 435 (=$1,056/$2.43) shares of common stock. This information is summarized in Table 1 under the heading *Date 1.*

Now suppose these numbers remain valid at *Date 2* and that the firm reports earnings of $1,000 between the two dates. A diluted EPS based on the securities' current values is 41 cents, obtained by dividing the $1,000 earnings by 2,435 equivalent shares of common stock. This result produces a price-earnings ratio of 5.9, given by $2.43/$0.41. Under the holding gain/loss approach, however, EPS is 50 cents, obtained by dividing the $1,000 of earnings by the 2,000 common shares outstanding. The EPS in this case is unaffected by the employee stock options outstanding because the holding gain/loss is zero. The related price-earnings ratio is 4.9, given by $2.43/$0.50. These results are summarized in Table 1 under the heading *Date 2.*

The point of this example is that the price-earnings ratio of 4.9 associated with the holding gain/loss approach misrepresents the firm's earning power. Although the market price of the common share has dropped in light of the real dilution caused by the employee stock options, the firm's earning power hasn't diminished. Under the holding gain/loss approach, though, the price-earnings ratio is based on a "diluted" market price but an unadjusted EPS. Thus, the 4.9 price-earnings ratio understates the firm's earning power. A meaningful price-earnings ratio would require a dilution in earnings parallel to that in the market price of the common stock. In sum, the holding gain/loss approach has an inherent weakness in that it ignores the market value dilution that actually occurs.

CONCLUSION

The point of this article is that EPS dilution can be both useful and necessary. Based on the reasoning of the conceptual framework and the upper bound test suggested here, certain option-like securities issued by the firm are in essence residual interests in the firm. In addition, security markets behave as if they share this view. Thus computing EPS dilution due to some of the option-like securities outstanding has both theoretical and practical appeal. This conclusion contradicts Mr. Wiseman's position that all option-like securities issued by the firm are

[11]A call option is said to be in-the-money if the current market price of the underlying stock exceeds the exercise price of the option.

TABLE 1

Comparison of EPS Dilution with Holding Gain/Loss Alternative

	Date 1	Date 2
Number of common shares	2,000	2,000
Market value per common share	$2.43	$2.43
Number of employee stock options outstanding	600	600
Current value per stock option	$1.76	$1.76
Equivalent number of common shares[1]	435	435
Operating income between two dates (assumed)		$1,000
Diluted EPS based on current values[2]		$0.41
Price-earnings ratio (dilution approach)[3]		5.9
EPS based on holding gain/loss[4]		$0.50
Price-earnings ratio (holding gain/loss approach)[5]		4.9

[1]($1.76 × 600)/$2.43
[2]$1,000/(2,000 + 435)
[3]$2.43/$0.41
[4]$1,000/2,000
[5]$2.43/$0.50

non-residual equity and that, because current values of such securities are readily available, the holding gain/loss approach naturally becomes a preferred method for EPS determination.

A problem with the holding gain/loss approach is that it ignores the market value dilution that actually occurs. As a result, the EPS figures produced may not be very meaningful. Specifically, an EPS figure unadjusted for the dilutive option-like securities is not in keeping with the diluted market price of the firm's common stock. Unlike the hypothetical EPS dilution under existing accounting rules, however, the EPS dilution advocated here is based on the current values of both the common stock and the dilutive securities outstanding. Hypothetical EPS dilution restricts EPS calculations to either full dilution or no dilution. Dilution based on relative current values is free from such a restriction. In sum, EPS dilution based on current values is preferable if the current value information is indeed available.[12]

[12]Whether such information is as readily available as Mr. Wiseman claims, or at least available at a reasonable cost, is debatable. Given the SEC's current support for marking corporate financial assets to market, I suspect that the current value availability issue will be debated in that context.

II-D

PENSIONS AND OTHER POST-EMPLOYMENT BENEFITS

II-D1

MEASURING THE EFFECTS OF POLITICAL COMPROMISE ON EMPLOYERS' ACCOUNTING FOR DEFINED BENEFIT PENSIONS

Paul B. W. Miller and Rodney J. Redding

Because the Financial Accounting Standards Board (FASB) uses a political process to resolve financial reporting issues, it is reasonable to expect that its standards would tend to fall short of theoretically sound solutions. Thus, an interesting topic for research into the political process would be an assessment of the magnitude of the deviation between theoretical accounting measures and those produced by complying with standards. While this deviation would not reveal whether the theory or the standard produced useful information, it would provide insight into the nature of the standards setting process and the credibility of its output. It nearly goes without saying that a substantial obstacle to this research is the lack of a clear consensus as to what would be a sound theory.

One way to overcome this obstacle is to turn to the FASB's own pronouncements to identify at least what the board members thought would be a good theory to use in the circumstances. One source that would describe such a theory would be the pronouncements issued as part of the Conceptual Framework; however, their relatively high theoretical level virtually

---

The authors wish to acknowledge the assistance of Mr. Tim Lucas, former Project Manager of the Pensions Project and now Director of Research and Technical Activities of the FASB, and Mr. Jules Cassell, Senior Technical Advisor of the FASB, for confirming the validity of our technical and theoretical interpretations of SFAS 87, which they, and others, drafted for the Board. Any errors are, of course, the responsibility of the authors.

Paul B. W. Miller and Rodney J. Redding, "Pensions and Other Post-Employment Benefits." American Accounting Association: *Accounting Horizons*. Reprinted by permission of the American Accounting Association.

precludes applying them to the details of a specific standard. Alternatively, the theory underlying a given standard is often described in the "Basis for Conclusions" appendix. If the description is sufficiently clear, then it can be used for investigating the effects of the compromises on the measures recognized or otherwise reported in the financial statements.

Perhaps the most obvious relatively recent example of a FASB pronouncement that includes many politically-based compromises is Statement of Financial Accounting Standards No. 87 (hereafter, SFAS 87) on accounting for pensions.[1] This standard is particularly suitable for this type of research because it provides a relatively clear discussion of the Board's theory in the Basis for Conclusions. Accordingly, we determined that this standard would provide an opportunity for analyzing the effects of the compromises reached among the board members and between the board and its constituencies in winning the necessary support for a consensus that would allow it to be issued. The analysis involved three steps: identification of the Board's preferred theory, application of the theory to the financial statements issued by a sample of large public corporations, and description of the results of substituting the preferred theory for the requirements of the standard.

Before describing these steps, it will be helpful to summarize what FASB said about the politics and their effects on its ability to develop a standard that came close to its preferred theory for pension accounting.

POLITICAL BACKGROUND ON SFAS 87

The Board's assessment of the political environment and the nature of the compromises in SFAS 87 are described in this comment from the Basis for Conclusions for that standard:

> After considering the range of comments on *Preliminary Views* and the Exposure Draft, the Board concluded that ***the changes required by this Statement represent a worthwhile improvement*** in financial reporting. [Accounting Principles Board] Opinion 8 noted in 1966 that "accounting for pension cost is in a transitional stage" (paragraph 17). The Board believes that is still true in 1985. FASB Concepts Statement No. 5, *Recognition and Measurement in Financial Statements of Business Enterprises,* paragraph 2, indicates that "the Board intends future change to occur in the gradual, evolutionary way that has characterized past change." The Board realizes that the ***evolutionary change in some areas may have to be slower than in others.*** The Board believes that it would be conceptually appropriate and preferable to recognize a net pension liability or asset measured as the difference between the projected benefit obligation and plan assets, either with no delay in recognition of gains and losses, or perhaps with gains and losses reported currently in comprehensive income but not in earnings. However, it concluded that those approaches would be ***too great a change from past practice to be adopted at the present time.*** (par. 107, emphasis added)

With these words, the Board admitted that the new standard did not establish ideal principles because the constituents were not ready for non-evolutionary change.

These two comments from the Basis for Conclusions also declare unambiguously that the standard did not live up to the Board's ideal:

[1]FASB, "Employers' Accounting for Pensions," *Statement of Financial Accounting Standards No. 87.* December 1985. For convenience, all otherwise unidentified paragraph numbers in this paper refer to paragraphs from SFAS 87.

> This Statement requires expanded disclosures intended to provide ***more complete and more current information than can be practically incorporated in financial statements at the present time.*** (par. 88, emphasis added)
>
> The Board acknowledges that the delayed recognition included in this Statement ***results in excluding the most current and most relevant information from the employer's statement of financial position.*** (par. 104, emphasis added)

Thus, it should be clear that the board members did not believe that SFAS 87 represented a pure theoretical resolution of pension accounting issues.

For clarity, it should be noted that the theoretical model presented below is the one described by the majority of the FASB. It is not necessarily the model that the authors would prefer, that anyone else would prefer, or that would lead to optimum decisions. The aim of this paper is merely to describe and measure some of the effects of the FASB's political process on its ability to implement theoretical solutions. This phenomenon differs substantially from others studied elsewhere in the literature. For example, one recent article[2] examined the effect on financial statements of the differences in measures of pension expense under SFAS 87 and Accounting Principles Board Opinion 8 (hereafter, APBO 8).[3] Another example is a study that attempts to explain the origins of FASB's pension accounting requirements in terms of the power of those who submitted comment letters during the project.[4]

FASB's Pension Accounting Theory

FASB's theory of pension accounting generally can be constructed from comments in SFAS 87, although we found that the Board's description of its rationale to be ambiguous on certain points. The following paragraphs explain the theory supporting the annual pension cost and the items that appear on the employer's statement of financial position.

Annual Pension Cost

According to SFAS 87, defined benefit[5] pension cost is deferred compensation arising from an exchange between the employer and employee (par. 79). It consists of eight components, which we have categorized as follows:

- Primary components (par. 16)

  Service cost (or, compensation cost)

  Interest cost

  Actual return on plan assets

[2]Curtis Norton, "Transition to New Accounting Rules: The Case of FAS 87," *Accounting Horizons,* December 1989, pp. 40–48.

[3]Accounting Principles Board, "Accounting for the Cost of Pension Plans," *Opinion No. 8,* November 1966.

[4]Nancy Wilburn, "An Analysis of the Relative Power of Constituents Participating in the Standard-Setting Process of SFAS No. 87," American Accounting Association Western Regional Meeting, April 1990.

[5]Because SFAS 87 requirements for defined contribution plans are consistent with the straightforward theory underlying them, this paper considers only defined benefit plans.

- Plan amendment component (par. 16)
  Amortization of prior service costs
- Smoothing components (par. 29–34)
  Deferred unexpected excess or shortfall in return on plan assets
  Deferred unexpected gains and losses from actuarial changes in the pension liability
  Corridor amortization (partial recognition of previously deferred unexpected gains and losses)
- Transition component (par. 77)
  Amortization of transition net asset (deferred transition gain) or transition net obligation (deferred transition loss)

The diagram in Exhibit 1 shows the relationships among these items of annual pension cost. Exhibit 2 presents what appears to have been FASB's theoretical measure of the cost. Comparing the two exhibits allows the differences produced by the compromises to be more easily seen.

PRIMARY COMPONENTS It is clear from the presentations of the Board's rationale in SFAS 87 that there were no compromises concerning the three primary components.

Service cost is the increase in the pension liability caused by new benefits earned during the period. In explanation, the statement says that:

> The Board concluded that, conceptually, compensation cost should be recognized in the period in which the employee renders services. (par. 95)

Interest cost is the increase in the pension liability caused by the passage of time. We concluded that there were no disagreements about including this factor because the Board said:

> If the service component and the related obligation are measured on a present value basis, a second component—*interest cost*—must also be accounted for. (par. 90, italics in the original)

Actual return on the plan assets is the change in their market value, after considering contributions made to the fund and benefits paid from it. Concerning its theoretical soundness, FASB simply said

> A third component is required for a funded plan. The employer must recognize the *return* (or possibly loss) *on plan assets*. (par. 91, italics in the original)

Additional evidence that these components are consistent with FASB's theory is found in the requirement for disaggregated disclosure of their amounts (par. 54b).

PLAN AMENDMENT COMPONENT Deciphering the Board's theory for **prior service cost** (hereafter, PSC) arising from plan amendments[6] was more problematic because the discussion is not as straightforward.

In overview, FASB was willing to acknowledge the presence of future benefit to the employer from a plan amendment and argued by analogy for assigning the cost to future periods:

[6] Par. 24 explains that the term "plan amendments" also encompasses the initiation of new pension plans.

EXHIBIT 1

Annual Pension Cost under SFAS 87

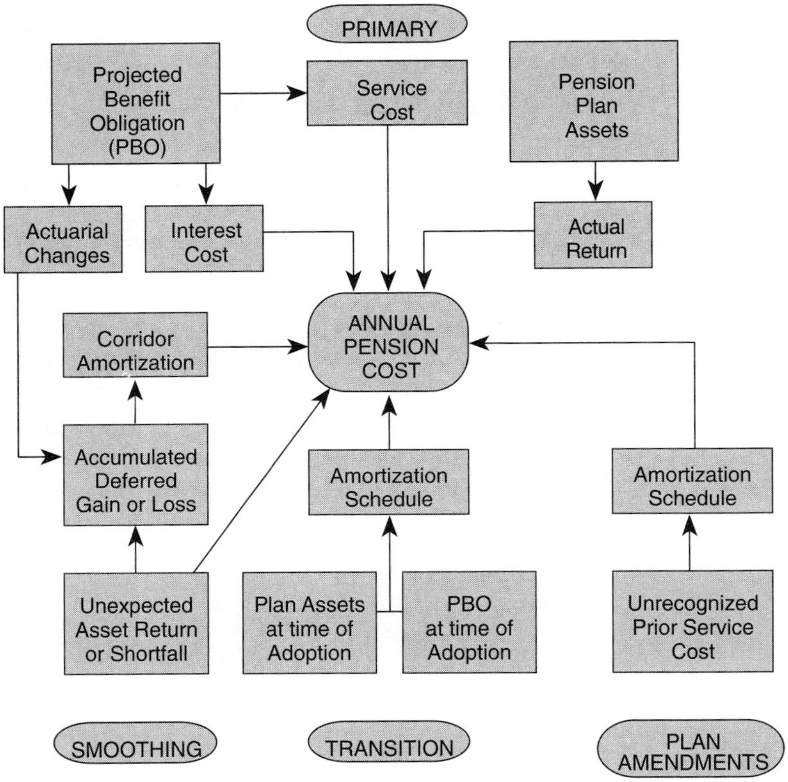

> The Board believes that a future economic benefit exists, that the cost of acquiring that benefit can be determined, and that amortization of that cost over future periods is consistent with accounting practice in other areas. (par. 159)

The same paragraph expresses FASB's reluctance to include the entire amount of PSC in pension cost for the year of the amendment:

> The Board also believes that a requirement to charge the cost of a retroactive plan amendment immediately to net periodic pension cost would not be representationally faithful and would represent an unacceptably radical change from current practice. (par. 159)

It should be noted that this sentence rejects only charging PSC against periodic pension cost; it does not say anything about reporting PSC as some other reduction in income in the year it is created. It should also be noted that the rejection is at least partially rationalized as being too revolutionary rather than inconsistent with a theory about the usefulness of the information.

EXHIBIT 2

Annual Pension Cost and Other Income under FASB's Preferred Theory

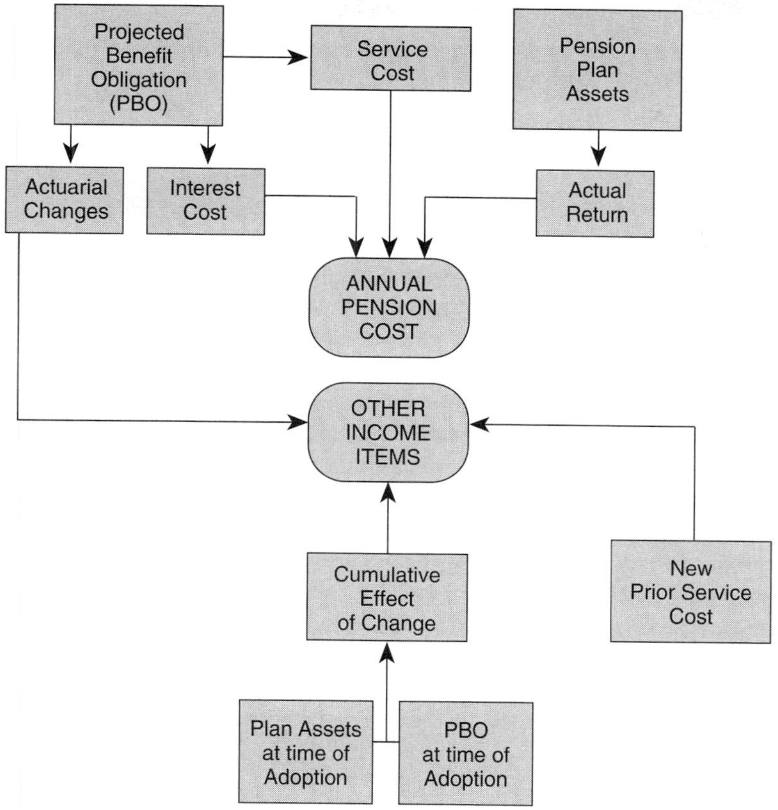

After deciding that PSC would be amortized, FASB faced the issue of whether the employer should recognize an asset for the unamortized balance. This approach was not adopted; instead, SFAS 87 calls for the use of an "Unrecognized" PSC balance that is maintained outside the formal system of accounts. The decision to use this approach produces ambiguity because it is not clear from the rationale whether the Board considered deferred PSC to be an asset.

The ambiguity is deepened by the requirement for the employer's recognition of an intangible asset if an additional liability is recognized in the process of putting the minimum liability on the statement of financial position (par. 37). Unfortunately for the purposes of this study, this unclear rationalization was all that was offered:

> Some respondents argued that the intangible asset proposed in the Exposure Draft does not qualify for recognition. The Board acknowledges the fact that similar future benefits are not recognized as assets in some cases. The Board concluded, however, that the asset should be recognized to the extent that a liability in excess

> of unfunded accrued pension cost is recognized. The Board also concluded that the asset recognized should be limited to the amount of prior service cost not yet recognized in net periodic pension cost. (par. 160)

If this intangible asset is recognized, its balance is not amortized but grows, shrinks, or disappears in tandem with the additional liability, which in turn changes with the funded status of the accumulated benefit measure of the pension liability (par. 38). Thus, it is not the same as any other recognized intangible asset.

Because of the contradictions in the rationale, we turned to two other factors to help us decipher FASB's theory. The first was Statement of Financial Accounting Concepts No. 6 (hereafter SFAC 6),[7] which was issued by FASB in the same month (December 1985) as SFAS 87. SFAC 6 superseded SFAC 3 by adding new elements and expanding discussions to include not-for-profit considerations without changing any of the original elements for business enterprises.[8] Given the timing of its issuance, we felt it appropriate to assume that this part of the conceptual framework expressed the general theory preferred by those board members who voted for both it and SFAS 87. Of particular relevance to this discussion is the fact that the structure of the elements would allow only assets to be recognized on the statement of financial position with no provision for deferred charges (also known more informally as "dangling debits") to be matched against future revenues. The juxtaposition of this fundamental concept with the rationalization for deferral in paragraph 159 shows the contradiction in the Board's analysis. To help resolve the ambiguity, we concluded that the concepts statements should override standards for the purpose of identifying FASB's preferred theory.

A second factor that we considered was the requirement in SFAS 87 for supplemental disclosures of pension information, including this item:

> The amount of net periodic pension cost for the period showing separately the service cost component, the interest cost component, the actual return on assets for the period, and ***the net total of other components*** (par. 54b, emphasis added).

The pertinent observation is that the Board did not require separate disclosure of the amount of PSC amortization. We believe that the decision to aggregate that amount with the other non-primary components strongly suggests that the Board did not consider PSC to have theoretical standing equivalent to the primary components. In any case, the practical effect of this provision is to make it more difficult (if not impossible) for users to find an annual cost equal to the primary components plus PSC amortization. That is, the amount of PSC amortization can be deduced as the change in the balance of the unrecognized PSC, but only if no new costs are created during the year and if there are no writedowns from plan curtailments under SFAS 88.[9] This outcome would be justified only if the Board considered PSC amortization to be irrelevant or otherwise not useful for decision makers.

In conclusion, we decided that the weight of the evidence falls in favor of a theory that excludes PSC amortization from annual pension cost but that nonetheless reduces income in

[7]FASB, "Elements of Financial Statements," *Statement of Financial Accounting Concepts No. 6,* December 1985.

[8]FASB, "Elements of Financial Statements," *Statement of Financial Accounting Concepts No. 3,* December 1980.

[9]FASB, "Employers' Accounting for Settlements and Curtailments of Defined Benefit Pension Plans and for Termination Benefits," *Statement of Financial Accounting Standards No. 88,* December 1985.

the amendment year by the full amount of new PSC. We admit that the evidence is ambiguous, but we do not assume responsibility for the lack of clarity, which certainly belongs to the Board.

SMOOTHING COMPONENTS The smoothing components of annual pension cost include deferred ***unexpected excess returns on or shortfalls in returns on plan assets.*** As reflected in Exhibits 1 and 2, the actual return is subtracted from the annual cost. However, to create a smoother annual expense, SFAS 87 requires any excess return above the expected amount to be added back to the expense and deferred to the future; likewise, an unexpected shortfall below that amount is deducted from the expense and deferred. SFAS 87 also defers all ***actuarial changes*** in the projected benefit obligation (hereafter, PBO) measure of the pension liability. A small part of the accumulated deferred gain or loss may be included in the annual cost through ***corridor amortization,*** the details of which are not described here.

This previously quoted language makes it clear that FASB adopted smoothing, which is euphemistically called "delayed recognition," because it was politically desirable, not because it was conceptually sound:

> The Board believes that it would be ***conceptually appropriate and preferable*** to [have] . . . no delay in recognition of gains and losses, or perhaps [to have] . . . gains and losses reported currently in comprehensive income but not in earnings. However, it concluded that ***those approaches would be too great a change from past practice to be adopted at the present time.*** (par. 107, emphasis added)

In addition, par. 104 refers specifically to the compromise embodied in the smoothing components when it says:

> The Board acknowledges that the delayed recognition included in this Statement results in ***excluding the most current and most relevant information*** from the employer's statement of financial position. (emphasis added)

This comment also confirms that the Board's preferred theory would not have included the smoothing components while denying that there was anything theoretical about the method required in the standard:

> The Board believes that both the extent of volatility reduction and the mechanism are ***essentially practical issues without conceptual basis.*** The Board does not believe that the market-related value of assets used in this Statement as a device to reduce the volatility of net periodic pension cost is as relevant as the fair value required for other purposes. (par. 177, emphasis added)

Accordingly, we determined that FASB's theory does not embrace delayed recognition of gains and losses from unanticipated events affecting the plan assets and the actuarial measures of the liability. Instead, this theory suggests that the actual return should reduce pension cost and that the actuarial changes should be reported as "other income" in the year in which they occur.

TRANSITION COMPONENT With respect to accounting for the transition from APBO 8 to SFAS 87, the employer is required to determine the net asset or net liability position when the standard is adopted by comparing the market value of the plan assets with the PBO measure of the pension liability.[10] Then, this net amount is amortized into the annual cost over no less than 15 years. SFAS 87 rationalizes this procedure by saying that:

> ***The Board continues to believe that transition is a practical matter*** and that a major objective of transition is to minimize the cost and to mitigate the disruption involved, to the extent that is possible without unduly compromising the objective of enhancing the ability of financial statements to provide useful information. (par. 256, emphasis added)

Thus, we also concluded that the transition component is not part of FASB's theory of annual pension cost. It follows that the Board's preference would be to charge or credit the net transition difference to income in the transition year. Although it might be speculated that this amount could be recognized as the cumulative effect of an accounting principle change, this detail is not central to the purposes of this paper.

SUMMARY As shown in Exhibit 2, our overall determination was that FASB's theory would include in the annual cost only the three primary components of service cost, interest cost, and the actual return on plan assets. As mentioned above, this conclusion is supported by the SFAS 87 requirement for separate disclosure of the individual amounts of these three items.

The presentation of the three primary components in the SFAS 87 footnote allows users who prefer the same theory to determine the cost incurred in the reporting year. However, if some cost is capitalized (perhaps as inventory), it is not possible to sort out how much of the pension cost flowed into the income statement.

STATEMENT OF FINANCIAL POSITION ITEMS

Consistent with the previously described asset/liability orientation of the conceptual framework elements, the pension items that could potentially appear on the employer's statement of financial position include the ***plan asset, an intangible asset for PSC, and the pension liability.***

However, the primary items recognized under SFAS 87 are a ***prepaid pension cost*** **or an** ***tunfunded accrued pension cost.*** These items are cumulative differences between the amount funded and the compromised annual cost measurements recognized over periods subsequent to adopting SFAS 87. To the extent that the balance of either account reflects the results of smoothing and PSC and transition amortization, it does not represent any of the three items listed above. The theoretical preferences of FASB are discussed below.

PLAN ASSETS This comment shows that FASB considered the plan assets to be the *de facto* property of the employer:

> Those who subscribe to the separate legal entity idea also argued that plan assets are not the assets of the employer. The Board noted that the employer's future contributions to the plan will be increased or decreased by the performance of the plan assets so that the ***employer bears the risks and reaps the rewards associated with those assets.*** The Board also observed that numerous recent situations

[10]Paragraph 77 also requires the employer to adjust this net difference for any residual accrued or prepaid pension cost recognized under APBO 8. For simplicity's sake, this technical point was omitted from Exhibits 1 and 2.

> in which significant amounts of assets have been withdrawn by employers provide compelling evidence that rebuts that argument. (par. 112, emphasis added)

There also is substantial clarity about the Board's view on measuring the plan assets:

> The Board recognizes that there may be practical problems in determining the fair value of certain types of assets. Notwithstanding those difficulties, the Board believes that the ***relevance of fair value of pension assets is so great*** as to override objections to its use based on difficulty of measurement. (par. 118, emphasis added)

Thus, we concluded that FASB's theoretical preference would be to recognize the plan assets on the employer's statement of financial position at their fair value.

PENSION LIABILITY In dealing with the issue of whether the employer has a liability for defined benefits, FASB included this comment in SFAS 87 to answer those respondents who argued that the employer's only obligation was to the pension fund:

> The Board concluded that viewing the obligation and the cost only in terms of scheduled contributions does not reflect the fundamental difference between the inherent promise and the resulting obligation under a defined benefit plan and the promise and obligation under a defined contribution plan. An employer that has undertaken an obligation to provide defined pension benefits based on service already rendered may view it as an obligation directly to the employees . . . or as an obligation to make future contributions to the plan, but ***the employer has a present obligation based on the defined benefits either way.*** (par. 110, emphasis added)

One of the more difficult controversies in the pension project was the selection among the ***vested, accumulated,*** and ***projected benefit obligation*** measures of the pension liability.[11] The choice affected not only the statement of financial position but also the income statement because changes in the liability are the basis for service and interest cost. The Board majority's consensus for the PBO was unambiguous:

> After considering respondents' views, both practical and conceptual, the Board concluded that estimated future compensation levels should be considered in measuring the service cost component and the projected benefit obligation if the plan's benefit formula incorporates them. The Board perceives a difference between an employer's promise to pay a benefit of 1 percent of an employee's *final* pay and a promise to pay an employee a fixed amount that happens to equal 1 percent of the employee's *current* pay. (par. 143, italics in the original)

Thus, it seems clear that FASB's preference was to recognize the liability at the PBO amount.

However, a compromise occurred when the Board chose the unfunded accumulated benefit obligation for measuring the ***minimum liability*** to be recognized on the balance sheet. Unfortunately for the purpose of this paper, this choice is not specifically justified in SFAS 87

[11]Evidence that this issue was controversial can be found in the fact that board member Robert Sprouse based his dissent to SFAS 87 partially on the statement's use of the PBO measure, while member Art Wyatt based his dissent partially on the failure to use the PBO for the minimum liability provision (see the next paragraph).

beyond its description in par. 152 as "an improvement in past practices for the reporting of financial position. . . ." It was our conclusion that this equivocal explanation did not create sufficient uncertainty to obscure FASB's theoretical preference for the PBO.

PRIOR SERVICE COSTS As we stated previously, the description of the preferred theory for PSC is simply not as clear as it could be. Even though FASB proposed recognizing PSC as an intangible asset in par. 15b of its *Preliminary Views* document,[12] this approach was not used in the final standard. After the analysis described earlier, we concluded that FASB's theoretical preference would be to charge new PSC against income instead of recognizing an intangible asset.

We also described the SFAS 87 requirement that an intangible asset be recognized when the minimum liability condition is met. Its amount equals only the additional liability (beyond any accrued liability[13]) that must be recognized, as long as it does not exceed the amount of unrecognized PSC. The ambiguity concerning conceptual preference is not relieved by FASB's explanation of its decision because it only restates the conclusion without providing a theoretical rationale:

> The Board concluded, however, that the asset should be recognized to the extent that a liability in excess of unfunded accrued pension cost is recognized. The Board also concluded that the asset recognized should be limited to the amount of prior service cost not yet recognized in net periodic pension cost (par. 160).

In the face of this silence, the authors interpret the partial recognition of PSC under the minimum liability condition to be nothing more than a practical compromise because there is no conceptual link between the amount of additional liability recognized to reach the minimum level and the total amount of intangible asset (perhaps with the nature of employee goodwill) that might be created by a plan amendment. That is, the existence and size of the additional liability depend on past funding choices, investment decisions, market results, and an incomplete actuarial estimate, whereas the amount of new PSC is simply the result of an increase in the more actuarially complete PBO measure of the liability. Our interpretation is that the recognized intangible is merely a convenient place to report the dangling debit needed to offset the credit to the additional liability.

SUMMARY Thus, it appears to us that FASB's theoretical preference calls for the employer to recognize only the plan assets and the PBO on its statement of financial position. However, there is some ambiguity on the issue of whether these two items should be offset or recognized separately; the following paragraphs deal with this part of the theory.

THE OFFSETTING ISSUE

Despite the stated preference in par. 107 for offsetting the plan assets against the liability (see the quotation in the fifth paragraph of this paper), there are other comments in SFAS 87 that raise the question of whether doing so reflects FASB's ideal.

---

[12]FASB, "Employer's Accounting for Pension and Other Postemployment Benefits," *Preliminary Views,* November 1982.

[13]If the employer were to face the unlikely situation of having a prepaid pension cost and an underfunded accumulated benefit obligation, the additional liability would equal the sum of the balances of the prepaid cost and the minimum liability.

In particular, the analysis in the Basis for Conclusions argues against offsetting more than it justifies it. First, the Board identifies offsetting as one of:

> three features of practice [that] have shaped financial reporting for pensions for many years even though ***they have been neither explicitly addressed nor widely understood and they conflict in some respects with accounting principles applied elsewhere.*** (para. 84, emphasis added)

In other words, the Board seemed to consider offsetting to be a vestigial practice that may not be conceptually sound. FASB then went on to examine offsetting from a theoretical perspective; this conclusion conveys a fairly clear denial of its soundness:

> The offsetting feature means that recognized values of assets contributed to a plan and liabilities for pensions recognized as net pension cost of past periods are shown net in the employer's statement of financial position, ***even though the liability has not been settled, the assets may be still largely controlled, and substantial risks and rewards associated with both of those amounts are clearly borne by the employer.*** (par. 87, emphasis added)

Because of these comments, we concluded that the Board's theory does not embrace offsetting. Rather, we think FASB saw offsetting as only a practical convention that was retained to produce a less revolutionary change.

This interpretation is reinforced by the Board's decision to require disclosure of the gross amounts of the plan assets and the PBO. If only the net amount were considered to be relevant, it would have been appropriate to require disclosure of only that amount. The view that offsetting may obscure useful information is bolstered by the results of other research. For example, this specific issue was addressed in a paper that recommends to analysts that they consider the assets and pension obligation separately.[14] Evidence that capital market participants may have an aggregate view consistent with a model that treats the plan assets and the pension liability as separate is provided in another study that reports that stock prices appear to reflect this valuation.[15]

In summary, we determined that the FASB's preferred theory would recognize the plan assets and pension liability as separate elements in the statement of financial position.

FINANCIAL STATEMENT ADJUSTMENTS BASED ON FASB'S PREFERRED THEORY

Once FASB's theory was identified, we then proceeded to the next step of attempting to measure the effects of the compromises in SFAS 87. The measurements were accomplished by comparing financial results and conditions actually reported under the standard with the amounts that would have been reported in compliance with the theory.

---

[14]Patrick J. Regan and Steven D. Bleiberg, "Overfunded Pension Plans," *Financial Analysts' Journal,* November/December 1985, pp. 10–12.

[15]Wayne Landsman, "An Empirical Investigation of Pension and Property Rights," *The Accounting Review,* October 1986, pp. 662–692.

SAMPLE SELECTION

Because the goal was to identify the effect of the compromises without attempting to infer results for all companies subject to SFAS 87, there was no need for a random selection or a minimum sample size. We chose a sample of 30 large *Fortune 500* companies for 1987. Because we wanted a cross-section covering six major industries, we chose the five largest companies in each. In completing this cross-section, the sample included companies ranging from 1st to 108th. A list of the industries and companies appears in Exhibit 3, which is presented later in the paper.

INCOME STATEMENT ADJUSTMENT

With respect to the income statement, the first adjustment used the information from the SFAS 87 footnote to calculate an annual pension cost consisting of only the three primary components. The difference between the sum of these amounts and the reported cost was used to adjust pension expense. To illustrate, Ford Motor Co. reported pension expense of $344.5 million under SFAS 87. We determined from the footnote that the theoretical amount was $509.8 million, and computed the adjustment as follows (in millions, and hereafter):

Service cost	$ 324.1
Interest	1,181.4
Actual return	(995.7)
Adjusted pension cost	509.8
Reported pension cost	(344.5)
Adjustment to pension cost (increase)	$ 165.3

As suggested previously, this difference only approximates the change in reported income because all pension cost does not flow directly to the income statement if it is capitalized in inventory or some other asset and recognized as expense in a subsequent year.

STATEMENT OF FINANCIAL POSITION ADJUSTMENTS

The first adjustment to the statement of financial position was the removal of any SFAS 87 items. Their balances were found in the footnote, and potentially included the prepaid pension cost asset or the accrued pension cost liability, an additional liability, and any recognized intangible.[16] Because they had more than one pension plan, some of the sample had both prepaid and accrued accounts (SFAS 87 prohibits offsetting their balances). We found that none of the sample companies had recognized a pension intangible.

Then, in accordance with the non-offsetting theory, the plan assets were added to total assets, and the PBO was added to total liabilities. These calculations were made for Ford:

Reported total assets	$44,955.7
Less: prepaid pension cost	(608.6)
Plus: pension plan assets	16,226.0
Adjusted total assets	$60,573.1
Reported total liabilities	$26,326.5
Plus: projected benefit obligation	14,826.0
Adjusted total liabilities	$41,152.5

[16] An employer's statement of financial position would include a contra equity item if the additional liability were to exceed the unrecognized prior service cost. No situations like these were encountered in the sample.

EXHIBIT 3

Results for Sample Companies

	Percentage Changes in:					
	Pension Expense or Income	**Income before Extraordinary Items**	**Total Liabilities**	**Total Assets**	**Liabilities/ Equity**	**Return on Equity**
Industry						
Company						
Automotive						
Chrysler	68.5%	−25.0%	46.2%	18.3%	141.6%	24.2%
Dana	15.8%	−4.1%	42.7%	24.1%	60.8%	8.3%
Eaton	346.5%	−24.5%	40.8%	28.9%	31.2%	−29.4%
Ford	48.0%	−3.6%	56.3%	34.7%	50.0%	−7.3%
GM	−784.0%	139.7%	61.9%	43.1%	44.8%	114.8%
Chemical						
Dow	0.0%	0.0%	24.0%	14.9%	21.9%	−1.4%
DuPont	−151.7%[a]	−17.6%	54.1%	39.3%	23.4%	−34.4%
Grace	−381.7%[a]	−41.6%	15.1%	17.1%	−5.2%	−51.8%
Monsanto	1,171.4%	−18.8%	53.6%	36.9%	30.8%	−31.3%
Union Carbide	507.1%	−61.2%	25.1%	20.6%	18.5%	−63.3%
Computers						
Digital	97.7%	−9.5%	52.9%	14.5%	51.2%	−10.9%
HP	−1,500.0%[a]	−4.7%	9.4%	5.3%	6.6%	−7.0%
IBM	632.6%	−27.3%	92.2%	41.9%	77.3%	−32.8%
NCR	128.0%	−3.1%	76.7%	40.7%	57.4%	−13.4%
Unisys	440.4%	−31.7%	56.2%	28.8%	62.5%	−29.1%
Electrical						
Emerson	47.2%[b]	0.5%	20.9%	11.6%	15.8%	−3.7%
GE	1,240.0%	−14.6%	67.9%	50.1%	32.8%	−32.3%
Motorola	−150.0%	1.9%	11.8%	8.2%	6.1%	−2.9%
TRW	292.9%	−16.9%	50.5%	40.1%	27.0%	−30.0%
Westinghouse	295.5%	−44.7%	73.6%	34.8%	162.3%	−16.1%
Food						
Borden's	−3,206.7%[a]	−18.0%	17.5%	10.5%	17.3%	−18.6%
Conagra	148.8%	−7.9%	6.9%	6.3%	2.1%	−12.2%
Occidental	185.7%	−7.1%	3.9%	2.7%	4.0%	−5.9%
RJR	235.7%	−10.2%	20.3%	14.1%	16.2%	−13.5%
Sara Lee	−1,294.9%[a]	−23.5%	17.9%	14.4%	9.1%	−29.3%
Petroleum						
Amoco	83.7%	−2.6%	14.9%	8.9%	12.0%	−4.5%
Chevron	−195.8%[a]	−4.7%	14.5%	10.6%	3.6%	−10.9%
Exxon	173.4%	−6.6%	14.1%	9.0%	10.0%	−9.9%
Mobil	478.8%	−12.6%	9.9%	6.6%	8.0%	−14.7%
Texaco	70.6%	0.8%[c]	4.6%	3.8%	2.8%	−0.8%[d]

[a]Reported net pension income, but adjusted to net expense

[b]Reported net pension income, and adjusted to larger net pension income

[c]The increase in pension expense increased the size of the net loss for the year

[d]The combined effect of the increased net loss for the year and the increased net assets was a less negative ROE

INCOME TAX EFFECTS

Because there were significant effects on the companies' financial statements from these adjustments, we considered whether income taxes needed to be included. We determined that the special tax deferred and exempt status of funded defined benefit plans makes the determination of any such effects elusive, to say the least.

That is, the tax treatment of pension cost allows the employer a deduction in a given year generally equal to the amount contributed to the fund, which is not likely to equal the amount of pension cost under SFAS 87. Furthermore, interest on the PBO is not separately deductible because it is not paid by the employer. Finally, the return on plan assets is not taxable to the employer but to the employees when they receive retirement benefit payments.

With respect to the statement of financial position, we also determined that there would be no tax effect produced by removing the SFAS 87 recognized items and adding the plan assets and the PBO. There are no tax consequences to the employer associated with the normal expenditure of plan assets for employee benefits. However, if reversion were to occur, there would be a tax consequence.

Because of these considerations, we determined that we would make the adjustments to the sample companies' financial statements without reflecting any tax effects. We were also encouraged to reach this conclusion by the still unsettled condition of the FASB project on accounting for income taxes, which suggests that the Board's own theory in this area is not yet completely supported by a consensus.[17]

THE RESULTS OF THE ANALYSIS

Six analyses were performed using the original and the adjusted financial data described above. They were:

- Effect on pension expense
- Effect on income before extraordinary items
- Effect on total liabilities
- Effect on total assets
- Effect on ratio of liabilities to equity
- Effect on return on stockholders' equity

In addition, we compiled average results for the six industries represented in the sample.

Exhibit 3 presents the data by industry and company. The amounts shown are the size of the adjustment from the reported to the theoretical measure, expressed as a percentage of the reported measure. For example, the percentage increase in pension expense for Ford was calculated as follows:

Adjusted pension expense	\$ 509.8
Reported pension expense	(344.5)
Adjustment	\$ 165.3
Adjustment as a percentage of the reported expense (\$165.3/\$344.5)	48.0%

The succeeding sections look at each of the six analyses.

[17]Financial Accounting Standards Board, *Exposure Draft,* "Accounting for Income Taxes" (Norwalk, Conn., June 1991).

EFFECT ON PENSION EXPENSE

Our first step in examining the effect of FASB's compromises on an employer's financial statements was the above comparison of the original annual pension cost with the amount computed under the theory. The adjusted amount included only service cost, interest cost, and actual return on the plan assets, and removed the effects of prior service costs, smoothing, and transition.

Exhibit 4 presents two frequency distributions of the observed differences reported in Exhibit 3; Part A shows the results for the 23 companies that originally reported a net pension expense, while Part B describes the seven companies that originally reported a net pension income. There is a clear pattern of larger expense and smaller income.

Of the 23 companies in the sample that originally reported net pension expense, 20 showed adjusted expense greater than the SFAS 87 amount, and one (Dow) was unchanged. Of the 20, 14 had adjusted expense more than double the reported amount. Two in this group (GE and Monsanto) had adjustments that increased their reported cost by more than 1,100 percent (GE went from $25 million to $335 million, and Monsanto went from $7 million to $89 million).

The other two companies (GM and Motorola) had adjustments of sufficient size to turn the pension cost into pension income. Specifically, GM went from a $632.7 million pension expense under SFAS 87 to a $4,327.8 million adjusted net pension income. The details of its pension cost components were:

Service cost	$ 825.9
Interest cost	2,868.9
Actual return	(8,022.6)
Adjusted pension income	(4,327.8)
Reported pension cost	632.7
Adjustment	$(4,960.5)

The combined effects of smoothing, amortization, and transition equaled nearly $5 *billion* and swamped the three primary components of cost.

For six of the seven companies that originally reported net pension income, the adjustment produced net pension expense. Borden's change of −3,206.7 percent is so large because its SFAS 87 measure of net pension income, $1.5 million, is relatively small compared to its adjusted net cost of $46.6 million. Emerson is the only company that showed a larger pension income under the theory.

Because there is so much variability in the results of this analysis, we are strongly inclined to doubt that SFAS 87 met this objective:

> To provide a measure of net periodic pension cost that is more understandable and comparable and is, therefore, more useful than those in past practice. (par. 6b)

Although the FASB's goal was to reduce the variability produced by the range of alternative measurement methods allowed under APBO 8, we believe that the wide distribution of changes in pension cost suggests that the compromises may have introduced virtually random noise into the measures. Consequently, SFAS 87 may have produced *less* comparability, not more. However, there is no way to assess the outcome without obtaining pension measures for a sample under both APBO 8 and SFAS 87 for the same year.

EXHIBIT 4

Frequency Distribution of Changes in Pension Expense or Income

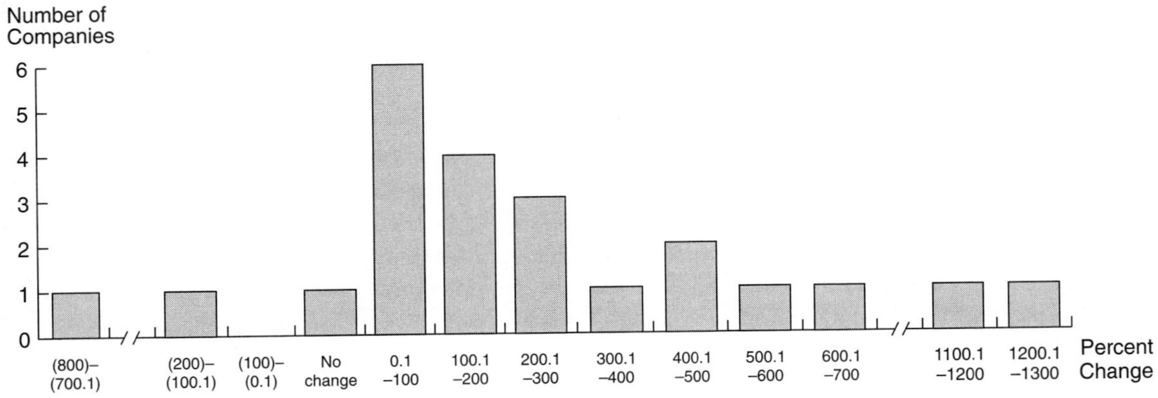

Part A–Companies Originally Reporting Pension Expense

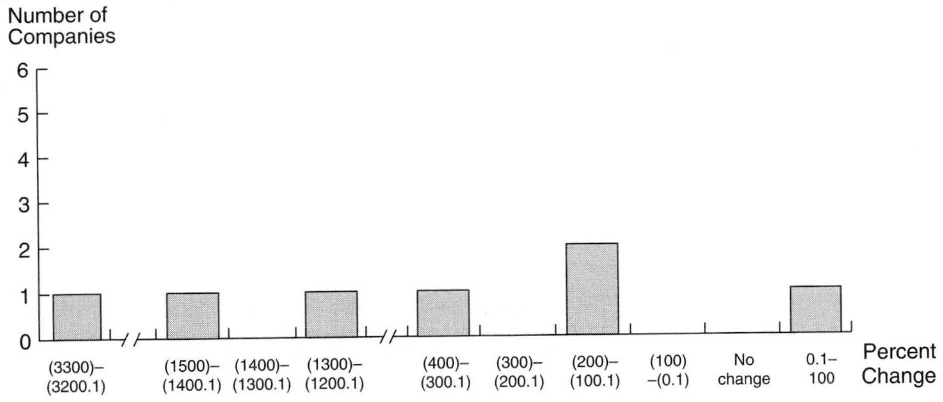

Part B–Companies Originally Reporting Pension Income

EFFECT ON INCOME BEFORE EXTRAORDINARY ITEMS

In order to describe more completely the effect of the compromises on the employer, our second analysis examined the change in reported income. Because the entire pension cost is allocated between continuing and discontinued segments, and because that allocation is not disclosed, it was determined that income before extraordinary items (IBEI) would be the most suitable definition of income for the analysis.

For example, these adjustments were made to Ford's reported numbers:

Reported IBEI	$4,625.2
Pension cost adjustment	(165.3)
Adjusted IBEI	$4,459.9
Adjustment as a percentage of the reported IBEI ($165.3/$4,625.2)	−3.6%

EXHIBIT 5

Frequency Distribution of Changes in Income before Extraordinary Items

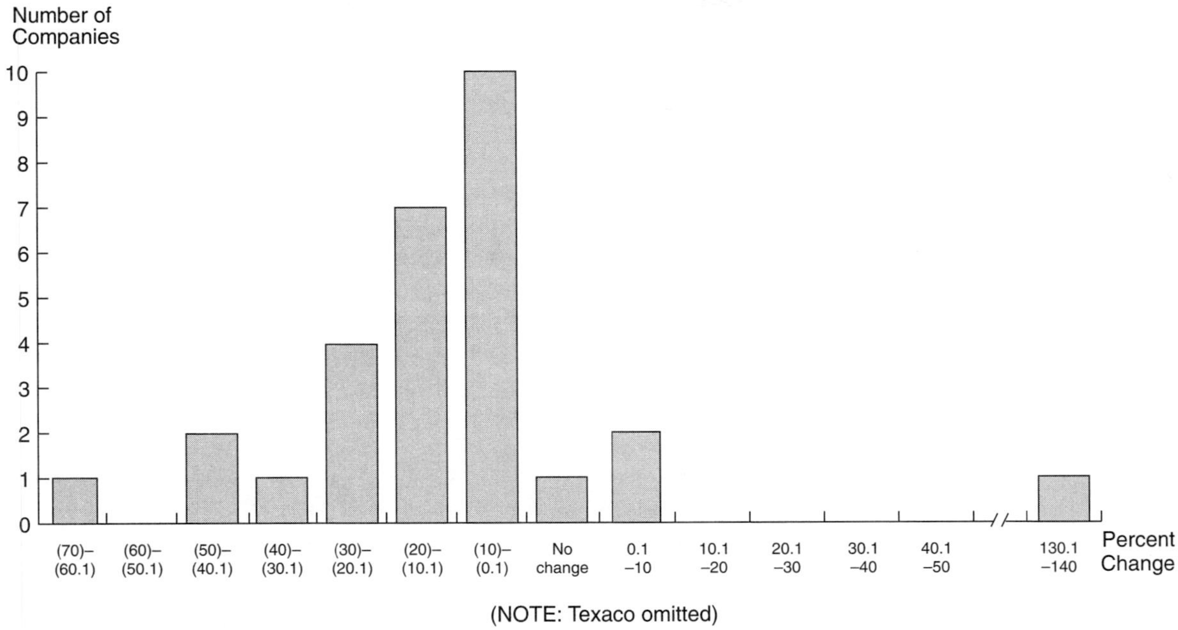

The frequency distribution in Exhibit 5 shows that compliance with the theoretical model produced significantly varied departures from the SFAS 87 measure of IBEI.[18] Increases in IBEI were calculated for only three companies in the sample (GM, Emerson, and Motorola). Naturally, Dow showed no change in IBEI because it had no change in its expense. Of the remaining 25 companies with lower adjusted incomes, ten had changes of ten percent or less. The remaining 15 experienced decreases ranging from RJR's 10.2 percent up to Union Carbide's 61.2 percent.

This analysis shows clearly that the SFAS 87 compromises led to recognized measures of income that can be materially different from the theoretical ideal described in the standard. It also shows that different companies are affected substantially differently, a fact that again suggests that comparability may have been inhibited rather than promoted.

EFFECT ON TOTAL LIABILITIES

The next three analyses considered the effects of the compromises on the employers' statements of financial position, beginning with an examination of the change that occurred when the total liabilities number was adjusted to include the PBO and remove any accrued pension

[18]Exhibit 5 includes changes for only 29 companies; for simplicity, it omits Texaco, which increased its loss by a very small amount.

liability. Because the PBO is always larger than any recognized pension liability, every company in the sample showed an increase, as reflected in the frequency distribution of percentage changes presented in Exhibit 6.

The calculation of the percentage change for Ford was:

Reported total liabilities	$26,326.5
Plus: PBO	14,826.0
Adjusted total liabilities	$41,152.5
Adjustment as a percentage of the reported liabilities ($14,826.0/$26,326.5)	56.3%

The effect for any company depends jointly on the size of the PBO and the amount of other recognized debt. The smallest change was only 3.9 percent for Occidental, while IBM's total liabilities would have been 92.2 percent higher if FASB's theory had been implemented. The changes for the sample were widely distributed over the other categories, with 25 showing increases of more than 10 percent.

EFFECT ON TOTAL ASSETS

The next analysis examined the increases in total assets that would be caused by including the pension plan assets and eliminating any recognized prepaid pension cost. Because the former must exceed the latter, all 30 companies showed increases. The frequency distribution of the percentage increases is presented in Exhibit 7.

The calculation of Ford's change is shown below:

Reported total assets	$44,955.7
Adjustment:	
Less: prepaid pension cost	(608.6)
Plus: pension plan assets	16,226.0
Net adjustment	15,617.4
Adjusted total assets	$60,573.1
Adjustment as a percentage of the reported assets ($15,617.4/$44,955.7)	34.7%

Under the normal condition in which total reported assets exceed total liabilities, and the amount of pension assets is relatively close to the PBO, the adjustments' effect on assets is not as great as on liabilities. Accordingly, and as shown in Exhibit 7, the frequency distribution of percentage changes for the sample companies was less dispersed than the effects on liabilities. Seventeen companies showed increases of 20 percent or less, while the remaining 13 had increases of less than 51 percent. The smallest increase was 2.7 percent for Occidental, and the largest was 50.1 percent for GE.

EFFECT ON RATIO OF LIABILITIES TO EQUITY

In order to determine how omitting the pension assets and liabilities affects the statement of financial position as a whole, we next examined the ratio of each company's total liabilities to its total stockholders' equity before and after adjusting both amounts. The frequency distribution of percentage changes is shown in Exhibit 8.

EXHIBIT 6

Frequency Distribution of Changes in Total Liabilities

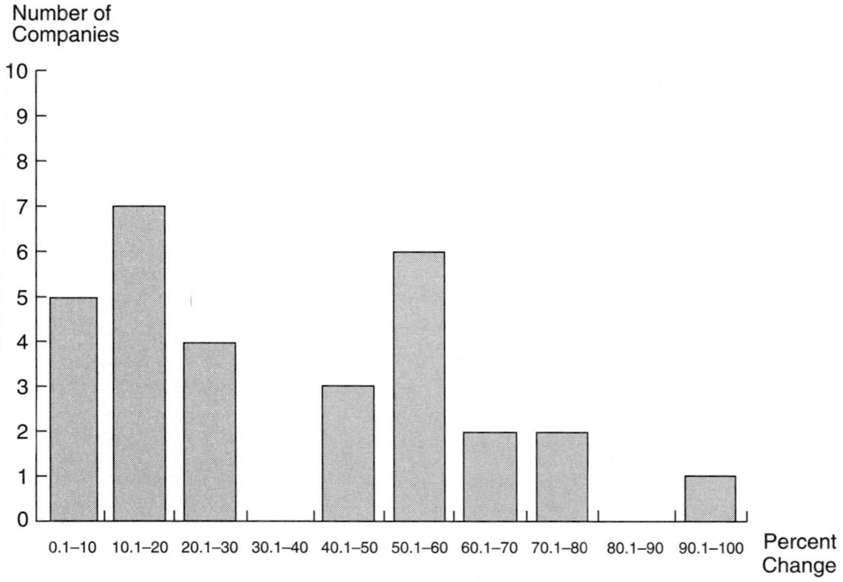

The calculations for Ford were:

Reported total assets	$44,955.7
Reported total liabilities.	(26,326.5)
Reported equity	$18,629.2
Reported ratio ($26,326.5/$18,629.2)	141.3%
Adjusted total assets.	$60,573.1
Adjusted total liabilities	(41,152.5)
Adjusted equity	$19,420.6
Adjusted ratio ($41,152.5/$19,420.6)	211.9%
Change in ratio [(211.9%–141.3%)/141.3%]	50.0%

Only one company (Grace) showed a decrease in its ratio, but the size of its change was relatively small (5.2 percent). All others showed increases, with slightly less than one-third (9) increasing by less than 10 percent. Five increased by 10 to 20 percent, with 13 increasing more than 20 percent but less than 80 percent. The two largest differences were experienced by Chrysler (141.6 percent) and Westinghouse (162.3 percent).

Again, the wide diversity of the results for these effects suggests that the compromises may have inhibited comparability by reducing the variability that would have been apparent if the theory had been implemented.

EXHIBIT 7

Frequency Distribution of Changes in Total Assets

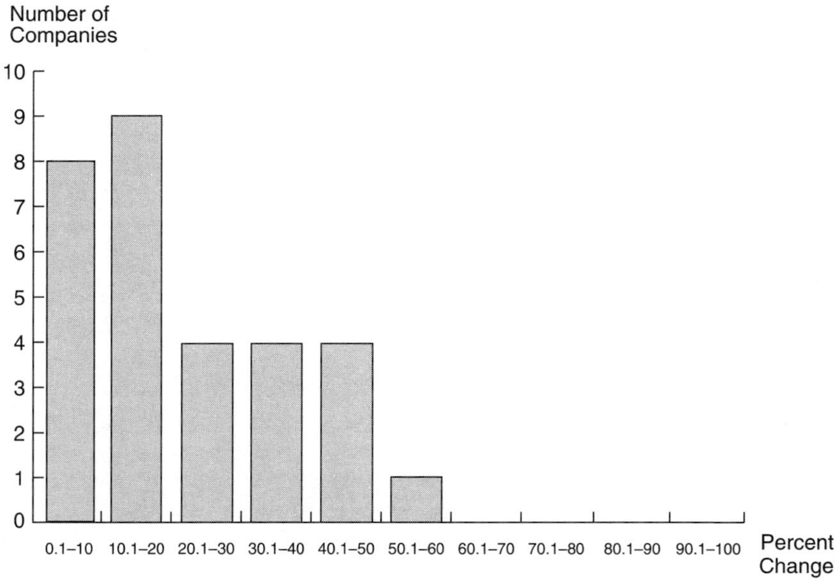

EFFECT ON RETURN ON STOCKHOLDERS' EQUITY

In order to examine the combined effect of all the adjustments, we looked at one version of the return on stockholders' equity (ROE) with and without the pension adjustments. ROE was calculated as IBEI divided by the difference between total assets and total liabilities.

The calculations for Ford are shown below:

Reported IBEI	$ 4,625.2
Reported equity	$18,629.2
Reported ROE ($4,625.2/$18,629.2)	24.8%
Adjusted IBEI	$ 4,459.9
Adjusted equity	$19,420.6
Adjusted ROE ($4,459.9/$19,420.6)	23.0%
Change in ROE [(23.0%–24.8%)/24.8%]	−7.3%

Only three companies (Chrysler, Dana, and GM) would have reported higher ROE measures if FASB had implemented its theory. Because of the large turnaround from its reported pension expense to its adjusted pension income, GM's ROE increased by 114.8 percent from the original 10.8 percent to its adjusted 23.2 percent.

Texaco would have a slightly less negative loss under the preferred theory, and the remaining 26 companies would have reported lower returns. As shown in Exhibit 9, most in this group would have experienced relatively small changes, with 8 of them showing percentage

EXHIBIT 8

Frequency Distribution of Changes in the Liabilities/Equity Ratio

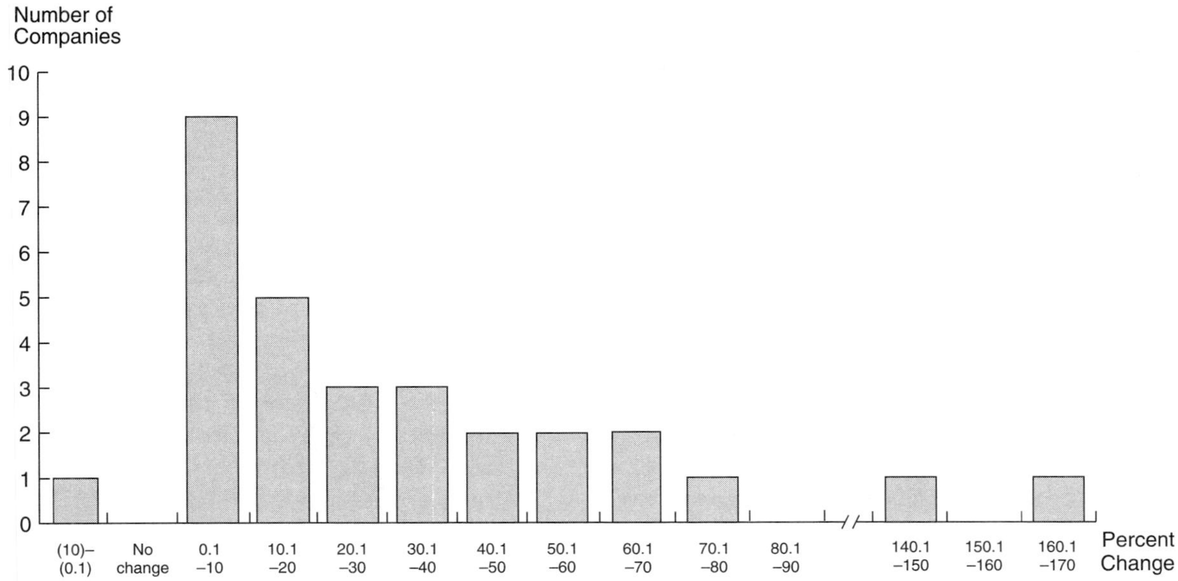

decreases in ROE of less than 10 percent and another 8 having decreases between 10 and 20 percent.[19] These three companies had the largest differences:

Company	Unadjusted ROE	Adjusted ROE	Percentage Difference
Union Carbide	12.8%	4.7%	−63.3%
Grace	11.0	5.3	−51.8
DuPont	12.5	8.2	−34.4

The inconsistency among the firms again suggests that SFAS 87's compromises may have introduced noise into the financial statements, at least in comparison to FASB's preferred theory.

INDUSTRY RESULTS

Exhibit 10 shows summary statistics for the six industries represented in the sample. For completeness, it also shows the numbers for the entire sample and for the automotive industry without GM, which has an expense adjustment so much larger than the others that it overwhelms the income statement averages.[20] In addition, the average changes in pension expense (shown in the first column) were computed using only the 23 companies that originally

[19]To avoid ambiguity, Exhibit 9 does not include Texaco's negative change in its loss.

[20]Specifically, GM's effects are sufficiently large to alter the sign of the average change in the industry's pension expense, IBEI, and ROE.

EXHIBIT 9

Frequency Distribution of Changes in the Return on Equity

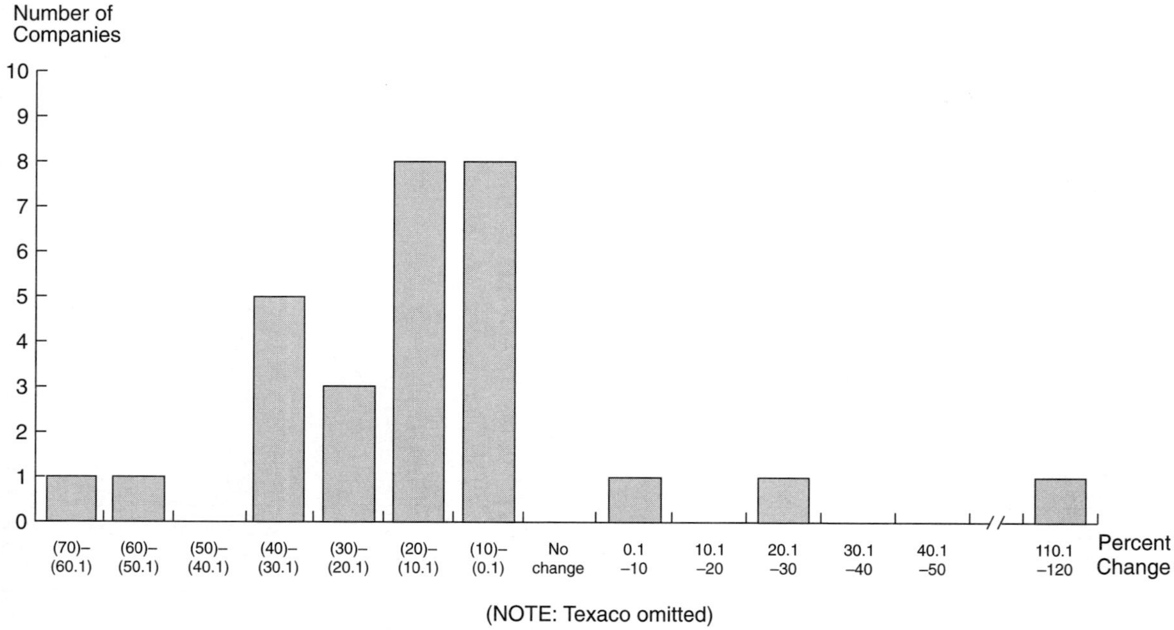

reported net pension cost, and excluded the seven that reported net pension income. The amounts shown are simple averages that do not reflect the different sizes of the sample companies. Nonetheless, they are appropriate for our goal of measuring how SFAS 87 compromises affected the financial statements.

Given the nonrandom and small samples, there is no basis for generalizing these results to entire industries. However, the data used in this study show again that there is substantial variation among the subjects.

The chemical industry seems to have received what could be considered favorable treatment from the compromises because its adjusted results show the largest increase in pension expense, the largest decrease in IBEI, and by far the largest decrease in ROE. The petroleum and food industries show the smallest decreases in IBEI and the smallest increases in assets and liabilities. Except for automotive, all industries showed declines in ROE, and even that industry had a small decline when GM was excluded.

LIMITATIONS

One of the limitations of the findings in this paper was described above. Specifically, the analysis of the actual companies' results is based on a nonrandom sample. A second limitation is that the measures are based on information provided in the companies' footnotes, which do

EXHIBIT 10

Industry Averages

	Percentage Changes in:					
	Pension Expense*	**Income before Extraordinary Items**	**Total Liabilities**	**Total Assets**	**Liabilities/ Equity**	**Return on Equity**
Automotive	−61.0%	16.5%	49.6%	29.8%	65.7%	22.1%
without GM	*119.7%*	*−14.3%*	*46.5%*	*26.5%*	*70.9%*	*−1.1%*
Chemical	559.5%	−27.8%	34.4%	25.8%	17.9%	−36.4%
Computers	432.9%	−15.3%	57.5%	26.2%	51.0%	−18.6%
Electrical	419.6%	−14.8%	44.9%	29.0%	48.8%	−17.0%
Food	190.1%	−13.3%	13.3%	9.6%	9.7%	−15.9%
Petroleum	201.6%	−5.1%	11.6%	7.8%	7.3%	−8.2%
Total sample	290.5%	−10.0%	35.2%	21.4%	33.4%	−12.3%
without GM	*320.6%*	*−15.1%*	*34.7%*	*20.8%*	*34.3%*	*16.2%*

*These averages exclude companies that originally reported net pension income.

not necessarily provide all the information that is needed. Third, and as described, we omitted any income tax effects. Fourth, the measures of income did not include any effects on "other" income from the amendment, smoothing, and transition components of cost.

CONCLUSION

We believe that this paper is important because it provides a measure of the effects of political compromises on financial statement items and their relationships, and thereby allows a more informed assessment of whether those compromises might make any difference. While departures from the theoretical answer are readily apparent just by reading SFAS 87, their effects can only be speculated on without these measures or others like them. While it is clear to observers of the FASB's process that the controversies over pension accounting were particularly deep and that the compromises were unusually intricate, we do not believe that many could have anticipated the wide diversity of results observed for our sample.

A second contribution of this paper is its description of a plausible (and politically supported) theory of useful measures of pension-related costs, assets, and liabilities. This model can serve as the basis for research into the information content of pension disclosures and other questions.

A third contribution is the use of the method of comparing the requirements of a SFAS and FASB's own description of a theoretically preferred approach. This method can be applied to other standards in order to assess the effects of compromises and financial statements prepared in accordance with their requirements.

Because of the differences between the theory and the SFAS 87 requirements, it appears that at least one FASB member had a vision for a more significant change in pension accounting. Board Member Art Wyatt's dissent to SFAS 87 laments that the majority would not go further than it did:

> Mr. Wyatt agrees with the assenters that, on an overall basis, the conclusions in the Statement will lead to improvements in accounting for and understanding of pension costs. He believes, however, that ***the degree of improvement is modest when related to the improvement that he believes should have been achieved.*** Thus, in his view, the Statement's deficiencies represent a lost opportunity for improvement in financial reporting. (page 26, emphasis added)

On the other hand, the fact that information can be useful without being recognized in the financial statements makes it possible that the efforts leading up to SFAS 87 might be worthwhile despite these compromises because the standard has created new public information, particularly the more reliable and disaggregated estimates of the primary components of pension cost and the PBO measure of the pension obligation. Because this information was not public before SFAS 87, one likely consequence is that the standard has reduced users' costs of gathering and processing information. Of course, the presence of any market effect of the new information remains an issue for further research that can build on the theoretical foundation described here.

II-D2

OPEB: IMPROVED REPORTING OR THE LAST STRAW?

Paula B. Thomas and Larry E. Farmer

The Financial Accounting Standards Board's Exposure Draft (ED) *Employers' Accounting for Postretirement Benefits Other Than Pensions,* usually referred to as OPEB, has been characterized as a way to improve financial reporting and, alternatively, as a pronouncement that will devastate reported corporate profits needlessly. Simply stated, the FASB is proposing accrual-basis reporting of the cost of, and the obligations for, postretirement benefits, instead of the prevalent current practice of report-as-you-pay (cash-basis) reporting. Though the ED encompasses all postretirement benefits currently owed and expected to be provided to current and future retirees, healthcare will constitute the bulk of the cost. The amounts involved can affect financial statements materially and adversely, and that has the preparers of financial statements worried.

Comparison to Pension Accounting

When companies initially offered postretirement benefits, healthcare costs were relatively low and the ratio of covered retirees to active workers was small. Since cash payments for these

---

PAULA B. THOMAS, CPA, CMS, DBA, is associate professor of accounting at Middle Tennessee State University, Murfreesboro. She is a member of the American Institute of CPAs, the National Association of Accountants and the American Accounting Association. LARRY E. FARMER, CPA, CMA, CIA, DBA, is professor of accounting at Middle Tennessee State University. He is a member of the AICPA, the NAA and the AAA. Drs. Thomas and Farmer are the authors of "Accounting for Stock Options and SARs: The Equality Question," which was published in the June 1984 Journal of Accountancy.

costs were generally immaterial, cash-basis expense recognition was acceptable. But a combination of escalating healthcare costs and changing demographics has altered the post-retirement landscape.

In deciding how companies should account for postretirement benefits, the board paid particular attention to FASB Statement no. 87, *Employers' Accounting for Pensions,* because there are similarities between the way pension and other postretirement benefits affect companies.

In some areas, accounting for both pensions and OPEB is inconsistent with the traditional accounting model. These include

- Delayed reporting of events that have occurred.
- Combined current and past compensation costs, financing costs and investment gains and losses reported on a net basis.
- Asset and liability offset without the presence of conditions specified in FASB Technical Bulletin no. 88-2, *Definition of a Right of Setoff.*

Similarities consistent with traditional accounting principles include

- Relating benefits to years of service.
- Matching costs with revenue.
- Reporting obligations as financial statement liabilities.

Because of similarities between the two models, it is conceptually appealing to pattern the unknown after what is now the accepted methodology of pension accounting. Nevertheless, the accounting implications of differences between pensions and postretirement benefits must be acknowledged. Following are some differences:

- Most postretirement benefits do not increase with years of service.
- Postretirement benefits are payable in services rather than cash.
- Postretirement benefits generally do not vest before retirement—an employee who quits shortly before retirement usually has no claim to them.
- Employers at present have little tax incentive to prefund nonpension benefits. (Some limited opportunities exist for deductible VEBA contributions, deductions to 401(h) accounts, pension benefit enhancements and corporate-owned life insurance.)

Any departures from traditional reporting in postretirement benefit reporting must be justified on their own merits, not just because they follow FASB Statement no. 87's departures.

REPORTING ISSUES

This article considers four key questions:

1. Does a postretirement benefit plan result in an obligation that meets the definition of a liability?
2. If so, how should the obligation be measured?
3. If the obligation can be measured, when should the liability be reported?
4. How should the transition from cash basis to accrual-basis reporting be handled?

ARE THEY LIABILITIES?

The first reporting issue in addressing other postretirement benefits is whether they are liabilities. In Concepts Statement no. 6, *Elements of Financial Statements,* paragraph 35, the FASB defines liabilities as "probable future sacrifices of economic benefits arising from present obligations of a particular entity to transfer assets or provide services to other entities in the future as a result of past transactions or events."

Pivotal to the board's stance for liability reporting is the view, stated in paragraph 125 of the ED, that postretirement benefits are a form of deferred compensation, not a gratuity. In exchange for the employee's current services, the employer promises the employee both current wages and current and deferred benefits. Critics counter that many of the benefits are discretionary, not meeting the definition's requirement that the liability arise from present obligations.

In defining liabilities, the FASB has implied that the legalistic definition serves as the floor. Thus, if employers are deemed legally liable for postretirement benefits, a liability should be recorded. And the courts generally have upheld the obligation of employers to provide postretirement benefits if there was no unambiguous communication before an employee's retirement that the company reserved the right to reduce or terminate his or her benefits.

As the enterprise continues in existence, some postretirement benefits ultimately will be paid, and the "probable future sacrifice" requirement will be met. Payment obviously would not occur without a specified employment period when the employee earned these benefits; thus the "result of past transactions or events" component of the liability definition is satisfied.

BEYOND THE LIABILITY DEFINITION

What about the exceptions—for example, companies that decrease the size of their operations? A frequent criticism of recording postretirement benefits as liabilities is that the benefits may never be paid because companies can alter these plans at will. Whether companies decreasing their operations can reduce postretirement benefits to nonretired individuals who are no longer employees is being decided in the courts.

What about businesses that may be found not legally liable for retiree benefits? Two existing components of generally accepted accounting principles can help here:

1. Nothing in GAAP requires certainty for the reporting of an element. Implicit in the probable component of the liability definition is the possibility the liability will not materialize. Although deferred compensation was excluded from the scope of FASB Statement no. 5, *Accounting for Contingencies,* paragraph 7, an analogy provides further support for this lack of certainty. When describing "the likelihood that the future event or events will confirm the loss or impairment of an asset or the incurrence of a liability" (Statement no. 5, paragraph 3), the board identified only three ranges: probable, reasonably possible and remote. If a future event is probable, which means only that it is likely to occur and can be estimated reasonably (discussed later), the board requires that a liability be reported (Statement no. 5, paragraph 8).
2. Accounting Principles Board Opinion no. 20, *Accounting Changes,* paragraph 10, recognizes that "accounting estimates change as new events occur, as more experience is acquired, or as additional information is obtained." Such changes could include revised estimates for postretirement benefit costs resulting from a change in

any component of cost for these plans, including eliminating the plans and thereby all the costs. The board incorporated methodology for reporting on curtailments and settlements of postretirement benefit obligations in ED paragraphs 85–94. So, even when a company alters its obligation to provide benefits, the existing reporting framework is equipped to handle these changes.

MEASURING THE OBLIGATION

The most difficult task in implementing the conclusion that a postretirement benefit obligation is a liability that should be reported is measuring that obligation. The task is complicated by the lack of historical claims data and the uncertainties surrounding future healthcare costs.

QUALITATIVE ISSUES

In trying to quantify the postretirement benefit obligation, the FASB again confronts the pervasive trade-off between relevance and reliability. Information regarding liabilities is relevant by definition. But critics have suggested that uncertainties inherent in measuring OPEB liabilities render the estimated amounts unreliable.

The use of estimates is an integral part of the reporting framework. Estimation does not necessarily impede reliability, which cannot be equated with precision. As the board notes in Concepts Statement no. 2, *Qualitative Characteristics of Accounting Information,* paragraph 59, reliability "is hardly ever a question of black or white, but rather of more reliability or less." Nevertheless, the proposed OPEB expense reporting will be based on softer numbers than most other financial statement amounts. The board acknowledges this difference in paragraph 66 of the ED by proposing sensitivity disclosures—the effect on the accumulated postretirement benefit obligation of a 1% change in the healthcare cost trend.

PROJECTING FUTURE COSTS

ED paragraph 33 would require that estimates include projections of the future cost of providing healthcare benefits. That would make it necessary to project such diverse items as utilization levels, technological advancements in medical knowledge and demographic information. However, cost-sharing programs with other healthcare providers are singled out as an element of OPEB cost requiring a seemingly higher level of evidence to recognize changes. The evidential level in this case requires a change in law, contract or regulation rather than a projection of such future change.

Despite its stated aversion to having a legalistic perspective, the board is emphasizing the legalities of cost-sharing arrangements. Prohibiting projected changes in cost-sharing programs is inconsistent with other specific projection requirements—if some cost elements can be projected to change, why not cost-sharing programs? Concerning occurrence of a future event, FASB Statement no. 5, paragraph 8, requires only that the event be probable for it to be recorded in the financial statements. Based on changes in economic conditions, financial institutions routinely alter their loan loss reserves for anticipated defaults on contractual loan agreements with customers. FASB Statement no. 48, *Revenue Recognition When Right of Return*

EXECUTIVE SUMMARY

■ THE FASB HAS ISSUED a controversial exposure draft requiring accrual-basis recognition of the cost of employee postretirment benefits other than pensions (OPEB) instead of the currently prevalent cash-basis method. The board has followed the methodology used in Statement no. 87 on pensions to develop the proposed requirements for OPEB. Because of the explosion in healthcare costs and a greater number of retirees in relation to active employees, the dollar amounts involved will affect companies' financial statements materially.

■ FOUR REPORTING ISSUES are involved:

1. Whether the OPEB obligation is a liability. According to the ED, it fits the definition of a liability in FASB Concepts Statement no. 6, *Elements of Financial Statements*. Pivotal to the board's position on liability reporting is the view in the ED that postretirement benefits are a form of deferred compensation, not a gratuity.
2. How the liability should be measured. Because of the lack of historical claims and the uncertainties of future healthcare costs, the most difficult task in implementing the proposed requirements will be measuring the obligation. However, current costs for OPEBs can provide a starting point for estimation.
3. When the liability should be reported. The ED concludes that using the full eligibility date is consistent with pension statement requirements; this seems to be forcing OPEB reporting into the pension mold, even when it doesn't fit. The FASB should consider allowing companies to use the expected retirement date because employees receive their benefits when they retire, not when they are eligible to retire.
4. The transition period. The ED opts for phasing in the proposed principle and requires the amortization of any unreported transition asset or liability—an approach with serious drawbacks. The cumulative effect method specified by APB Opinion no. 20 should be applied instead.

■ MANY SOCIAL AND ECONOMIC consequences will result from the reporting choices selected by the FASB. Perhaps the companies disgruntled by the effects on reported earnings will be the catalysts for changing economic policy.

Exists, paragraph 6, requires that sellers must be able to reasonably estimate returns of a product before revenue can be reported from the product's sales. In the ED, the board is inconsistent in allowing estimation of changes in only some elements of cost. It should allow projections of all facets of cost.

MEASUREMENT ANALOGIES

Some items that fit the definition of a given financial statement element are not reported because they are not measurable. Are postretirement benefits in this category or are they measurable enough to be reported as liabilities?

FASB Statement no. 2, *Accounting for Research and Development Costs,* paragraph 44, implies that assets are not recognized for R&D costs because future economic benefits cannot be measured objectively. The same reasoning applies to advertising expenditures. Even though many advertising campaigns are targeted to enhance the company's image and build long-term sales, those benefits cannot be measured, so advertising costs generally are expensed when incurred.

Even when reporting guidelines specify asset reporting, sometimes practical application is impeded because of measurement difficulties. For example, APB Opinion no. 16, *Business Combinations,* paragraph 68, specifies that in a business combination accounted for by the purchase method, the purchase price should be allocated to identifiable assets. But even in purchases in which valuable trademarks are acquired, goodwill is frequently reported instead of attributing a portion of the purchase price to the trademarks because of the difficulty of determining their value.

Clearly, the above accounting issues indicate areas where measurement difficulties prevent recognition of an element that otherwise probably qualifies as an asset. But these are more in the nature of cost allocation concerns. Whether an obligation represents a financial statement liability evokes a new set of concerns, best addressed through analysis of FASB Statement no. 5. That statement restricts liability recognition to situations in which the loss is probable and the amount can "reasonably" be estimated. But, given the wide range of contingent loss possibilities (such as risk of loss from future injury to others, threat of expropriation and litigation), it is appropriate to acknowledge that in some cases the items simply are not subject to reasonable estimation.

Postretirement benefits are undeniably difficult to measure, but measuring them is more objective than measuring amounts for the possibilities listed above. At least with postretirement benefits, the current costs for these expenditures provide a starting point for estimation. OPEB costs are different from lawsuit or injury losses, for example; for these there may be no basis for making estimates.

WHEN SHOULD THE LIABILITY BE REPORTED?

The OPEB liability reported at any point in time ideally should be the sum of the total liability for retirees and an assigned portion of the ultimate total liability for active employees. Attribution is more difficult with postretirement benefits than with pensions because pension benefits generally are specified by plan formulas. And postretirement benefits usually cliff-vest—that is, only on retirement is the employee eligible to receive benefits. The amount ultimately paid usually is dictated by factors unrelated to an employee's years of service in a company.

Probably because most plans give retroactive credit for service with a company before a healthcare plan is initiated or amended, the ED recommends the attribution period begin at the hire date. Specifying the end of the attribution period has been a contentious issue for the FASB; two dates considered were the full eligibility date and the expected retirement date. The board opted in ED paragraph 20 to end the attribution period at the full eligibility date, essentially concluding that all benefits had been earned at that time and no additional benefit could be gained by working past the full eligibility date. Also, the board concluded in ED paragraphs 204 and 206 that using the full eligibility date was consistent with the requirements of FASB Statement no. 87.

Despite differences between the two, the FASB appears to be forcing postretirement benefit reporting into the pension mold, even where it doesn't fit. The FASB should consider allowing companies to use the expected retirement date. Employees do not receive postretirement benefits when they are eligible to retire; benefits are received on retirement. Using the retirement date more clearly reflects the true substance of the exchange.

TRANSITION METHOD

Standard-setting bodies have identified four different transition methods:

- Cumulative effect of the change in reporting principle reported in the period of the accounting change, as specified by APB Opinion no. 20.
- Restating prior period presentations so all presentations conform to the new reporting principle, as specified by Opinion no. 20 and FASB Statement no. 16, *Prior Period Adjustments*.
- Grandfathering in the transactions previously entered so transactions before a given date are recorded by the old principle and transactions after that date are recorded by the new principle, for example, APB Opinion no. 17, *Intangible Assets*.
- Phasing in the effects of the new principle on previous transactions so that, for some period of time, financial statements reflect some of the old principle and some of the new principle but, by a later date, all financial data reflect the new principle, for example, FASB Statement no. 87.

ED paragraph 220 opts for the last method and requires the amortization of any unreported transition asset or liability. For the sake of not burdening one income statement and not reflecting an existing unrecorded liability all at one time, the FASB has chosen to phase in the effect of previous promises to employees. Because of similarities in the two kinds of benefits, specifying the same transition method for pensions and other postretirement benefits has merit.

However, the arguments presented in Opinion no. 20 concerning the treatment of a change in reporting principle also should apply to these two kinds of benefits. The FASB recognized in ED paragraph 22 that the OPEB transition is a cash-basis problem. Accordingly, GAAP specify that financial statements be restated. With postretirement benefits, the board concluded in ED paragraph 224 that the cost of either restating financial statements or reporting a cumulative effect in the current period would be prohibitive. The board also said the actuarial techniques for measuring these obligations are still evolving.

The cost of gathering the data to restate prior periods might be prohibitive but, if the obligation will be amortized, an amount representing the obligation at the transition date must be developed. It follows that there is no data-gathering cost differential between reporting a cumulative effect and phasing in through amortization. Because the FASB recognizes that actuarial techniques are still evolving, a more pragmatic alternative may be to delay implementation, as was done for FASB Statement no. 96, *Accounting for Income Taxes*. The FASB has answered this criticism partially by postponing the effective date of the proposed standard to 1993.

Despite recognizing the conceptual merit of currently accounting for the change in principle, the board seems to have bowed in ED paragraph 120 to the sensitivity of employers that have been able to avoid reporting this liability for so long. But this approach has serious drawbacks:

1. It understates liabilities until the phase-in period expires, to the detriment of the report users.
2. During the phase-in period, the income statement must report expenses of previous promises and previous activities while it is reporting current expenses.

Until conceptual issues to support the phase-in method are raised and found to have merit, the cumulative effect method specified by Opinion no. 20 should be applied to all reporting changes.

POLICY CONCERNS

In addition to sorting out the conceptual issues, which might lead to sound reporting on postretirement benefits, there are myriad social and economic consequences that will result from the reporting choices selected by the FASB. Few financial statement users would suggest that tax consequences should dictate reporting pronouncements or that reporting guidelines are intended to drive employers' OPEB plans. Nor has the FASB set out to promulgate standards for the sole purpose of reducing reported corporate earnings. Nonetheless, these and related concerns arise when considering the proposed new reporting rules in a broader social and economic context.

EARNINGS REDUCTION VIS-À-VIS NEUTRALITY

Although data-gathering and record-keeping costs are significant, businesses seem most rankled by the proposed statement's effects on reported earnings. As accountants, we are trained to be neutral, and it goes against our grain when a statement that appears to improve financial reporting is criticized because it affects reported earnings negatively. But the political reality of standard setting is that neutrality is an ideal desired by standard setters, not by individual companies.

The board notes in Concepts Statement no. 2, paragraph 98, that "neutrality means that either in formulating or implementing standards, the primary concern should be the relevance and reliability of the information that results, not the effect that the new rule may have on a particular interest." Taking this one step further, not being neutral implies that standard setters should aim for specific policy goals; this first implies that agreement on desirable social and economic policy goals exists. It doesn't. Even if such a consensus did exist, it is not the function of reporting standard setters to implement social and economic policy objectives; such a task should be handled through the public sector.

SOCIAL-POLICY CONSIDERATIONS

Some companies may consider the proposed guidelines so onerous that their benefit plans will be reduced or eliminated. While the board acknowledges in ED paragraph 130 that such actions may be a consequence of companies assessing and reporting their obligations, these changes are not the board's objective. The new pronouncement would not cause companies to incur additional costs for retirees; it simply would require reporting costs that the companies themselves have committed to incur.

Other companies will continue their cash outlays for retiree benefits regardless of whether this ED is issued. By continuing the currently prevalent cash basis, the profession would be endorsing the concept that companies have no obligation to provide postretirement benefits. Enactment of the proposed standard would allow society to assess this cost. And if the cost to employers is determined to be too high, perhaps the reporting standard will be the impetus for creating more efficient alternatives for society.

FINANCIAL STATEMENT AND MARKET CONSIDERATIONS

The Employee Benefit Research Institute has estimated the total unfunded employer liability, including that of the public sector, to be about $280 billion; the private sector's share is estimated to be about $169 billion. The U.S. General Accounting Office has recently estimated the private sector's liability to be $221 billion. The primary difference between the two estimates is Medicare benefits.

Information from companies willing to use the proposed guidelines to compute the reportable cost illustrates the diversity of financial statement effects. A study conducted by the Financial Executives Research Foundation reports that the 26 companies tested would experience decreases in pretax income ranging from 2% to 20%. Two-thirds of these companies predicted an increase in expense of two to six times current costs.

FUNDING

The funding issue is separate from measuring the OPEB obligation. Nonetheless, funding has reporting ramifications because, for companies to minimize reported liabilities, OPEB plans must be funded—a costly alternative in the current tax environment. Although the FASB knows about the practical difficulties posed by existing funding constraints, as stated in ED paragraph 129, it holds how and when to fund retiree benefits is a financing decision influenced by many factors, of which tax is one.

Unlike contributions to pension plans that are deductible when paid, general tax rules prohibit current deductions for deferred compensation. Since no tax deduction is permitted until postretirement benefits are provided to retirees, companies have little tax incentive to prefund the plans.

It is counterproductive to focus on the current tax prohibition for deducting prefunded retiree healthcare. If retiree healthcare is indeed a desirable policy goal, and if employers are deemed the best providers of that service, the ED may serve to recognize that goal and initiate a change in the tax structure that will make prefunding more attractive. Perhaps companies disgruntled by the effects on reported earnings will be the catalyst for that change.

A WORKABLE SOLUTION

Accounting for postretirement benefits is so complex there just isn't an ideal solution to the many problems involved. Therefore, we must move in the direction in which the preponderance of evidence takes us—accrual-basis recognition—and keep working to improve the problem areas. The current cash-basis approach is misleading because of its implication that no liabilities for retiree benefits exist. Although the evidence presented suggests that the board reexamine some specific issues, the ED's primary provisions generally can be supported using the conceptual framework.

II-E

BUSINESS COMBINATIONS AND CONSOLIDATIONS

II-E1

CONSOLIDATIONS: AN OVERVIEW OF THE FASB DM

Paul Pacter

Procedures for preparing consolidated financial statements evolved quietly over 50 years ago and have not changed much since. The prevailing authoritative guidance, Accounting Research Bulletin no. 51, *Consolidated Financial Statements,* issued more than 30 years ago, described accepted practice at the time and expressed some preferences but set few hard and fast rules. Since then, considerable merger and acquisition activity has taken place. And, except for a 1987 amendment to ARB no. 51 by the Financial Accounting Standards Board, no U.S. standard-setting body has completed a conceptual consideration of consolidations.

In recent years, numerous consolidation policy and procedure questions have been brought to the FASB's attention by the American Institute of CPAs, the Securities and Exchange Commission and others. In an effort to address those questions, the FASB recently published a discussion memorandum, *Consolidation Policy and Procedures*. The DM is part of a multiphased FASB project on accounting for affiliations between entities.

PAUL PACTER, CPA, PhD, is professor of accounting at the University of Connecticut Stamford MBA program. As a consultant to the Financial Accounting Standards Board he wrote the DM on consolidations. He is a member of the American Institute of CPAs, the New York State Society of CPAs and the American Accounting Association.

The views expressed in this article are Dr. Pacter's own, not necessarily those of the Financial Accounting Standards Board. Official positions of the FASB are determined only after extensive due process and deliberation.

FUNDAMENTAL ISSUES IN THE DM

The fundamental issues in the DM are *whether* and *how* separate financial statements of two or more affiliated entities should be combined into a single set of consolidated statements.

"Whether" focuses on the importance of control and ownership as conditions for consolidation and on defining control.

"How" considers procedural matters such as the following:

- Measuring a subsidiary's identifiable assets and liabilities at acquisition date.
- Measuring a subsidiary's goodwill at the acquisition date.
- Treating an investee that becomes a subsidiary through a series of purchases of small blocks of stock.
- Handling subsequent increases and decreases in a parent's proportionate interest in a subsidiary.
- Eliminating intercompany transactions.
- Structuring the information for the most meaningful financial statement display.
- Conforming parent and subsidiary accounting practices and fiscal periods.

CONTROL VERSUS OWNERSHIP

Historically, consolidation in the United States has almost always been limited to the financial statements of an investor and the investees in which it owns more than a 50% voting interest. In the past few years, Canada, Australia, New Zealand, the United Kingdom, Germany, France, Japan, the European Community and the International Accounting Standards Committee have adopted control as the principal consolidation criterion—broadening the reporting entity to include all controlled affiliates, even if they are less-than-majority owned.

Control versus ownership is probably the most important issue in the DM. Does one entity's ability to control another's operating and financing policies justify consolidation (with ownership of a substantial voting interest serving as an indicator of control)? Or are control and level of ownership two distinct conditions that must be separately tested and met?

Varying viewpoints have led to three concepts of consolidated financial statements—the economic unit concept, the parent company concept and the proportionate consolidation concept. Exhibit 1 describes them. The examples in exhibits 2 and 3, pages 287 and 289, and the more extensive examples in the DM itself, show the three concepts can result in significantly different accounting measurements.

Views differ on the appropriate ownership level for consolidation, whether as a separate condition or as a control indicator. For some, the minimum is ownership of a majority of voting stock. Others support consolidation if a parent is able to exercise a majority of voting rights through a legal device such as a pyramid (a sequential tier of corporations whereby each corporation is controlled through majority stock ownership by corporations at higher levels); use of multiple classes of voting stock with disproportionate voting rights; or through a voting trust.

Still others make the consolidation cutoff at ownership levels below a majority. For example, the owner of a large minority interest could have effective control, depending on the dispersion, disorganization or apathy of other owners.

EXHIBIT 1

Three Concepts of Consolidated Financial Statements

Economic Unit Concept

- Consolidated financial statements are intended to provide information about a group of legal entities, a parent and its subsidiaries, operating as a single unit. All of their assets and liabilities, not just the parent's portion, belong to the consolidated entity.
- Unless the subsidiary is wholly owned, the consolidated entity's proprietary interest is divided into a controlling interest (the parent's stockholders) and one or more noncontrolling interests in subsidiaries.
- Control is the basis for consolidation, with ownership an indicator of, but not a separate criterion from, control.

Parent Company Concept

- Consolidated financial statements are intended to provide information about the beneficial interest of the parent's stockholders in the various assets and liabilities controlled by the parent, including their undivided interest in the net assets of the parent's subsidiaries.
- The noncontrolling (minority) stockholders' equity in the subsidiaries' net assets is considered outside the proprietary interest in the consolidated entity.
- Ownership is a criterion separate from control. Without ownership, the parent's stockholders do not have a beneficial interest in the investee's net assets. Beneficial interest means the right to share in profits, receive dividends and recover one's investment through stock resale or asset liquidation. Views differ about the level of beneficial interest below which consolidation is not meaningful.

Proportionate Consolidation Concept

- Only the parent's share of a subsidiary's assets, liabilities, revenues and expenses is included in consolidated financial statements. The noncontrolling interest's share is excluded.
- To proponents of this concept, perhaps even more than to parent company advocates, ownership is an essential and distinct condition for consolidation, because it is ownership of a subsidiary, not just control, that gives the parent's stockholders a beneficial interest in the subsidiary's net assets.
- An advantage often cited for proportionate consolidation is its extensibility beyond parent-subsidiary relationships to jointly controlled investees, such as joint ventures, and to investees now accounted for by the equity method.
- Some people view proportionate consolidation as a variant of the parent company concept.

The DM defines control as "the power of one entity to direct or cause the direction of the management and operating and financing policies of another entity." In addition to examining control through majority or large minority ownership, the DM discusses other circumstances that may indicate current control, including the power to obtain a majority voting interest in another entity (by unilateral action or by occurrence of a specified event) and the power to control by contract or lease. Also considered is whether a subsidiary should be included in consolidated statements if its parent's control is temporary.

ACQUISITION OF A SUBSIDIARY IN A SINGLE TRANSACTION

Under the parent company concept, if a subsidiary is acquired in a single transaction, its identifiable assets and liabilities are included in consolidation at the parent's proportionate share of their fair values at the acquisition date plus the subsidiary's book value for the noncontrolling interest's proportionate share. Goodwill is the difference between the parent's investment cost and its proportionate interest in the net fair values of the subsidiary's identifiable assets and liabilities. Under proportionate consolidation, the only difference is the book values of assets and liabilities representing the noncontrolling interest's proportionate share are omitted from the consolidated balance sheet, as is the noncontrolling interest.

Under the economic unit concept, if controlling interest in a subsidiary is acquired in a single transaction, 100% of identifiable assets and liabilities—both the parent's and the noncontrolling interest's shares—are included in consolidation at their fair values at the acquisition date. Goodwill is recognized under either a full or purchased goodwill interpretation.

FULL GOODWILL INTERPRETATION

All the subsidiary's goodwill (not just the parent's purchased share) is recognized at the time control is attained. Ideally, an appraisal should serve as the basis for estimating the entire subsidiary's fair value, though the value of the subsidiary as a whole often is inferred from the per-share price the parent paid to obtain control. The full goodwill interpretation generally is considered the purest form of the economic unit concept.

PURCHASED GOODWILL INTERPRETATION

Only goodwill the parent purchases on the acquisition date—the difference between the price paid to obtain the controlling interest and the related share of the fair values of the subsidiary's identifiable net assets—is recognized. Goodwill for the non-controlling (minority) interest is omitted. Proponents believe the fair value of all an entity's goodwill cannot be reliably appraised or inferred from the purchase price of a controlling interest because the amount may include a control premium. Exhibit 2 illustrates the alternatives.

STEP ACQUISITIONS

If the controlling interest is obtained by purchasing two or more blocks of the subsidiary's stock on different dates (a step acquisition), under the economic unit concept all the subsidiary's identifiable tangible and intangible assets and liabilities are included in the consolidated statements at their fair values at the date control is attained. On that date the fair value of the subsidiary's goodwill is measured by appraisal or is inferred from the price the parent paid in the control transaction. The economic unit is considered to have acquired all the subsidiary's assets and liabilities at the time it gains control. Before that, it was just an investor in stock.

On the date control is attained in a step acquisition, a holding gain or loss must be recognized on any previously purchased shares, under the economic unit concept, if the shares' current fair value differs from that carried on the parent's books. Why? Because the economic unit concept accounts for all a subsidiary's stock owned by its parent as alike. Shares purchased earlier are accounted for as having the same carrying amount (fair value at the date control is attained) as those purchased later, requiring the parent's investment account to be increased or decreased to reflect fair value at the control date.

Once control is attained, the parent's additional subsidiary stock purchases are accounted for under the economic unit concept as distributions to owners—like treasury stock acquisitions in the sense outstanding shares in the economic entity are reduced through asset trans-

EXHIBIT 2

Sixty Percent Interest in Subsidiary Acquired in a Single Transaction

Stock Purchased	Amount Paid	Fair Market Value of Subsidiary's Identifiable Net Assets	Book Value of Subsidiary's Identifiable Net Assets
60%	$900	$1,200	$800

Parent company concept

The subsidiary's identifiable net assets are included in consolidation at $1,040 [(60% × $1,200) + (40% × $800)]. Another way to look at the $1,040 is it represents the book value of the subsidiary's identifiable net assets plus the parent's share of the excess of the fair values over the book value of those assets [(100% × $800) + (60% × [$1,200 − $800])]. Goodwill recognized is $180 [$900 − (60% × $1,200)]. Noncontrolling interest is $320 (40% × $800).

Proportionate consolidation concept

The subsidiary's identifiable net assets are included at $720 (60% × $1,200), goodwill is $180 and noncontrolling interest is zero.

Economic unit concept

The subsidiary's identifiable net assets are included at $1,200.

- *Full goodwill interpretation.* The subsidiary's full value must be determined either by appraisal or by extrapolation from the $900 paid to acquire 60%. If fair value of the subsidiary is $1,500 ($900 ÷ .6), identifiable assets and liabilities are recognized in consolidation at $1,200 fair value, and $300 of goodwill is recognized ($1,500 − $1,200). The $300 includes a $180 parent's 60% share plus a $120 noncontrolling interest's 40% share. Noncontrolling interest is reported at $600 (40% × $1,500) in the balance sheet.
- *Purchased goodwill interpretation.* Goodwill is $180 [$900 − (60% × $1,200)]. Noncontrolling interest is $480 (40% × $1,200).

fers to owners. Share sales by the parent maintaining a controlling interest are accounted for as investments by owners—again, as treasury stock—with no gain or loss recognized. Newly issued subsidiary shares are accounted for similarly.

Under the parent company concept, each parent purchase of an investee's stock is accounted for separately. Separate acquisitions are aggregated after control is attained to determine the amounts of acquired assets and assumed liabilities included in the consolidated statements. Thus, a parent's investment account contains a series of layers, one for each stock purchase, and corresponding layers are found in consolidated statements for each of the subsidiary's assets and liabilities, including goodwill, at the parent's stock purchase dates. Under the parent company concept, a fraction of the then-current fair values of the assets acquired and liabilities assumed and another slice of goodwill are recorded for each acquisition. The noncontrolling interest is accounted for at its share of the subsidiary's book value, unaffected by the fair values of either identifiable net assets or goodwill on the acquisition dates. The same measurements are made under proportionate consolidation, except the noncontrolling interest's share is excluded.

After control is attained, additional purchases of the subsidiary's stock result in additional layers of identifiable net assets and goodwill. If the parent sells some of the subsidiary's stock while maintaining a controlling interest, gain or loss is recognized under the parent company concept; transactions with noncontrolling interests are regarded as transactions with outsiders. Proponents believe recognizing gain or loss is necessary to enable the parent company's shareholders to assess performance and cash flows. To measure gain or loss on sale, layers acquired earlier must be peeled away using a method such as first-in first-out, last-in first-out, or average cost. Exhibit 3 illustrates the alternatives.

DISPOSITION OF A SUBSIDIARY

Disposition of a subsidiary occurs if a parent-subsidiary relationship is terminated, even if a noncontrolling interest is retained. Under both the economic unit and parent company concepts, the parent's gain or loss on disposition is recognized in the consolidated statements. Under the economic unit concept, the gain or loss results from the economic unit's disposal of individual assets and liabilities; under the parent company concept, the gain or loss results from the parent's selling the subsidiary's stock. The amount of gain or loss may differ because of different investment carrying amounts on the parent's books. The DM provides illustrations.

INTERCOMPANY TRANSACTIONS

An intercompany transaction is one between a parent and its subsidiary or between two subsidiaries of the same parent. Under the economic unit concept, such a transaction is considered an internal transfer, and profit or loss is not realized pending resale to an outside entity. Under the parent company concept, the transaction is partly an internal transfer to be eliminated in consolidation and partly an exchange between the parent and an outside party (the subsidiary's noncontrolling stockholders).

If a 75%-owned subsidiary sells inventory to its parent, under the economic unit concept 100% of the unrealized intercompany profit is eliminated from the parent's inventory and from the subsidiary's income and retained earnings. The elimination is divided between controlling and noncontrolling interests. Under the parent company concept, the transaction is 75% internal transfer and 25% exchange between the parent and the subsidiary's noncontrolling stockholders. The parent's 75% share of unrealized intercompany profit is eliminated against its income and retained earnings; the rest is recognized as realized profit to the noncontrolling interest.

If the sale is from the parent to the subsidiary, the transaction and all unrealized intercompany profit is eliminated under the economic unit concept. Since the profit is entirely on the parent's books, the controlling interest absorbs 100% of the elimination. Most parent company advocates also eliminate the entire transaction and all unrealized intercompany profit; some recognize 25% of the profit as having been realized in a sale by the parent to the noncontrolling interest.

In addition to intercompany inventory sales, the DM also examines intercompany

- Receivables and payables.
- Sales of plant assets or intangible assets, including adjustment of gain or loss and depreciation.
- Investments in bonds.

EXHIBIT 3

Sixty Percent Interest in Subsidiary Acquired in a Step Acquisition—Two Blocks of Stock Purchased One Year Apart

Stock Purchased	Amount Paid	Fair Market Value of Subsidiary's Identifiable Net Assets	Book Value of Subsidiary's Identifiable Net Assets
30%	$350	$1,000	$700
30%	450	1,200	800
Increase			$100

The $100 increase in the book value of the subsidiary's net assets is entirely due to undistributed net income for the year between the two purchase dates. The investor uses the equity method to recognize its $30 share of earnings (30% × $100) and amortizes the implicit $50 of goodwill [$350 − (30% × $1,000)] over 40 years, or $1.25 per year. As a result, income recognized is $28.75. The carrying amount of the investment is $378.75 ($350 + $30 − $1.25).

Parent company concept

The subsidiary's identifiable net assets are measured in consolidation at $1,010, consisting of a $300 fair value layer from the initial 30% purchase (30% × $1,000), the parent's $30 share of the investee's preconsolidation net income (30% × $100), another 30% fair value layer (30% × $1,200), plus noncontrolling interest at book value (40% × $800). Consolidated goodwill is $138.75 ($50 + $90 − $1.25 amortization under the equity method), and noncontrolling interest is $320 (40% × $800).

Proportionate consolidation concept

This is identical to the parent company concept except for omitting the $320 of net assets attributable to the noncontrolling interest and the corresponding noncontrolling interest itself.

Economic unit concept

The subsidiary's identifiable net assets are included at $1,200.

- *Full goodwill interpretation.* Consolidated goodwill is $300, which is the excess of $1,500 total value of the subsidiary (based on an appraisal or inferred at $450 ÷ .30) over the $1,200 fair value of its identifiable net assets. Noncontrolling interest is $600 (40% × $1,500), and a holding gain of $71.25 is recognized on the 30% of the stock purchased earlier and held while its price increased ($450 − $378.75 carrying amount).
- *"Purchased goodwill" interpretation.* Only the portion of the subsidiary's goodwill purchased by the parent on the date it obtains control is recognized. No goodwill is recognized from the earlier stock purchase, nor any related to the noncontrolling interest. Accordingly, consolidated goodwill is $90 [$450 − (30% × $1,200)]. Noncontrolling interest is $480 (40% × $1,200). And a holding loss of $18.75 is recognized on the original 30% interest. That interest was purchased for $350, and while 30% of the identifiable net assets are now worth $360 (30% × $1,200), the $10 gain is more than offset by the $28.75 previously recognized by the investor under the equity method. Hence the $18.75 loss.

NOTE: In addition to the full goodwill and purchased goodwill interpretations, the DM describes four other ways to measure goodwill and holding gain or loss under the economic unit concept in a step acquisition. One recognizes $138.75 of goodwill ($90 from the second 30% purchase plus $48.75 unamortized goodwill implicit in the first 30% purchase when it was accounted for by the equity method) and a holding gain of $30. A second alternative recognizes $180 of goodwill (the parent's 60% of the full $300 of goodwill) and a $71.25 holding gain. A third variant results in goodwill of $108.75 ($378.75 carrying amount of the initial 30% interest plus $450 cost of the second 30% interest minus the $720 (60% share of the $1,200 value of the identifiable net assets on the date control was obtained). This third approach results in no holding gain or loss. A fourth variant credits the holding gain to a stockholder's equity account, deferring recognition until the subsidiary's stock is ultimately sold.

Balance Sheet and Income Statement Display

Three choices for displaying noncontrolling interest in the consolidated balance sheet are as a liability, a separate item between liabilities and stockholders' equity and a component of stockholders' equity. The first two options are consistent with the parent company concept; the last, with the economic unit concept. Display of noncontrolling interest is not an issue under proportionate consolidation.

The choices for displaying noncontrolling interest in the consolidated income statement are to deduct income attributable to the noncontrolling interest in computing net income (parent company concept) or to deduct it from net income to compute net income attributable to the controlling interest (economic unit concept).

Long-Standing Practice

Preparing consolidated financial statements is a pervasive and long-standing accounting practice. If the United States decides to replace majority ownership with control as the principal consolidation criterion—as Canada, Australia, the United Kingdom, the EC and the IASC have done—that practice would be extended to many more intercorporate affiliations. Moreover, some of the alternatives discussed in the DM would dramatically change current practices for measuring a subsidiary's assets and liabilities. CPA practitioners should take notice: The DM has awakened a sleeping dog.

Single copies of the DM are available without charge by writing the FASB at 401 Merritt 7, P.O. Box 5116, Norwalk, Connecticut 06856 or by calling (203) 847-0700, ext. 555. Because of the subject's importance and complexity, the board established a July 15, 1992, comment due date.

II-E2

MINORITY INTEREST: OPPOSING VIEWS

Paul Rosenfield versus Steven Rubin

Three views on the amounts ascribed in consolidated financial statements to minority stockholdings, called "minority interest," have contended for more than 75 years. One view is that minority interest should be presented as a separate item of liabilities; another is that minority interest should be presented between liabilities and equity; still a third view is that minority interest should be presented as a separate item in equity.

A look at the quotations in the sidebar on page 293 (and many others could have been offered) will suggest that the controversy has become humorous by now. Indeed, the very fact that the controversy is of long standing—and in such a practical discipline as

---

The views expressed herein are those of the authors and do not necessarily reflect the views of the American Institute of CPAs. Official positions of the AICPA are determined through certain specific committee procedures, due process and deliberation.

PAUL ROSENFIELD, CPA, is director of the American Institute of CPAs accounting standards division and is responsible for the technical and administrative activities of the AICPA accounting standards executive committee (AcSEC). He is a member of the American Accounting Association.

STEVEN RUBIN, CPA, is technical/administrative manager of the AICPA accounting standards division, staff aide to AcSEC and its task force on consolidation problems, and adjunct assistant professor of accounting at Brooklyn College of the City University of New York. He is a member of the New York State Society of CPAs, the National Association of Accountants and the AAA. Messrs. Rosenfield and Rubin are the authors of Consolidation, Translation, and the Equity Method: Concepts and Procedures (New York: John Wiley & Sons, 1985).

accounting—should lead its practitioners to wonder whether something is wrong with the question rather than with its trio of possible answers.

OPPOSING VIEWS, CONTRA-SOLUTIONS

We hold that the fault lies in the question of how to treat minority interest. The question presupposes that a consolidated reporting entity with minority stockholdings must present minority interest in its financial statements. We take the opposing view—that the entity shouldn't present minority interest in its financial statements.

We offer contra-solutions, however, to how minority stockholdings should be dealt with in consolidated financial statements.

In considering that issue, we also explore related issues concerning the nature of equity, proportional consolidation and the focus for financial reporting. The Financial Accounting Standards Board, in its project on consolidation and allied topics, is currently considering those issues.

Now is the time to settle them.

ROSENFIELD'S VIEW: FUNDAMENTAL RETHINKING

Because the issue of how minority stockholdings should be dealt with in consolidated financial statements has been unsettled for so long, one thing is sure: Fundamental rethinking is required. The discussion that follows is intended to contribute to that process.

SEPARATE EXISTENCE

Some believe, plausibly, that a corporation doesn't exist separately from its stockholders but is, rather, its stockholders acting collectively. But the opposite view—that a corporation exists and acts separately from its stockholders—conforms with some common beliefs and expressions. Examples of those beliefs and expressions are that a corporation owns its assets and its stockholders don't; that it owes its debts and its stockholders don't; that on its own behalf it engages in its transactions, realizes its revenue and gains, and incurs its costs, expenses, and losses and its stockholders don't.

Whichever view is adopted should be used consistently in considering issues in financial reporting.

I subscribe to the view that corporations exist and act separately and adopt it as a basis on which to consider the treatment of minority stockholdings in financial reporting.

A complementary issue concerns the focus for financial reporting.

FOCUS FOR FINANCIAL REPORTING

It may seem unexceptional to observe that a financial report on an entity such as a corporation should focus on that entity, that it should present, for example, the reporting entity's assets, liabilities, equity, revenue, expenses, gains and losses, and not those of other entities—

HOW TO PRESENT MINORITY INTEREST

Separate item of debt

1917: "The proper practice is to take up as a *liability* the par value of the outstanding stock [held by the minority stockholders], together with its relative share of surplus."[1]

1981: "Any minority interest in subsidiaries is shown as the last item of *liabilities*."[2]

Separate item between debt and equity

1941: "The minority interest should be shown as *a distinct element between the liabilities proper and the capital and surplus* attaching to the dominant interest."[3]

1976: "The minority interest in the equity of consolidated companies should be classified in the consolidated balance sheet as a *separate item* and should *not* be shown as *part of stockholders' equity*."[4]

Separate item in equity

1908: "Under *capital stocks* will be included . . . such part of the stocks of the subsidiary companies as are not owned by the holding company. . . ."[5]

1966: "In theory the minority interest is *clearly* part of the *ownership equity* on the consolidated balance sheet. The minority interest is *certainly not an* unliquidated *obligation* in any sense, and *classifying it in the no-man's land between liabilities and capital simply avoids the issue*."[6]

1980: "Minority interests . . . are part of *equity*."[7]

[1] Arthur Lowes Dickinson, *Accounting Practice and Procedure* (New York: Ronald Press Company, 1917), p. 183 (emphasis added).

[2] Roderick K. Macleod, "Financial Statements: Form and Content," in Lee J. Seidler and D. R. Carmichael, eds., *Accountants' Handbook,* 6th ed. (New York: John Wiley & Sons, 1981), p. 4.15 (emphasis added).

[3] W. A. Paton, *Advanced Accounting* (New York: MacMillan, 1941), p. 803 (emphasis added).

[4] International Accounting Standards Committee, International Accounting Standard no. 3, *Consolidated Financial Statements,* 1976, par. 43 (emphasis added).

[5] William M. Lybrand, "The Accounting of Industrial Enterprises," JofA, Dec. 1908, p. 120 (emphasis added).

[6] Walter B. Meigs, Charles E. Johnson and Thomas Keller, *Advanced Accounting* (New York: McGraw-Hill, 1966), pp. 263–64 (emphasis added).

[7] Financial Accounting Standards Board, Concepts Statement no. 3, *Elements of Financial Statements of Business Enterprises,* 1980, par. 179 (emphasis added).

GM shouldn't report Ford's sales. But that view contains unexamined implications, which lead in novel directions.

A financial report that focuses on the reporting entity can't ignore other entities because the reporting entity has relationships with other entities, such as debtor-creditor relationships, and changes in such relationships that must be presented in the financial report. To retain the focus on the reporting entity without ignoring the other entities, such relationships and changes in them should be reported from the reporting entity's side. A reporting entity should report, for example, its claims on other entities, not other entities' obligations to it; it should report its debts to other entities, not other entities' claims on it; it should report its purchases from other entities, not other entities' sales to it; it should report its sales to other entities, not other entities' purchases from it.

Much of that is commonly done. Reporting entities report their sales, their purchases and their receivables. They also report their liabilities, of course, but here's where the slippage starts. Accountants and authoritative accounting bodies sometimes describe a reporting entity's liabilities in terms of the other entities' side rather than the reporting entity's side; they sometimes refer to an entity's liabilities as the claims of others rather than as the reporting entity's obligations.

In fact, in paragraph 40 of Concepts Statement no. 1, *Objectives of Financial Reporting by Business Enterprises,* the FASB goes even further and describes liabilities as both obligations of the reporting entity and claims of other entities: "Financial reporting should provide information about the economic resources of an enterprise, *the claims to those resources* (*obligations of the enterprise* to transfer resources of other entities . . .). . . ." (Emphasis added.)

Reporting is unambiguously made to appear focused on other than the reporting entity, however, in treating the relations between a corporation and its stockholders. The equity section of a corporation's balance sheet states explicitly that it provides information on an aspect of its stockholders, not on an aspect of the reporting entity: It says it reports on *their* equity, the "stockholders' equity." And by referring to their equity in the "statement of changes in stockholders' equity," the entity states explicitly that it provides information on changes in aspects of the stockholders, not of itself.

Because current accounting for the relations between a corporation and stockholders doesn't consistently conform with the views that a corporation exists separately from stockholders and that financial reporting should focus on the reporting entity, how the relations between a corporation and stockholders should be treated in general in financial reporting is considered first; the point is to provide perspective for an inquiry into how consolidated financial statements should treat minority stockholdings.

ENTITY'S DUTIES TO STOCKHOLDERS

If the corporation's side of its relations with stockholders is to be reported, which aspects to report aren't readily apparent. On its side it has duties. Perhaps, then, it should report its duties to stockholders. Examples of its duties are

- Holding meetings at least once a year, at which the stockholders vote to appoint or retain the members of its board of directors and perhaps its senior officers and vote on other matters brought to the stockholders' attention.
- Paying dividends ratably, based on percentages of shareholdings, to the stockholders when, as and if declared by its board of directors.
- Paying a liquidating dividend ratably, based on percentages of shareholdings, to the stockholders on the entity's liquidation, to the extent assets are available after paying its liabilities.

The number columns of financial statements can't adequately portray any of those duties. Further, because no aspect of the corporation's side of its relations with stockholders is apparent other than its duties to them, nothing concerning those relations should be presented in the number columns. A corporation should disclose the number of outstanding shares of stock and all other matters pertaining to its duties to stockholders in its financial report—but outside the number columns of its financial statements.

Two kinds of information only indirectly related to the reporting entity's relationships with its stockholders traditionally have competed to be the subject matter of the equity section of the balance sheet: (1) sources of equity and (2) restrictions on dividends. Neither should be its subject matter.

SOURCES OF EQUITY

Information in the number columns of a balance sheet concerning the sources of equity usually is presented in at least two amounts: paid-in capital and retained earnings. Because dividends are deducted from earnings and only the difference is presented, financial statement users can't tell from the balance sheet the amount of equity obtained from successful operations. They also can't tell from such a presentation when equity was obtained from its various sources. The amounts presented as components of equity can be misleading for both of those reasons.

To illustrate: Company M and Company N were incorporated with the same initial amount of capital, $500,000, at the same time, January 1, 19A. Exhibit 1 shows that, 20 years later, on December 31, 19T, they have the same balance sheets. Specifically, the two balance sheets show identical amounts for retained earnings.

Users of such reports could easily believe that, if those amounts mean *anything,* they

EXHIBIT 1

Original Balance Sheets

COMPANY M
BALANCE SHEET
DECEMBER 31, 19T

Assets		Liabilities and Equity	
Cash	$1,000,000	Liabilities	$ 300,000
		Equity	
		Paid-in capital	500,000
		Retained earnings	200,000
		Total equity	700,000
Total assets	$1,000,000	Total liabilities and equity	$1,000,000

COMPANY N
BALANCE SHEET
DECEMBER 31, 19T

Assets		Liabilities and Equity	
Cash	$1,000,000	Liabilities	$ 300,000
		Equity	
		Paid-in capital	500,000
		Retained earnings	200,000
		Total equity	700,000
Total assets	$1,000,000	Total liabilities and equity	$1,000,000

mean that the two companies have been equally profitable. But they haven't. During those 20 years Company M had net earnings of $200,000 and paid no dividends, whereas Company N had net earnings of $2.5 million and paid dividends of $2.3 million.

But even if the equity section contained three pure amounts—paid-in capital, plus cumulative earnings, minus cumulative dividends—knowing those amounts would help users of the financial statements of few companies. Disclosure by most companies of such amounts could as easily mislead as inform.

To continue the illustration: The balance sheets of the two companies using the three pure amounts are presented in exhibit 2. Here Company N shows more cumulative earnings than Company M, suggesting that Company N is the healthier of the two. But it isn't. Company N's presentation masks large and growing losses in recent years, offsetting steady earnings over many previous years, ending with the retirement of competent management and its replacement by inept management. In contrast, new management has taken over Company M, bankrupt on its arrival, and in three years recouped all its losses, started to turn a profit and gives evidence of keeping the company on the high road.

Information on sources of equity is history, which can't be reported satisfactorily in a balance sheet, a dated statement of financial position. Users need to know the trend in capital contributions, the trend in earnings and the trend in dividends. To complete the illustration: Exhibit 3 presents statements of changes in equity of Company M and Company N for the five years ending on December 31, 19T. The statements show trends, the only sound kind of presentation of the companies' sources of equity.

RESTRICTIONS ON DIVIDENDS

Restrictions on dividends a corporation may pay depend on common and statutory law in the jurisdiction in which the entity is incorporated and on contracts. A single amount, retained earnings, purportedly indicating the limit on dividends the reporting entity may pay, can't encompass that complexity. Adequate disclosure concerning restrictions on dividends requires narrative, possible only in the notes to the financial statements.

A NEW VIEW OF EQUITY

Because of those inadequacies, a new view of equity is needed. For that purpose, common experience provides a hint. A homeowner with a mortgage is said to have equity in a house if a significant aspect of the house, such as its current selling price, exceeds the debt on the house. The equity is a helpful amount, though that is all it is. It's one amount, simply a residual—the excess of the owner's asset over the owner's debt; only the house and the debt exist. And the equity is the homeowner's.

That view of equity should be applied in financial reporting. The equity section should present only one amount, simply a residual—the excess of the total of the reporting entity's assets over the total of its liabilities, the reporting entity's own equity in its own assets, an amount of interest to all users of its financial reports.

That definition of "equity" contrasts with the FASB's in paragraph 43 of Concepts Statement no. 3, *Elements of Financial Statements of Business Enterprises:* "Equity is the residual interest in the assets of an entity that remains after deducting its liabilities. In a business enterprise, the equity is the ownership interest."

EXHIBIT 2

Balance Sheets with Pure Equity Amounts

COMPANY M
BALANCE SHEET
DECEMBER 31, 19T

Assets		Liabilities and Equity	
Cash	$1,000,000	Liabilities	$ 300,000
		Equity	
		Paid-in capital	500,000
		Cumulative earnings	200,000
		Total equity	700,000
Total assets	$1,000,000	Total liabilities and equity	$1,000,000

COMPANY N
BALANCE SHEET
DECEMBER 31, 19T

Assets		Liabilities and Equity	
Cash	$1,000,000	Liabilities	$ 300,000
		Equity	
		Paid-in capital	500,000
		Cumulative earnings	2,500,000
		Cumulative dividends	(2,300,000)
		Total equity	700,000
Total assets	$1,000,000	Total liabilities and equity	$1,000,000

That definition does refer to the residual nature of equity, but it calls equity an attribute not of the reporting entity but of other entities—that is, of the reporting entity's owners.

NEITHER MAJORITY NOR MINORITY INTEREST

As with its majority stockholders, no aspect of a consolidated reporting entity's side of its relations with minority stockholders, other than its duties to them, is apparent, and none of those duties can be portrayed adequately in the number columns of the consolidated financial statements.

Because they are aspects of other entities, neither the majority nor the minority interest should be presented in the number columns of the reporting entity's balance sheet or income statement. The interests of the majority and minority stockholders are in the consolidated reporting entity, not in its assets, and if they are to be presented in financial statements, they belong in those of the stockholders, not in those of the consolidated reporting entity.

Like the equity section of the balance sheet of a separate corporation, the equity section of the balance sheet of a consolidated reporting entity should present only one amount, simply

EXHIBIT 3

Statements of Changes in Equity

COMPANY M
STATEMENTS OF CHANGES IN EQUITY
FOR YEARS ENDING DECEMBER 31

	19P	19Q	19R	19S	19T
Balance Jan. 1	$ 25,000	$ (25,000)	$(100,000)	$ 100,000	$ 350,000
Net income or (loss)	(50,000)	(75,000)	200,000	250,000	350,000
Dividends	—	—	—	—	—
Balance Dec. 31	$ (25,000)	$ (100,000)	$ 100,000	$ 350,000	$ 700,000

COMPANY N
STATEMENTS OF CHANGES IN EQUITY
FOR YEARS ENDING DECEMBER 31

	19P	19Q	19R	19S	19T
Balance Jan. 1	$1,400,000	$1,450,000	$1,375,000	$1,225,000	$1,000,000
Net income or (loss)	150,000	(75,000)	(150,000)	(225,000)	(300,000)
Dividends	100,000	—	—	—	—
Balance Dec. 31	$1,450,000	$1,375,000	$1,225,000	$1,000,000	$ 700,000

a residual—the excess of the total of the reporting entity's assets over the total of its liabilities. It is the consolidated reporting entity's own equity in its own assets. Also, like a reporting entity that is a separate corporation, a consolidated entity should disclose the number of outstanding shares of stock of the parent and all other matters pertaining to the parent's duties to its stockholders—but outside the number columns of the consolidated financial statements.

SHARING WITH MINORITY STOCKHOLDERS

A parent company will have to share dividends of its subsidiaries with minority stockholders when, as and if they are declared. Information on percentages of shareholdings in its less than wholly owned subsidiaries and on other pertinent matters concerning all the consolidated subsidiaries, both wholly and less than wholly owned, such as their outstanding options, warrants or convertible debentures, should be disclosed. The information is needed to help statement users assess the prospective effects of sharing on the parent. Earnings per share (EPS) calculations of consolidated financial statements should be influenced, for example, by minority stockholdings.

Such information is similar to that on shareholdings in a separate corporation and on other pertinent matters concerning it, including its EPS and its outstanding options, warrants or convertible debentures. Such information is now given to help its stockholders assess the prospective sharing each will have with the other stockholders in dividends when, as and if they are declared. All those kinds of information on prospective sharing straddle financial reporting and financial statement analysis. None should be mistaken for historical information that belongs in the number columns of the financial statements, which should be confined to information on the current position and past results of the reporting entity, the only sound focus for financial reporting.

RUBIN'S REBUTTAL OF ROSENFIELD'S VIEW

Rosenfield's proposed alternative is better than current practice, but it doesn't satisfactorily solve the problem of how to treat minority stockholdings. He's right that the number columns of a reporting entity's financial statements shouldn't report amounts that relate to minority stockholdings. But his proposed treatment doesn't do that because, under what he calls his new view of equity, amounts that relate to minority stockholdings are still included in the equity section of the balance sheet, albeit combined with similar amounts that relate to the reporting entity.

Further, under his new concepts of equity and income, reported equity and reported income are the same regardless of whether a parent company owns 51 percent or 100 percent of the stock of one or more subsidiaries. Those results don't correspond to reality.

Moreover, Rosenfield's proposal to expand disclosure is an unsatisfactory substitute for recognition and measurement of essential information in the number columns. Disclosure should elaborate on or amplify amounts in the number columns, not substitute for such amounts. Also, his new concepts would make helpful financial statement analysis difficult, if not impossible. The complexities in incorporating minority stockholdings in EPS calculations, a possibility he mentions, proves that.

The only sound way to exclude amounts that relate to minority stockholdings from the number columns is to exclude all such amounts, and the only acceptable way to do that is through proportional consolidation.

RUBIN'S VIEW: PROPORTIONAL CONSOLIDATION AS THE SOLUTION

Proportional consolidation is the only sound solution to the problem of how to treat minority stockholdings in consolidation. Under proportional consolidation, as the phrase implies, consolidated financial statements report the parent company's proportionate share in each of the subsidiary's assets, liabilities, revenues and expenses by combining, line by line, those amounts directly with the parent's assets, liabilities, revenues and expenses.

That is one of about five methods commonly used today to account for investments in real estate partnerships and in construction joint ventures. It hasn't generally been used to account for other kinds of investments, but it has some appealing characteristics. The most attractive is that financial statements using proportional consolidation don't present amounts for minority interest and therefore report only attributes of the reporting entities.

The elements of consolidated financial statements are most helpfully viewed as including (1) all the assets, liabilities and equity of the parent company, including investments in companies in which the parent owns voting shares insufficient to give it control over their financial and operating activities, and (2) the parent's proportionate share of the assets and liabilities of all subs in which the parent owns voting shares sufficient to give it control over their financial and operating activities, exclusive of intercompany balances.

That would involve, for example, including 80 percent of each of a sub's assets and 80 percent of each of its liabilities in the financial statements of an investor that owns 80 percent of the voting stock of the investee.

Exhibit 4 contrasts consolidated balance sheets whose reporting entity includes P, the parent company, and S, a subsidiary, 80 percent of whose voting common stock P has acquired for $500,000. The balance sheets apply and contrast

1. Current practice.
2. Rosenfield's view.
3. Rubin's view.

For simplicity, the reported amounts of S's assets and liabilities equal their fair values. There are no intercompany balances other than P's investment in S's voting common stock.

Including 80 percent of the investee's assets, liabilities, and so on is unsatisfactory to some, but it is more satisfactory than

- Current practice, which (1) includes 100 percent of each of the subsidiary's assets and 100 percent of each of its liabilities in the financial statements of the investor and (2) reports on the right side of the investor's balance sheet a nondescript amount equal to 20 percent of the carrying amount of the investee's equity, attributable to stockholdings outside the consolidated group.
- Rosenfield's view, which (1) includes 100 percent of each of a consolidated sub's assets and 100 percent of each of its liabilities in the consolidated financial statements, (2) ascribes all the sub's equity to the extent not eliminated in consolidation, including that attributable to minority stockholdings, as an undifferentiated part of the equity of the reporting entity and (3) merely discloses information in the notes concerning the prospective effects of dividend sharing on the parent and on the majority stockholders.

A basic concept underlying financial reporting—that financial statements should emphasize the substance of events and conditions rather than just their form—further supports proportional consolidation. A company that acquires voting stock of another company obtains the right to receive a pro rata share of dividends when, as and if declared. The declaration of dividends generally is possible only if a company is profitable.

Efficient operations, among other factors, engender profits—that is, increases in assets and decreases in liabilities. Therefore, a company that acquires, say, 80 percent of the voting stock of another company in effect acquires the same percentage of the sub's assets and future increases in its assets and of its liabilities and future decreases in its liabilities. In other words, the parent has acquired an 80 percent interest in the present position and in the results of future efficient operations of the subsidiary.

EXHIBIT 4

Consolidated Balance Sheets

			Consolidated Results		
	P	**S**	**Current Practice**	**Rosenfield's View**	**Rubin's View**
Investment in S	$ 500,000				
Goodwill			$ 100,000	$ 100,000	$ 100,000
Other assets	500,000	$ 600,000	1,100,000	1,100,000	980,000
	$1,000,000	$ 600,000	$1,200,000	$1,200,000	$1,080,000
Liabilities	$ 300,000	$ 100,000	$ 400,000	$ 400,000	$ 380,000
Common stock P	400,000		400,000		400,000
Common stock S		300,000	60,000*		
Retained earnings P	300,000		300,000		300,000
Retained earnings S		200,000	40,000*		
Equity				800,000**	
	$1,000,000	$ 600,000	$1,200,000	$1,200,000	$1,080,000

*Disclosed as minority interest.

**Plus expanded disclosures on the reporting duties to the majority and minority stockholders and on factors affecting sharing of dividends of subsidiaries and of the parent company.

One way for a company to acquire 80 percent of future increases in another company's assets and of future decreases in its liabilities is to directly acquire that percentage of its assets and liabilities. Another way to accomplish essentially the same thing is to acquire 80 percent of the voting stock of the other company; in effect, the parent has acquired 80 percent of the following: the sub's equity at the date of acquisition, future increases in its assets and subsequent decreases in its liabilities. In other words, the parent has an 80 percent interest in the results of the subsidiary's future efficient operations.

To be sure, a company can't acquire 80 percent of a machine, building or desk. But existing accounting standards, FASB Statement no. 13, *Accounting for Leases,* for one, require companies to recognize, in specified circumstances, ownership interests in assets they don't own.

In sum, of the three approaches discussed in this article, only proportional consolidation results in reporting based solely on relevant aspects of a soundly defined consolidated reporting entity. The FASB should therefore adopt proportional consolidation as the major thrust of its current project on comprehensive review of consolidation reporting.

II-E3

PROPORTIONATE CONSOLIDATION AND FINANCIAL ANALYSIS

Harold Bierman, Jr.

For many years accountants have attempted to define the necessary conditions for consolidating the financial statements of corporations owning the stock of other corporations. The Financial Accounting Standards Board (FASB) in 1991 issued a Discussion Memorandum titled "Consolidation Policy and Procedures" that lists seven issues and many subissues. Issue 1 is "What condition(s) determine or indicate that a subsidiary should be included with its parent in consolidated financial statements?" Two primary factors traditionally considered in requiring consolidation are:

a. Percentage of ownership interests.

b. Presence or absence of control.

One objective of this paper is to offer a workable useful alternative to specific percentages of ownership and to specific amounts of control. What type of consolidated information should be supplied for financial analysts when the common stock ownership of a subsidiary is less than 100 percent? The paper concludes that the financial statements of corporations consolidated on a proportionate basis provide financial information useful to financial analysts.

The author thanks colleagues Tom Dyckman and Bob Libby, financial marketers Tom Ostrander, Ernie Liu, and Scott Smith, and three reviewers.

Harold Bierman, Jr., "Proportionate Consolidation and Financial Analysis." American Accounting Association: *Accounting Horizons*. Reprinted by permission of the American Accounting Association.

THE THREE CHOICES

The accounting profession has three broad choices for consolidation practices:

1. Current practice where there is full consolidation if consolidation is appropriate. All the assets and liabilities of the investee firm are added to those of the investor firm.
2. Proportionate consolidation in which any material investment in common stock by a corporation gives rise to the need to consolidate.
3. No consolidation of the financial affairs of separate legal entities.

The primary advantage of the third alternative is that the investor firm does not show as a liability the investee's debt, consistent with the fact that the investor has no legal obligation to pay this debt. The primary disadvantage is that closely linked corporations, as when one corporation owns 100 percent of the common stock of the other firm, would be reported separately and it would be more difficult to analyze the leverage position of the investor firm. Because of this disadvantage, it is assumed that some form of consolidation is more useful than no consolidation.

THE OWNERSHIP REQUIREMENT

FASB Statement No. 94, *Consolidation of All Majority-Owned Subsidiaries* (1987), states that the necessary condition for consolidation is ownership of a majority interest. Statement 94 requires consolidation of qualified nonhomogeneous activities, but prohibits consolidation when control is likely to be temporary and when the majority owner does not have effective control.

The principal shortcoming of an ownership requirement is that it is impossible to state an exact cut-off percentage of ownership necessary for consolidation without being arbitrary. Moreover, the definition of qualifying ownership interests may be ambiguous—should ownership of any part or all of preferred stock, convertible debt, or warrants be counted as qualified ownership?

THE CONTROL REQUIREMENT

The control requirement has received support for many years. For example, Paton (1955, 568) distinguished between acquiring shares for investment purposes and acquiring shares for control and took the position that the extent of control should affect the accounting. Chambers (1966, 288) considered control to be a sufficient condition for consolidation. Hendriksen (1970, 514) added the requirement of majority ownership, and concluded that the information obtained from the resulting consolidated statements is valuable.

None of these theorists provide an operational definition of control, although Chambers cites the ability to name a majority of the directors. This paper argues that consolidated financial information is useful even when control does not exist, and that proportionate consolidation is the only consolidation method that reports the amount of debt directly related to the amount of the common stock investment.

Consider a company owning 51 percent of the voting stock of a subsidiary. Because the investor firm has control, debt of the subsidiary is consolidated even though the investor may not be liable for any of the debt in case of default. Suppose there is a second subsidiary with the same amount of debt where 49 percent of the voting stock is owned and there is not control. Under current GAAP, none of the debt of the second firm is consolidated. If the investor is liable for payment in case of default this will be disclosed in a footnote, regardless of whether the debt is consolidated. For most financial analysis, control is much less important than either legal liability of the investor or the existence of debt with a prior claim to the subsidiary's earnings. There is no question that if control exists in the first situation and not in the second, this is relevant financial information, and should be revealed. The issue is whether or not the status of control should affect the consolidation process, not whether it is relevant information. The absence of control inhibits consolidation, but it is not obvious that it should prevent it.

THE ISSUES

The two relevant issues for this paper may be defined as:

1. Should full (conventional) consolidation be used for majority-owned and/or controlled subsidiaries?
2. Should proportionate consolidation be used for all material intercorporate common stock investments?

FULL CONVENTIONAL CONSOLIDATION

If all investments controlled by the investor are consolidated, then the financial statements may be used to evaluate management's performance. All controlled assets are reported, and full consolidation is reasonable for the purpose of performance evaluation.

If, on the other hand, the objective is to analyze from an investment perspective the asset portfolio owned by the shareholders of the investor firm, then the full consolidation process has deficiencies. The first problem with full consolidation is determination of the situations eligible for consolidation. There is no defensible specific cut-off for the percentage of ownership to divide a corporation's investments into the group that will be consolidated and the group that will not be consolidated. Any percentage will be arbitrary. If the percentage of ownership (or control) is defined to be .5 (or any other percentage) then the firm with marginally less than .5 of ownership will not be consolidated but the firm with .5 or more will be fully consolidated. This discontinuity is not logically attractive. The second difficulty with full consolidation is that the resulting leverage information may not be useful for the purpose of financial analysis.

Suppose a parent makes three common stock investments of \$100 each. The investees' debt is not guaranteed by the parent. The first investment is in a firm with \$150 of common stock and \$600 of debt; the investment qualifies for consolidation, all \$600 of the subsidiary's debt is added in consolidation, and the consolidation process is implicitly assumed to be useful for financial analysis even though the investor firm does not owe the \$600.

The second investment is in a firm with \$300 of common stock and \$600 of debt. Because this \$100 investment does not qualify for consolidation under current GAAP, only the \$100 investment would be shown on the investor's balance sheet; none of the subsidiary's debt (even though the subsidiary has $2 of debt for each dollar of common stock) would be shown on the investor's balance sheet.

The third investment is in a firm with $300 of common stock and zero debt. This investment also does not qualify for consolidation. The $100 investment would be shown on the investor's balance sheet, similar to the second investment. But the second investee had $600 of debt and the third investee had zero debt. Without consolidation, the different leverages of the second and third investees do not affect the investor's balance sheet. Information relevant for financial analysis is omitted when only the $100 is shown on the investor's balance sheet for both the second and third investments. The first investment adds $600 of debt when consolidated but the investor is not obligated to pay the $600 and only owns 2/3 of the stock.

The amount of a firm's debt affects the variability of both the firm's earnings per share and its return on equity. Substitution of debt for equity also increases the firm's Beta, the standard risk measure of the capital asset pricing model and an important input into valuing a firm's stock. For the effect of a changing capital structure on the value of a stock's Beta see Brealey and Myers (1991, 191–193). Unfortunately, current consolidation practice reports too much debt when a firm owns less than 100 percent of the subsidiary's common stock and too little debt when the firm owns less than enough shares to qualify for consolidation.

PROPORTIONATE CONSOLIDATION

If one accepts the argument that consolidated statements for corporations that currently qualify for consolidation are more useful than parent company statements alone, then one can argue that consolidated statements for corporations with non-qualifying common stock investments are also useful. If consolidations are to take place even in the absence of an ownership or control requirement, then proportionate consolidation could be used for all material investments in common stock.

The use of proportionate consolidation requires that when the investor owns p of the common stock, p of the debt and p of the firm's assets are attributed to the investor. But this attribution is not strictly valid. An investor normally cannot spend the cash of an investee firm until the cash is distributed. For example, closed end investment trusts frequently sell at a discount compared to the market value of the securities owned. Owning .01 of an investment trust that owns securities valued at $10,000 is normally not as valuable as possessing $100 cash. Full consolidation can be criticized on similar grounds as it requires, when consolidation is permitted, that all of the investee's assets be combined with the investor's assets. Also, the attribution of liabilities has an equivalent complexity since, given limited liability, the debt of a corporation does not have to be paid by the firm's stockholders, an observation that also applies to full consolidation.

Thus, although proportionate consolidation has an attribution rule that is not completely valid, full consolidation has a comparable attribution rule. The issue is not whether proportionate consolidation has faults, but whether the information from proportionate consolidation is more useful than the information from the alternatives.

The examples that follow make the following assumptions:

1. Stock may be purchased in any amount with zero transaction costs.
2. Balance sheets are prepared on a fair value basis.

3. The extent of ownership or control does not affect the value of the investment.
4. Analysis of the consolidated statements is made from a shareholder's perspective, rather than that of a creditor.

To broaden the usefulness of consolidated information, the debt resulting from the consolidation process should be reported as "Debt Arising from Consolidation," and it should be disclosed whether or not the investor is legally liable for the debt of the firms whose stock is owned.

WHY PROPORTIONATE CONSOLIDATION AIDS FINANCIAL ANALYSIS

To illustrate why proportionate consolidation facilitates financial analysis, Exhibit 1 shows an investor firm's balance sheet.

EXHIBIT 1

Investor's Balance Sheet

Assets	284[1]	Stock Equity	284

[1] .71(400) = 284. See firm Able's balance sheet.

Although the investor has zero debt, and the impression is one of a safe financial strategy, the investor's sole asset is an investment in 71 percent of the common stock of firm Able. Exhibit 2 shows Able's non-consolidated balance sheet:

EXHIBIT 2

Firm Able's Balance Sheet

Assets	1,420[2]	Liabilities	1,020
		Stock Equity	400
			1,420

[2] .71(2,000) = 1,420. See firm Baker's balance sheet.

Firm Able's assets consist solely of an investment in 71 percent of Baker's common stock. (See Exhibit 3)

EXHIBIT 3

Firm Baker's Balance Sheet

Assets	10,000	Liabilities	8,000
		Stock Equity	2,000
			10,000

Exhibit 4 presents the conventional consolidated balance sheet.

EXHIBIT 4

Consolidated Balance Sheet (Full Consolidation)

Assets	10,000	Liabilities	9,020$^{(3)}$
		Minority Interests	696$^{(4)}$
		Investor's Stock Equity	284
			10,000

$^{(3)}$1,020 + 8,000 = 9,020

$^{(4)}$.29(2,000) + .29(400) = 580 + 116 = 696

There is an implicit assumption in full consolidation that the investor firm has access to all the investee firm's assets and is liable for all its liabilities.

Exhibit 5 presents the balance sheet with proportionate consolidation.

EXHIBIT 5

Consolidated Balance Sheet (Proportionate Consolidation)

Assets	5,041$^{(5)}$	Liabilities	4,757$^{(6)}$
		Minority Interests	—
		Investor's Stock Equity	284
			5,041

$^{(5)}$.71 × .71(10,000) = 5,041

$^{(6)}$.71(1,020) + .5041(8,000) = 724.20 + 4,032.80 = 4,757

Conventional consolidation overstates assets owned and liabilities owed but does not overstate assets controlled when ownership is less than 100 percent. Following GAAP, consolidated assets and liabilities are equal to or larger than they would be under proportionate consolidation if consolidation takes place. When the proportion of the investor's ownership falls below the required percentage, current GAAP prohibits consolidation, and only the investor's assets (including investments) and liabilities are presented. But under proportionate consolidation, the user is presented with the investor's pro-rata share of the debt of the firms in which the investor had invested. Although an analyst might try to adjust the investor's balance sheet for the debt of its subsidiaries in the absence of consolidation, this adjustment can be done more efficiently by the investor's accountants. Current practice leads to overstatement of the subsidiary's debt on the consolidated balance sheet when the investor owns more than 50 percent and less than 100 percent of the subsidiary's common stock, since 100 percent of the subsidiary's debt is shown as a liability on the consolidated statement. Without proportionate consolidation, there is an understatement of debt on the investor's consolidated balance sheet when the investor owns 50 percent or less of the investee's common stock.

PROPORTIONATE CONSOLIDATION AND FINANCIAL THEORY

Consider proportionate consolidation for any material common stock investment, regardless of the degree of control and the percentage of ownership. Using concepts from finance theory, proportionate consolidation will be seen to better facilitate financial analysis of the investor and its investments than all-or-nothing consolidation. Basic financial decision models are used to illustrate desirable aspects of proportionate consolidation. Although the theoretical origin of these models is the seminal Modigliani-Miller (MM) paper (1958, 261–297) they are now found in any introductory corporate finance text. MM use a partial-equilibrium analysis with perfect information and rational investors where the prices of income streams are determined assuming no bankruptcy costs and no taxes. Relaxing these assumptions adds complexity without enhancing the main argument.

Assume Corporation B has the following balance sheet (Exhibit 6):

EXHIBIT 6

B's Balance Sheet

Assets	200	Liabilities	100
		Stock Equity	100
			200

B's stock has a market value of $100. Exhibit 7 shows the balance sheet of the two other companies, A and C. Book values are assumed to equal fair values. The equality of fair values and book values avoid unnecessary complications; I will address the implications of relaxing this assumption later in the paper.

EXHIBIT 7

A's Balance Sheet

Assets	100	Liabilities	90
		Stock Equity	10
			100

C's Balance Sheet

Assets	100	Liabilities	10
		Stock Equity	90
			100

All three firms have identical (but proportional) operating characteristics; when B earns $30 before interest, A and C will both earn $15 each before interest (zero taxes are assumed). Firm A may appear to have too much debt and C not enough. But the MM theory tells us that, under its assumptions, capital structure does not affect a firm's value. Therefore,

Value of A = Value of C

and

Value of A plus Value of C = Value of B

To see why A plus C equals B, assume that a corporate investor buys all the common stock of firms A and C for $100. The investor's consolidated balance sheet for the investment in A + C is Exhibit 8.

EXHIBIT 8

Consolidated Balance Sheet Corporate Investor in (A + C)

Assets	200	Liabilities	100
		Stock Equity	100
			200

Because this balance sheet is identical to that of B, and the earnings are identical, the value of A plus C must equal that of B. Assumptions are being made that limited liability and bankruptcy costs do not exist and that there are zero transaction costs. Relaxing these assumptions causes the examples to be less exact. Logically the interest paid on B's debt must equal the interest paid in total on A's debt plus C's debt. Although A's interest rate is higher than B's, C's rate will be lower than B's, and the weighted average will be equal to that of B. An investor can buy all of B's debt for $100 and earn interest of I. If the investor buys all $100 of A and C's debt, which has the same risk as B's debt, the interest on this debt must also be I, given capital markets with well informed investors acting rationally. Instead of buying all of B's debt, the investor can buy any fraction and the same logic holds.

Rather than buying 100 percent of A and C and 100 percent of B, the investor can buy any percentage, say 40 percent. The scale of the numbers changes, but not the equality of values. Consider a corporate investor with $60 cash and $60 of stock equity. After buying 40 percent of B's common stock for $40, the investor would show assets of $100 and debt of $40 under proportionate consolidation. (Exhibit 9)

EXHIBIT 9

Consolidated Working Paper (Proportionate Consolidation; 40% of B Owned)

			Eliminations		
	Investor	**B**	**DR**	**CR**	**Proportionate Consolidation**
Assets	60	80		40	100
Liabilities		40			40
Stock Equity	60	40	40		60

If the investor did not consolidate and report the $40 of B's debt, the investor would show only a common stock investment of $40 and no liabilities. Because only 40 percent of B's stock is owned, full consolidation would not take place.

If the investor spent $4 buying 40 percent of A's common stock, without consolidation the investor would report an investment of $4 and zero debt. In contrast, with proportionate consolidation the corporate investor reports the information shown in Exhibit 10.

EXHIBIT 10

Consolidated Working Paper (Proportionate Consolidation; 40% of A Owned)

			Eliminations		
	Investor	A	DR	CR	Proportionate Consolidation
Assets	60	40		4	96
Liabilities		36			36
Stock Equity	60	4	4		60

Now assume a $36 investment in C's common stock (40 percent of the stock) which has a total market value of $90. Exhibit 11 shows the proportionate consolidation.

EXHIBIT 11

Consolidated Working Paper (Proportionate Consolidation; 40% of C Owned)

			Eliminations		
	Investor	C	DR	CR	Proportionate Consolidation
Assets	60	40		36	64
Liabilities		4			4
Stock Equity	60	36	36		60

If $4 is invested in A and $36 is invested in C, we obtain the economic equivalent of the $40 investment in B. Because the investments are equivalent, the consolidated statements should be the same for the investment in A and C as for the $40 investment in B. Under proportionate consolidation they are identical. (Exhibits 9 and 12)

EXHIBIT 12

Consolidated Working Paper (Proportionate Consolidation; 40% of A and C Owned)

				Eliminations		
	Investor	A	C	DR	CR	Proportionate Consolidation
Assets	60	40	40		40	100
Liabilities		36	4			40
Stock Equity	60	4	36	40		60

THE VALUE EQUALITY OF A AND C

Continuing the above example where A has $90 of debt, C has $10 of debt and the operating results are identical, with zero taxes the values of firms A and C must be identical. Assume one buys 40 percent of A's common stock at a cost of $4. Exhibit 10 showed the $4 investment in A's stock using proportionate consolidation.

Although A has $90 of debt (90 percent of its capital), and C has only $10 of debt, both companies must have the same value. If the investor buys $4 of C's stock and then borrows $32 and uses the proceeds to buy $32 more of C's common stock, the investor then owns $36 or 40 percent of C's common stock in total. Exhibit 13 shows the results using proportionate consolidation.

EXHIBIT 13

Consolidated Working Paper (Proportionate Consolidation; $36 Investment in C)

			Eliminations		
	Investor	C	DR	CR	Proportionate Consolidation
Assets	92	40		36	96
Liabilities	32	4			36
Stock Equity	60	36	36		60

The proportionate consolidated balance sheet for C and the investor is now the same as the proportionate consolidated balance sheet incorporating the investment in A. Firm C with only 10 percent debt cannot sell for a different amount than A, that has 90 percent debt, assuming zero taxes, because there is at least one financial strategy that will cause the two investments to be equivalent. This is an example of MM's "homemade leverage" solution where the investor borrows to make the investment in C equivalent to the investment in A.

Continuing the example, assume that the debt cost is .08 and both A and C earn $15 before interest. The investor and the two corporations are assumed to borrow at the same rate so the sum of the investor's interest and C's interest must equal A's interest. This is reasonable when the investor borrows to buy the common stock of C and uses the stock as collateral. Exhibit 14 shows the investor's incomes and expenses from the A and C investments.

EXHIBIT 14

	A	C
Earnings Before Interest	$15.00	$15.00
Interest on Corporate Debt (.08)	− 7.20	− .80
Common Stock Earnings	7.80	14.20
Ownership Proportion	× .40	× .40
Investor's Common Stock Earnings	3.12	5.68
Interest on Private Debt (.08)	0	− 2.56
Investor's Net	$ 3.12	$ 3.12

The investor will have the same net from the A and C investments for any amount of earnings before interest. Firms A and C must have the same value and the same average cost of capital. Consistent with this conclusion, when the financial affairs of the corporations are consolidated on a proportionate basis, the statements show identical financial results when the economic characteristics of the investments are identical.

CORPORATE INCOME TAXES

The development to follow is consistent with Modigliani and Miller (1963, 433–443) but the derivation is somewhat different. Relaxing the assumption of zero corporate income taxes used above changes the details of the analysis, but not the underlying theory. The investor can convert a heavily levered firm into the equivalent of an investment in a zero debt firm by a suitable strategy where both stock and debt are purchased. As an example, consider a zero debt firm that earns X before tax and $(1 - t)X$ after corporate tax, where t is the corporate tax rate. If the investor buys p of the firm's stock, the investor will earn $p(1 - t)X$.

Consider a second firm that also earns X before tax but has substituted B of debt paying I interest for B of stock. The investor buys p of the remaining stock and $(1 - t)p$ of the new debt and earns:

$(1 - t)p\,I$	from the debt
$p(X - I)(1 - t)$	from the stock
$pX(1 - t)$	Sum

The earnings from the investment in the levered second firm are identical to the earnings from the investment in the unlevered firm, and the investments in the two firms must have equal costs when the investor buys p of the stock and $(1 - t)p$ of the debt. When the value of the debt of the levered firm is B and the value of the stock is S, since the earnings are equal, if V_U is the value of the unlevered firm then:

$$pV_U = pS + (1 - t)pB \tag{1}$$

Since the value of the levered firm is $V_L = S + B$, dividing (1) by p yields:

$$V_U = S + (1 - t)B = S + B - tB$$

or

$$V_L = V_U + tB \tag{2}$$

With the inclusion of corporate tax considerations it is necessary to reflect the fact that the theoretical values of the unlevered and levered firms differ. The value of the levered firm is increased by the present value of the tax savings on the levered firm's interest payments. To own the same proportions of the securities of the levered firm as the unlevered firm a larger investment will have to be made.

AN EXAMPLE: PROPORTIONATE CONSOLIDATION OF INVESTMENTS IN LEVERED FIRMS

Now suppose that A has $90 of debt and D has zero debt, and the two firms have identical operating results. The value of firm D is $100 and there is a .34 corporate tax rate. The investor purchases $40 of D's stock. Exhibit 15 shows the balance sheet using proportionate consolidation.

EXHIBIT 15

Consolidated Working Paper (Proportionate Consolidation; $40 Investment of D)

			Eliminations		
	Investor	**D**	**DR**	**CR**	**Proportionate Consolidation**
Assets	60	40		40	60
Liabilities					
Stock Equity	60	40	40		60

Since D has a value of $100, the levered firm A with $90 of debt and identical operating results has a value of:

$$V_L = V_U + tB = 100 + .34(90) = \$130.60$$

Because the tax savings from interest deductibility accrue to common shareholders, A's stock has a value of:

$$S = V_L - B = 130.60 - 90.00 = \$40.60$$

To produce an investment in A with annual returns equivalent to the investment in D, the investment strategy is to buy

.40 of A's stock:	.40(40.60) =	$16.24
.40(1 − .34) of A's debt:	.40(.66)(90.00) =	23.76
Total investment		$40.00

Because the $40 investment in A's stock and debt produces the same after tax income as the $40 investment in D's stock, proportionate consolidation reflects the purchase of only .4(1 − .34) = .264 of A's debt rather than .40. Thus, in Exhibit 16 only $23.76 of the $36.00 debt is eliminated, and $12.24 of A's debt remains after consolidation.

The annual returns are identical to those earned by buying .40 of D's stock, but now proportionate consolidation shows $12.24 of debt. The purchase of .264 of A's debt and .40 of A's stock results in identical annual returns, but whereas the investment in D's stock resulted in owning .40 of the firm, now the debt ownership percentage of A is less than .40. To obtain identical proportionate consolidation balance sheets, there has to be ownership of .4 of all of A's securities. Since A with its debt (and tax savings) has more value than D, the investment will now have to be larger than $40 to have the same percentage of ownership.

EXHIBIT 16

Consolidated Working Paper (Proportionate Consolidation; $40 Investment of A)

	Investor	A	Eliminations DR	Eliminations CR	Proportionate Consolidation
Assets	60	52.24[(1)]		40.00	72.24
Liabilities		36.00	23.76		12.24
Stock Equity	60	16.24	16.24		60.00

[(1)].4(130.60) = 52.24

Thus the tax savings on the levered firm's interest payments cause the levered firm's value to exceed that of the unlevered firm. Although an investment in p of the levered firm's stock and $(1 - t)p$ of the debt costs the same as an investment in p of the unlevered firm's stock, and produces the same annual returns to the investor, the proportionate consolidated balance sheets of the two alternatives differ. Proportionate consolidation includes p of the levered investee's debt whereas only $(1 - t)p$ of that debt is eliminated and tp remains. Compared to proportionate consolidation, all-or-nothing consolidation continues to overstate (understate) consolidated debt when consolidation occurs (does not occur).

Although investment in p of the levered firm's stock and $(1 - t)p$ of the debt costs the same as investment in p of the unlevered firm's stock and provides equivalent annual returns, the two alternatives are not equivalent in cases of financial distress. To obtain equivalent bankruptcy protection, the investor must acquire p of *both* stock *and* debt of the levered firm at a higher cost. In this latter case, proportionate consolidated balance sheets involving investments in the levered and unlevered firms are equivalent. The following example illustrates this point.

If $36 of A's debt (40 percent) and $16.24 of A's stock (40 percent) are purchased, then proportionate consolidation for the investment in A's debt and stock is shown in Exhibit 17 to be exactly the same as that shown in Exhibit 15 for the investment in D's stock.

EXHIBIT 17

Consolidated Working Paper
(Proportionate Consolidation; Buying .40 of A's Securities)

	Investor	A	Eliminations DR	Eliminations CR	Proportionate Consolidation
Assets	60	52.24		52.24	60
Liabilities		36.00	36.00		
Stock Equity	60	16.24	16.24		60

Now the investment is $52.24 and for this investment the investor gets the same annual return as owning .40 of D's stock, an additional return on the extra $12.24 of debt, and in case of financial distress the investor gets the same percentage of ownership rights as with the .40 ownership in D.

BENEFITS OF PROPORTIONATE CONSOLIDATION

The primary benefit of proportionate consolidation is that it eliminates an arbitrary boundary between investments that are consolidated and those that are not. Secondly, when the investor owns less than 100 percent of a consolidated subsidiary, only a proportionate amount of the debt appears on the consolidated balance sheet rather than 100 percent of the debt. Finally, when the subsidiary would not qualify for conventional full consolidation, none of the subsidiary's debt would appear on the consolidated balance sheet. With proportionate consolidation a proportionate amount of the debt is included.

CASH FLOW INFORMATION

In addition to the proportionate consolidated balance sheet and income statement data, the investor company's cash flow might also be of interest to an analyst. Whereas creditors are interested in the cash flows of each corporate entity, the investor company stockholders are interested in the consolidated cash flows. Both sets of cash flow data should be reported because both supply useful information. Whatever confusion exists with two sets of cash flows exists under full consolidation as well as under proportionate consolidation.

Proportionate consolidation results in proportionate inclusion of net income and cash flows. If the investor owned 19 percent of the investee, then 19 percent of the investee's income and cash flows are included on the proportionate consolidated income and cash flow statements. Also, 19 percent of intercompany sales and the intercompany profits are eliminated under proportionate consolidation. Because the other 81 percent is already excluded by proportionate consolidation, proportionate consolidation removes 100 percent of the intercompany sales and profits on upstream sales from the subsidiary to its parent.

In appraising the creditworthiness of the investor, the credit analyst wants to know the cash flows of the investor and the extent to which the cash flows of the investees are available to the investor. For this analysis, the investor's legal right to access an investee's cash flow is relevant financial information. The need for this information transcends the specific consolidation method, and can be supplied by footnote disclosure.

A LESS THAN IDEAL WORLD

In the above examples it was assumed that there were four companies with identical operating characteristics leading to identical earnings before interest and taxes, but the companies had different capital structures. Although this is not likely to happen in the real world, it is always possible for one company to consider many alternative capital structures. The same logic that applied to the four companies now applies to the one company with four different capital structures.

Also, in all the examples, the accounting information was always consistent with the assumed fair value measures. This assumption is necessary in order to show that the theory works in an exact manner. If the accounting does not measure fair value, then the consolidation process will result in accounting measures that also will be inconsistent with the value measures.

In this situation, illustrating the usefulness of proportionate consolidation would be more complex. To simplify this very complex subject, the assumption that accounting measures equal fair value measures is retained. The FASB is currently considering the appropriate extent to which fair value measures should be used.

WOULD ALL STOCK INVESTMENTS BE CONSOLIDATED?

While theoretically all common stock investments result in proportionate consolidation, as with all other accounting rules the safety valve of "materiality" exists. If the common stock investment is not material, the proportionate consolidation procedure would be set aside. In addition, it might be useful to exclude from proportionate consolidation types of firms for which the cost of proportionate consolidation exceeds the expected benefits of the information. The process by which the FASB arrives at its rules is excellent at finding exceptions to its rules.

The primary disadvantage of proportionate consolidation is that accounting complexities are introduced compared to just showing an investment in common stock. While full consolidation of majority-owned subsidiaries as required by GAAP also has complexities, the fact that proportionate consolidation would be used for minority-owned investees is a new complexity.

PURCHASE PRICE ALLOCATIONS

Proportionate consolidation of a common stock investment is easily accomplished. Assume the investor buys 1 percent of a firm's stock. In proportionate consolidation the assets added are 1 percent of the investee's assets balanced by 1 percent of the investee's debts and 1 percent of the investee's stock. The consolidation process eliminates the 1 percent of the investee's stock and an equal amount of the investment cost. A "goodwill" account would adjust the investee's assets to be consistent with the market price of the stock. For example, if stock with a book value of $60 is purchased at a cost of $80, there would be $20 shown in a goodwill or "excess of purchase price over book value" account. The assets and liabilities can be estimated using the accounting reports of the purchased firm. Improving the investee's asset and liability accounting measures is a separable issue. The "goodwill" reconciling account would include conventional goodwill as well as undervalued (or overvalued) recorded assets and liabilities.

CONCLUSIONS

Modern theory of finance tears down the fiction of separate corporations financed with debt and equity and allows development of a method of analysis that effectively considers the consolidated financial situation of the investor. Investing in the common stock of a highly levered firm has different financial consequences than investing in the common stock of a zero debt firm. Balance sheets for the corporate investor will reflect this difference if proportionate consolidation is used. Rather than limiting consolidation to the set of firms that meet ownership and control criteria, this paper recommends that proportionate consolidation be used for any material common stock investment.

We are accustomed to specific rules regarding consolidations that define which equity investments lead to consolidation. Proportionate consolidation when there is common stock ownership has the desirable characteristic of not dividing investments into those to be consolidated and those not to be consolidated. Using proportionate consolidation eliminates the importance of "bright line" rules deciding the criteria for normal consolidation procedures.

While it is true that limited liability rules for corporations might result in the corporate investor not having to pay the debts of its subsidiary, this does not currently preclude qualified consolidations, and should not preclude proportionate consolidations. The debt for which the firm is not liable should be labeled using a title such as "Debt of corporations in which common stock is owned" and detailed explanations offered in footnotes. The debt of a company in which stock is owned by the parent is different than the debt of the parent. The presence or absence of debt guarantees should also be revealed in footnotes.

When corporate taxes are introduced, the levered firm is valued more highly than its unlevered counterpart, *ceteris paribus,* because of the tax savings from deductibility of interest. For equal cost investments having equal annual returns, less than p of the levered firm's debt can be acquired as the common equity is worth more—the tax savings from financial leverage accrue to the common equity—thereby producing non-equivalent proportionate consolidation and bankruptcy results. Thus the concept of totally "equivalent investments" in levered/unlevered firms does not exist. For equal percentage investments—buy p of all securities—the levered firm investment costs more, produces higher annual returns but provides equivalent bankruptcy protection and an equivalent proportionate consolidation result. All-or-nothing consolidation shows too much debt when consolidation occurs and too little when it does not, thus proportionate consolidation has significant advantages.

There are several opportunities for future research and several issues to be resolved even if the proportionate consolidation concept is accepted. For example, suppose a joint venture being considered will be accounted for on an equity basis and not consolidated. Would the decision to undertake the joint venture be different if proportionate consolidation resulted in the addition of significant debt to the investor's balance sheet? Now consider a firm that currently consolidates several subsidiaries and does not consolidate other investees. Would the different amounts of debt shown on the proportionate consolidation balance sheet affect the stock price or bond credit rating?

Also, we have to resolve the issue of outstanding preferred stock, options, warrants, and convertible debt. Should all these equity type of securities be converted into common stock equivalents for the purpose of determining the extent of ownership? Finally, are there unknown obstacles to proportionate consolidation that should be considered? For example, bond covenants were drawn up with one set of accounting conventions; do the same set of covenants apply as the accounting conventions change?

The above issues are interesting, but none of them affect the basic objective of improving the reporting of the financial affairs of corporations that own the common stock of other corporations.

REFERENCES

Brealey, R. A., and S. C. Myers, 1991. *Principles of Corporate Finance.* New York, McGraw-Hill, Inc.

Chambers, R. J. 1966. *Accounting, Evaluation, and Economic Behavior.* Englewood Cliffs, New Jersey: Prentice-Hall, Inc.

Financial Accounting Standards Board. 1992. *Discussion Memorandum, Consolidation Policy and Procedures.* Norwalk.

———. 1987. *Statement of Financial Accounting Standard No. 94,* "Consolidation of All Majority-Owned Subsidiaries." Norwalk.

Hendriksen, E. S. 1970. *Accounting Theory.* Homewood, Illinois: R. D. Irwin, Inc.

Modigliani, F., and M. H. Miller. June 1958. "The Cost of Capital, Corporation Finance, and the Theory of Investment," *American Economic Review.*

———, and ———. June 1963. "Corporate Income Taxes and the Cost of Capital: A Correction," *American Economic Review.*

Paton, W. A. 1955. *Corporation Accounts and Statements.* New York: The Macmillan Company.

II-E4

APB 16: TIME TO RECONSIDER

Michael Davis

Consider this dilemma: A company entering its fourth quarter finds earnings have deteriorated significantly, the company's stock is out of favor with analysts and a long-expected recession is under way. The company already is using the most advantageous accounting methods. Executives have cut back, slimmed down, restructured, refocused and economized in every way they can think of, but it has not been enough. As an afterthought, management decides to call its auditors for suggestions. Almost without hesitation, the engagement partner suggests a transaction and accounting treatment to give the company's financial statements the facelift they need.

What was the engagement partner's suggestion? A merger using the pooling of interests method. When the 12 conditions of American Institute of CPAs Accounting Principles Board Opinion no. 16, *Business Combinations,* are met, a pooling of interests creates instant earnings on the company's income statement. In fact, no matter how late in the fiscal year a pooling is consummated, earnings of the acquired company *for the entire year* are included in consolidated net income. On top of that, there's no goodwill to be recorded and amortized over the next 40 years.

As good as this outcome sounds, the above scenario masks some problems the Financial Accounting Standards Board is going to have to address. The rules governing poolings are now over 20 years old, and today's business environment is far different, especially in terms of capital structure and financial instruments, than when APB Opinion no. 16 was passed. In addition, of all the major industrialized countries, only Great Britain allows anything resembling

---

pooling, and its rule makers are modifying the rules to prevent most poolings. Finally, the International Accounting Standards Committee (IASC) has an exposure draft outstanding that blacklists poolings and would eliminate them in most circumstances.

A SHORT HISTORY OF POOLINGS

Originating in the 1940s, the term "poolings" was coined to describe the final form of a union of similar-sized utilities combined via an exchange of securities. In response to the utility companies' attempts to justify higher rates by writing their assets up to fair market value at the time of the combination, the Federal Power Commission ruled valuation on this basis was improper and no new values should be assigned to properties because no change in substance had actually occurred.

In essence, by denying the utilities' requests, a new book-value-based combination called a "pooling of interests" was created. The AICPA formalized this merger concept in 1950 in Accounting Research Bulletin no. 40, *Business Combinations,* as a fusing of equity interests normally involving

- Companies of relatively the same size.
- A continuity of combined management.
- Similar or complementary business activities.

No new basis of accountability arose and assets remained at book value.

What went wrong? Denial of fair-value-based accounting for utility poolings turned into a veritable gold mine for everybody else. Book-value-based depreciation often was far less than fair-value-based depreciation under the other merger accounting alternative, the purchase method. Additionally, goodwill was neither recorded nor amortized in a pooling. Moreover, ARB no. 40 and subsequent pronouncements allowed for diverse interpretation, so by the "go-go" years of the late 1960s, when earnings were everything, the substance of a merger became irrelevant—virtually any combination could be accounted for as a pooling and the resulting public outcry was unrelenting.

As Exhibit 1 indicates, it took some fairly strong pressure from the Securities and Exchange Commission in February 1969 to finally prod the AICPA into action. Rather than incorporating the three conceptually sound guidelines of ARB no. 40, however, Opinion no. 16 instead instituted 12 conditions that give little regard to the substance of the merger.

Although a comparable-size test was included in the exposure draft of Opinion no. 16, intense pressure from the business community ultimately forced its removal from the final version. Absent also was the notion a true pooling could hardly occur without a continuity of management or complementary lines of business. The requirement that a fusing of equity take place remains, but in reality, the fusion need last only a moment in time, as shareholders are basically free to sell once the merger is consummated. As for the 12 rules themselves, numerous practitioners readily admit many of them defy logic. One large accounting firm published a 200-page interpretation of Opinion no. 16 (and a related statement, APB Opinion no. 17, *Intangible Assets*); the two opinions themselves total only 20 pages.

The complex rules of APB Opinion no. 16 have achieved one desired objective: The use of pooling has decreased steadily. As Exhibit 2 illustrates, the number of poolings for the 600 companies tracked in *Accounting Trends & Techniques* declined from 185 in 1969, the last

EXHIBIT 1

A Brief History of APB Opinion No. 16*

June 1963	Accounting Research Study no. 5, *A Critical Study of Accounting for Business Combinations,* by Arthur Wyatt, is issued and recommends abolishing pooling unless the merging parties are related.
February 1969	The Securities and Exchange Commission chairman, testifying before a congressional committee, says unless the accounting profession takes prompt action to resolve the business combinations controversy, the SEC will establish rules in this area.
June 1969	The AICPA holds a symposium on accounting for business combinations.
September 1969	In announcing a forthcoming exposure draft that will propose abolishing pooling of interests, AICPA Executive Vice-President Leonard M. Savoie says, "Anything less than this solution will mean simply a 'repositioning' of the abuses that have become so rampant in recent years."
November 1969	The Accounting Principles Board tentatively decides to abolish pooling of interests accounting. A Federal Trade Commission study authorized by a Senate antitrust committee recommends the SEC eliminate pooling of interests accounting when stock is given as consideration.
December 1969	The APB reverses itself and tentatively decides pooling of interests accounting should be allowed, but not as an alternative that can be freely chosen if desired. For a given set of circumstances and conditions, only one merger accounting method will apply.
February 1970	The APB issues an exposure draft. The detailed conditions set forth for a pooling will severely limit its use. A three-to-one comparable-size test is included. Lawsuits are subsequently threatened over this condition. The Financial Executives Research Foundation commissions a study by John C. Burton, *Accounting for Business Combinations,* to supply data to the APB. Questionnaire results indicate a three-to-one size test would have barred pooling by 90% of the companies that used it in 1967.
June 1970	The APB effectively nullifies the size criterion by changing it to nine to one.
August 1970	APB Opinion no. 16 barely passes with the minimum 12-to-6 vote. The requirement that the combining companies effect a continuity of ownership interests becomes the cornerstone for pooling treatment; the size test is dropped entirely and there are no requirements for continuity of management or similar or complementary lines of business. The combining interests must meet 12 detailed conditions to effect a pooling; otherwise purchase accounting must be used.
1970–73	APB Opinion no. 16 is difficult to apply. Because of its complexity and in order to close loopholes, the AICPA issues 30 interpretations and the SEC issues 4 accounting series releases. (Later, between 1974 and 1987, the FASB issues three interpretations and three technical bulletins.)
1973	The FASB replaces the APB and immediately requests views on previous APB pronouncements. The responses show APB Opinions nos. 16 and 17 are of greatest concern.
1974	The FASB decides to reevaluate the 12 conditions for pooling in APB Opinion no. 16.
1976	The FASB issues a discussion memorandum, *Accounting for Business Combinations and Purchased Intangibles.*
1981	The FASB removes the project from the active agenda because of its "low priority in relation to other existing and potential projects."
1990	Accounting for business combinations and purchased intangibles continues to be law in priority for the FASB, even though 17 years have passed since respondents indicated they were most concerned with these issues.

*Adapted from A. J. Pahlar and J. E. Mori, *Advanced Accounting,* Harcourt Brace Jovanovich, 1991, pages 298–99.

EXHIBIT 2

Poolings vs. Purchases

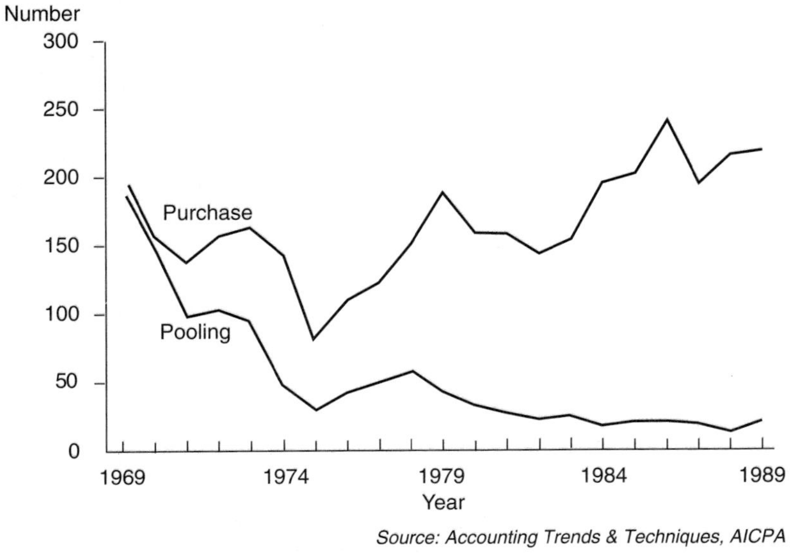

1969 (pre-APB Opinion no. 16) to 1989

full year before Opinion no. 16 became effective, to 18 in 1989. While these statistics might give the impression poolings eventually will disappear, the total number of poolings in any given year is significantly larger than these data indicate and at least one industry—banks and savings and loans—uses the pooling method extensively. These data also highlight the first of four major controversies that justify reexamining the pooling method's appropriateness.

FOUR MAJOR CONTROVERSIES

In recent years, four major controversies have arisen challenging the validity of accounting for certain types of transactions as poolings.

1. ***Most poolings are really acquisitions.*** Exhibit 2 shows a fairly steady decrease not only in poolings but also in the percentage of material poolings, in which the pooled company was large enough to warrant restatement of prior year's financial statements as required by Opinion no. 16. Exhibit 3 illustrates this. Assuming lack of restatement implies immateriality, there were several years in the 1980s when immaterial poolings outnumbered material ones. In other words, using a reasonable materiality threshold of 10%, over half the poolings in some years involved target companies at least 10 times *smaller* than the acquiring entity.

Research studies have found the average relative size of pooled companies, both before and after Opinion no. 16, is about 20% of the acquirer. Rarely do pooled companies approach

EXHIBIT 3

Material Poolings

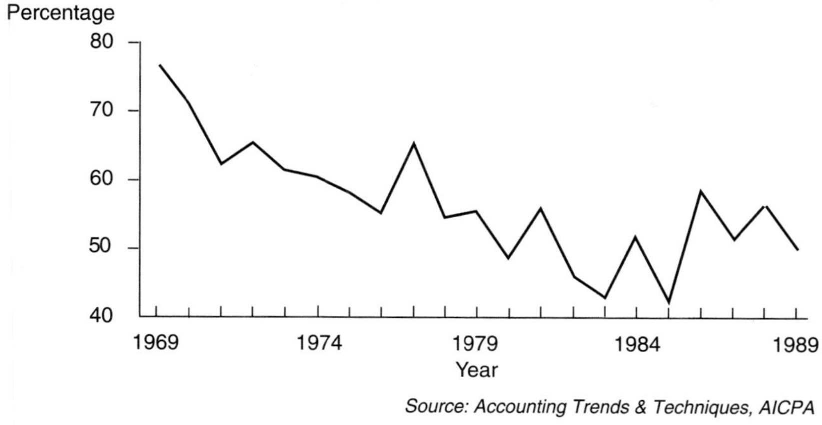

1969 (pre-APB Opinion no. 16) to 1989

50% of the acquirer and many are less than 5%. Except in the most unusual circumstances, it seems inconceivable a true pooling of interests could occur when one merger partner is 5 to 20 times larger than the other.

Rule makers in the United Kingdom agree with this position; the U.K. Accounting Standards Board's February 1990 Exposure Draft (ED) no. 48, *Accounting for Acquisitions and Mergers,* proposes to restrict poolings to combinations in which "none of the combining parties is more than 50% larger than any other enterprise [that] is a party to the combination unless special circumstances prevent the larger from dominating the other(s)." This rule translates to a relative size of 40% to 60% for the pooled entity. The ED also says, "A merger [which is the British term for a pooling] is a rare business combination. . . . The great majority of business combinations are acquisitions."

Poolings are rare indeed. According to my study of a sample of 108 U.S. pooling method mergers during 1971–82 as published in the July 1990 issue of the *Accounting Review,* a 40% size restriction would have eliminated all but one of them.

As further evidence of worldwide opposition to poolings, the IASC's ED E32, *Comparability of Financial Statements,* though not incorporating a specific size test, would require purchase method accounting if the acquirer can be identified and says, "Conditions where an acquirer cannot be identified are expected to be very rare." Perhaps if the original size guidelines in ARB no. 40 had been retained, this controversial issue would now be moot. But in the view of pooling critics, even ARB no. 40 has a fatal flaw.

2. ***The equity exchange is based on market value, not book value.*** Although both ARB no. 40 and Opinion no. 16 require an equity exchange in a pooling, little credence is accorded book value when the two sides argue over the stock exchange ratio. In fact, the value of the shares exchanged often is far above the pooled company's share price at the announcement date. Yet that fair value, along with any implied goodwill, is ignored and the assets and liabilities are combined at book value.

3. ***The illusion of higher earnings.*** It was noted previously that pooling of interests accounting normally results in higher—and often much higher—earnings than when purchase accounting is used. This is due to

- Lower, book-value-based tangible asset depreciation.
- Higher gain recognition when book-value-based assets, such as marketable securities, are sold.
- The absence of goodwill amortization.

What is often forgotten is the incremental earnings caused by these three factors produce virtually *zero* extra cash flow. Why? Because the lower earnings in a purchase method merger, caused by higher depreciation-amortization charges and lower gain recognition, generate negligible tax savings. While the extra depreciation and lower gain recognition can produce tax benefits, amortization of goodwill is never tax deductible and the goodwill element usually is far larger than the first two factors.

In the recent Time-Warner merger, which started out as the largest-ever pooling at $9 billion but ended up being accounted for as a $14 billion purchase, $11 billion—80% of the purchase price—was for non-tax-deductible goodwill. Of the $12.9 billion Philip Morris paid for Kraft Inc. in 1988, 90%—$11.6 billion—was for goodwill. Even today, many players and observers in the merger arena still don't understand one simple fact: Goodwill amortization has no real impact on the financial statements because it has no cash flow impact. As a result, they mistakenly believe either goodwill is bad because of its impact on income and earnings per share or, alternatively, the pooling method is beneficial because it avoids these charges. Samples from the rash of financial press surrounding these two mergers are provided in the sidebar on page 325.

Two recent research studies, one published in the January 1990 *Accounting Review* and the other in the fall 1988 *Journal of Accounting and Public Policy,* found that on the average, acquiring entities pay a larger premium over book value in pooling method mergers than in purchase method mergers. If the stock market is any judge, however, such premiums are wasted. Other studies have documented the market does *not* react positively to window dressing—earnings differences caused solely by accounting method choices. One study specifically examined the purchase-pooling method choice and found pooling mergers did not generate any extra stock market returns during the period when postmerger combined earnings were announced.

4. ***The global push for harmonization of accounting standards.*** Not only have the rules of Opinion no. 16 become increasingly difficult to use in a more sophisticated and complex merger environment but the global economy also is saying "no" to pooling. There has never been a worldwide movement to embrace the pooling method; on the contrary, as evidenced by exposure drafts from the United Kingdom and the IASC, the impetus is to virtually eliminate it.

ELIMINATE POOLING?

Leonard M. Savoie, the chief staff officer of the AICPA in 1969, said the AICPA would propose abolishing the pooling method. One year later, however, Opinion no. 16 was enacted. Dissent was strong and it passed by the slimmest possible vote. Instead of a vehicle to ensure a pooling was truly a fusing of two relatively equal equity interests, Opinion no. 16 was a rule-based labyrinth that bore very little relationship to economic reality.

MISCONCEPTIONS ABOUT PERCEIVED "BENEFITS" OF POOLING OF INTERESTS

The following excerpts from the financial press contain misconceptions about poolings, highlighted here with italics.

"Investment bankers involved in the transaction said the *stock swap also will avoid the giant shot of goodwill that would be generated in a cash deal . . .* which . . . would have to be subtracted from Time earnings over the next 40 years." ("Media Stocks Catch Fire in Wake of Time-Warner Deal," *Wall Street Journal,* March 7, 1989, p. C1. This article was published when the two parties were still trying to do a pooling.)*

"Warner and Time are determined to preserve their ability to use the pooling method because *the alternative method, purchase accounting, could produce significant dilution of Time's per-share earnings.*" ("Time, Warner Alter Merger-Pact Terms After Accounting Challenge by the SEC," *Wall Street Journal,* April 14, 1989, p. B3.)*

"Because many analysts value companies on the basis of their earnings, *acquisitions involving lots of goodwill can really hurt an expanding company's stock price,* and make acquisitions for stock more expensive." ("Britain's Goodwill Games," *Forbes,* October 2, 1989, p. 65.)

"Does anyone care about reported earnings anymore? . . . The conventional wisdom says yes. A recent survey of 60 securities analysts by Ketchum Communications showed that 52% consider profitability measures like earnings and return on investment more important than cash flow in their evaluations of companies. Only 27% thought that cash flow is more important than earnings. . . . One investment banker reports that *20 acquisitions he personally worked on in the last two years fell through because goodwill amortization would have reduced reported earnings, a risk the acquiring companies' managers were loath to take. Goodwill doesn't always kill the deal, but it sure weighs heavily.* Generally investors are still looking for earnings per share." (*Forbes,* July 10, 1989, p. 44; statement by Eugene Beard, executive vice-president for finance and operations, Interpublic Group, in the article, "A Peculiar Beauty Contest.")

" 'We've never backed off an acquisition because of the goodwill,' says Douglas H. McCorkindale, CFO of Gannett Co., the media giant. Still, McCorkindale says it has taken a long time for Wall Street to realize that 'goodwill is an accounting charge without any substance.' That could be true for Gannett, Philip Morris, and a few others. *But if scores of companies started reporting big losses just because of goodwill, shareholders would surely start screaming.*" ("Goodwill Is Making a Lot of People Angry," *Business Week,* July 31, 1989, p. 76.)

*This statement, although technically correct, gives the impression pooling is beneficial because it avoids the purported negative impact of goodwill.

Most mergers that meet the pooling rules are not poolings in substance. Moreover, not recording the true economic value results in materially misleading financial statements. Instead of providing a reasonable alternative to the purchase method, the intervening years have borne out Savoie's concerns and substantiated the objections voiced by other critics. Perhaps these concerns are best summed up by three dissenting members of the APB: "The opinion . . . seeks to patch up some of the abuses of pooling. The real abuse is pooling itself. On that, the only answer is to eliminate pooling."

FIRST IMPRESSIONS

First impressions are often correct—the AICPA was on the right track in 1969 when it announced its intention to abolish poolings. The evidence clearly indicates the rules of Opinion no. 16 do not produce true poolings but acquisitions disguised as poolings, resulting in potentially misleading cosmetic improvements in earnings. The international community is taking steps to severely restrict pooling. The FASB must also make good on the APB's 22-year-old first impression and critically reevaluate the appropriateness of pooling of interests accounting in the United States.

II-F

INTERNATIONAL ISSUES IN FINANCIAL REPORTING

II-F1

EC, EZ?

Larry Sundby and Bradley Schwieger

The "global market" concept is old news. Today, CPAs and their clients are more interested in focusing on opportunities and problems arising from Europe 1992. Expected changes in the European Community (EC) during the coming year have caused many U.S. companies to consider how they can best operate in this newly created market.

One alternative involves mergers and acquisitions (M&As). In 1988, more than 2,000 crossborder M&As took place in Europe, many involving U.S. companies. In 1989, almost 6,000 similar transactions occurred, and 12% of the total involved American dollars. A Conference Board survey of 1,000 publicly held U.S. manufacturers shows the following activities in EC countries in 1989:

- Seventy-two companies acquired EC companies.
- Twenty-four companies started joint ventures.
- Fourteen companies build new EC plants.
- Six companies expanded old plants.

Almost 40% of total U.S. direct investment in foreign countries goes into EC industries.

U.S. accountants play a significant role as strategic planning consultants and in helping clients acquire or expand European operations. Helping clients evaluate EC opportunities is likely to involve an examination of the foreign company's financial statements. In these examinations it is essential that U.S. CPAs understand the accounting rules followed by European companies.

EC Financial Reporting

All companies in the EC follow the EC's fourth directive, issued in 1978, which sets forth general guidelines for reporting financial results. When the EC issues a directive, member countries must incorporate its guidelines into their domestic laws and financial reporting requirements. In this sense, harmonization exists.

However, because of the general nature of the fourth directive, there is much latitude. How EC companies prepare financial statements varies considerably. Some of what is allowed represents procedural differences from U.S. generally accepted accounting principles and is relatively easy to understand and interpret; however, it's also true there are some unexpected conceptual and philosophical differences.

This article examines the major differences between accounting policies in the United States and the EC and seeks to provide a basis for U.S. accountants to understand financial statements prepared in various countries. To begin, exhibit 1 lists EC countries and some of their accounting policies.

Revaluation Reserves

Inflation's general impact on the balance sheet and income statement is typically well understood in most countries. Approaches for dealing with inflation are quite different among EC countries, however, and U.S. accountants need to examine financial statements carefully to determine which approach is being used.

For example, exhibit 2 shows a partial balance sheet for a hypothetical French company. The assets listed seem much like those found in the annual report of a U.S. corporation. However, France periodically mandates an upward revaluation of assets. The shareholders' equity section of the balance sheet shows the total assets amount of FF 15,235,906,000 to be FF 1,857,146,000 (about 12%) above original cost, since a reserve for revaluation of assets account was used to offset an increase on the asset side of the balance sheet.

France, Greece, Portugal, and Spain use a countrywide revaluation approach—all companies are required by the government to revalue to current cost at the same time. The government normally specifies an indexing system or provides other write-up guidelines. Companies essentially have no choice but to revalue. When a countrywide approach is used, the revaluation occurs once every few years. Most other EC countries allow companies to revalue assets periodically at their own discretion.

Normally, companies use replacement cost as a basis for write-ups. The replacement cost approach represents current cost adjusted for years of use for property, plant and equipment. In the Netherlands, some companies go one step further and use current market values. For inventory, sale prices can be significantly in excess of current costs. Only Germany and Luxembourg prohibit write-ups and instead stick with historical cost.

Not all companies write up assets in countries that allow voluntary write-ups; the key account for U.S. CPAs to watch for is the revaluation reserve account, which must be disclosed and is found in the equity section of the balance sheet. U.S. accountants also must be aware that depreciation charges are based on the increased basis of assets in the 10 EC countries requiring or allowing write-ups.

EXHIBIT 1

EC Countries Accounting Treatments

Country	Funds Flow Statement	Equity Method	Revaluation Reserves	Reserve Account: Statutory	Reserve Account: General	Reserve Account: Hidden
Belgium	No	Rare	Yes	Yes	Yes	Some
Denmark	Yes	Yes	Yes	Yes	Yes	Some
France	Yes	Yes	Yes, countrywide	Yes	Yes	Prohibited
Germany	Rare	Prohibited	No	No	No	No
Greece	No	Rare	Yes, countrywide	Yes	Yes	Some
Ireland	Yes	Rare	Yes	No	No	Prohibited
Italy	Yes	Rare	Yes	Yes	Yes	Some
Luxembourg	Rare	Rare	No	Yes	Yes	Rare
Netherlands	Yes	Yes	Yes	Yes	Yes	Prohibited
Portugal	Rare	Rare	Yes, countrywide	Yes	Yes	Some
Spain	Rare	Rare	Yes, countrywide	Yes	Yes	Some
United Kingdom	Yes	Yes	Yes	No	No	Prohibited

OTHER RESERVES

The shareholders' equity section in exhibit 2 shows accounts for legal reserves, other reserves and reserves for long-term capital gains. In the United States, loss contingencies are accrued if the criteria of Financial Accounting Standards Board Statement no. 5, *Accounting for Contingencies,* are met. Otherwise, reserves are not normally found and the term is not used. EC countries frequently use reserves, which tend to be of three types.

Statutory reserves. Several countries have statutory reserves. Denmark, for example, requires 10% of profit to be allocated to a reserve account. This account accumulates until it is 10% of share capital. Statutory reserves protect creditors in that some portion of profits must be permanently retained as assets. Statutory reserves are clearly labeled and should present no problems for U.S. CPAs.

General reserves. These reserves may create some questions. Since several countries permit a fairly liberal contingency loss rule, companies may adjust net income more easily in most EC countries than in the United States. Normally, changes in general reserves must be disclosed. As a result, careful analysis should provide a means to evaluate these reserves.

Hidden or Secret Reserves. These present a problem in any country, including the United States. They occur when there are asset understatements or liability overstatements. In the United States, these reserves usually are limited to taking excessive depreciation, bad-debt charges, warranty expense and other accrued items related to accounting estimates.

EXHIBIT 2

Partial Balance Sheet for a French Company

Assets at December 31 (in thousands of francs)			1990	1989
	Gross	Amortization Depreciation	Net	Net
Preliminary expenses:				
Reimbursement premiums, debentures and others	FF 36,472	FF 14,304	FF 22,168	FF 4,446
Fixed assets:				
Land	10,507	—	10,507	11,363
Buildings	15,449	3,232	12,217	14,881
Furniture, fixtures and office equipment	14,531	5,634	8,897	7,382
Other assets	399	164	235	1,210
Intangible assets	3,721	—	3,721	3,721
Construction in progress	5,048	—	5,048	3,878
Total	49,655	9,030	40,625	42,435
Other noncurrent assets:				
Long-term loans	769,656	549	769,107	316,063
Trade investments	11,809,851	349,947	11,459,904	10,074,820
Other investments	21,395	3,177	18,218	2,529
Total	12,600,902	353,673	12,247,229	10,393,412
Current assets:				
Other accounts receivable	1,055,859	—	1,055,859	319,814
Clearing account	63,083	—	63,083	76,094
Short-term loans	911,024	—	911,024	78,313
Marketable securities	112,931	—	112,931	10,743
Bank balances and cash	405,980	—	405,980	625,498
Total	2,548,877	—	2,548,877	1,110,462
Commitments received: FF 232,308				
General total	FF 15,235,906	FF 377,774	FF 14,858,899	FF 11,550,755
Shareholders' equity:				
Share capital			3,583,628	3,583,628
Additional paid-in capital			1,434,086	1,434,086
Legal reserves			358,363	358,363
Reserve for long-term capital gains			400,032	400,032
Other reserves			712,667	782,975
Reserve for revaluation of assets			1,857,146	1,868,634
Total			FF 8,345,922	FF 8,427,718

U.S. auditors generally take issue with suspected hidden reserves. In the EC, there is a different philosophy. To be tax deductible in many EC countries, expenses must be reported in the accounting record in conformity with the tax returns. For example, if tax law permits bad-debt writeoffs of 5%, a company probably will book a 5% bad-debt writeoff to minimize taxes, even if actual bad-debt losses are less. This creates a hidden reserve, which EC accountants generally accept because of the company's tax minimization objectives.

According to a 1985 United Nations report, *International Accounting and Reporting Issues: 1985 Review,* hidden reserves likely are created in other ways in some countries. For example, by writing off capital expenditures in the year of acquisition, an excessive charge over reasonable depreciation occurs and an asset that is in use does not appear on the balance sheet. It has been suggested the Deutsche Bank wrote down its new headquarters in Frankfurt to one deutsche mark (from a probable cost of over DM 1 billion) on the premise it was a specially built facility with no tangible value to any other user. Likewise, some EC companies record expenses and create a reserve but hide the reserve account by netting the reserve against assets. Another approach is to bury the reserve in other liability accounts or simply to show totals for liability categories (which will include but not disclose the reserve).

EC companies that create hidden reserves seldom intend to be fraudulent. Rather, the company creates such reserves simply to smooth earnings (when needed, the reserve will be reversed). The rationale is long-term performance is much more relevant than annual results. Without question, however, hidden reserves are hard to detect and U.S. CPAs are generally unfamiliar with the concept.

INCOME STATEMENT PHILOSOPHY

Less emphasis in the EC on an accurately calculated annual profit results in several other differences. First, as stated in the EC's fourth directive, extraordinary items "arise otherwise than in the course of the company's ordinary activities." Therefore, some items will be labeled extraordinary that to the U.S. CPA seem nonextraordinary. As shown in the hypothetical British report in exhibit 3, neither of the items listed as extraordinary income would appear to meet extraordinary criteria according to U.S. GAAP.

A second area that affects the income statement is the use of the equity method of accounting for investments, which the fourth directive allows but does not require. As a result, particularly when investment ownership is between 20% and 50%, the U.S. CPA's expectation is the equity method will be used. EC companies need to be evaluated carefully to determine whether subsidiary earnings or dividends are included in income.

A third area of difference results from EC companies' inconsistent consideration of "substance over form." Capitalizing leases and interest, for example, are not common accounting practices. Not all EC companies impute interest on non-interest-bearing notes. As a result, net income is apt to be different from that in the United States. All of these possible differences make it difficult to make comparisons.

FORMATS AND STATEMENTS

The final major differences between the United States and the EC relate to the income statement format, the value-added statement and the lack of a cash flow statement in some countries.

EC companies have four options in formatting an income statement. They can use (1) a vertical or (2) a horizontal approach coupled with a choice between (3) listing expenses by function, such as cost of sales and general and selling expenses, or (4) listing expenses by class, such as purchases, depreciation and wages and salaries. Any U.S. CPA could easily cope with the horizontal format, even though a U.S. income statement almost always is vertical. However, expenses listed by class present a problem.

EXHIBIT 3

Extraordinary Section of a British Company's Income Statement (in thousands of pounds)

Extraordinary Items	**1990**
Extraordinary income:	
Profit on sale of unlisted investments held as fixed assets	£ 70
Compensation received for breach of patent held by the group	90
Extraordinary charges:	
Expropriation of finished stocks held by foreign agent	(80)
Extraordinary profit before taxation	80
Corporate tax on extraordinary profit	(30)
Extraordinary profit after taxation	£ 50

In the income statement shown in Exhibit 4, depreciation and amortization, wages and salaries and purchases are not allocated to production, selling and administrative categories. Therefore, no cost of goods sold appears and any ratio analysis on gross margin is impossible. Unfortunately for those accustomed to a vertical and functional income statement, the typical European income statement is apt to be horizontal and lists expenses by class.

The annual reports of many EC companies include a value-added statement. Exhibit 5 is a value-added statement that includes income statement information from exhibit 4, plus payments to shareholders (dividends). The purpose of a value-added statement is to show the company's use of money and contributions toward society through the payment of salaries, taxes, interest to creditors and dividends to shareholders. The value-added statement is not difficult to interpret but does represent a fairly common reporting difference from the statements U.S. CPAs typically prepare. The £8,772 retained in the corporation represents net income (£10,131) plus depreciation and amortization (£2,641) minus dividends to shareholders (£4,000).

Finally, while EC companies may prepare value-added statements, in 6 of the 12 countries (see exhibit 1), it's unlikely cash (funds) flow statements would be found. In the 6 countries preparing funds flow statements, none restricts the definition of funds to cash as U.S. GAAP does. However, U.S. CPAs should not have difficulty evaluating funds flow on a different basis.

DIFFICULT COMPARISON

It's clearly difficult to compare EC financial statements to those of U.S. companies or to U.S. industry averages. Asset write-ups, reserves, liberal definitions, lack of substance over form and expenses listed by class render any ratio analysis useless if these ratios are compared to U.S. ratios. However, just as U.S. CPAs would not compare a utility company with its regulatory accounting requirements to a manufacturer but would compare the utility to other utilities, so should U.S. accountants evaluate EC companies, by making comparisons only where accounting presentations are similar.

EXHIBIT 4

Income Statement Showing Expenses by Class

	1990
Revenue	**Amount**
Fees from services rendered	£162,266
Manufacturing of program products	864
Other revenue	5,067
Total revenue	168,197
Operating Expenses	
Purchases	5,799
Wages and salaries	105,861
General and administrative expenses	34,635
Interest expense	2,417
Depreciation and amortization	2,641
Total operating expenses	151,353
Net income before taxes	16,844
Provision for income taxes	(6,713)
Net income	£ 10,131

EXHIBIT 5

Value-Added Statement

Disposal of value added

Payments to employees	£	105,861
Payments to creditors	£	2,417
Payments to government	£	6,713
Payments to shareholders	£	4,000

The retained portion of the value added is the corporation's principal source of financing:
- To increase working capital (cash, inventories, etc.)
- For capital expenditures

This article highlighted areas of major differences between U.S. and EC financial reports. There are numerous minor and procedural differences as well. To help clients consider how to best operate in the EC market, U.S. CPAs need to understand foreign financial statements. CPAs can then ask appropriate questions to provide depth to the understanding attained through statement review. The task is challenging but necessary until international harmonization of accounting standards, including those of the United States, is achieved.

II-F2

FOREIGN CURRENCY TRANSLATION GAINS AND LOSSES: WHAT EFFECT DO THEY HAVE AND WHAT DO THEY MEAN?

William Beaver and Mark Wolfson

Most analyses of the effect of foreign currency translation under Financial Accounting Standards Board Statement No. 52 on earnings and the interpretability of the resulting income numbers contend that volatility of income is likely to be reduced, relative to what it would have been under Statement No. 8.[1] Such contentions fail to appreciate the complexity introduced by the interplay of three different factors—(1) the change in the method of translation (from temporal to all-current); (2) the shift to reporting translation gains and losses as direct charges to an equity account, bypassing the income statement; and (3) the underlying assumptions about what determines changes in foreign exchange rates. We will demonstrate that the relation between such economic forces as inflation rates and foreign exchange rates determines the effect on earnings volatility of charging translation gains and losses directly to equity. Contrary to conventional wisdom, increased volatility results under quite plausible economic conditions.

William Beaver and Mark Wolfson, "Foreign Currency Translation Gains and Losses: What Effect Do They Have and What Do They Mean?" *Financial Analysts Journal.* Reprinted, with permission, from *Financial Analysts Journal,* March/April.

[1]Statement No. 52 permits a transition period that ends with the fiscal years starting after December 15, 1982. Earlier adoption was encouraged, and many companies adopted the statement in their 1981 annual reports. However, all firms must adopt Statement No. 52 by 1983.

Of course, the focus on earnings volatility is somewhat myopic. It is presumably motivated by concern over analysts' ability to predict earnings, the premise being that increased stability implies greater predictability. But it misses a major point: How are the translation gains and losses to be interpreted? In particular, are translation gains and losses to be regarded as income? Most discussions of Statement No. 52 are either silent on this question or take the paradoxical position that the gains are part of equity but not part of income. We address the issue of whether the inclusion in earnings of such gains and losses facilitates interpretation and understanding of the earnings reported under Statement No. 52.

ARE TRANSLATION GAINS INCOME?

There is relatively little controversy over how short-term monetary items should be translated.[2] Rather, the controversy centers on whether any gains are to be included in income.[3]

Table 1 presents a hypothetical multinational company, one that lends funds both domestically and through one of its foreign entities. On January 1, both the domestic parent and the foreign subsidiary lend the equivalent of \$1,000, with principal and interest to be paid in local currency on December 31. The nominal interest rate is 10 per cent domestically and 3 per cent in the foreign market. The exchange rate on January 1 is 1(\$):1(f).

On December 31, the domestic parent receives, \$1,100 including \$100 in interest, and the foreign subsidiary receives 1,030(f), including 30(f) in interest. The 1,030(f) is equivalent to \$1,100, given the year-end exchange rate of 1.068(\$):1(f); that is, 1,030(f) × 1.068(\$)/1(f). Thus the January 1 consolidated balance sheet reports amounts lent of \$2,000 (\$1,000 domestic and \$1,000 foreign), while the December 31 balance sheet reports assets (including interest) totaling \$2,200 (\$1,100 domestic and \$1,100 foreign).

The asset sides of the balance sheets are identical under Statements No. 8 and No. 52, but reported net income differs considerably. Under Statement No. 52, a translated foreign income of \$32 is reported; Statement No. 8 would have raised this figure by \$68—the amount of the translation gain.

Which figure, \$32 or \$100, reflects the economic effect of the foreign transaction? A naive analysis might suggest that domestic lending was three times as profitable as foreign lending, but, setting aside issues such as transaction costs and currency restrictions, the foreign loan and the domestic loan are economically indistinguishable. The dollar-denominated return on both loans is exactly 10 per cent. The \$68 translation gain is realizable and is as much a part of income as the \$32. Indeed, in this example, the inclusion in income of the translation gain is essential to interpreting the economic consequences of the transaction, which are only partially reflected in foreign interest income.

[2] Statement No. 8, Statement No. 52 and all other proposed methods of translation agree that the current exchange rate is the rate to be used. In particular, the temporal, the all-current, the monetary-nonmonetary, the modified monetary-nonmonetary, and the current-noncurrent methods all translate short-term monetary items at the current rate of exchange.

[3] Statement No. 8 requires inclusion, whereas Statement No. 52 does not. We will ignore the fact that Statement No. 52 effectively permits a company to remain on Statement No. 8 for some or all of its foreign operations.

TABLE 1

Translation of Short-Term Loans

Exchange Rate[a]			
January 1	1($):1(f)		
December 31	1.068($):1(f)		
Amount Lent	*Foreign*	*Domestic*	*Total*
	1,000(f)	$1,000	
Nominal Interest Rate	3%	10%	
Consolidated Balance Sheet: Assets			
January 1	$1,000	$1,000	$2,000
December 31	$1,000[b]	$1,100	$2,200
Reported Net Income			
Excluding Translation Gain	$ 32[c]	$ 100	$ 132
Translation Gain ($1,068–$1,000)	68		68
Total Including Translation Gain	$ 100	$ 100	$ 200

[a]f denotes some basic unit of the foreign currency.

[b]1030(f) × 1.068($)/1(f).

[c]30(f) × 1.068($)/1(f).

INTEREST RATES AND EXPECTED EXCHANGE RATES

In Table 1, foreign and domestic rates of return coincided, despite the fact that the one-year nominal interest rates (as of January 1) differed considerably—3 per cent versus 10 per cent. Part of this disparity in nominal interest rates may be attributed to *anticipated* changes in the exchange rate. In other words, the interest rates on January 1 may have anticipated the weakening in the dollar.

A casual inspection of forward rates in foreign exchange markets suggests that foreign exchange traders often expect future exchange rates to differ considerably from current (or spot) rates.[4] This implies that a portion of foreign exchange "gains or losses" (the term "adjustment" might be less misleading) are anticipated and may be reflected in the differences in the nominal interest rates.

Consider, for example, the *Foreign Exchange Trader* information shown in Table 2. First, note that the German mark, Swiss franc and Japanese yen are all expected to strengthen against the dollar throughout the next year; the French franc and Italian lira are expected to weaken; and the Canadian dollar and the British pound are expected to remain approximately stable. Second, note that the currencies that are expected to strengthen all have prime rates below the United States rate of 11 per cent (6.0, 5.5 and 5.75 per cent); the currencies expected to weaken both have prime rates above the U.S. rate (12.25 and 18.75 per cent); and the stable currencies have approximately the same prime rates (11 and 10 per cent). The relationship is not exact, of course, for a variety of reasons, including the limitations of focusing on the prime rate as the measure of short-term interest rates.

[4]The most frequently cited explanation is different expected inflation rates across different countries (often called the purchasing power parity theory).

TABLE 2

Foreign Exchange Trader

	Per Cent					Foreign Units Per U.S. Dollar(top)/U.S. Dollars (bottom)						
	U.S. Treasury Bills	Certificates of Deposit: U.S.	Certificates of Deposit: Euro-Market	Certificates of Deposit: Singapore	Euro-market Time Deposits[a]	German Mark	Swiss Franc	Japanese Yen	Canadian Dollar	French Franc	British Pound	Italian Lira
Spot	X	X	X	X	X	2.61	2.10	233	1.23	7.96	.6764	1582
						.3836	.4756	.004296	.8117	.1257	1.4784	.000632
Three-Month	8.67	9.20	9.37	9.49	9.63	2.58	2.07	231	1.23	8.05	.6762	1614
						.3872	.4824	.004328	.8123	.1242	1.4790	.000619
Six-Month	8.87	9.40	9.52	9.63	9.75	2.56	2.05	230	1.23	8.19	.6758	1648
						.3907	.4886	.004358	.8124	.1220	1.4797	.000607
One-Year	8.99	9.80	9.95	10.07	10.06	2.52	1.99	226	1.23	8.42	.6752	1710
						.3972	.5019	.004429	.8129	.1188	1.4811	.000585
Bank Prime	11.00%	X	X	X	X	6.00%	5.50%	5.75%	11.00%	12.25%	10.00%	18.75%

Data: From Boston Corp., Irving Trust Co. As of Oct 4, 1983.

[a]At London interbank offered rates.

Source: *Business Week,* October 17, 1983.

Several years of empirical research support our suggestion that there is a significant relation between interest rates and expected exchange rates.[5] The relationship is not perfect, and it can occasionally be disturbed by attempts of central monetary authorities to prevent the exchange rate from reaching its natural level via market forces. For practical purposes, however, the relationship is strong enough to be economically important, and any analysis of earnings from foreign operations is subject to considerable errors of interpretation if it is ignored.

TRANSLATION AND INCOME VOLATILITY

Assume that interest rate parity (i.e., equal effective interest rates, denominated in a common currency, in all countries) holds *ex post* and *ex ante.* Assume further that the nominal interest rates in both domestic and foreign currencies are constant over time. Now consider the domestic parent in Table 3 that has two foreign subsidiaries. One operates in a relatively inflation-free economy, where the nominal one-year interest rate is 3 per cent. The other operates in a relatively inflationary economy, where the nominal one-year interest rate is 17.5 per cent. The nominal rate in the parent company economy is 10 per cent.

Loans made by each of the foreign subsidiaries vary from year to year, but on average they have the same dollar equivalent. Table 3 assumes that the subsidiary in the low-inflation

[5]A comprehensive review of earlier research appears in G. Feiger and B. Jacquillat, *International Money and Capital Market Analyses for Business Policy Makers* (Boston: Allyn and Bacon, 1981).

TABLE 3

Volatility of Net Income

	Year	
	1	2
Nominal Interest Rate		
Domestic	10.0%	10.0%
Low-Inflation Foreign Economy	3.0%	3.0%
High-Inflation Foreign Economy	17.5%	17.5%
Exchange Rates		
Low-Inflation Foreign Economy		
Beginning	1($):1(f)	1.068($):1(f)
Ending	1.068($):1(f)	1.141($):1(f)
High-Inflation Foreign Economy		
Beginning	1.068($):1(f)	1($):1(f)
Ending	1($):1(f)	0.936($):1(f)
Reported Net Income		
Foreign Interest Income	$ 32	$164[a]
Translation Gain or Loss	68	(64)[b]
Net Income	$100	$100
Net Income from economically equivalent domestic loans	$100	$100

[a]Interest income = 1000(f) × 0.175 × 0.936($)/1(f).

[b]Translation loss = $1000 − $936 = $64.

country lends the equivalent of a $1,000 one-year loan in year one and lends nothing in year two. The subsidiary in the high-inflation country makes no loan in year one but lends the equivalent of a $1,000 one-year loan in year two.

Translated net income, excluding the translation gain or loss, goes from $32 to $164—a difference of 513 per cent! Yet net income including translation gain or loss remains constant, because the translation gains and losses vary inversely with translated net income.

Contrary to the conventional wisdom, inclusion of gains and losses does *not* increase earnings volatility if (1) fully anticipated interest rate parity holds and (2) nominal interest rates remain constant. The critical feature here is that high nominal interest rates in foreign countries are naturally associated with expected translation losses and low nominal interest rates with expected translation gains.

The illustration in Table III thus counters the contention that Statement No. 52 (by excluding translation gains and losses) will reduce earnings volatility. But earnings volatility *per se* is not our major interest. In fact, we could just as easily have provided an illustration showing that nominal interest rates fluctuated over time, and earnings volatility increased with the inclusion of translation gains. In either case, however, we would encourage the analyst to view translation gains or losses as a component of foreign earnings.

The reason is that foreign earnings are aggregated with domestic earnings, and it is easy to demonstrate that if earnings on foreign loans are compared with earnings from economically identical domestic transactions, the volatility of the *difference* in earnings is reduced by including translation gains and losses. As Table 3 illustrates, the difference between foreign income (including gains and losses) and domestic income on an equivalent loan is zero.[6]

UNCERTAINTY ABOUT FUTURE EXCHANGE RATES

When future exchange rates are *not* fully anticipated, part of any translation gain or loss will be *unanticipated*.[7] Of course, a company uncertain about future exchange rates may hedge a transaction by trading in the forward foreign exchange markets. If the company chooses not to hedge the transaction, any resulting translation gain or loss is another source of earnings volatility.[8] However, any incremental increase in volatility reflects the effects of not hedging against unanticipated movements in the exchange rate. The nominal dollar-denominated return arising from foreign loans *is* uncertain, and translation gains or losses reflect that uncertainty.

In interpreting earnings, the analyst is concerned not only with the expected magnitude of future earnings, but also with the volatility of that earnings stream. By failing to incorporate translation gains or losses, the analyst ignores one manifestation of the period's performance. As a result, forecasts of future earnings, as well as assessments of the volatility of the future earnings stream, may suffer.

MORE COMPLICATED SETTINGS

Interest rate parity may not hold for a variety of reasons—e.g., transaction costs, restrictions on currency flows or "fixed" exchange rates. Indeed, many multinational corporations, especially banks, make borrowing and lending decisions at a multinational level to exploit "perceived" violations of interest rate parity among currencies.

If the objective is to take advantage of interest rate disparities, however, exclusion of translation gains and losses from earnings will obscure an evaluation of the effectiveness of this speculative activity. The earlier illustrations assumed interest rate parity merely for convenience of exposition. They were meant to demonstrate that *when transactions denominated in different currencies are economically alike, inclusion of gains and losses will result in their being treated alike.*

---

[6]Another way to dramatize this point is to consider a situation where the foreign loan is financed via domestic borrowing or conversely. Assuming interest rate parity, the one transaction is the economic mirror image of the other. The net economic effect of such dual transactions on earnings is zero. As Table 3 illustrates, the inclusion of gains and losses will achieve this property.

[7]In this case, we can think of interest rate parity holding *ex ante* (e.g., as reflected in the forward foreign exchange rates) but not necessarily *ex post*.

[8]We have been careful to talk in terms of volatility, not risk. For purposes of illustration, we are focusing on reported nominal earnings. Many contend that a major cause of unanticipated exchange rate movements (exchange rate risk) is unanticipated inflation. In this case, an unhedged foreign loan in an economy with little or no inflation risk may be less risky than a domestic loan for a domestic parent operating in an economy with large inflation risk. When uncertain inflation is introduced, risk is defined in terms of the impact on real earnings rather than nominal earnings.

TABLE 4

Translation When Interest Rates Diverge

Exchange Rate[a]			
January 1	1($):1(f)		
December 31	1.068($):1(f)		
Amount Lent	*Foreign*	*Domestic*	*Total*
	1,000(f)	$1,000	
Nominal Interest Rate	10%	10%	
Consolidated Balance Sheet: Assets			
January 1	$1,000	$1,000	$2,000
December 31	$1,175	$1,100	$2,275
Reported Net Income			
Excluding Translation Gain	$ 107	$ 100	$ 207
Translation Gain	68		68
Total Including Translation Gain	$ 175	$ 100	$ 275

However, we wish to emphasize the flip side of the coin: *When transactions are economically different, the inclusion of translation gains and losses will show them to be different.*

Table 4 provides one illustration. Here, the respective nominal rates are the same in each currency but the foreign currency is growing stronger. The nominal rate of return (denominated in dollars) on the foreign loan is 17.5 per cent, versus 10 per cent for the domestic loan. The amount of foreign loan proceeds is 1,100(f), which translates to $1,175. Excluding the translation gain, the net incomes on the foreign and domestic investments look alike, although they are economically quite different. The inclusion of the translation gain reflects the high (after-the-fact) effective nominal interest rate of the foreign loan.

INTERPRETING EARNINGS

Interpreting earnings in the presence of transaction costs, restrictions on currency flows, and "fixed" exchange rates is difficult.[9] As the above illustration suggests, however, interpretation will be hampered, not helped, by ignoring translation gains and losses.

Consider, for example, a firm that claims to be exploiting perceived interest rate differentials as one of its foreign currency management goals. If it is known that translation gains and losses are ignored in evaluating management, then spuriously favorable performance may be achieved through a simple strategy—lend (borrow) in the economies where the nominal interest rate is high (low), even though a weakening (strengthening) of the foreign currency may be anticipated and reflected in the forward rates. It is easy to construct cases of misleading performance measures when translation gains and losses are ignored.

[9]One might think that the separation of translation gains and losses into their anticipated and unanticipated components might also be difficult. However, the forward foreign exchange markets provide a potentially valuable source of information in this regard. Of course, for a multinational firm with positions in several currencies, the annual report data may be too aggregated to permit the analyst to exploit this approach fully.

Of course, there may be some reluctance to view translation gains and losses as realizable in some situations. For example, foreign exchange restrictions may preclude the conversion of gains and losses into dollars. While this is a valid concern for the analyst attempting to interpret earnings, it is not an indictment of the inclusion of the translation gain or loss. It does cast doubt on the use of the current exchange rate as the translation basis; however, translated net income excluding the translation gain or loss, also translated at the current rate, is equally problematic.

We are not calling for a literal interpretation of the translation gain or loss as "cash in the domestic bank." Nominal interest rate differentials, such as those illustrated in Table 2, do not explain 100 per cent of the differences in expected future foreign exchange rates (e.g., forward rates). However, it is sufficient that they explain an economically important proportion of the differences.

Interest rate differentials vary systematically with anticipated changes in exchange rates. There are economically plausible reasons for this relationship, and failure to consider them can lead to errors of interpretation. The incorporation of foreign currency gains and losses is one way of considering these factors. Obviously, analysis could be enhanced by discussion of the reasons for and interpretation of such gains. It would also be helpful to know the firm's exposure by currency, because expected gains and losses differ across currencies and because the validity of the current exchange rate as a translator may vary across currencies.

Including translation gains and losses in earnings does not eliminate the challenges of performance evaluation. It is still necessary to disentangle expected from unexpected gains and losses, to separate transitory from permanent earnings components, and to distinguish management luck from management skill. These problems are the same encountered in the evaluation of domestic operations, however; they are not unique to the foreign setting.

TRANSLATING OTHER ITEMS

Our analysis so far has focused on short-term monetary items, which are an important component of foreign operations, especially for such industries as banking. But there is also considerable controversy surrounding the exchange rate to be used in translating long-term and nonmonetary items. A comprehensive examination of the properties of these other balance sheet items has led us to the following conclusions.[10]

Translation under Statement No. 8 preserves historical cost for most accounts whose accounting basis is historical cost according to U.S. generally accepted accounting principles (GAAP). It also preserves mark-to-market (i.e., market value accounting) for those accounts whose GAAP basis is current cost or market value. Market value accounting would not be preserved without the inclusion of the translation gain or loss, which Statement No. 8 requires. Statement No. 8 is thus a hybrid of historical cost and current cost accounting. This is not so much a flaw of Statement No. 8 as a reflection on GAAP as currently defined.

If agreement with GAAP is viewed as desirable, then a major flaw of Statement No. 8 is its requirement that long-term monetary items be translated at the current exchange rate. The resulting translation gains or losses are not interpretable if the long-term monetary item is

[10]See W. Beaver and M. Wolfson, "Foreign Currency Translation and Changing Prices in Perfect and Complete Markets," *Journal of Accounting Research,* Autumn 1982, pp. 528–550.

recorded at historical cost and if that cost differs materially from current market value. This flaw could be rectified by recording long-term monetary items at current cost or market value.[11]

The all-current method of Statement No. 52 does not appear to provide interpretable numbers. Simply stated, it does not make sense to translate an account recorded at historical cost at the current exchange rate. The economic forces that led to a change in the exchange rate since the time of acquisition of the item (such as plant and equipment) are likely to have caused a change in the market value or current cost of that item as well. Translating historical cost accounts at the current exchange rate is the ultimate example of "mixing apples and oranges."[12] Thus, while Statement No. 8 committed an "error" with respect to long-term monetary items, Statement No. 52 extends this error to all asset and liability accounts whose accounting basis is historical cost.

From this perspective, it may seem to make sense to toss those meaningless items directly into equity and not clutter up the income statement. However, there are at least two problems with such a simplistic approach. First, some of the translation gains and losses currently being charged directly to equity are interpretable (e.g., accounts whose basis is current cost or market value). Rather than being commingled with the meaningless translation gains and losses, they should be considered in conjunction with items appearing on the income statement (i.e., they are part of net income and do not warrant a direct charge to equity). Second, to the extent that "meaningless" gains and losses are directly charged to equity, then equity, assets and liabilities are still misstated. Failure to report the items in the income statement (i.e., via a direct charge to equity) does not alleviate the problems of interpreting the amounts reported on the balance sheet.

Many praise Statement No. 52 for preserving the relative relations between the balance sheet and income statement items of the foreign subsidiary's books and the amounts translated into dollars on the domestic parent's statements. For example, local return on assets will be preserved under translation. Yet we have demonstrated that this is undesirable. In Table 1, a 3 per cent foreign loan is economically equivalent to a domestic loan of 10 per cent; the foreign loan should be translated so as to report an effective return of 10 per cent (rather than 3 per cent), denominated in dollars. Inclusion of the translation gain or loss produces this result, whereas exclusion does not. Preservation of proportional relationships (such as rate of return on assets) is a reason for being suspicious of a translation method, not a reason for praising it.

[11]This solution would have the property of requiring market value accounting for foreign items when it is not now required under GAAP for similar domestic items. Another solution would have been to translate such items at the historical exchange rate. The result would be no translation gain or loss. However, the translated interest income or expense associated with such claims would be difficult to interpret in isolation from any translation gain or loss, for the same reasons we gave for short-term items.

[12]Recent work by F. Gjesdal ("Valuation of Assets Denominated in Foreign Currencies" (Norwegian School of Economics, Bergen, October 1981)) indicates that under specified economic conditions the limitations of the all-current method may be mitigated.

II-G

EXPANSION IN THE CONTENTS OF FINANCIAL REPORTS

II-G1

TOWARD A THEORY OF CORPORATE SOCIAL ACCOUNTING

Kavasseri V. Ramanathan

A contemporary problem of concern to all technology-rich industrialized societies is that of continuing to provide a high level of motivation for private enterprise while ensuring that its aggregate impact upon society is consistent with social goals and aspirations. This is an exceedingly complex problem for several reasons. Traditional performance criteria for private enterprise have emphasized results which may be in conflict with societal priorities. There are many divergent views as to the most desired social goals and aspirations. The qualitative dimensions of social goal formulation and evaluation add further to the complexity. Yet, the problem is of such significance that there is a pressing need to explore its many dimensions and find ways of formulating solutions.

The nature of the problem can be related further to performance as it is typically viewed from a management perspective. A corporate management's attention, decisions and actions are focused more on those components of the firm's performance which are included in the firm's formal measurement system. To the extent that a firm's social impacts are not subjected to formal measurement process, these aspects are not likely to enter into the firm's planning decisions or performance evaluation.

The traditional view of corporate performance is idealized in the quest to maximize profits. It also is widely acclaimed that a firm's only social responsibility in a free market system is

Kavasseri V. Ramanathan, "Toward a Theory of Corporate Social Accounting," *The Accounting Review,* July 1976, pp. 516–528. Reprinted with the permission of *The Accounting Review.*

Kavasseri V. Ramanathan, "Toward a Theory of Corporate Social Accounting," July 1976, pp. 516–528. American Accounting: *The Accounting Review.* Reprinted by permission of the American Accounting Association.

to maximize its profits, for in so doing, it is presumed to maximize its contribution to society. Under this notion, the profits of a firm which operates within the society's legal framework would provide the all-inclusive criterion for evaluating its social performance. However, the economic depression phenomenon of arriving at full equilibrium with substantial unemployment; the relentless disparities in income and employment opportunities among different social groups; and the serious erosion in the quality of environment caused by productive activities have led to sharp criticisms of the use of profits as an all-inclusive criterion of corporate social performance.[1]

A comprehensive analysis of the social impact of private enterprise suffers, at the present time, from a general absence of reliable data on aggregate social costs and benefits of business and on how these are shared among various social groups. However, some progress has been reached in recent years toward gathering and reporting data on corporate social performance, both as a result of internal initiatives of progressive corporations and in response to external influences. Thus, Beresford's [1973] annual survey reports that 298 of the Fortune 500 industrial firms disclosed some type of social performance data in their 1973 annual reports. The majority of these disclosures were in the environmental control category. Other broad categories used in the Beresford survey were minority employment, responsibility to employees, community activities and product improvement. Disclosure practices varied considerably as regard to scope, format, use of quantitative and financial measures and the significance of items disclosed. The trend appears to be toward greater disclosure. Apparently, this follows from firms' increasing concern with their social responsibility and their attempts to institute some form of social audit [Ackerman, 1973; Dierkes and Bauer, 1973].

There have been several other attempts to gather data on corporate social performance from firms on an ad hoc or routine basis by private research groups such as the Council of Economic Priorities [American Accounting Association, 1975; pp. 57–63]. Further, several statutory agencies, such as the Federal Trade Commission, Environmental Protection Agency, Occupational Safety and Hazards Agency and the Office of Equal Employment Opportunity, are requiring data from firms in specific aspects of social concern. Recently, the Securities and Exchange Commission has proposed increased disclosure of corporate environmental policy, plans and performance.

The challenges involved in accounting for corporate social performance has engaged the particular attention of the major accounting institutions in the United States. The Study Group on Objectives of Financial Statements [1973, pp. 53–55 and 66] proposed as an objective of financial statements the reporting on those activities of the firm which have major social impacts. An American Institute of Public Accountants' committee is studying the problems of developing measurement systems for corporate social accounting. The National Association of Accountants' Committee on Accounting for Corporate Social Performance published its report in the February 1974 issue of *Management Accounting*. Several American Accounting Association Committees have been concerned with the broad area of social accounting [1971, 1972, 1973, 1974, 1975, 1976]. The Association also has sponsored a major research study on social cost measurement problems.

Despite such widespread and growing concern and support for accounting for corporate social performance, progress has been slow and sporadic. "Apparently, no corporation has yet designed or implemented anything approaching a systematic information system for its socially

[1]The literature on this debate is voluminous. Sethi [1974] contains discussions on most of the pertinent issues.

relevant actions" [American Accounting Association, 1975, p. 64]. Historically, the theory and practice of accounting has evolved in four interrelated areas—a framework of objectives, valuation concepts, measurement methodology and reporting standards. There is no reason to believe that evolution in social accounting will not follow the same course. This paper will concentrate on developing a theoretical framework consisting of a proposed set of social accounting objectives and concepts in the belief that an acceptable framework of objectives is fundamental to the development of social accounting theory in the areas of valuation, measurement methods and reporting standards.

BASIC PREMISES

Although there is considerable debate about which corporate actions constitute socially responsible corporate behavior, there appears to be a general acceptance of two assumptions.

1. The solutions to many of the current social problems require the active and willing involvement of private business organizations; and
2. To the extent that measured corporate profits are an inadequate guide to policy, a broader scheme of corporate performance measurement is necessary.

The absence of a broader scheme of corporate social performance measurement is partly due to the recency of the public's concern over corporate social impact. But in a large measure it also is due to the failure to arrive at an operational definition of the role of a corporation in its broader social context [Preston, 1975; Bell, 1971, Ch. 6]. The elements of such a definition and the philosophical justification for a broader scheme of corporate social performance measurement is to be found in the notion of a social contract whereby a firm agrees to perform certain socially desirable functions in return for certain rewards. This notion of a social contract, which is of fundamental importance to this paper, is explained well by Shocker and Sethi [1974, p. 67]:

> Any social institution—and business is no exception—operates in society via a social contract, expressed or implied, whereby its survival and growth are based on:
>
> 1. the delivery of some socially desirable ends to society in general, and
> 2. the distribution of economic, social, or political benefits to groups from which it derives its power.
>
> In a dynamic society, neither the sources of institutional power nor the needs for its services are permanent. Therefore, an institution must constantly meet the twin tests of legitimacy and relevance by demonstrating that society requires its services and that the groups benefiting from its rewards have society's approval.

SOCIAL PERFORMANCE CRITERIA—THE MACRO CONTEXT

The development of a set of social performance criteria is essential for bringing the notion of social contract from the level of ideas to the realm of operationality and to provide answers to the following types of questions:

1. What are the performance dimensions implied by the social contract?
2. What is socially responsible performance?
3. How is it to be measured and evaluated in the aggregate social context?

The task of developing social performance criteria, particularly at the macro-level, is unlikely to be the exclusive province of any one group of specialists or of any one discipline. There is ample evidence to suggest that such criteria will result from the combined efforts of philosophers, historians, sociologists, psychologists, political scientists, measurement theorists and others [See footnote 4].

SOCIAL PERFORMANCE CRITERIA—THE MICRO CONTEXT

Once such macro-level dimensions and criteria for social performance measurement become generally available and accepted, the unique tasks of the accountant are (1) to develop corresponding micro-level criteria applicable to specific firms and (2) to design and operate internal accounting systems which will make the resulting corporate social performance measures routinely available. Several difficult issues must be resolved before these tasks can be completed. Chief among these are the choice of performance dimensions to be included in the corporate measurement system, the selection of measures and measurement procedures and development of methods for independent verification of reported data. The firm-level measurement system developed ultimately must be such that reported social performance data would be useful not only for internal decision making, but also for external evaluation of the firm's performance within the framework of macro-level social performance criteria.

DEFINITION OF SOCIAL ACCOUNTING

The purpose of social accounting is to help evaluate how well a firm is fulfilling its social contract. It would accomplish this purpose by providing visibility to the impact of a firm's activity upon society. While the micro-level measurement system provides the information regarding the corporation's social performance, the macro-level performance criteria provide the evaluative framework. In light of this background, social accounting is:

> the process of selecting firm-level social performance variables, measures, and measurement procedures; systematically developing information useful for evaluating the firm's social performance; and communicating such information to concerned social groups, both within and outside the firm.

PROPOSED OBJECTIVES FOR SOCIAL ACCOUNTING

The notion of a social contract offers crucial assistance in objectives formulation by recognizing as two unique roles of a firm (1) the delivery of some socially useful goods and services and (2) the distribution of economic, social or political rewards to social groups from which the firm derives its power. The nature of these two roles warrants further examination.

As a deliverer of socially desirable goods, the firm is cast in the role of an agent of production. In this role, the ultimate test of a firm's success is whether its aggregate contribution to the society is more than its aggregate consumption of the society's resources. Under the traditional classical economics view, a firm's contribution and consumption are presumed to be completely valued in the market place—profits are presumed to be the all-inclusive measure of a firm's net contribution to society.

However, certain types of decisions of an individual firm may affect the actions of other firms or social groups or individuals in ways which are not reflected in the market process. For example, a major bank's decision to close down its branch in the ghetto area may prompt similar actions by other banks operating branches there and, thus, accentuate the economic and social decline of that neighborhood. The adversity caused to this social segment may not be reflected in the bank's net profits. Indeed, the bank's profits presumably will increase as a result of closing down the ghetto area branch. Many such instances are conceivable where the pursuit of private benefits may not result in the optimization of social benefits. Consideration of such external costs and benefits arising from an individual firm's action are necessary for the attainment of a socially optimal allocation of a society's resources. Whether such optimization is arrived through internalization of externalities or through direct government intervention, a common prerequisite to policy making within and outside the firm is information on, and separate consideration of, the externalities which give rise to social costs and benefits [Ronen, 1974].

OBJECTIVE 1

An objective of corporate social accounting is to identify and measure the periodic net social contribution of an individual firm, which includes not only the costs and benefits internalized to the firm but also those raising from externalities affecting different social segments.

While the first role of a firm under the notion of social contract is that of an agent of production, its second unique role is that of an agent in the resource sharing and benefit distribution processes in society. The resource sharing and benefit policies (e.g., hiring, training, retention and promotion policies; plant location strategies; political philosophies; ethical norms) which a firm adopts have a direct impact upon how the aggregate benefits and sacrifices generated in the society are shared among individuals, communities, social segments and generations. The complexities of making tradeoff decisions among these competing groups are overwhelming, and the absence of theories which deal with interpersonal preferences and aggregate social utility functions are well recognized. Hence, in this second role, the firm's decision process is concerned more with notions of fairness, equity and consistency with social goals than with considerations of optimality.

The social monitoring of individual firm performance in this second role is less direct and more complex than the market-mechanism-based social monitoring of its economic performance. Indeed, the successful attainment of social welfare goals and priorities depends, in a large measure, upon how well embedded they are in the strategies and performance of individual firms—one of the largest organized sectors in modern societies. This relationship between individual firm performance and social welfare is the basis for a second major objective for corporate social accounting.

OBJECTIVE 2

An objective of corporate social accounting is to help determine whether an individual firm's strategies and practices which directly affect the relative resource and power status of individuals, communities, social segments and generations are consistent with widely shared social priorities on the one hand and individuals' legitimate aspirations on the other.

The foregoing two unique roles—a production agent and a distribution agent—of individual firms in modern society, together with the two corresponding objectives of corporate social accounting, indicate the basic directions, dimensions and challenges involved in measuring corporate social performance. Attainment of these two social accounting objectives is necessary for systematically evaluating how well a firm is fulfilling its social contract.

The two preceding objectives may be viewed as *measurement objectives* of social accounting. Implementing these measurement objectives would ensure that a data base relevant to appraising corporate social performance would be available. However, there remains the task of providing relevant information from this data base to the users of social accounting information. For internal reporting purposes, the firm's management presumably will develop specific reporting objectives consistent with the unique features of the firm's technology, the strategies the firm adopts for fulfilling its social contract and its internal management structure. Obviously, this is not a public policy issue.

However, from the external reporting standpoint, there is need for a public policy on corporate social reporting. The purpose of such a policy is to ensure that social reporting by individual firms would be adequate and relevant for aiding public accountability, evaluation, coordination and monitoring of corporate contributions toward social goals attainment. A further purpose of such a public policy would be to insure that external reporting required of individual firms is cost/benefit-effective from the aggregate social standpoint. In the absence of such a policy, different user groups—the different social constituents of firms—will have different degrees of access to corporate social performance data. Further, an overabundance of data on some aspects of social performance and a paucity of information on other relevant aspects could result. Still further, potentials for biased reporting also exist, e.g., as when a firm reports only favorable aspects of its social performance. Finally, there exists the problem of resolving, without adverse social consequences, conflicts of interest in information needs of the various social constituents. There is thus a compelling need for an explicitly stated *reporting objective* of social accounting:

OBJECTIVE 3

An objective of corporate social accounting is to make available in an optimal manner, to all social constituents, relevant information on a firm's goals, policies, programs, performance and contributions to social goals. Relevant information is that which provides for public accountability and also facilitates public decision making regarding social choices and social resource allocation. Optimality implies a cost/benefit-effective reporting strategy which also optimally balances potential information conflicts among the various social constituents of a firm.

Of the three proposed social accounting objectives, two relate to the measurement process and the third to the reporting process. All three follow from the notion of a social contract under which the firm has both a productive role and a distributive role in society. While these social accounting objectives provide the basic theoretical framework, implementing these objectives would be facilitated by a set of social accounting concepts discussed in the following section.

PROPOSED CONCEPTS FOR SOCIAL ACCOUNTING

The central notion in the first measurement objective proposed is that of a firm's periodic net contribution to social goals. Traditional accounting income provides only a partial measure of this contribution because its computation is based only on an analysis of historical transactions in the market place. Many of the "transactions" between a firm and the society, e.g., positive and negative externalities, are not handled presently through the market place.

The earlier example of a bank branch withdrawing from a ghetto area provides one example of the nature of such nonmarket transactions between a firm and the society. In this case, the local community is deprived of easily accessible banking services and also perhaps of some employment opportunities. Further, the community would incur additional transportation costs due to more distant commuting for both banking facilities and jobs. Another adverse consequence might be the decline in the value of real estate upon withdrawal of prominent business units from a neighborhood. All of these results may be characterized as the consequences of a nonmarket transaction between the bank and the local community.

Nonmarket transactions also could lead to social benefits—e.g., when a bank decides to open a new branch in a ghetto. Furthermore, nonmarket transactions may involve shifting costs or benefits from one social segment to another. This may not affect the firm's contribution to society as a production agent, but could do so in its distributive role. Affirmative action programs by firms represent transactions whose main direct impact upon society is in the redistribution of income and growth opportunities among different social segments. Social accounting requires recognition of such nonmarket transactions in addition to the traditional market-based financial transactions. Thus, a fundamental concept in social accounting is that of a *social transaction.*

1. A *social transaction* represents a firm's utilization or delivery of a socioenvironmental resource which affects the absolute or relative interests of the firm's various social constituents and which is not processed through the market place.

The significance of recognizing social transactions lies in the fact that their net cumulative effect, along with traditionally determined financial net income, provides the proper measure of a firm's aggregate social impact. For the purpose of bridging the measurement gap between a firm's aggregate social impact and its financial net income, two more concepts are necessary:

2. *Social overheads* (*returns*) represent the sacrifice (benefit) to society from those resources consumed (added) by a firm as a result of its social transactions. In other words, social overheads is the measured value of a firm's negative externalities, and social returns is the measured value of its positive externalities.
3. *Social income* represents the periodic net social contribution of a firm. It is computed as the algebraic sum of the firm's traditionally measured net income, its aggregate social overheads and its aggregate social returns.

These two concepts are bound to receive considerable attention from both theoreticians and practitioners in social accounting because of the variety of alternative descriptions and measures applicable for these purposes. A proper evaluation of social overheads/returns would require, in the first instance, an identification of the different externalities and social segments affected by each social transaction. A complete enumeration of these would require an impractically elaborate input-output model. Considerable experimentation will be necessary before practical solutions are found in this area.

Secondly, each consequence needs to be "priced" using rates or prices or opportunity costs derived from an appropriate macro-level framework. The problem of developing rates and pricing social transactions of a firm is roughly analogous to, but incredibly more complex than, the problem of developing overhead rates and transfer prices in multidivision organizations [Ronen, 1974].

The problem of developing social overhead/return rates is a derivative of and is coterminous with, the problem of developing an operational definition of social income. The definition proposed above is admittedly vague. As in financial accounting, one approach would be to accept a definition of social income based on a matching of identifiable social costs and identifiable social benefits. While such an approach might be a necessary first step, a more comprehensive and precise definition of social income should be the subject of further research by social scientists.

The next concept, although not yet formally introduced, was used in stating the reporting objective of social accounting. Also, the central notion in the second objective relates to the impact of a firm's activity upon different social groups, with reference for whom the firm is presumed to be a distributive agent. These are the groups with whom the firm has an expressed or implied social contract.

Traditional accounting does not provide formal recognition to these groups. Only the claims of financial equity-holders and the periodic changes in their equity in the firm are measured in conventional accounting. In order to implement the second objective of social accounting, it is necessary to recognize formally in the accounting system all concerned groups. Thus:

4. *Social constituents* are the different distinct social groups (implied in the second objective and expressed in the third objective of social accounting) with whom a firm is presumed to have a social contract.

Formal recognition of social constituents in the accounting system is facilitated through social equity accounts where:

5. *Social equity* is a measure of the aggregate changes in the claims which each social constituent is presumed to have in the firm.

Obviously, social equity claims may not be enforceable under the existing legal system. But measures of social equity would serve as a useful basis for social decision making and for evaluating corporate social performance.

Finally, as a firm's social transactions enhance social well being or consume social resources, formal recognition of these nonmarket events in the firm's accounting system is facilitated by means of a social assets account. A positive externality of the firm (e.g., a decrease in neighborhood crime) would increase the value of its social assets. A negative externality (e.g., pollution) would deplete the firm's social assets. Thus:

6. *Net social asset* of a firm is a measure of its aggregate nonmarket contribution to the society's well being less its nonmarket depletion of the society's resources during the life of the firm.

The net social asset of a firm obviously is not recognizable under the current legal system and does not represent legal title to any future benefits to the firm. However, measures of net social assets would serve as a useful basis for social decision making and for evaluating corporate social performance.

Methodological Implications

Considerable experimentation will be necessary before the objectives and concepts proposed can be translated into a methodology of social accounting. The basic approach implied by the proposed concepts is described below, however, and major problems of implementation are discussed in the next section.

A fundamental step in social accounting would be to identify a firm's social transactions. All decisions and activities of a firm, whether or not they involve a market exchange, would be examined to identify the associated externalities. Such externalities then would be formulated as social transactions.

The process of formulating a social transaction involves identifying three elements. The first element is the *social constituent(s)* affected by the externality being considered.[2] Examples of social constituents are consumer groups, employees, minorities, the local community, investors groups, the general public, groups representing environmental aspects, youth groups and senior citizen groups.

The second element in formulating a social transaction is the specific nature of the *impact* of a firm's action upon the social constituent. In general, such impacts might be either technology-derived or management policy-derived. Thus, product safety and improved service efficiency are illustrative of technology-derived impacts upon consumers. Truth in advertising and sensitivity to customer service needs are illustrative of policy-related variables impacting upon consumers. Other examples of social transactions relevant to various social constituents are pollution-caused damage to health and environment, quality of human resource management, degree of commitment to affirmative action and concern for quality of life and welfare of the local community.

The final, and perhaps most difficult, element is the determination of the relevant social overhead/return *rates* to be used for pricing each social transaction. Since social transactions are not subject to market tests, no automatic process reveals the rates relevant for pricing such transactions. Instead, the rates would have to be developed within a macro social framework. In principle, this issue would be similar to the problem of developing cost and credit transfer rates in integrated multiplant operations. However, the practical problems would pose a serious challenge to any group of experts working on the problem. An interim solution might be to develop social overhead/return rates at specific industry levels which could be used by individual firms in that industry.

The proposed methodology would require each firm to undertake an audit of its externalities in order to develop a reasonably complete set of social transactions reflecting the firm's ongoing impact upon society which are not subject to the market process. The methodology also requires the valuation of each social transaction using social overhead/return rates. The formal accounting for social transactions then would require determination of a social asset effect on the one hand and social income and social equity effects on the other. Certain transactions may involve an exact tradeoff between one type of social benefit (or cost) and another—both affecting the same social constituent. The accounting for such transactions might not involve a social equity effect. On the other hand, certain other social transactions might involve shifting benefits (or costs) from one social constituent to another, e.g., affirmative action. Accounting for this type of transaction might not involve any social income effect.[3]

To illustrate the approach further, consider the case of a bank. Based on the nature of a bank's function and its operating characteristics, the following social constituents and transactions are plausible.

---

[2]It is possible that more than one social constituent might be affected by one externality, thus giving rise to multiple social transactions.

[3]This may not be true if affirmative action programs lead not only to reduced disparities in income and opportunities among social segments, but also to other secondary benefits like greater political stability, fewer crimes, etc.

ILLUSTRATIVE SOCIAL CONSTITUENTS	ILLUSTRATIVE SOCIAL TRANSACTIONS
1. Clients	1. Quality of services which affect thriftiness, savings habits, etc., of clients 2. Client satisfaction with services
2 Employees	1. Job satisfaction 2. Opportunities for personal development and professional growth
3 Local community	1. Effect on neighborhood economic development 2. Effect on education, training, crime prevention, etc., in the neighborhood 3. Effect on commuter traffic, congestion, pollution, etc.
4. Minority groups	1. Minority hiring, training and utilization 2. Financial services designed especially to meet minority needs

CLIENTS The financial earnings of the bank usually are a major indicator of a bank's contribution to its clientele. However, the bank's impact upon them may go beyond that. Through aggressive campaign and management policies, the bank may influence its clientele to achieve greater thrift and more responsible personal fiscal management. Part of the resulting benefits may accrue to the bank in terms of greater client loyalty and business, but the aggregate benefit to the client group may exceed that realized by the bank.

EMPLOYEES Payroll costs and employee productivity may be reflected by traditional accounting. However, if the job situation leads to personal or professional enrichment, for instance, this positive benefit should be recognized through a social transaction.

LOCAL COMMUNITY Traditional accounting recognizes only local taxes, utility payments and other such market transaction effects on the community. But the bank's impact upon the community may include greater stability of, and fillip to, the local economy and employment potential. These, in turn, could help lessen crime, enhance educational and training opportunities and, generally, improve the quality of life. On the other hand, the bank's presence might also contribute to traffic problems, congestion and pollution. In all these cases, of course, there is a problem of identifying how much of each effect is attributable to the bank under study.

MINORITY GROUPS These may be employees, clients or other social segments. Efforts to reduce disparities in income and employment opportunities are examples of an employee-related social transaction. Client-related social transactions are illustrated by special programs to promote minority enterprises and minority capital formation. In all such cases, those evaluating the social transactions would attempt to recognize the social costs and benefits which are not reflected in the bank's market transactions and, hence, are not recognized by traditional accounting.

PROBLEMS OF IMPLEMENTATION

The objectives, concepts and methodology proposed here hopefully provide a tentative framework for developing pilot empirical applications of corporate social accounting. However several complex problems at the macro and micro levels must be resolved before a comprehensive and generally acceptable approach to social accounting can be developed. These include, at the macro level, the development of generally accepted social goals and social indicators to provide the normative framework within which firm-level performance dimensions and measurement criteria must be developed.[4] It is not the accountant's task to prescribe social goals, programs, or structure, just as it is not his or her task to prescribe a firm's goals, policies or management structure. The accounting theorist would necessarily look to sociologists, political scientists, economists and philosophers, among others, to interpret what is socially desirable and to formulate an operational set of goals—just as he or she relies on economists, behavioral scientists and others to interpret and operationalize a firm's goals and decision/performance system. It is essential that the accountant be familiar with the logic and content of the operationalized social goal set, as he or she is to be guided by it in designing appropriate firm-level social accounting systems. Indeed, he or she might be expected to contribute to the macro-level social goal operationalization process by commenting upon the relative merits and problems of measurement implied by alternative operationalization approaches.

The problem of developing relevant social performance measures is particularly challenging at the micro level. On the one hand, they must follow logically from the firm's strategies and technological realities. At the same time, they must be technically congruent with the macro-level social indicators such that firm-level performance scored as positive using these measures also would imply positive contribution toward social goals. One solution might be to develop a social input/output model in which the coefficients capture all the interrelationships between a given set of firm-level social performance criteria and the macro-level social goal dimensions.[5] However, considerable research will be necessary before data for such models become available.

Another major micro-level problem relates to social overhead/return rates. This is a fertile field for research aimed at better understanding the economics of externalities and the behavioral impact of alternative rates upon firm managements and social constituents. Empirical research testing the feasibility and usefulness of alternative approaches to developing rates in selected performance dimensions would be of immediate benefit to the refinement of social accounting methodology.

CONCLUDING COMMENTS

The proposals in this paper are based on the premise that accounting for a firm's social performance requires a broader definition of a firm's role in society than is reflected in the legal entity notion underlying current accounting practices. Accordingly, the notion of a social

---

[4]Milestones in the "social goals" literature include *Goals for Americans* [The American Assembly, 1960]; *Agenda for the Nation* [Gorden, 1968]; *Toward Balanced Growth: Quantity with Quality* [National Goals Research Staff, 1970); and *Setting National Priorities* [Schultze, et al.]. Milestones in the "social indicators" literature include *Indicators of Social Change* [Sheldon and Moore, 1968]; *Toward a Social Report* [U.S. Dept. of H.E.W., 1969] which is the first attempt to implement the social indicators concepts; and *Social Indicators 1973* [Office of Management and Budget] which provides a substantial volume of relevant social and behavioral information.

[5]Knowledge of this type is assumed in the input/output model presented by Charnes, Colantoni, Cooper and Kortanek [1972].

TABLE 1

Proposed Objectives and Concepts for Social Accounting

Objective 1

An objective of corporate social accounting is to identify and measure the periodic net social contribution of an individual firm, which includes not only the costs and benefits internalized to the firm, but also those arising from externalities affecting different social segments.

Objective 2

An objective of corporate social accounting is to help determine whether an individual firm's strategies and practices which directly affect the relative resource and power status of individuals, communities, social segments and generations are consistent with widely shared social priorities, on the one hand, and individuals' legitimate aspirations, on the other.

Objective 3

An objective of corporate social accounting is to make available in an optimal manner, to all social constituents, relevant information on a firm's goals, policies, programs, performance and contributions to social goals. Relevant information is that which provides for public accountability and also facilitates public decision making regarding social choices and social resource allocation. Optimality implies a cost/benefit-effective reporting strategy which also optimally balances potential information conflicts among the various social constituents of a firm.

Concept 1

A *social transaction* represents a firm's utilization or delivery of a socioenvironmental resource which affects the absolute or relative interests of the firm's various social constituents and which is not processed through the market place.

Concept 2

Social overheads (returns) represent the sacrifice (benefit) to society from those resources consumed (added) by a firm as a result of its social transactions. In other words, social overheads is the measured value of a firm's negative externalities, and social returns is the measured value of its positive externalities.

Concept 3

Social income represents the periodic net social contribution of a firm. It is computed as the algebraic sum of the firm's traditionally measured net income, its aggregate social overheads and its aggregate social returns.

Concept 4

Social constituents are the different distinct social groups (implied in the second objective and expressed in the third objective of social accounting) with whom a firm is presumed to have a social contract.

Concept 5

Social equity is a measure of the aggregate changes in the claims which each social constituent is presumed to have in the firm.

Concept 6

Net social asset of a firm is a measure of its aggregate nonmarket contribution to the society's well being less its nonmarket depletion of the society's resources during the life of the firm.

contract was introduced which led to the three objectives and five concepts of social accounting proposed earlier. Table 1 summarizes these objectives and concepts. They provide a general framework within which several refinements are possible. More important, they suggest useful directions for further research into the various aspects of social accounting, some of which have been noted earlier. In particular, the concepts of social constituents and social transactions require further debate and empirical testing, and methods appropriate for determining social overheads/returns need to be developed. Alternative versions of the concept of social income are bound to emerge with corresponding implications for measuring social overheads/returns and social equity. In the absence of supporting legal sanctions, the notion of social equity and the determination of its shares attributable to various social constituents will have to be resolved through sociopolitical reasoning. Choices of measures and measurement procedures will have to be resolved based on which alternatives best help meet social accounting objectives. The usefulness and problems of integrating financial accounting and social accounting in one combined system need to be explored. Research into questions of materiality, verifiability and bias will receive fresh impetus as corporate accounting systems are broadened to include social performance data. This paper will have served its purpose if it helps to organize the emerging debate on such issues within a logical framework of objectives and concepts.

REFERENCES

Ackerman, R., "How Companies Respond to Social Demands," *Harvard Business Review* (July–August 1973), pp. 88–98.

American Accounting Association, Committee on Nonfinancial Measures of Effectiveness, "Report of the Committee on Nonfinancial Measures of Effectiveness," *The Accounting Review,* Supplement to Vol. XLVI (1971), pp. 164–211.

———, Committee on Measures of Effectiveness for Social Programs, "Report of the Committee on Measures of Effectiveness for Social Programs," *The Accounting Review,* Supplement to Vol. XLVII (1972), pp. 336–396.

———, Committee on Environmental Effects of Organizational Behavior, "Report of Committee on Environmental Effects of Organizational Behavior," *The Accounting Review,* Supplement to Vol. XLVIII (1973), pp. 73–119.

———, Committee on Measurement of Social Costs, "Report of the Committee on Measurement of Social Costs," *The Accounting Review,* Supplement to Vol. XLIX (1974), pp. 98–113.

———, Committee on Social Costs, "Report of the Committee on Social Costs," *The Accounting Review,* Supplement to Vol. XLX (1975), pp. 50–89.

———, Committee on Accounting for Social Performance, "Report of the Committee on Accounting for Social Performance," *The Accounting Review,* Supplement to Vol. LI (1976).

Bauer, R. A. and D. H. Fenn, Jr., *The Corporate Social Audit* (Russell Sage Foundation, 1972).

Bell, D., *The Coming of Post-Industrial Society* (Basic Books, 1971).

Beresford, D., *Compilation of Social Measurement Disclosures in Fortune 500 Annual Reports—1973* (Ernst & Ernst, 1973).

Charnes, A., C. Colantoni, W. W. Cooper, and K. O. Kortanek, "Economic, Social and Enterprise Accounting and Mathematical Models," *The Accounting Review* (January 1972), pp. 85–108.

Dierkes, M. and R. A. Bauer, eds., *Corporate Social Accounting* (Prager Publishers, 1973).

Gordon, K., ed., *Agenda for the Nation* (The Brookings Institution, 1968).

National Goals Research Staff, *Toward Balanced Growth: Quantity with Quality* (U.S. Government Printing Office, 1970).

Office of Management and Budget, Executive Office of the President, *Social Indicators 1973* (U.S. Department of Commerce, Social and Economic Statistics Administration).

Preston, L. E., "Corporation and Society: The Search for a Paradigm," *Journal of Economic Literature* (July 1975), pp. 434–453.

Report of the Study Group on *Objectives of Financial Statements* (American Institute of Certified Public Accountants, October 1973).

Ronen, J., "Accounting for Social Costs and Benefits," in J. J. Cramer, Jr. and G. H. Sorter, eds., *Objectives of Financial Statements* (American Institute of Certified Public Accountants, May 1974), pp. 317–340.

Schultze, C. L., et al., *Setting National Priorities* (The Brookings Institution, annually issued).

Sethi, S. P., ed., *The Unstable Ground: Corporate Social Policy in a Dynamic Society* (Melville Publishing Company, 1974).

Sheldon, E. and W. E. Moore, eds. *Indicators of Social Change: Concepts and Measurements* (Russell Sage Foundation, 1968).

Shocker, A. D., and S. P. Sethi, "An Approach to Incorporating Social Preferences in Developing Corporate Action Strategies," in S. P. Sethi, ed., *The Unstable Ground: Corporate Social Policy in a Dynamic Society* (Melville Publishing Company, 1974), pp. 67–80.

The American Assembly, *Goals for Americans,* The Report of the President's Commission on National Goals (Prentice-Hall, 1960).

U.S. Department of Health, Education and Welfare, *Toward a Social Report* (U.S. Government Printing Office, 1969).

II-G2

ACCOUNTING FOR TOMORROW'S POLLUTION CONTROL

Sid R. Ewer, Jon R. Nance, and Sarah J. Hamlin

When the Clean Air Act was signed by President Bush in 1990, many accountants with no professional interest in the electric utility industry—the target of that environmental law—examined the legislation carefully. They were interested because they suspected the law's unusual procedures for attacking industrial pollution would be precursors of environmental laws that will have a major impact on their clients or employers.

The provision of specific interest to accountants was the government's authorization to grant air-pollution emission rights—in effect, a limited license to pollute—and the eventual creation of a market in which these rights can be sold or traded. (For details on the law's schedule, see the sidebar on page 361.) In fact, several states, including California and Washington, have already implemented similar regulations affecting local industry, and the United Nations is now considering implementing some type of worldwide pollution allowance system.

As a result, the law opens a Pandora's box of accounting problems for industry nationwide. The major question faced by utility accountants today, and probably other accountants tomorrow, is, How should these emission rights, which in many ways resemble securities, property and inventory, be accounted for? For example, are they assets? What should their cost basis be? Can they be amortized?

To date, there are no definitive answers to these questions. This article, however, explores some of the complexities the law raises and offers some solutions. Also, the article may

---

inspire fresh thinking on what surely will be a topic many accountants will have to address in the years ahead.

To understand the accounting issues, accountants must first understand this background on air pollution and its regulation.

WHAT'S BEING REGULATED

Sulfur dioxide emission, a by-product of electric-generating utilities that burn fossil fuels (coal and oil), has been a target of federal regulators for decades. The first Clean Air Act, passed in 1970, set pollution standards, but they were applied with only moderate regard for their economic consequences. Some utilities were forced to make very costly plant modifications that did not yield equivalent benefits to air quality. Others could have improved air quality at modest cost, but the law gave them no incentive to do so. Consequently, many utilities missed deadlines for air-quality improvements, and sulfur dioxide emitted by electric utilities was nearly as high in 1985 as it was the year the law was passed.

The Environmental Protection Agency (EPA) always has regulated sulfur dioxide emission by setting emission standards. The 1990 law, which begins to go into effect in 1993, continues that process. Utilities currently operating will be granted rights to release sulfur dioxide emissions, but only in amounts based on those of the period from 1985 to 1987. New power plants will not be granted such rights. The goal is to reduce total emissions for all U.S. power plants to about two-thirds of their 1985–87 level.

The law bundles emission rights into units called "allowances," which are authorizations to emit one ton of sulfur dioxide in a given year. The law also directs the EPA to establish a market and a bank for the allowances. An allowance may not be used before the authorized year but may be carried forward to a later year.

The EPA goal is to hold back 2.8% of those allowances in order to develop the bank. Beginning in 1993, it will sell some of these allowances directly, and in 1993, in addition to its direct sale, the EPA will auction allowances to the highest bidder. Auction and sale proceeds will be distributed pro rata to the existing companies from which allowances were withheld. Qualifying sources also may trade allowances directly.

The auction and direct sale

- Will allow new companies to produce electricity using fossil fuels.
- Will allow existing companies to purchase additional allowances for planned expansion.
- By promoting a trading market, will reduce hoarding incentives and mitigate the partial monopoly the law confers on existing utilities.

The law's carryforward provision encourages companies to lower emissions below mandated levels and makes allowances granted for that year available for use in a later year. Under regulations to be promulgated soon by the EPA (and by individual state environmental protection authorities), companies may bank these allowances and later sell them to companies unable to reduce their emissions efficiently. Such sales may be direct or through the EPA auction.

Two relatively simple methods for freeing up allowances are aggressive conservation and installation of pollution-control equipment. More complex methods include replacing "dirty" fuels, such as coal, with "clean" fuels, such as natural gas; burning coal of lower sulfur content; and replacing old generating stations with modern, cleaner-burning plants.

ACCOUNTING FOR ALLOWANCES

What exactly is an allowance, from an accounting point of view, and how should it be treated?

An allowance confers a specific right on its holder: the license to emit pollution at a specified time. Without that license, most utilities would be forced to close down their generating plants. Allowances evidently fit the definition of an asset in Financial Accounting Standards Board Concepts Statement no. 6, *Elements of Financial Statements:* "Assets are probable future economic benefits obtained or controlled by a particular entity as a result of past transactions or events."

The act says allowances are "limited authorizations" and not "property rights." Nevertheless, the law intends those authorizations to be marketable and provides holders with substantial protection against expropriation. An allowance is obtained or controlled by one of the following three past events: (1) the EPA grants to existing companies, (2) purchases by companies at auction or directly from the EPA or other companies and (3) receipts of bonus allowances from the EPA because of qualified emission reduction. Thus an allowance seems to meet all criteria for an asset and should be recognized as such.

The market value of an allowance isn't known at this time because the market hasn't been established yet. The Chicago Board of Trade recently filed to establish a futures market before the first EPA auction in 1995. It is known, however, that the offering price of allowances in the EPA's direct sales is set at $1,500 per ton of sulfur dioxide, adjusted for inflation and discounted for the time between year of sale and authorized year.

COST OR MARKET?

Clearly, allowance assets and related expenses will be very material items in a company's financial statement. But how should the value be recognized—at current market or historical cost? Each has advantages and disadvantages.

Because there will be a futures market for the allowances, market values always will be available. An allowance's economic value will be its value when it's used for electricity production or when it's exchanged, whichever is greater. After all, a rational manager who cannot derive more value from internal use of an allowance will choose to sell it; thus current market value is useful for management planning and control. Obviously, use values will be different for different companies and will depend on management decisions, production technologies and rate regulators' decisions. Market value is an opportunity cost that must be considered in evaluating any plan to use an allowance internally.

Current market valuation for financial reporting purposes, however, conflicts with traditional principles of realization and historical cost. Historical cost valuation is the norm for financial reporting. For an EPA allowance granted to an existing company, the original cost is zero; for a purchased allowance, it is the purchase price.

Use of a zero-cost basis for granted allowances leads to difficulty when a utility intends to offer its own allowances for sale in the market. How should costs (the price of a scrubber installation or plant conversion, for example) be treated if they are incurred entirely so that a utility can sell an allowance? The reasonable solution is to allocate such costs to the allowances freed up for trade.

TIMETABLE FOR CLEAN AIR	
1990:	The Clean Air Act of 1990 is signed into law.
1992–93:	Within 18 months of enactment, the Environmental Protection Agency (EPA) is to promulgate the necessary procedures to establish an emission allowance market.
1993:	The EPA will conduct annual auctions of the emission allowances.
1994:	By January 1, the EPA will submit to Congress an evaluation of the law with the view to extend its regulations to include nitrogen oxides.
1995:	Compliance begins on January 1 for 110 specifically named power plants that are considered the worst pollution offenders. In order to emit sulfur dioxide, these facilities must possess sufficient emission allowances.
2000:	Compliance begins on January 1 for all U.S. power plants.

This presents some problems. Different authorization dates for different allowances create a need for discounting and prevent equal allocations to each allowance. Also, most costs of installation or conversion probably are incurred for multiple purposes. What fraction of such costs should be charged to the allowances they free up for sale? Should such allowances be charged to the allowances they free up for sale? Should such allowances be charged with a share of increased maintenance or operating costs of plants with lower emissions? Costing allowances made available for trade by changes in policy or technology suffer from all the usual hazards of costing joint processes and may not lead to valuations useful in management decision making.

While historical cost valuation of allowances is ambiguous and of limited relevance to management decisions, the traditional concept of realization requires some use of historical cost when a utility issues financial reports. Just how historical cost is to be used depends on which of many financial reporting principles currently apply. That, in turn, depends on how the allowance asset is classified.

INVENTORY, SECURITY OR INTANGIBLE?

A case can be made for classification of allowances as inventory, marketable securities or intangible operating assets.

INVENTORY

If classified as inventory, allowances are carried as current assets at the lower of cost or market, and their cost is expensed as they are sold or consumed. Some cost-flow assumption (for example, first-in first-out accounting) is required to choose those costs to expense in each period.

The definition of inventory in Accounting Research Bulletin no. 43, *Restatement and Revision of Accounting Research Bulletins,* is "items of tangible personal property which . . . are held for sale in the ordinary course of business . . . or . . . are to be currently consumed in the production of goods or services to be available for sale."

Clearly, an allowance is held either for sale or for consumption. Unfortunately, it is neither obviously tangible nor necessarily held for current consumption. So, is it actually a tangible asset?

Allowances are conferred as "pieces of paper" whose physical characteristics are wholly unrelated to the right to emit sulfur dioxide. Nevertheless, they are just as tangible as certificates of deposit (CDs) and marketable securities. As with CDs, companies will be able to bank or transfer emissions allowance certificates, and each represents a specific quantity of future benefit.

Allowances may be held for sale. As the Clean Air Act is implemented, allowances will become essential for a utility to operate, and certainly they will be held in the "ordinary course of business." Allowances held for internal use are certainly consumed in the production of goods or services to be made available for sale. Indeed, the law requires companies to possess sufficient emissions allowances before fuel can be legally consumed. Sanctions for burning fuel without appropriate allowances include fines, offsets in the next producing year and criminal prosecution.

The problem with inventory classification is most allowances booked at a particular time will be authorized for future years and cannot plausibly be regarded as current assets. The act calls for sale of allowances many years before authorized use and many utilities may want to purchase a stream of allowances to cover the entire service life of a new installation.

MARKETABLE SECURITY

If classified as marketable securities, allowances are carried in two distinct portfolios, one current and one noncurrent. Each is valued at the lower of cost or market. Sales and some value changes flow through income.

An allowance is a specific, marketable right to a certain form of consumption. This makes the marketable security classification plausible. However, allowances may be consumed and nothing quite like that happens to ordinary marketable securities. Of course, some securities (for example, bonds) mature and at maturity their proceeds may be consumed, and other securities (for example, options and warrants) expire. To be sure, the analogy between allowances and marketable securities is imperfect.

INTANGIBLES

If classified as intangibles, emission allowances are carried as noncurrent operating assets at cost less amortization, according to the provisions of Accounting Principles Board Opinion no. 17, *Intangible Assets*.

Allowances possess certain characteristics of intangible operating assets. The rights conferred by allowances are unrelated to physical form. Allowances enable companies to continue operations at a given level of emissions, which is characteristic of a franchise or license. They may be held for future production and purchased many years before they are used.

An allowance is a right to a specific quantity of consumption. In fact, an EPA pollution certificate conveys more information about the physical character and service potential of an allowance than a bulldozer's certificate of title conveys about its physical character and service potential.

Intangibles rarely refer to such specific quantities. For example, a patent permits a company to produce a specific product exclusively for a specific period but does not limit the number of units that may be produced. For this reason, straight-line amortization, although not mandated by Opinion no. 17, is the customary method of allocating intangible cost to expense.

By contrast, it makes no sense to amortize the cost of emissions allowances over time. The only reasonable method of charging allowance costs to expense is in proportion to sulfur dioxide emission. Presumably, pursuant to the requirements of Opinion no. 17, companies could demonstrate the appropriateness of a units-of-production method of amortization.

DESERVING SPECIAL TREATMENT

Ultimately, both internal and external reporting of allowances should reflect the underlying economic events, and the consequences of those events must be reported to a company's management. FASB Concepts Statement no. 2, *Qualitative Characteristics of Accounting Information,* says, "The overriding criterion by which all accounting choices must be judged [is that] . . . the better choice is the one that . . . produces from among the available alternatives information that is most useful for decision making."

After careful consideration, we have concluded reporting allowances at current market value best meets this criterion. Accordingly, we advocate this reporting for internal planning and control.

However, we also believe current market value is not satisfactory for external financial reporting. No matter what asset classification we select, we find current market value reporting is inconsistent with current accounting standards. Moreover, it raises a specter of "windfall profits" arising from the original "free" EPA grants and might lead to retaliation by state and local regulators. Thus our external financial reporting recommendation begins with historical cost valuation.

CLASSIFICATION

The classification problem is critical. The new asset does not fit comfortably into any existing asset classification, and we believe that fact, along with the materiality of allowances both in market value and in their necessity for operations, justifies special treatment.

Uncommitted allowances should be given some descriptive name such as "sulfur dioxide emission allowances" and divided into current and noncurrent portfolios by an authorized date. Each portfolio should be carried at the lower of cost or market with disclosure of current market value. This treatment is intended to resemble closely the treatment of marketable securities; we believe that uncommitted allowances most resemble such assets.

The cost of committed allowances should be regarded as an element of fuel cost. It is a cost that must be incurred to bring fuel into readiness for burning. For a given technology and fuel, charging allowances consumed to expense in proportion to sulfur dioxide emitted is equivalent to charging in proportion to fuel consumption.

Allowance accounting would be simplified if all allowance costs could be attached to fuel, but this is unsatisfactory for several reasons.

1. Fuel covered by allowances may not be available; for example, when it has yet to be delivered to cover even currently authorized allowances. Further, adding allowance costs to fuel that does not require allowances would adversely affect comparability and consistency of financial statements.

2. Decisions involving changes in fuel-consumption technology require separation of allowance cost from fuel cost, and such decisions are critical to rational use of uncommitted allowances.
3. Allowances may be held only for resale, with no intent to consume.

In addition to fully disclosing the number of allowances held and projected annual usage, we suggest that accountants attach committed allowance cost to fuel cost and carry uncommitted allowance cost as a separate balance sheet item, classified as current or noncurrent by the date of authorized use.

This threefold classification is complex, but nothing simpler captures adequately the economic substance of transactions in this newly created asset.